CW00428580

FREEDOM of EXPRESSION in ISLAM

THE ISLAMIC TEXTS SOCIETY
FUNDAMENTAL RIGHTS & LIBERTIES IN ISLAM SERIES:
PRINCIPLES & APPLICATIONS

Volume 1: *The Dignity of Man: An Islamic Perspective*

Volume 2: *Freedom, Equality and Justice in Islam*

Volume 3: *Equity and Fairness in Islam*

Volume 4: *Freedom of Expression in Islam*

Volume 5: *The Right to Life, Security, Privacy and Ownership in Islam*

Volume 6: *The Right to Education, Work and Welfare in Islam*

Volume 7: *Citizenship and Accountability of Government: An Islamic Perspective*

OTHER TITLES BY M. H. KAMALI

Principles of Islamic Jurisprudence

Islamic Commercial Law

Mohammad Hashim Kamali

FREEDOM of EXPRESSION in ISLAM

Revised Edition

ISLAMIC TEXTS SOCIETY

CAMBRIDGE • 1997

First published by
The Islamic Texts Society
Miller's House
Kings Mill Lane
Great Shelford
Cambridge CB22 5EN, U.K.

Reprint 2010

British Library Cataloguing-in-Publication Data.
A catalogue record for this book is
available from the British Library.

ISBN 978 0946621 59 0 cloth
ISBN 978 0946621 60 6 paper

ABOUT THE AUTHOR

Dr. Mohammad Hashim Kamali is currently Professor of Law at the International Islamic University of Malaysia, where he has been teaching Islamic law and jurisprudence since 1985. Born in Afghanistan in 1944, he studied law in Kabul University, where he was later appointed Assistant Professor. Following this he worked as Public Attorney with the Ministry of Justice in Afghanistan. The author then went to England where he completed his LL.M, and then his doctoral studies in London University where he specialised in Islamic Law and Middle Eastern Studies. Dr. Kamali then held the post of Assistant Professor at the Institute of Islamic Studies at McGill University in Montreal, and later worked as Research Associate with the Social Science and Humanities Research Council of Canada. He is the author of *Law in Afghanistan, A Study of the Constitutions, Matrimonial Law and the Judiciary* (Leiden: E.J. Brill, 1985), and *Principles of Islamic Jurisprudence* (Cambridge: The Islamic Texts Society, 1991). The author has published a number of articles in learned international journals. He comes from a family of long-standing legal and judicial service in Afghanistan and his knowledge of Islamic law is an interesting blend of the theory and practice of this discipline in Afghanistan and of studying and teaching this subject in England, Canada and Malaysia.

Contents

Acknowledgements

It is my pleasant duty to express my gratitude to the individuals and institutions who have contributed to the completion of this volume. I wish to record my appreciation of the Social Sciences and Humanities Research Council of Canada for a generous research grant awarded to me in 1983-84 in support of a larger research project of which this book is only a part. The grant was assigned to a project entitled 'Fundamental rights of the individual in Islamic law'. In writing the present volume I have utilised much of the data I had collected in preparation for that project. I also thank most warmly my former colleague, Professor Charles J. Adams, of McGill University, Institute of Islamic Studies, whose enthusiasm, advice, and support for this research has not failed to be heartwarming and beneficial.

I also take this opportunity to acknowledge the interest and involvement of the Law Department of the School of Oriental and African Studies, University of London, in this research. I thank especially Mr. Ian Edge and Chibli Mallat for the two colloquia they organised for me to discuss some of the topics of my research. I would also like to express my appreciation to the Research Committee of the International Islamic University, Malaysia, for a grant awarded to me specifically in support of this research, and for enabling me to take a research leave during the summer of 1990 to consult library collections in the universities of London and Oxford. Professor Ahmad Ibrahim, Dean of the Kulliyyah of Laws, International Islamic University, Malaysia, has always been helpful and supportive of my research activities; his encouraging and constructive influence in bringing this work to completion has been significant. I also take this opportunity to thank the organising committee of the Public Lecture Series at the Kulliyyah of Laws for enabling me to discuss the themes of my research in a public lecture at the International Islamic University, Malaysia. Lastly, I take this opportunity to thank the organising committee of the seminar on 'Freedom of Association: the Islamic Perspective', in Kuala Lumpur, December 1991.

The library staff of the I.I.U., Malaysia, especially Sister Noraini Ismail and the secretarial staff of the Kulliyyah of Laws, especially Siti Rohaya Zakaria and Norasiah Mohamad Sulaiman, among others, have always been very helpful and courteous in giving me assistance with the typing and preparation of the manuscript.

Mohammad Hashim Kamali
International Islamic University, Malaysia
1993

Preface to the Revised Edition

One of the main events following the initial publication of this book in Kuala Lumpur in September 1994 was that it won, in February 1995, the Ismāʿīl al-Fārūqī Award for Academic Excellence. The Award was jointly administered by the Malaysian branch of the International Institute of Islamic Thought and the International Islamic University, Malaysia. The External Assessor's report that was read out at the award presentation ceremony described the work as one of 'painstaking scholarship' which exhibited the 'thoroughness of the author and his firm grip on the relevant materials'. The report added that 'freedom of expression has not been dealt with in such depth in the works of Islamic law in English, Arabic or Urdu'.

Since the publication of the Kuala Lumpur edition I have also had the pleasure of associating more closely with the editors of The Islamic Texts Society, especially Dr. Abd al-Rahman Azzam who solicited an expert opinion from an Egyptian reviewer, the substance of which was conveyed to me in a letter by Dr. Azzam. I have had the benefit of reflecting the improvements suggested by both the reviewer and Dr. Azzam. It was proposed that technical Arabic terms which occurred in the text needed explanatory footnotes so as to make the work more accessible for the non-specialist. Some linguistic refinements were also recommended, so that the text might reflect the style of 'an objective legal handbook which will, God willing, become a standard reference and inspiration for many'. The reviewers, on the other hand, also described the book as 'excellent, certainly the first of its kind'.

To prepare the book for the present edition, I have made alterations of a stylistic nature which involved revision of some passages, addition of explanatory footnotes to some of the Arabic terms and concepts, and the insertion of a new section in the final chapter of the book: The added section is concerned with an analysis of the Qur'ānic evidence on the issue of blasphemy, and a discussion of Ibn

Taymiyyah's renowned work, *Al-Ṣārim al-Maslūl*, on that subject. The section on the Salman Rushdie affair which appeared in the text in its first edition has now been shifted to an appendix at the very end. These changes were undertaken mainly with the view of enhancing objectivity and balance in the treatment of subjects. Technical terms are normally accompanied by parenthetic explanations, both in the first and the present edition; there is also a glossary at the end which explains most of the Arabic terms that occur in the text.

It is a pleasure to note that entering this work into the Ismāʿīl al-Fārūqī Award contest brought me into closer contact with many distinguished scholars, and I take this opportunity to extend my warmest thanks to Dr. Abdul Hamid Abu Sulayman, Rector of the International Islamic University, Malaysia, and Chairman of the Ismāʿīl al-Fārūqī Award Committee, and Dr. Jamal Barzinji, Director of the International Institute of Islamic Thought, Malaysia, for their co-operation and support. I would also like to thank Professor Mohammad Kamal Hassan, the Deputy Rector for Academic Affairs, IIUM and member of the Award Committee, for his useful remarks which I have taken into account in my revision. And, lastly, I thank the editors of The Islamic Texts Society for their excellent editorial work and co-operation, in particular Mrs Farhana Mayer and Dr Reza Shah-Kazemi.

Mohammad Hashim Kamali
International Islamic University, Malaysia
June 1995

PART ONE: PRELIMINARY

I. Introduction

The second chapter in the preliminary part of this volume is devoted to the definition, scope and objectives of freedom of expression in Islam. The main objectives of freedom of expression highlighted in this section are the vindication of truth and the protection of human dignity. Chapter Three addresses the issue of the recognition, or otherwise, of rights in the *Sharīʿah*. This discussion is set against the background of the view which asserts that Islam is a religion of duties, and that the concept of rights, especially of fundamental rights, is foreign to the *Sharīʿah*.

The rest of this book is concerned with two principal themes, namely, affirmative evidence in support of freedom of expression, and the limitations, whether moral or legal, which Islam imposes on the exercise of this freedom. These two themes, it may be said, are investigative in their purpose, which is why I should add that a third feature of the volume at hand is its attempt at reassessing certain issues and to highlight the need for a fresh review of the source materials of the *Sharīʿah*, whenever this was deemed to be necessary and desirable. My review of the source materials and the perspective I derive from them is generally intended to interpret the *Sharīʿah* in the light of contemporary developments, and to seek to relate its directives to modern issues.

The section on affirmative evidence on the freedom of expression draws attention, in the first place, to some of the principles enunciated in the Holy Qur'ān, and the Sunnah, i.e. the normative teachings of the Prophet Muḥammad ﷺ, which provide the authority for this freedom. In this connection, I have discussed the fact that, despite the existence of affirmative evidence in the sources, nowhere does one find, nor indeed would one expect to find in the scholastic works of the *ʿulamāʾ*, an exclusive treatment of this freedom in the way which is now familiar in modern writings on constitutional law. The principles of *ḥisbah*, that is, commanding good and forbidding evil, *naṣīḥah* or sincere advice, *shūrā* or consultation, *ijtihād* or independent juristic reasoning, and *ḥaqq al-muʿāraḍah*, or the right to constructive criticism, all affirm the freedom of speech and I have devoted a section to each.

My discussion in this part also addresses the subject of personal opinion (*raʾy*) and its historical development, which originates in the question of whether, and how, the use of personal opinion should be regulated in the development of the rules of the *Sharīʿah*. The section on affirmative evidence ends with an exposition of the freedom of association and assembly, which is undoubtedly one of the most important, and yet most neglected, aspects of freedom of expression in Islam. My treatment of the topics discussed in this part is somewhat experimental in that I had no precedent on which to rely. My main concern has been to locate the evidence and present it in a coherent form, as well as to develop new perspectives on issues and to interpret the existing materials in the light of relevant hypotheses.

The next section addresses freedom of religion and explores the extent of this freedom in a system of law which is intertwined with religion, and is often coterminous with the dogma and belief-structure of Islam. The principal question I have addressed here is whether or not the *Sharīʿah* subscribes to freedom of conscience. My conclusion is that the *Sharīʿah* takes an affirmative stand on freedom of religion despite a certain controversy that has arisen over the understanding of the Qur'ān on this freedom. Some commentators have, for example, advanced the argument that the Qur'ānic declaration that there shall be 'no compulsion in religion' (Qur'ān *sūrah* II: verse 256) has been abrogated. This is clearly not the case, and I have developed a certain perspective on it. I have also reviewed some of the evidence pertaining to apostasy, its meaning and its bearing on freedom of religion.

The second of my two themes, namely, restrictions on the freedom of expression, occupies a much larger portion of this volume. I have attempted to divide these restrictions into two main categories —moral and legal. Violations of freedom of speech like backbiting, acrimonious talk, exposing the weaknesses of others, and even certain types of lying, obviously fall into the category of moral violations and I have treated them as such. Other violations, such as slanderous accusation, libel, insult, sedition, and blasphemy, call for legal sanctions. They are clearly justiciable and therefore fall into the category of legal prohibitions.

Certain concepts that relate to freedom of expression such as sedition (*fitnah*), heresy (*bidᶜah*), and disbelief (*kufr*), have remained loosely defined and versatile. I also found so much diversity in the treatment of these concepts in early sectarian literature that it was difficult to identify the precise import of concepts, and also to ascertain positions which might be at variance with the correct teachings and principles of Islam. For example, in relation to sedition (*fitnah*), the Khārijites departed from the mainstream of Islamic teachings on many points and advocated some ideas which were decidedly controversial and others which were merely dubious. Also, in the sectarian literature pertaining to *kufr*, charges of heresy and disbelief were sometimes laid on the opponent's faction with a certain degree of laxity and self-assertiveness. The *ᶜulamā'* of the leading schools have identified such departures and I have tried to ascertain their positions. In connection with apostasy, blasphemy and heresy, I have also drawn attention to a certain need to separate and distinguish concepts which are often pervasive and overlapping.

I have attempted, on occasion, to develop a fresh perspective on the source materials of the *Sharīᶜah* concerning concepts or issues where evidence warranted such a course. In the absence of any precedent that could be used as a guideline in the selection of themes, posing questions, and the degree of emphasis that should be given to subsidiary and related issues, I alone take the blame for possible errors. There is, to the best of my knowledge, no exclusive study of freedom of expression in Islam available either in the English or Arabic languages. The task has, therefore, been somewhat daunting, as issues tended to criss-cross the boundaries of law, theology and ethics, so much so that certain themes in my discussion hardly recognised any clear boundaries at all. Although I have, as noted earlier, attempted a division of themes into the various categories of moral, legal and so on, this classification is not intended to be either definitive or exhaustive, as there may be some subjects which could simultaneously be placed under more than one heading. Despite the fact that I have included non-legal themes, this enquiry is nevertheless predominantly legal in character, and departures from this context are only made whenever necessary and warranted.

Appendix I, which appears at the end of this volume, elaborates the discussion in Chapter Two on *ḥaqq*, its definition and how it relates to the two allied concepts of *ḥukm* and *ᶜadl* respectively.[1] In Appendices II, III and IV, I have expounded, as far as my access to information permitted, the applied laws of some countries, including Malaysia, Egypt and Pakistan. But my aim in doing so was merely to provide a basis for comparison, and to ascertain the broad outline of modern law on the issues of our concern. Statutory legislation in contemporary Muslim countries is, on the the whole, not explicit on matters such as defining disbelief, sedition, blasphemy and heresy. The focus of discussion also tends to vary in the *Sharīᶜah* and modern law. Sedition *(fitnah)* in the juristic literature of the *Sharīᶜah*, for example, is as much a religious as it is a political issue, whereas in modern law we find that sedition is almost exclusively a political concept. This would partly explain why my discussion of modern law on some of these subjects tends to be somewhat selective. Appendix V is devoted to a discussion of the Salman Rushdie affair.

One of the principal objectives of this research has been to identify the legal norms and guidelines of the *Sharīᶜah* on the issues we have raised. This has, in turn, entailed an attempt at consolidating the materials in a manner that can be used by a modern student of law. In evaluating the data I have made suggestions regarding their relevance and application to the lives of Muslims today, and the need, in certain areas at least, for fresh enquiry and solutions. Also, I have presented an opinion when I was able to formulate one, but there are areas that can still be developed further through research.

Except for certain issues which might require structural changes in order to ensure harmony between the *Sharīᶜah* and modern law, the constitutions and laws of present-day Muslim countries do, on the whole, maintain a certain level of harmony with the principles of Islam. This tendency might have been less prominent in the early years of the post-colonial period, but now there is a general awareness of the need to enhance the Islamic identity and origins of the applied law in Muslim lands. The Islamic resurgence of recent decades has largely consisted of political demands which generated pressure to bring about a closer identity with the Islamic heritage. But these demands have not yet been translated into specific measures as to where and how this heritage can be utilised in creating viable alternatives in relation to specific issues. Constitutional law has naturally been a prime candidate for such attempts. The demand here has generally been either to establish an Islamic state, or to enhance the Islamic content of the constitution and other laws. How this can be achieved, which specific areas need to be reformed, and in what way, are questions to which detailed responses are still wanting.

This work is an attempt to explore some of the Islamic responses to issues of contemporary concern, not only by ascertaining the *Sharīʿah* guidelines on specific themes, but also by bridging the gap that has developed between the *Sharīʿah* and social reality owing to the long-standing prevalence of imitation (*taqlīd*). It is often noted, as a result, that social conditions have developed in a certain direction, and given rise to new questions to which the independent reasoning (*ijtihād*) of the legal schools (*madhāhib*) does not relate in the same way as it might have in the past.[2]

The need then arises either to develop further the existing positions in the light of prevailing conditions, or, failing that, to take a direct approach to the source materials of *Sharīʿah* in the quest for an alternative solution. These two approaches need not be mutually exclusive. Even in cases where new solutions are needed, the existing body of opinion and *ijtihād* can be of great assistance and may well show jurists to have already contemplated and debated the alternative interpretations that we now find more suitable to our conditions.

NOTE ON TERMINOLOGY

Arab writers are not consistent in the use of terminology for 'freedom of expression'. While some employ such terms as *ḥurriyyat al-ra'y,* literally 'freedom of opinion', and *ḥurriyyat al-qawl,* 'freedom of speech', others have used alternative terms such as *ḥurriyyat al-tafkīr,* literally 'freedom of thought', *ḥurriyyat al-taʿbīr,* 'freedom of expression or interpretation', and *ḥurriyyat al-bayān,* 'freedom of expression'. Ṣubḥī Mahmassānī uses both *ḥurriyyat al-ra'y*, and *ḥurriyyat al-ra'y wa'l-taʿbīr,* that is, freedom of opinion and expression. He then explains why this longer phrase is preferable to *ḥurriyyat al-tafkīr* or 'freedom of thought':

> . . . thought is a hidden phenomenon and a mental activity which is communicated in words, and until then, thought which has not been expressed in words, remains outside the concern of law. It is the external manifestation of thought which we refer to as *ra'y* (opinion). To use

> the phrase *ḥurriyyat al-ra'y wa'l-taᶜbir* is thus preferable as it leaves no doubt that the thought, idea, or opinion at issue has been expressed and communicated.[3]

ᶜAbd al-Ḥamīd Mutawallī, too, uses *ḥurriyyat al-ra'y* and *ḥurriyyat al-ra'y wa'l-taᶜbīr,* while Muḥammad Kāmil Laylah prefers *ḥurriyyat al-ra'y.* ᶜAbd al-Wāhid Wafi uses *al-ḥurriyyah al-fikriyyah,* 'freedom of thought', while ᶜAbd al-Qādir ᶜAwdah and Sayyid al-Sābiq tend to use its other equivalent, *ḥurriyyat al-tafkīr.*[4] Fārūq al-Nabhān has, on the other hand, used *ḥurriyyat al-ra'y wa'l-tafkīr* to imply the basic freedom of opinion and thought, but the freedom to express and propagate opinion and thought is referred to as *ḥurriyyat al-taᶜbīr.*[5] All of these writers tend to distinguish freedom of expression from freedom of religion, which they consistently treat as a separate category variously referred to as *ḥurriyyat al-tadayyun,* 'freedom of religion', *ḥurriyyat al-ᶜaqīdah,* 'freedom of belief', and *al-ḥurriyyah al-dīniyyah,* 'religious freedom'. Yet, it is generally acknowledged that freedom of expression in Islam is in many ways complementary to freedom of religion; that it is an extension and a logical consequence of the freedom of conscience and belief which the *Sharīᶜah* has validated and upholds.[6]

I have elsewhere elaborated, in a section on freedom of opinion, why the phrase *ḥurriyyat al-ra'y,* literally 'freedom of opinion', is used in Islamic scholastic literature for freedom of speech, despite the existence of a more precise equivalent, that is, *ḥurriyyat al-qawl.* This is, presumably, because opinion is the most important aspect of freedom of expression, and also because the word '*ra'y*' has a history of its own. *Ra'y* means a considered opinion, often related to, and co-extensive with, personal reasoning (*ijtihād*) and it signifies harmony with the norms and principles of Islam.[7]

II. Definition and Scope

1. DEFINITION

Since freedom can apply to competing or even conflicting interests, it tends to defy the idea of a comprehensive definition, which is precisely why there is no clear definition for freedom. There are, of course, many attempts by writers and commentators to define freedom, yet they are all open to some level of uncertainty and doubt. Freedom for whom? Freedom from what? And freedom to do what? To the mystic, freedom has often meant the release from egoity and dependence on the material world. The philosopher and theologian would extend the debate to encompass the relationship between God and man, and the extent to which a person can be deemed free. What meaning, if any, can the word 'freedom' have in that context?

For the lawyer and the judge, freedom operates within the limits of the law. I shall presently give a definition of freedom from a legal perspective, but bear in mind that it is only an attempt to define a certain aspect of this concept without any claim to comprehensiveness. It should be noted at the outset that the basic notion of freedom, in an objective sense, is common to all legal systems, traditions and cultures. Whether one talks of freedom in western law, Chinese law, or Islamic law, this must essentially mean 'the ability of the individual to say or do what he or she wishes, or to avoid doing so, without violating the right of others, or the limits that are set by the law'.[8] Although I have quoted this definition from an Islamic source, its basic message is nevertheless universal. Liberty has elsewhere been defined as 'the extent to which the individual can detrmine his own destiny and act as he wishes, unconstrained by others.'[9] Freedom of expression means 'the absence of restraints upon the ability of individuals or groups to communicate their ideas to others, subject to the understanding that they do not in turn coerce others into paying attention or that they do not invade other rights essential to the dignity of the individual'.[10]

Freedom of expression includes freedom of the press and the liberty to communicate ideas in all forms including books, pictures, signs and other means of communication. The purpose may be to inform, to persuade, to convince others, to reveal the truth or to clarify and eliminate doubt. The last two definitions that I have quoted above are from western sources, and yet, the concepts that they convey are universal. We may also note in this connection, Montgomery-Watt's brief comparison of the Muslim concept of freedom with that of its western counterpart, in which he has highlighted some of the differences between them but concluded that 'despite such points, however, it seems likely that there is a combination of ideas somewhere in Islamic thought, which performs much the same function as the concept of freedom does in the west.'[11] Thus, the basic notion of freedom and of freedom of expression would appear to strike a common note in all legal traditions, including that of Islam. However, the scope and character of freedom of expression under the *Sharīᶜah* differs widely from other laws in respect of detail, especially with reference to the limits that are imposed by the *Sharīᶜah* and the values that are to be upheld. If I were to characterise the rules of the *Sharīᶜah* on freedom of expression, I would be inclined to say that, unlike modern legal discourses on the subject, the *Sharīᶜah* does not convey a great deal of awareness about state authority and the political interests of its agencies and institutions. To that extent, the *Sharīᶜah* is egalitarian and substantive in the sense that attention is paid to actual values rather than to institutional interests or the dictates of the status quo and power politics. But, being a religious law, the *Sharīᶜah* is only expected to be emphatic about moral and religious values, which might mean imposing restrictions on freedom of expression in areas where this might come into conflict with the principles of Islam. This can, perhaps, be clearly seen in reference to the *Sharīᶜah* rules pertaining to blasphemy, heresy and disbelief, where the dominant concern is to defend the dogma and belief-structure of Islam, even at the expense of imposing restrictions on what may, under western law, be seen as personal matters which fall outside the concern of the law. The rules of the *Sharīᶜah* pertaining to the rights of citizens to criticise the government are, on the other hand, indicative of latitude. By comparison to some of the over-regulated areas of modern law in relation to such matters as sedition and criticism of government authorities, *Sharīᶜah* rules encourage flexibility and tolerance. Moral advice and encouragement also pervade the bulk of *Sharīᶜah* rules on freedom of expression; the legal rules therein are often less elaborate compared to the teachings and recommendations that aim at developing the individual's personality and character.

2. OBJECTIVES

There are basically two objectives that are served by the right to free speech: discovery of truth and upholding human dignity. Restrictions on freedom of speech imposed by society and the state, and the consequent fear that exposition of facts and ideas may invoke wrath or disfavour, naturally inhibits the discovery of truth. The right to free speech is also an integral part of self-development. Imposing restrictions on the articulation of what an individual may wish to say, write, express or propagate, compromises both his dignity and the desire for personal growth. Of these two objectives which are recognised and validated in Islam, it is, perhaps, the discovery and vindication of truth on which Islam tends to be more emphatic, but this should only be seen as a general characterisation of Islam with its commitment to the discovery of truth. Even so, it is reasonable to assume that in the event of a direct conflict between the quest for truth and human dignity, the former would normally prevail. This order of priority can, perhaps, be seen in the Qur'ānic text which declares that 'God loves not the public utterance of evil speech except by one who has been wronged' (IV:148).

لَا يُحِبُّ اللّٰهُ الْجَهْرَ بِالسُّوءِ مِنَ الْقَوْلِ اِلَّا مَنْ ظُلِمَ.

Note that this text imposes one major restriction on free speech and that is when it is evil, obscene, immoral or hurtful to others. But, the text allows this restriction to be dropped if doing so would mean that the victims of injustice can make their voices heard. They may be given this opportunity, free of any restriction, if it serves the cause of justice and truth. A court witness may, for example, reveal faults in the character and personality of another person, or make remarks which might compromise their personal dignity, but this may be done only if it would serve the cause of justice. The Qur'ān, in other words, tolerates utterance of hurtful speech in pursuit of a higher objective, which is to establish justice. The quest for justice, at an objective level, may thus continue even at the expense of violating the personal dignity of the individual. The Qur'ānic ideal of justice is inextricably intertwined with righteousness and truth. However, one is also reminded of the relative nature of this discussion, in particular of instances where the dignity and freedom of individuals may take precedence over the quest for truth. This is to be seen in the Qur'ānic prohibition on espionage and on violating the sanctity of private dwellings (XLIX:12; II:189). The quest for truth and justice, in this instance, is not permitted to disturb the privacy of the individual home, nor may it seek to uncover a person's weaknesses even if doing so would otherwise promote the cause of justice. Ascertaining an order of priority between these values is, on the other hand, not expected to diminish anything of the validity of either. Freedom of expression and the quest for truth are both normative values, each in its own right, and, as such, they are each to be pursued and upheld without detriment to the other. Instances of direct conflict between them are not expected to be frequent, as the normal pattern of the relationship between these values is that they endorse one another, and each functions as an instrument for the realisation of the other.

The basic commitment to truth (*al-ḥaqq*) is expressed in several places in the Qur'ān. *Al-Ḥaqq* is one of the Most Beautiful Names of God (*al-Asmā' al-Ḥusnā*), as well as being one of the principal attributes of the Qur'ān. This is the clear purport of the Qur'ānic text which reads: 'This is Our Book that pronounces for you the truth' (*bi'l-ḥaqq)* (XLV:29).

هٰذَا كِتٰبُنَا يَنْطِقُ عَلَيْكُم بِالْحَقِّ.

The normative character of *al-ḥaqq* and persistence in its pursuit is vividly portrayed in the Qur'ān where true believers are described as those who 'advise one another to truth and perseverance' (CIII:3) in its cause.

وَتَوَاصَوا بِالْحَقِّ وَتَوَاصَوا بِالصَّبْرِ.

Several meanings can be listed for *al-ḥaqq*, including for example 'just', 'real', 'right', 'obligation', 'truth', 'certainty' (*al-thubūt wa'l-wujūb*),[12] and even 'beneficence' and 'public good' (*al-khayr wa'l-maṣlaḥah*).[13] Islamic law also distinguishes '*ḥaqq Allāh*', that is, the Right of God or public rights from '*al-ḥaqq al-ādamī*', the private or civil rights of an individual. However, of all these meanings, it is 'telling the truth' that most embodies the primary meaning of *al-ḥaqq*. The Qur'ān also advocates the finality of *al-ḥaqq* in the sense of there being no further value beyond the truth once this has been attained: 'And what is there after attaining the truth, except misguidance?' (X:32)

فَمَاذَا بَعْدَالْحَقِّ اِلاَّ الضَّلَل.

The Qur'ānic stance on the pre-eminence of *ḥaqq* finds ample support in the Sunnah of the Prophet ﷺ and in the precedent of his Companions. The following *Ḥadīth* tells us, for example, that truth must not be hindered by the prospect of invoking the disfavour of others, or even of causing discomfort to oneself: 'Tell the truth even if it be unpleasant.'[14]

قُلِ الحَقَّ وَلَوْ كَانَ مُرّاً.

This robust attitude to the advocacy of truth is taken a step further by the *Ḥadīth* which proclaims that the best form of holy struggle (*jihād*) is to tell 'a word of truth to a tyrannical ruler'.[15]

أفْضَلُ الجهادِ كَلِمَةُ حَقٍّ عِند سُلْطَانٍ جَائِرٍ.

The foregoing evidence obviously implies that both ruler and subjects are committed to the pursuit and discovery of truth. This attitude was, in turn, endorsed and substantiated in the inaugural speeches of the first two caliphs, Abū Bakr al-Ṣiddīq (died 12 A.H./634 A.D.) and his successor ʿUmar b. al-Khaṭṭāb (died 23/643). Upon assuming the caliphal office, both asked the people to assist them when they were right and to correct them if they deviated from the truth.

Another way of vindicating the truth may be by correcting an error of judgement. If one acknowledges the premise that to err is an inevitable aspect of human existence, then it should follow that the avenues toward exposing and correcting errors should be open, be it through suggestion, advice or criticism, and that this cannot be achieved without granting the right to free speech. The Qur'ānic principle of *ḥisbah*, that is, commanding good and forbidding evil, and the principle of *naṣīḥah*, or good advice, which I have discussed in separate sections, are simply some of the avenues that Islam opens up in its quest for righteousness and truth.

Freedom of expression also complements human dignity, for the essence of character and personality is reflected in a person's opinion and judgement. Individuals can have but little dignity if they are denied the right to give opinions and voice their feelings in matters that concern them. The Qur'ān declares that dignity, in the broadest possible sense, is the natural right of every human being: The Qur'ānic dictum that 'We bestowed dignity on the progeny of Adam' (XVII:70) clearly transcends all the racial, social or religious barriers that divide humanity.

لَقَدْ كَرَّمْنَا بَنِي آدَمَ،

It is a general and absolute declaration, and there is no evidence anywhere in the *Sharīᶜah* to qualify the broad and universal terms of this statement. Further affirmation of the normative character of this text is found in a passage where the dignified status (*al-ᶜizzah*) of the believers is stated alongside that of God Most High and of the Prophet Muḥammad ﷺ (LXIII:8). Also found in the Qur'ān are numerous references to the grace and dignity that is bestowed on the community of believers, so much so that their collective judgement and consensus (*ijmāᶜ*) stands next to the will of God and is recognised as a source of His *Sharīᶜah*.

The *Sharīᶜah* entitles the individual to say what he or she pleases, provided that the words so uttered do not involve blasphemy, back-biting, slander, insult or lies, nor seek to give rise to perversity, corruption, hostility or sedition. In the affirmative sense, the *Sharīᶜah* encourages freedom of expression in a variety of ways including the promotion of good and prevention of evil (*ḥisbah),* sincere advice (*naṣīḥah*), consultation (*shūrā*), personal reasoning (*ijtihād)*, and the freedom to criticise government leaders.

The dignity that is attached to *ᶜadālah,* or the upright character of an individual, is a mark of his or her distinction in the eyes of God and fellow human beings. In all juridical matters, whether a person is a court witness, a judge, a head of state, a qualified scholar, a trustee of charities, a guardian, or a custodian of the person or property of others, each must pass the test of *ᶜadālah.* In this sense, the *Sharīᶜah* obviously contemplates a society whose affairs are administered by upright individuals. Indeed, according to a *Ḥadīth*, Muslims are presumed to be upright and just unless proven otherwise.[16] Therefore, it comes as no surprise that the *Sharīᶜah* takes a serious view of attacks on the honour and good name of upright citizens. Slanderous accusation (*qadhf*) is one of the handful of proscribed offences (*ḥudūd*) for which a mandatory punishment has been enacted in the Qur'ān (XXIV:4). Even when the slandering accuser (*qādhif*) is duly tried and punished, he is never again admitted as a witness in the courts of law. For the offence he committed may well have inflicted irreparable damage on the good name of his victim.

3. ROLE AND SIGNIFICANCE

Freedom of expression has often been characterised as a barometer by which to measure the democratic quality of a government and its commitment to the rights and liberties of its citizens. It is, perhaps, equally true to say that the endeavours of a people in safeguarding this freedom, and the way they balance its use against its possible abuse, is an index of their cultural refinement. The degree of tolerance that a society encourages on the part of its members to enable everyone to say what they have to say, and for the rest to show sensitivity in receiving it, is not just a question of legal finesse but reflects the liberality and latitude of a society's collective conscience. Only in a secure and tolerant atmosphere where thoughtful contribution and constructive criticism are gracefully received and appreciated by the community and its leaders, can such contributions be positively encouraged and utilised.

A government which grants and protects its citizens' right to freedom of expression can also ascertain their wishes, views and attitudes in public affairs. It is only to be expected that free speech may bring contentious issues out into the open and stimulate differences of opinion, but this may also be the only way to facilitate a meaningful consensus over issues. In this sense, constructive free speech is, to a large extent, a question of attaining the correct balance of values, and the necessary incentives and disincentives at various levels of interaction in society. But public participation in government necessitates that every citizen has the assurance that he can say what he has to say without incurring anger or being oppressed by the ruling authorities. This need for openness is even more pronounced in regard to minority opinions and views that might oppose the majority or the government in power. For a government which only wishes to explore the views of its supporters is a dictatorship. On the other hand one which encourages impartiality inspires confidence and becomes a vehicle by which a society may attain its aspirations.

Freedom of speech is also a powerful instrument when used to combate injustice and to expose the misconduct of rulers and leaders who exceed the limits of their authority. In this sense, freedom of expression plays an important role in enabling the public to monitor the conduct of its government. For it is through such freedom that errors and malpractices in public affairs are discovered. Thus, free speech plays a distinctive role in nurturing a well-informed and vigilant society—one that is likely to exercise good judgement in matters which concern it, including the choice and election of leaders. As Ibn Qayyim al-Jawziyyah points out, freedom of expression (*ḥurriyyat al-ra'y*) can be utilised for the realisation of benefit (*maṣlaḥah*), or for the prevention of evil (*mafsadah*), which may come to light and then be secured through the exercise of this freedom.[17]

ᶜAwdah has similarly observed that when freedom of speech is exercised within its legitimate framework, it leads to progress and encourages affection, fraternity and respect among fellow citizens. It is also a means by which the ruler and his subjects can co-operate (*taᶜāwun*) to attain benefit and to combat evil, discrimination and prejudice.[18]

In the area of basic liberties, historical reality is not a good indicator of normative values and the history of Islamic goverment is no exception. It is generally acknowledged that the first four decades of Islamic government under the Rightly-Guided Caliphs (*al-Khulafā' al-Rāshidūn*; see glossary) was closely guided by the normative teachings of the Qur'ān and Sunnah, but then dynastic and political interests began to dominate government practices in Muslim lands in much the same fashion as is generally known in the history of government in the Middle Ages. Fārūq al-Nabhān has acknowledged this and observed that the rights of non-Muslims in regard to freedom of expression have suffered from oppressive government practices. However, the same author adds that such practices were politically motivated, and that they had 'nothing to do with Islam' and could not in any form be validated by the norms and principles of Islam.[19] The Qur'ānic attitude as regards freedom of enquiry in the pursuit of knowledge and the exchange of information is indicated by its prolific use of such expressions as 'those who exercise their intellect' (*yaᶜqilūn*), 'those who think' (*yatafakkarūn*), 'those who know' (*yaᶜlamūn*), 'those who ponder' (*yatadabbarūn*), and 'those who understand' (*yafqahūn*). As these expressions show, the Qur'ān clearly encourages enquiry and investigation. Thought, judgement, opinion and knowledge, as the Qur'ān suggests, must be expressed and communicated, and only then can they serve effectively as the means by which to promote faith in God and to benefit mankind.

4. RESTRAINTS

It is inconceivable that any society would have attempted or achieved total and unrestrained rights to free speech, for a certain amount of restriction goes hand in hand with the facts of life. Society's perception of the right to free speech is liable to change in accordance with changing conditions, for what we consider to be acceptable today may have been quite out of the question a century or even a generation ago. A great many of the inhibitions and restrictions that are imposed on freedom of speech are extra-legal. Public opinion determines, to a large extent, the acceptable limits of such freedom, and rejects what is unacceptable or excessive. And yet, public opinion is not a free agent, as it reflects a combination of moral, religious, cultural and legal influences. Legal rules provide a good indication of the vision of a society and the standards by which it regulates the conduct of its members. But the law often intervenes only when freedom of speech violates the rights of others, the general objectives of the law or the dictates of public policy and interest. The far wider range of restraints that society and culture impose are, from a strictly legal standpoint, a matter of choice. These would fall, from the viewpoint of the *Sharīʿah*, under the general principle of original permissibility, or *ibāḥah*. Compared to other legal systems, it is probably true that Islamic law concerns itself more extensively with moral and spiritual guidance, but even so, no one would expect the law to offer exhaustive guidance on freedom of expression, as public opinion, moral attitudes and custom all play a significant role in determining the scope and dimension of this freedom.

An adequate understanding of the principles of *Sharīʿah* on freedom of expression inevitably brings us into contact with the conditions of Arab society and its vision as to the types of freedom it could visualise and accept. Although it is true that Islam has not been shaped by the dictates of social reality, it has, nevertheless, taken into consideration both the reality and potential of the society in which it came into being. Nowhere is it claimed that the divine principles and objectives of Islam are totally isolated from the realities of Arab society or from the stage of world history with which they were immediately associated. The *ʿulamā'* have also tried, on the whole, to interpret the general principles of the Qur'ān and Sunnah in the light of the socio-political conditions of their time.

From its very inception, Islam attempted to open a dialogue with those who refused to accept it. The Qur'ān explicitly stated that the Prophet ﷺ must conduct his campaign through sound reasoning and persuasion. Furthermore, the Qur'ān has encouraged rational argumentation in religious matters, and it has consistently recommended investigation and inquiry into almost all aspects of creation. In other words, the Qur'ān takes for granted the validity of an individual's right to freedom of speech. Muslim writers[20] on the subject have consistently stated that Islam not only validates freedom of expression but it also urges Muslims not to remain silent or indifferent when expressing an opinion which is likely to serve the cause of truth and justice, or be of benefit to society. A look at the passages which are often quoted in support of this position would indicate that the Qur'ānic message is to create simultaneously a right, as well as a duty, for the individual to pursue the recommended values of Islam. The Qur'ān, for instance, not only permits *ḥisbah* , *ijtihād*, and *shūrā* etc., as a right for every eligible person to practise, but also makes it their duty to do so. Here, we note a difference of style and approach between the *Sharīᶜah* and statutory law in that the *Sharīᶜah* does not seek to separate the dual concepts of right and obligation from one another in the same way as does modern statutory law.

III. Rights and Fundamental Rights

The question I propose to discuss has often been raised but has not been answered by writers in the field. This is the question of the recognition or otherwise of rights, as opposed to obligations, in Islamic law. The next, and naturally related, question is whether distinguishing fundamental rights as a separate category from the general body of rights is sustainable under the *Sharīᶜah*. These, and certain other issues of methodological significance, have not been addressed in the works of the Muslim jurists and are, as such, lacking in precedent. I have reflected on some of them and the analysis I have given below, although not essential to the main theme of this book, nevertheless warranted consideration from the point of view of methodology and comparison with some of the well-established features of modern constitutional law.

1. A PERSPECTIVE ON *ḤAQQ*

Western commentators have generally held that there is no recognition in Islam of the idea of right and liberty, fundamental or otherwise, that is inherent to the human person. Thus, according to

Schacht, 'Islamic law is a system of duties, of ritual, legal and moral obligations, all of which are sanctioned by the authority of the same religious command.'[21] Hamilton Gibb has also commented that 'the Islamic theory of Government gives the citizen as such no place or function except as taxpayer and submissive subject'.[22] This line of argument is taken a step further by another commentator who stated that 'no such abstractions as individual rights could have existed in Islam ... In such a system the individual cannot have rights and liberties ... [he] has only the obligation'.[23] It is not my purpose to enter into polemics, but merely to record a viewpoint which is clearly not borne out by the evidence I have examined in the following pages.

At the outset it is noted that rights and duties in Islamic law originate in the Qur'ān and in the authentic Sunnah of the Prophet ﷺ. The juristic manuals of the *Sharīᶜah* often speak of *ḥukm sharᶜī*, that is a ruling, typically communicated in the form of a command or a prohibition, which regulates the conduct of a legally responsible individual (*mukallaf*). These may convey a variety of concepts, including legal rights and obligations. Although the nature of these communications and the language in which the *ḥukm* is conveyed may tend toward obligation rather than right, a closer examination of *ḥukm* reveals that a mere propensity in the style of communication does not negatively affect the substance and validity of rights in the *Sharīᶜah*. An insight into the language of the Qur'ān and Sunnah would confirm that Islam has its own perspective on *ḥukm* and on the allied subject of rights and liberties. Also, in the Qur'ān and Sunnah there is no formal distinction between fundamental rights and other rights, or for that matter, between constitutional law and ordinary law. This is indicative of a certain outlook: in expounding the *juris corpus* of the law, the source materials of the *Sharīᶜah* reflect the influence of *tawḥīd*, the unity in source and origin of all knowledge, and of a tendency to turn away from approaches that may interfere with the holistic and unitarian philosophy of this principle.[24] Since the *Sharīᶜah* subscribes to the overriding authority of divine revelation, the sense of mission and duty to God and to society admittedly acquires a certain prominence in the concept of *ḥukm* over the idea, so to speak, of an individual's right or his claim *vis-à-vis* God. It is largely a question of the pattern of relations between the Lawgiver and the recipient of the law, which is inspired by the ideal of unity and integration rather than a duality of their respective interests. For, after all, modern constitutional law, and constitutionalism as such, championed the rights of the citizen in the face of the ever-expanding power of the state, which was, on the whole, viewed as a menace to individual rights and liberties. On the other hand, Islamic law does not proceed from a position of conflict between the respective rights or interests of the individual and state, which are realised through the implementation of the *aḥkām* of the *Sharīʿah*.[25] When the state succeeds in doing this, it satisfies the basic purpose of its existence, including upholding the rights of the individual. In doing so, both the individual and state obey the *ḥukm* of the *Sharīʿah* and gain the pleasure of God. Thus, the duality of interest which is often envisaged in modern constitutions does not present the same picture as in the Islamic theory of government.

Islamic law operates on the premise that God commanded humanity to act, or to refrain from acting, toward His own illustrious Self, and then toward each other, in certain ways. Individuals must worship and obey God, there being no room in their pattern of relationships for anything other than submission to His will. But then we say that God has expressed His will and *ḥukm*, which has bestowed upon human beings certain rights, as an expression of His divine grace. Commentators who are persuaded to deny the place and reality of rights in the *Sharīʿah* have not shown an awareness of this perspective in their arguments, and have advanced a superficial discourse which confuses a certain outlook that Islam maintains on rights and duties with the affirmative substance of the *Sharīʿah* on this theme. For centuries, Muslim jurists and scholars have consistently spoken of the virtues of submissiveness to God and of obeying His *ḥukm* and law. But they have, in spite of this, never hesitated to speak of the rights of individuals, and of the safety and sanctity of their lives and properties. They affirm equally effusively that the interests and benefits of people are the ultimate objective of the *Sharīʿah*; these scholars have, in other words, never entertained any doubts about the centrality of people's rights in the whole concept of *ḥukm*. They were admittedly somewhat less elaborate in advancing theories on the definition and philosophy of law, but that has probably been due partly to an attitude of piety and unquestioning submission to the will of the divine Lawgiver. It would appear that this general outlook has been taken by some commentators to mean a negation of the idea of rights. This bias in favour of obligations over rights can be found in varying degrees in almost any legal system, and Islamic law is no exception. For obligation has a stronger foundation than right, and it carries a binding force which is lacking in the concept of a right. But the reality of rights, and its existence and significance in Islamic law is undeniable. The *Sharīʿah* is merely the form in which these concepts are communicated, expressing a certain outlook on the same reality rather than a denial of that reality.

2. A PERSPECTIVE ON FUNDAMENTAL RIGHTS

The origin of fundamental rights is traceable to the works of European writers of the seventeenth and eighteenth centuries, particularly Locke and Rousseau, who wrote on natural law, and the economic theory of *laissez faire*. Somewhat vague and imprecise notions of natural rights were taken by settlers to the American continent where they were refined and articulated in the constitution of the United States and its subsequent amendments. American judges expounded and further refined these rights for almost a century and a half, and these developments influenced the constitutions of some European states and of Japan after each of the two World Wars. In 1948, the General Assembly of the United Nations approved a list of about thirty human rights which included the most important fundamental rights and liberties.[26]

The distinction between fundamental rights and other rights tends to be changeable in both contents and attributes, as it reflects the values and outlook of a particular society through its various stages of historical and cultural development. For example, with reference to Western jurisprudence, we note that Blackstone does not mention freedom of speech in his discussion of personal liberties, and his classic passage on freedom of the press occurs in the section which deals with wrongs and libel. The closest reference that Blackstone makes to free speech is in his treatment of 'Right of Persons', when he mentions the right to petition the King or the Houses of Parliament for the redress of grievances.[27] In his classic study of the constitution, Dicey has acknowledged that English law took little notice of such concepts as 'freedom of speech' and 'liberty of the press'. He wrote that 'Freedom of discussion is ... in England little else than the right to write or say anything which a jury, consisting of twelve shopkeepers, think it expedient should be said or written.'[28] The implications of this statement regarding the publication of minority or unorthodox opinions were almost totally ignored.

Writers on modern constitutional law have identified a number of methods by which to distinguish fundamental rights from other rights. The most obvious of these, in the context of western law and also perhaps in the constitutions of Muslim countries, is to refer to the constitution and ascertain whether the right in question is expressed and recorded as such. In countries where the constitution is unwritten, fundamental rights can still be identified by reference to rules, conventions and judicial precedent which may have identified certain rights to be of primary importance to the structure and content of the legal system.[29]

To designate a right as fundamental often means that the court has decided either that the right is politically essential to the existence of society, or that it is essential to individuals and to their dignity and self-respect. Thus, there are two sorts of fundamental rights which often overlap: those which are founded on basic human dignity, and those which are based on considerations of social policy. As a matter of principle, we respect the right of a person not to be killed, or his right of privacy and speech, and we respect rights which maintain the integrity of a political system, such as freedom of assembly and freedom of the press, as matters of social policy. If a right is respected on principle, it may be restricted only for very compelling reasons, but rights that are founded on social policy may be overridden or changed on the grounds of social and political desirability. However, a certain order of importance is ascertained in each category. Thus, the right to life may take priority over privacy, and the right of a police officer to carry weapons may be seen as an ordinary social right in comparison to freedom of assembly and freedom of the press. When rights of the first category conflict with those of the second, it seems proper that the court give priority to the former. For it would seem that social and political utility should not be bought at the price of respect for individuals.[30]

A legal right may also be called fundamental when it legally embodies what is basically a moral right or value. Such rights are often considered fundamental when the moral principles that give rise to them are considered to be basic principles of the moral system in question. Thus, Western jurisprudence has entertained many different philosophical perspectives, including utilitarianism, individualism and the social contract theories of law. By combining these, attempts have been made to ascertain the basic value structure of the law, what it may regard to be fundamental to the system and in what order of priority.[31] However, most of these theories have aspects in common with the influences that determine the *Sharīʿah* approach to the evaluation of rights. For instance, Muslim jurists have almost unanimously considered *maṣlaḥah* as an objective, or philosophy, of the *Sharīʿah*, and one which is strongly utilitarian, notwithstanding the fact that *maṣlaḥah* in Islam is subservient to a set of divinely-ordained values.[32]

Another area wherein the *Sharīʿah* may have aspects in common with Western legal theories is in the category of rights which are founded on the fundamental principles of morality. The principal difference, however, which distinguishes the *Sharīʿah* from secular jurisprudence is that the former subscribes to the overriding authority of divine revelation as the determinant of basic moral and legal values. Under the *Sharīʿah*, a right is fundamental if it is founded on the clear injunctions and primary principles of the Qur'ān and Sunnah. Admittedly, there are no categorical pronouncements in these sources which would identify fundamental rights as a separate category. But there are a set of principles in the Qur'ān which are in turn reiterated and upheld in the Sunnah and the consensus of scholars, which are fundamental to Islam and to its legal system. These tenets and principles carry an overriding influence and permeate, as I shall presently elaborate, almost every level of legal thought and its development in Islam.

A formal distinction between fundamental rights and other rights in the *Sharīʿah* can be made with reference to the Qur'ān, which is, by unanimous consensus, the most authoritative source of Islamic law. A right which is founded on a clear Qur'ānic injunction, such as the right to life, to property, to privacy, the right of movement, the right of parents over their children, the right to justice, the right to personal dignity and honour, and equality before the law and so forth, may be classified as a fundamental legal right. The Qur'ān also expounds certain norms and principles which give the *Sharīʿah* its distinctive identity and have a far-reaching influence on its rules and doctrines. Thus, the Qur'ānic principles of the promotion of good and prevention of evil (*ḥisbah)*, trust (*amānah*), co-operation in good work (*taʿāwun*) and so forth, may well provide textual authority for the identification of many a fundamental right whether concerning an individual, the community, or the environment, and whether it be within or beyond a nation's territorial boundaries. In numerous instances, the Qur'ān also expresses such principles as 'the removal of hardship' (*rafʿ al-ḥaraj*), which is in turn substantiated by the Sunnah. Moreover, the Sunnah elaborates on a variety of other themes in almost every legal area. These may or may not directly embody a fundamental right, but they may well provide the authority for the identification of a particular right as basic or fundamental. It is also noted that the Qur'ān and the Sunnah provide the authority, as I shall presently elaborate, on all the five essential values: life, religion, intellect, property and lineage. Many of these norms and principles have been identified and articulated by Muslim jurists in the form of legal maxims (*qawā*ᶜ*id kulliyyah*) which express the objectives of the *Sharī*ᶜ*ah* on an impressive variety of themes and which could be utilised as guidelines for an Islamic theory of fundamental rights. Some efforts have already been made by individuals and organisations, such as the ᶜ*ulamā'* of Egypt and Pakistan, and the Islamic Council of Europe, among others, but there is scope for further research in order to enhance both the range and the identification of fundamental rights in the *Sharī*ᶜ*ah*.

In his 1975 study of human rights and fundamental freedoms in the Arab Middle East, C. Luca has concluded that 'the Koranic text has a stronger hold on the mind of the Arabs than declarations contained in their formal constitutions.'[33] It would be no exaggeration to generalise the substance of this statement with regard to other Muslim countries and to proceed on the assumption that the Qur'ān has a profound influence on the thought and conduct of Muslims everywhere. The Qur'ān can best be characterised as a stable source of authority and influence which is partly open to interpretation, but whose definitive injunctions and basic value structure are not changeable. Therefore, the continuity of values is the dominant feature of the Qur'ān. It follows, then, that the basic notion of fundamental rights and their identification in the Qur'ān and the Sunnah is not only acceptable, but recommended, in so far as this articulates the essentials of the *Sharī*ᶜ*ah* in this area and gives them a concrete expression which can be utilised as a basic indicator of the place of a particular right, norm, or principle, in the general scheme of Qur'ānic values.

With reference to a parallel subject, namely, considerations of public interest, or *maṣlaḥah*, we note that the ᶜ*ulamā'* have classified them into three categories: essential interests (*ḍarūriyyāt*), complementary interests (*ḥājiyyāt*) and desirable embellishments (*taḥsīniyyāt*). The essential *maṣāliḥ* (pl. of *maṣlaḥah*) are defined as interests which are essential to life and, when disregarded, lead to the collapse of normal order in society. There are five, and according to a minority opinion, six, essential *maṣāliḥ*, namely life, religion, intellect, property, and lineage. To this, some scholars have added a sixth, namely dignity (*ʿirḍ*), but according to the majority this is subsumed under 'life'. These interests must be protected at all costs, as society cannot afford to expose them to danger or collapse. To protect these *maṣāliḥ*, and to promote and develop them further, is one of the basic duties of an Islamic government. Next in order of importance come the complementary interests, which are followed by the desirable embellishments. These categories are often interrelated and open to judgement, and they vary in reference to the circumstances in which they are evaluated. What may seem a complementary interest in one setting may well belong to a higher or a lower class of interests in another. The means and methods of protecting the essential values may differ according to circumstances, but the basic structure of these values is not changeable. Some writers have drawn a parallel between the essential interests (*al-maṣāliḥ al-ḍarūriyyah*) of Islamic law and the 'fundamental rights' of modern constitutional law. Muḥammad ʿImārah's *al-Islām wa-Ḥuqūq al-Insān: Ḍarūrāt lā Ḥuqūq* (*Islam and Human Rights: Necessities not Rights*) is perhaps the most explicit of such attempts. The author equates the idea of necessity with that of essential rights, but he also suggests that the recognition of a basic value structure in the *Sharīʿah* would justify all measures that seek to protect these values and facilitate their proper development. There is, thus, no objection to terminology or classification—call them what you will; the point is that the *Sharīʿah* advocates them and validates their protection. On the subject of basic rights, ʿImārah's is a slightly different perspective to that of the majority of scholars. The general approach is to ascertain the place and validity of each of these rights in the sources of the *Sharīʿah* as values in their own right, rather than to be subsumed under a particular juristic doctrine such as *maṣlaḥah*. Nonetheless, we can utilise this three-fold classification of *maṣāliḥ*, as a basis to classify fundamental rights and liberties along similar lines. Obviously, there is no shortage of basic authority in support of these rights in the *Sharīʿah*.[34]

Contemporary Muslim countries already have available a legacy of experience and precedent in constitution-making, which is generally predicated on the binary division of rights and liberties into either constitutional or ordinary. But since constitutionalism, which was closely imitated in the post-colonial period by newly emerging Muslim states, is a Western phenomenon, many of these countries have not attempted to forge a link with their Islamic heritage. However, the foreign origin of this legacy does not necessarily forbid, nor make reprehensible, endeavours to forge just such links. Indeed, much of the legacy may be retained or formulated in the light of the *Sharīʿah* guidelines. This would develop harmony and coherence in the legal and cultural experiences of contemporary Muslims, and consequently may be considered highly worthwhile.

NOTES

1. *Ḥaqq* is the Arabic equivalent of 'right'; *ḥukm* means law or ruling, such as in the phrase '*ḥukm sharʿī*', 'a law or ruling of the *Sharīʿah*'. ʿ*Adl* is the Arabic equivalent of 'justice'.

2. *Ijtihād* or independent reasoning by a qualified scholar is the principal method of developing the *Sharīʿah* in relation to new issues and matters which have not been determined by a clear textual injunction.

3. Mahmassānī, *Arkān Ḥuqūq al-Insān fi'l-Islām*, p. 141 and *passim*; Mutawallī, *Mabādi' Niẓām al-Ḥukm fi'l-Islām*.
Referenes in end-notes are given only in brief; for full author-names, titles and publishing data please see the bibliography.

4. Laylah, *al-Nuẓūm al-Siyāsiyyah*, p. 1122 and *passim*; Wafī, *Ḥuqūq al-Insān fi'l-Islām*, p. 114 and *passim*; ʿAwdah, *al-Tashrīʿ al-Jinā'ī al-Islāmī Muqāranan bi'l-Qānūn al-Waḍʿī*, II, p. 29; Sayyid al-Sābiq, ʿ*Anāsir al-Quwwah fi'l-Islām*, p. 143 and *passim*.

5. Al-Nabhān, *Niẓām al-Ḥukm fi'l-Islām*, p. 239.

6. Cf. Mahmassānī, *Arkān*, p. 142; al-Nabhān, Niẓām, p. 234 ff.

7. Cf. Section on *ḥurriyyat al-ra'y* below.

8. Cf. Mahmassānī, *Arkān*, p. 72.

9. *Encyclopedia Americana*, vol XVII, P. 303.

10. David H. Bailey, *Public Liberties in the New States*, p. 27. See also Wan Abdul Manan, 'Freedom of Expression: views from Academia', paper presented at the Malaysian Bar Council Seminar in commemoration of World Human Rights Day, Kuala Lumpur, Dec.10. 1989, p.1.

11. Montgomery-Watt, *Islamic Political Thought: the Basic Concepts*, p. 97.

12. Cf. Macdonald, 'Ḥakk', The Encyclopedia of Islam; Said, *Precepts and Practice of Human Rights in Islam*, p. 63.

13. Cf. Ḥammād, *Ḥurriyyat al-Ra'y fi'l-Maydān al-Siyāsī*, p. 433 ff.

14. Al-Suyūṭī, *al-Jāmiʿ al-Ṣaghīr*, vol. 1, p. 111; Ḥammād, *Ḥurriyyah*, p.7.
Ḥadīth (pl. aḥādīth), literally meaning 'speech', refers to the sayings or teachings of the Prophet Muḥammad ﷺ. It is often used synonymously with Sunnah.

15. Abū Dāwūd, *Sunan Abū Dāwūd*, II, 438.

16. Al-Bayhaqī, *al-Sunan al-Kubrā*, X, 155. The *Ḥadīth* provides to the effect: 'Muslims are upright, honest and just with each other.'

المسلمون عُدول بَعْضُهُمْ عَلىٰ بَعْضٍ .

17. Ibn Qayyim, *I'lām al-Muwaqqi'īn 'an Rabb al-'Ālamīn*, vol.3, p. 147.

18. 'Awdah, *al-Tashrī' al-Jinā'ī*, vol.2, p. 34.

19. Al-Nabhān, *Niẓām*, p. 237.

20. Note, for instance, Mahmassānī, *Arkān*, p. 142; and Mutawallī, *Mabādi'*, p. 280.

21. Schacht, 'Law and Justice' in P.M. Holt ed., *The Cambridge History of Islam*, II, 541.

22. Gibb, 'Constitutional Organisation', in M. Khadduri & H. Liebesney eds., *Laws in the Middle East*, p. 12.

23. Henry Siegman, 'The State and Individual in Sunni Islam', *The Muslim World*, 54 (1964), p. 23.

24. *Tawḥīd*, or belief in the Oneness of God, is the first pillar and foundation of Islam.

25. *Aḥkām* (pl. of *ḥukm*) as a general term refers to the laws and ordinances of the *Sharī'ah*.

26. Cf. *Universal Declaration of Human Rights*, December 10, U.N.G.A, New York. The Declaration consists of a Preamble and thirty Articles. The text of the Declaration also appears in Khan, *Human Rights in Islam*, pp. 4-10.

27. Barendt, *Freedom of Speech*, p. 29.

28. Dicey, *Introduction to the Study of the Law of the Constitution*, Ch. VI.

29. For example, in English law the right to vote and the right to issue a writ of *habeas corpus* are both fundamental rights 'as a matter of practice and history', as they are necessary for the proper working of the constitution: see Bridge, *Fundamental Rights*, p. 8.

30. Cf. Murphy, *An Introduction to Jurisprudence*, pp. 88-98.

31. Bridge, *Fundamental Rights*, n. 28 at 9ff, thus expounds theories on the philosophy of law according to Kant, Kelson, Hart and Rawls.

32. For a discussion on *maṣlaḥah* see M.H. Kamali *'Have We Neglected the Sharī'ah Law Doctrine of Maṣlaḥah?'* Islamic Studies 27, (1988), pp. 287-304.

33. Luca, 'Discrimination in the Arab Middle East', in Willem A. Veenhoven, ed., *Case Studies on Human Rights and Fundamental Freedoms*, vol. 1, 1975.

34. See for details Kamali, 'An Analysis of Rights in Islamic Law', *American Journal of Islamic Social Sciences*, vol. 10 (1993), pp. 340-367.

PART TWO: AFFIRMATIVE EVIDENCE

I. Introductory Remarks

This chapter enquires into some of the principles and institutions of the *Sharīʿah* which provide the basic evidence in support of freedom of expression. Since the compendia of jurisprudence (*fiqh*) [1] do not treat freedom of speech and expression in the same manner as we find in modern constitutional discourse, the relevant data of *fiqh* on this theme has consequently remained scattered and underdeveloped. Thus, the *Sharīʿah* evidence on freedom of expression is found under a variety of topics including the Qur'ānic principle of commanding good and forbidding evil (*ḥisbah*) which takes for granted the basic freedom of individuals to formulate and express their own opinions. Another topic of interest here is sincere advice (*naṣīḥah*), which is a manifestation of fraternity among Muslims, and may be proffered to anyone, including the *ʿulamā'* and government leaders. Similarly, the Qur'ānic principle of consultation (*shūrā*) entitles community members to be consulted in public affairs, and their leaders are entitled to solicit counsel from those who are capable of giving it. In addition, the doctrine of independent reasoning (*ijtihād*), as well as the citizen's right to criticise government leaders (*ḥaqq al-muʿāraḍah*), are all premised on the recognition in the *Sharīʿah* of the fundamental freedom of speech and expression.

I have addressed each of these topics in the following pages. Yet a perusal of my discussion may leave the reader questioning whether, and if so, why some of these topics such as *ḥisbah* and *naṣīḥah* are treated in the scholastic works of *fiqh* as moral categories which have not been translated into practical legal rules. This may be true, but even so it does not provide a conclusive argument that the attitude taken by the jurists of the past must prevail indefinitely. We need only take note that the juristic expositions of the Muslim jurists (*fuqahā'*, sing. *faqīh*), on these issues came into being long before the onset of contitutionalism and its allied concepts of fundamental rights and liberties. The juristic discourse of the *fuqahā'* is conveyed in a language which they felt was suitable to the prevailing conditions of their time. Surely it is now the task of the contemporary student of the *Sharīᶜah* to address these issues, as they present themselves today, in an appropriate manner and form. However, such differences of approach are not necessarily expected to lead to disputes over basic principles. For Muslim society in its changing phases of development is within its rights to elevate some of the moral and religious teachings of the Qur'ān, the Sunnah and the legal schools, into positive laws for purposes of enforcement. Furthermore, it is a known fact that a substantial part of the *Sharīᶜah*, especially those of its teachings which fall within the categories of recommendable, permissible and reprehensible (*mandūb, mubāḥ, makrūh*), consists of moral guidance which may be turned into legal provisions if this would benefit the people. It is also known that the *Sharīᶜah* combines in its corpus, in addition to legal rules, moral teachings which tend to support and supplement one another and often merge into unified formulae. There is often, for example, a relationship between strict compliance to a legal duty and the Islamic concept of moral excellence (*taqwā*). Thus, the moral teachings of Islam have been taken a step further and have been given a place in the *juris corpus* of the *Sharīᶜah*. It is partly for this reason that the present study, although dominantly juristic, is not confined to the legal subject-matter of the *Sharīᶜah*. This relationship between law and morality acquires special significance in the area of freedom of speech, which, by its nature, extends beyond the scope of formal legal rules. It is, therefore, neither advisable nor in keeping with the holistic approach of the *Sharīᶜah*, to confine the scope of this study to legal subjects alone. For such an attempt would not only be out of character with the *Sharīᶜah* but would also alienate the rich reservoirs of moral teachings which could provide the basis of legislative reforms on various aspects of the freedom of expression.

II. The Qur'ānic Principle of *Ḥisbah*

Commanding good and forbidding evil (*al-amr bi'l-maʿrūf wa'l-nahy ʿan al-munkar*) is a cardinal Qur'ānic principle which lies at the root of many Islamic laws and institutions. As an epithetical description of Islam itself, this principle is the supreme objective of the *Sharīʿah*, and the ethical core of governmental power. Accordingly, citizens are, in so far as their conditions and capabilities permit, entitled to speak and to act in pursuit of what in their enlightened judgement seems good, or they can forbid, whether in words, acts or silent denunciation, any evil which they see being committed. This Qur'ānic principle, also known as *ḥisbah*, lays down the foundation of some of the basic liberties that form the principal theme of many modern constitutions. Although *ḥisbah* is much wider in scope and cannot, therefore, be confined to freedom of speech alone, it is nevertheless no exaggeration to say that this freedom is of central importance to the concept of *ḥisbah*; indeed it is its *sine qua non*. For without freedom of speech it would be inconceivable to command good or to forbid evil. The wider scope and implications of *ḥisbah* are treated in considerable detail in the works of jurists and theologians and, since a full treatment of *ḥisbah* falls beyond my immediate purpose, I shall confine this discussion to the relevance of *ḥisbah* to freedom of expression. However, a brief word about the manner in which the *ʿulamā'* have treated *ḥisbah* will, perhaps, justify my being eclectic in the treatment of this principle. Al-Ghazālī characterises *ḥisbah* as 'the greatest pole in religion' (*al-quṭb al-aʿẓam fi'l-dīn*), and the most important objective of all of God's revealed scriptures. Therefore, as this is the essence of all religion, a total neglect of *ḥisbah* would bring about the collapse of religion and widespread corruption and ignorance.[2] In Ibn Qayyim al- Jawziyyah's assessment, *ḥisbah* constitutes the basic objective of all governmental authority (*jamīʿ al-wilāyāt*) in Islam. He regards it as a collective obligation (*farḍ kafā'ī*) in which everyone must participate to the extent of his or her ability.[3]

With all the prominence it has commanded, however, *ḥisbah* has not been treated as a principle of positive law in the *Sharīʿah* in the sense that its neglect carries no legal sanctions. It is instead treated as a normative principle of Islam which provides moral argument and the foundation for the bulk of the detailed rules of the applied

Sharīʿah in its various branches.[4] Part of the reason for this may be that *ḥisbah* is broad enough to comprise the whole of the *Sharīʿah*, which is why it is almost impossible to reduce it to concrete and specific rules. It is, therefore, treated as an integral part of religion, as a moral theme and guideline, and as a philosophy and objective rather than a concrete rule of positive import. There is only one situation where *ḥisbah* becomes an individual obligation (*farḍ ʿaynī*), and that is when there is only one person in the entire community, or when a single individual witnesses evil being committed. Only in these situations does *ḥisbah* become the personal responsibility of the individual concerned; in all other capacities, it remains a collective duty (*farḍ kafāʾī*) of the community as a whole.

Whether collective or individual, *ḥisbah* has been generally characterised as an obligation. On the whole, the classical expositions of the *ʿulamāʾ* on this subject do not address the question as to whether or not *ḥisbah* also constitutes an individual's right, fundamental or otherwise, or whether it can be designated as a collective right of the community as a whole. This question of the recognition, or otherwise, of fundamental rights in Islamic law has already been raised and discussed. Suffice it here to say that Islamic law recognises both rights and obligations, including fundamental rights, notwithstanding the fact that the *ʿulamāʾ* have not treated the latter as a separate category. In many cases, the question of separation between rights and obligations in the *Sharīʿah* tends to be a matter mainly of perspective and style rather than substance. This is, to a large extent, also true of *ḥisbah*, for although it has been characterised as an obligation, it is quite obvious, nevertheless, that it entitles every Muslim to speak for a good cause or to disapprove and criticise a bad one. This dual characterisation of *ḥisbah*, both as a right and a duty, has found explicit recognition in the recent *Universal Islamic Declaration of Human Rights*, a publication of the Islamic Council of Europe. This document refers to *ḥisbah* as simultaneously constituting 'the right and duty of every person' to speak for and defend the rights of others and those of the community when these are threatened or violated.[5] This is further supported by A. J. Ḥammād who observes that '*ḥisbah* being a pillar of the faith and a cardinal principle of the *Sharīʿah* offers a basis which is sufficiently authoritative to validate freedom of expression in political and governmental affairs'.[6] Zaydān is even more emphatic in saying that a correct understanding and implementation of 'the principle of *ḥisbah* necessitates the freedom of the individual to formulate and express an opinion'.[7] To Muṣṭafā al-Sibāʿī, the primary focus of *ḥisbah* is the well-being of society, for it lays down the foundation of what he calls social liberty (*al-ḥurriyyah al-ijtimāʿiyyah*). 'It confers upon those who are capable to form an opinion, the liberty to express that opinion or even to criticise others on an issue of social concern.' Al-Sibāʿī adds that if anyone witnesses an evil action which violates the *Sharīʿah*, or the standard of decent conduct and approved custom, it is up to that individual to prevent or denounce it to the extent of his or her capability.[8]

Commanding good and forbidding evil is the main theme of a number of verses (*āyāt*) in the Qur'ān. The following excerpt is often quoted by the *ʿulamā'* as the principal Qur'ānic authority for *ḥisbah*:

> Let there be *(waltakun)* among you a group that calls others to good, commanding good and forbidding evil. Those are the successful ones *(mufliḥūn)*. (III:104; see also III:110 and XXII:41)

Al-Ghazālī has observed that since this verse begins with a command ('let there be', '*waltakun*'), it conveys an obligation (*wājib*) which is, however, a collective obligation of the entire community. The collective nature of the obligation is also indicated in the same text, specifically where it reads: let there be 'among you', meaning that the obligation is fulfilled even if only a section of the community acts upon it. Performing *ḥisbah* as the *āyah* once again indicates, leads to success (*falāḥ*) in both this world and the Hereafter.[9] It is best, therefore, if the whole of the community observes *ḥisbah*, but it may be observed by only some members - men or women or both. This is backed up by the Qur'ānic passage which states that: 'The believers, both men and women, are friends and protectors (*awliyā'*) of one another. They enjoin good and they forbid evil' (IX:71). Thus, it is understood that a successful implementation of *ḥisbah* requires a collective effort by the entire society. If implementing certain aspects of *ḥisbah* require an active role to be assigned to women alone, or through co-operation between men and women, then the Qur'ān authorises this. Furthermore, it is interesting to note that in the Qur'ān *ḥisbah* is mentioned side by side with the first pillar of faith, namely, belief or *īmān*. The Qur'ānic references to *ḥisbah* are also explicit about the great benefit to mankind that it contains, and that a society which loses sight of the essence of *ḥisbah* is bound to find itself in a losing battle against the forces of corruption and evil. Clearly, this is the message of the Qur'ānic verse which declares, 'Verily man is in loss, except for those who have faith, and act righteously, and who advise each other to [pursue] truth, perseverance, and patience.' (CIII:2-3)

The Prophet ﷺ instructed the believers to carry out *ḥisbah* in accordance with their ability and to the extent that circumstances permitted. *Ḥisbah* may thus be implemented in at least three ways, as we read in the following *Ḥadīth*:[10]

> If any of you sees something evil, he should set it right with his hand; if he is unable to do so, then with his tongue, and if he is unable to do even that, then (let him denounce it) in his heart. But this is the weakest form of faith.[11]

مَن رَأى مِنْكُم مُنْكَرًا فَلْيُغَيِّرهُ بِيَدِه، فَإن لَمْ يَسْتَطِع فَبِلِسَانِه، فَإن لَم يَسْتَطِعْ فَبِقَلبِه وذٰلِكَ أضْعَفُ الايْمَان.

It is interesting to note that the first of the three varieties of *ḥisbah* specified in this *Ḥadīth* is entirely practical, that is, to act against evil by one's physical action (*taghyīr bi'l-yad*). However, it is only logical to expect that a verbal attempt to denounce or correct the wrong which is observed precedes the actual attempt, and that the verbal attempt is, in turn, preceded by disapproving thoughts. This is the natural order of human responses to events, but the *Ḥadīth* here does not necessarily conform to this order, as it prescribes a sequence which is almost the reverse. However, this is a familiar feature of the rulings (*aḥkām*) of the *Sharīʿah* as they often contemplate the external manifestation of thought, and may for this purpose set a certain order of priority which differs from the natural pattern of human response. Note also that the *Ḥadīth* cited above uses the words 'whoso sees' (*man ra'ā*), instead of using words such as 'knows' or 'hears'. Again, this concerns the external nature of the evil being committed, and the ability of the person witnessing it to change it in some way.[12]

Forbidding evil, which is only one of the two aspects of *ḥisbah*, constitutes the principal theme of this *Ḥadīth*. Again, this reflects the familiar norm of the *Sharīʿah* that priority should be given to the prevention of evil over the attraction of some gain. The three steps that are indicated in this *Ḥadīth* bring *ḥisbah* within reach of virtually every individual who witnesses evil being uttered or committed. Prevention is obligatory (*wājib*) when a person observes something forbidden (*ḥarām)* being committed, but it is only commendable (*mandūb*) if it aims at preventing something which is reprehensible (*makrūh*). There is also a difference between wickedness (*munkar*) and sin or disobedience (*maᶜṣiyah*) in that the former is wider in scope than the latter. If, for example, a child is seen to be committing a wicked act, it may not qualify as *maᶜṣiyah* but it may still qualify as *munkar*, which would consequently fall within the scope of *ḥisbah.*[13]

There are four degrees of *ḥisbah* which also specify, in the way they are given, the correct order of priority in attempting to implement *ḥisbah.* These are as follows: Firstly, informing or apprising (*taᶜrīf*), either verbally or in writing, the person who is committing a wrong, of the enormity of his conduct. If this proves insufficient, then one proceeds with the second step - kindly admonition (*waᶜẓ*) to invoke the fear of God in the person and to appeal to his reason and better sentiment. If this still proves ineffective, then the third step authorises the use of harsh words. These may involve a threat but may amount neither to accusation nor to insult. Words and phrases which are expressive of denunciation such as 'O tyrant' (*yā ẓālim*), or 'O ignorant one' (*yā jāhil*), or 'Do you not fear God?' may be used. The forth and last stage of *ḥisbah* consists of expressing anger or the use of force, but these are permitted only when absolutely necessary and to the extent that they may prevent evil. However, the use or threat of force must aim precisely at preventing evil, and not in order to punish the perpetrator.[14] The only three exceptions to the application of all four degrees of *ḥisbah* are made in regard to one's father, husband and the head of state, to whom only the first two degrees are applied. Al-Ghazālī explains this by saying that subjecting the Imām to anger is likely to incite sedition (*fitnah*). But harsh words may be used even to the Imām, and in some cases it is recommended (*mandūb*), if there is no fear of inciting *fitnah*. However, if the ill arising out of such *fitnah* is likely to harm others, it must be avoided. But according to the majority of *ᶜulamā'*, it is permittted to use harsh words to the head of state and other officials if the harm that is feared only concerns the person himself. But the ultimate purpose must always be the removal of evil (*izālat al-munkar*) and *ḥisbah* should not be attempted if it is likely to give rise to a greater evil.[15]

While commenting on the *Ḥadīth* quoted earlier, al-Ghazālī observes that fear of death, injury or loss of property are legitimate excuses to relieve a person of the duty of carrying out *ḥisbah*, in which case the *ḥisbah* may be confined to a tacit disapproval only. But, on the other hand, it is not permissible under any circumstances to assist the perpetrator of evil either in words or in action. Moreover, the evil which is to be prevented or denounced, must be self-evidently evil so that there remains no need to resort to interpretation or *ijtihād* in order to establish its status. The question as to exactly what amounts to good (*maʿrūf*) or to evil (*munkar*) is to be determined with reference to the *Sharīʿah*, in particular to those rules that pertain to the protection of the five values, namely, life, faith, intellect, property and lineage.[16]

Furthermore, the Mālikī jurist, al-Qarāfī, records the following three conditions which must be observed in the implementation of *ḥisbah*. Firstly, the person who bids good or forbids evil must act from a position of knowledge, since an ignorant individual who is not sure of his grounds may neither enjoin good nor forbid evil. Secondly, one must be reasonably sure that their attempts at prevention do not give rise to a greater evil. Thirdly, one must act on the basis of an overwhelming probability (*al-ẓann al-ghālib*) that the attempt to enjoin good or to forbid evil is likely to achieve the desired result. The absence of either of the first two conditions renders *ḥisbah* unlawful (*ḥarām*) which must be avoided, but the absence of the last condition downgrades *ḥisbah* from an obligation into a mere permissibility (*mubāḥ*).[17]

III. Sincere Advice (*Naṣīḥah*)

The dictionary meaning of *naṣīḥah* is 'sincere advice, friendly admonition, and friendly reminder'.[18] *Naṣīḥah* (also *munāṣaḥah*) is a Qur'ānic concept which occurs in a number of places in the Holy Book, especially where references are made to the purpose and function of prophethood. Thus we read that the prophets Noah, Ṣāliḥ, Hūd and Shuʿayb, may peace be upon them, all informed their people that the nature of their mission was to give warning as a sincere advisor (*nāṣiḥ*) does. The prophet Noah said to his followers 'I give to you sincere advice', and 'I am to you an honest adviser (*nāṣiḥun amīn)*'. (VII:62, 68; note also verses 79 and 93 in the same *sūrah*.)

Naṣīḥah is to be distinguished from reprimand (*tawbīkh*), as the two may have aspects in common and may be liable to confusion and overlap. According to al-Ghazālī the principal difference between *naṣīḥah* and *tawbīkh* is that the former is confidential and courteous, whereas the latter is public and tactless. Here, al-Ghazālī's observation is in harmony with that of Imām Shāfiʿī, who observed that when a person advises his brother confidentially, he has given him *naṣīḥah*, but if he preaches to him openly, he has ridiculed and belittled him.[19] Both of these views may be seen as commentaries on the *Ḥadīth* which states: 'One who gives advice is a confidant.'

اَلْمُسْتَشارُ مُؤْتَمَن.

According to yet another *Ḥadīth*, 'When one of you gives advice to his brother, let him isolate him (from) the company of others.'[20]

اِذَا اِسْتَشَارَ اَحَدُكم اَخاهُ فَلْيَشِرْ اليه.

The essence of *naṣīḥah* in Islam is to encourage a vigilant but caring attitude on the part of the believers, who are expected to maintain and protect the moral and religious values of Islam. Thus, the individual is entitled to give sincere counsel to others when he is convinced of the essential benefit of his advice. *Naṣīḥah* is generally seen as an integral part of *ḥisbah*, with the only proviso being that the emphasis in *naṣīḥah* is laid on the first of its twin aspects, namely, enjoining good (*al-amr bi'l-maʿrūf*) rather than on forbidding evil. In this way, *naṣīḥah* takes for granted the right of every individual to form an opinion or advice in which he or she sees a benefit, and the right to convey it in confidence to others, be it a fellow citizen or a government leader. In addition, the opinions or advice in question may be given in social, political or personal affairs, but, as Ḥammād points out, freedom of expression in political affairs (*ḥurriyyat al-ra'y al-siyāsī*), is a distinctive feature of *naṣīḥah.*[21]

The centrality of *naṣīḥah* to the promotion of good and prevention of evil is once again confirmed in a *Ḥadīth* in which *naṣīḥah* is declared to be the essence of religion, and a necessary ingredient of the fraternity (*ukhūwah*) that Islam encourages among the believers. *Naṣīḥah* is also the antidote of *ghībah* (backbiting), in that when a Muslim observes a fault on the part of another, or a benefit that he envisages for him, the matter should be communicated between them. However, this should be done with a certain tact and courtesy that is appropriate to the spirit of fraternity. As an example, it is reported that on one occasion the Prophet ﷺ told his Companions 'Religion is *naṣīḥah,*' which invoked the inevitable question 'To whom [does the right/duty of *naṣīḥah* belong], O Messenger of God?' To this, the Prophet ﷺ replied, 'To God, to His Book, to His Messenger, and to the leaders and commonalty of the believers'.[22]

اَلَّدِينُ اَلنَّصِيحَةُ، قُلْنَا لِمَن يَا رَسُولَ اللهِ، قَال لله
وَلِكتابِهِ وَلِنَبِيّهِ ولِأئِمّةِ المُسلِمِينِ وَعَامَّتِهِم.

While commenting on this *Ḥadīth*, al-Nawawī, the author of *Riyāḍ al-Ṣāliḥīn*, quotes al-Khaṭṭābī as having said that the phrase 'Religion is sincere advice' (*al-dīn al-naṣīḥah*) means that *naṣīḥah* is the sustainer of religion and a pillar thereof (*qiwām al-din wa-ʿimāduhu*). For example, when it is said, 'The pilgrimage is ʿArafah' (*al-Ḥajj ʿArafah*), it means that ʿArafah is a pillar, that is, a *sine qua non* of the Ḥajj.[23] Another commentary maintains that this *Ḥadīth* stresses the significance of *naṣīḥah,* which is declared to be the embodiment of Islam itself. Giving *naṣīḥah* to community leaders and the generality of its members means to assist them in righteousness and give them sincere counsel in the spirit of promoting good and forbidding evil.[24]

The link between *naṣīḥah* and true belief in Islam is once again the focus of attention in the following *Ḥadīth*, as Jarīr b. ʿAbd Allāh reported: 'I came to the Prophet ﷺ and declared "I pledge myself to you in Islam (*ubāyiʿuka ʿalā'l-Islām*)". The Prophet ﷺ then said "on condition that you offer *naṣīḥah* to the faithful" . . . I then pledged this in my oath of allegiance.'[25]

We also read in a *Ḥadīth* that *naṣīḥah* is a right every Muslim has over his or her fellow believers. The *Ḥadīth* in question begins by saying, 'There are six rights that all Muslims have over one another'. These consist of such rights as responding to one's greeting (*salām*), visiting the sick, and so on. Then the *Ḥadīth* ends as follows: 'when you are asked for *naṣīḥah* then you must give it.'

إذا اسْتَنْصَحَكَ فانْصَحْ لَهُ.

Furthermore, al-Maqdisī quotes Imām Aḥmad b. Ḥanbal as having said that *naṣīḥah*, like *ḥisbah*, is a collective obligation (*farḍ kafā'ī*) and, as such, it may be given even if it is not solicited or asked for. This view is supported by another *Ḥadīth* in which there is a reference to the leader or head of state who is required to give *naṣīḥah* to his subjects. It states that he must exert himself in this direction, and if he fails, he shall not be a companion to those of his subjects who enter Paradise.[26] This *Ḥadīth*, according to Imām Ibn Ḥanbal, does not specify that *naṣīḥah* should be given only when it is solicited. The first of the two *Ḥadīths*, however, does specify this condition, but the conclusion has nevertheless been drawn that *naṣīḥah* does not depend on asking, and that Muslims should give it at their own initiative.[27] This ruling is apparently based on an analogy between *naṣīḥah* and *ḥisbah*. As both are collective obligations, neither must depend on a particular request, otherwise they would lose much of their significance and rationale. Furthermore, the first of the two *Ḥadīths* begins with the phrase, 'the right of a Muslim' ('*ḥaqq al-Muslim*'). From this context, it is understood that *naṣīḥah* in this particular *Ḥadīth* embodies a right to be claimed, as opposed to an obligation which requires fulfilment even without such a claim. However, the possibility still remains that the *Ḥadīth* under discussion might have identified only the best form of *naṣīḥah* which naturally must be one that is requested or solicited by its recipient. It is further suggested that the precedent of the Companions, especially that of the Rightly-Guided Caliphs (*al-Khulafā' al-Rāshidūn*),[28] indicates that members of the community (*ummah*), both men and women, and their leaders, have given and received *naṣīḥah* in an informal atmosphere and publicly in the mosque, in the street and also in the presence of others. This precedent would lend support to the conclusion that there is no compelling reason to lay down any particular procedure for *naṣīḥah*.[29]

The *Sharīʿah* does not regulate the manner in which *naṣīḥah* is given, since in all cases this must remain a matter for the good conscience and sincerity of the individual. The only guidance that is found in the Sunnah has been conveyed with a view to identifying the best form of *naṣīḥah*, rather than dictating a particular procedure for giving it. It is thus recommended:

1) That *naṣīḥah* must not involve exposing or exploring the privacy and personal weaknesses of people (*tatabbuʿ al-ʿawrāt*);
2) that it is given in the best possible form, with an awareness of the suitability of the occasion, time and place;
3) that it is founded on certainty and not on speculation, estimation, or suspicion;
4) that it is given to the extent necessary and that excess is avoided;
5) that it is in harmony with the guidance of the Qur'ān and the Sunnah.[30]

Furthermore, according to the terms of another *Ḥadīth*, 'when someone wishes to give *naṣīḥah* to a person in authority, then let him not declare it openly but let him take his hand and speak to him in privacy. If it is accepted, the purpose is achieved, and if not the donor of *naṣīḥah* has still fulfilled his duty.'[31]

مَن اَرَادَ ان يَنْصِحَ لِذِى سُلْطَانٍ فَلَا يَبْدَه عَلا نِيَةً وَلٰكِن يَأْخُذْ
بِيَدِهِ فَيَخْلُوبه، فَإِن قَبِلَ منه فَذَاكَ وإِلاّ كانَ قَد اَدّى الَّذِى عليه.

Naṣīḥah to the leaders of the Muslim community, both the government leaders and *ʿulamā'*, means assisting them in righteousness, courteously reminding or alerting them of their duties, and bringing them closer to the people. Regarding the generality of Muslims, *naṣīḥah* means offering them sincere advice and guidance concerning their benefits in this world and the Hereafter, in both words and actions, and to like or dislike for them that which one would like or dislike for oneself.[32] In this connection, it is interesting also to quote the following report that al-Maqdisī has recorded. Ibn Mubārak was once asked: 'What if, in my presence, a bankrupt person comes to do business with a merchant. If I know that he is bankrupt, but the merchant is unaware of this, should I reveal the facts to the merchant?' Ibn Mubārak answered this query in the affirmative and quoted the following *Ḥadīth*: 'None of you is a (true) believer unless you love for your brother that which you would love for yourself.'[33]

لَا يُؤْمِنُ أَحَدُكُمْ حَتَّى يُحِبَّ لِأَخِيهِ مَا يُحِبُّ لِنَفْسِهِ.

There is no value in advice which is devoid of sincerity (*ikhlāṣ*), and it is even worse if the advice is based on hypocrisy (*riyā'*), in which case it would amount to a sin.[34] Moral courage and conviction are required to make *naṣīḥah* effective and this can only be achieved when the donor's conscience is not burdened with the fear of authority, or the fear of losing a material advantage. The greatest source of inner strength is faith in God, and the belief that He alone controls the destiny of everyone. The following *Ḥadīth* once again expresses this concern on the part of the Prophet ﷺ, who is reported to have said: 'When you see my community afraid of calling a tyrant "tyrant" then take leave of it.'[35]

إذا رَأَيْتَ أُمَّتِي تَهَابُ أَن تَقُولَ لِلظَّالِمِ يَاظَالِمُ فَقَدْ تُوُدِّعَ مِنْهَا.

The Sunnah of the Prophet ﷺ also impresses upon the believers not to neglect *naṣīḥah*, and that it must, at no time, be brought to a close. Thus, we read in this *Ḥadīth*, which begins on a striking note:

> 'Let no one humiliate himself or herself.' The Companions who heard this asked, 'How does one do that (ie humiliate oneself), O Messenger of God?' Then the Prophet ﷺ said, 'When someone sees an occasion on which he should speak out for the sake of God, but does not; God Most High will say to [such a person] on the Day of Judgement: "What stopped you from speaking on that issue?" And when the person answers, "fear of people", then God will say: "It was more correct that you should have feared Me".'[36]

لاَيَحْقِرُ احدُكم نَفْسَه، قَالُوا يَا رَسُولَ اللهِ كَيْفَ يَحْقِرُ
اَحَدُنَا نَفْسَهُ؟ قَالَ يَرَى اَمْرًاللهِ عَلَيْهِ مَقَال ثُمَّ لاَيَقُولُ
فِيهِ، فَيَقُولُ اللهُ عَزَّوَجَلَّ يَوْمَ الْقِيَامَةِ: مَا مَنَعَكَ اَن
تَقُولَ فِي كَذَا وَكَذا، فَيَقُولُ خَشْيَةَ النَّاس، فَيَقُول،
فَاِيَّايَ كُنْتُ اَحَقُّ اَن تَخْشَى.

Imām Aḥmad b. Ḥanbal is reported to have held that Muslims are not bound by an obligation to give *naṣīḥah* to non-Muslims (i.e. *dhimmī*s) but to Muslims only. This conclusion is said to be based on a *Ḥadīth* which reads to the effect that every Muslim is required to participate in *naṣīḥah:* 'Good counsel is for every Muslim (*al-nuṣḥ li-kulli Muslim)*'. The terms of this *Ḥadīth*, do not actually categorically conclude that the *dhimmī*s are outside the purview of *naṣīḥah*. What is clear in this *Ḥadīth* is the conclusion, as al-Maqdisī points out, that *naṣīḥah* is a collective obligation of all Muslims. As to the other conclusion, which excludes the *dhimmī* from the scope of *naṣīḥah*, al-Maqdisī merely records the reported view of Imām Ibn Ḥanbal, but ends it with the phrase 'and God knows best', which is usually invoked when the speaker himself is not certain about the matter. In the view of the present writer, there is no conclusive evidence to confine the scope of *naṣīḥah* in this way. On the contrary, my understanding of the evidence I have reviewed suggests no such limitation on *naṣīḥah*, except perhaps in matters which have a direct bearing on the creed (*ʿaqīdah*) of Islam.

IV. Consultation (*Shūrā*)

Being one of the salient principles of government prescribed in the Qur'ān, *shūrā* requires the head of state and government leaders to conduct community affairs through consultation with community members. However, the Qur'ānic provisions on *shūrā* are primarily concerned with laying down the basic foundation of *shūrā* as a principle of public law, but the details as to its manner of implementation and the subject matters on which consultation must take place are left out. The Qur'ān provides no instruction on whether all community affairs should be determined through consultation, or whether *shūrā* applies to government affairs alone. However, this absence of specific detail has actually given *shūrā* the unfettered flexibility of being applicable to all circumstances, and to all matters that are of concern to the community. The general language of the Qur'ānic provisions on *shūrā* has also led to the conclusion that *shūrā* is an integral part of Islam and that it must, in principle, permeate every sphere of public, and even personal life under the *Sharīʿah*. It is also to be noted that the Qur'ānic texts that require the implementation of consultation are mentioned alongside references to the pillars of Islam, such as the profession of faith (*īmān*), obligatory prayer (*ṣalāh*), and legal alms (*zakāh*). This has, once again, been taken as evidence that *shūrā* should be treated on a similar basis, and be given an equally prominent place in regulating the social and political affairs of Muslim societies. Thus, according to al-Bahī, the Qur'ānic provisions on *shūrā* are conveyed in terms which not only comprise the affairs of government, but also relations within the family and between neighbours, business partners, employer and employee, and in virtually all spheres of life where it is deemed to be of benefit to the people.[37]

The following text, one of the two Qur'ānic passages concerning *shūrā*, praises the early community of believers for their diligence in conducting their communal affairs on the basis of *shūrā*:

> Those who respond to the call of their Lord, and establish the prayer, and who consult each other and spend of what We have granted them of sustenance ... (XLII:38)

وَالَّذِينَ اسْتَجَابُوا لِرَبِّهِمْ وَأَقَامُوا الصَّلَوٰةَ وَأَمْرُهُمْ
شُورَىٰ بَيْنَهُمْ وَمِمَّا رَزَقْنَٰهُمْ يُنْفِقُونَ.

In this text, the fact that consultation occurs side by side with the three pillars of faith has been taken to mean that it is an obligation of a similar order. It is interesting to note that this particular text is a Meccan verse which was revealed before the Islamic state had come into existence. Later, when an Islamic government was established in Medina, the injunction on consultation came in the form of a Qur'ānic command, and this laid the textual foundation of *shūrā* as a principle of Islamic government. The Prophet ﷺ, now head of state, was then ordered to:

> Consult them [the Companions] in the [community] affair[s], and when you have reached a decision, then place your trust in God [and implement it]. (III:159)

وَشَاوِرْهُمْ فِى الْأَمْرِ فَإِذَا عَزَمْتَ فَتَوَكَّلْ عَلَى اللهِ.

Al-Ṭabarī characterises consultation as one of the fundamental principles of the *Sharīʿah (ʿazā'im al-aḥkām)*, which are essential to the substance and identity of Islamic government.[38] Ibn Taymiyyah held a similar view, observing that God Most High commanded the Prophet ﷺ to consult the community, despite the fact that he was the recipient of divine revelation. This Qur'ānic command is therefore all the more emphatic with regard to the subsequent generations of Muslims who no longer have the Prophet ﷺ among them, and so no longer have access to direct revelation.[39] Muḥammad ʿAbduh has also held that in this verse, consultation is not just a recommendation, but an obligatory command addressed primarily to the head of state to ensure that it is properly implemented in government affairs.[40] Asad, Zaydān, al-Bahī, Mawdūdī and ʿAwdah, among others, have all concurred with this conclusion. Further support for this interpretation is found in the Sunnah of the Prophet ﷺ and the precedent of his Companions.[41] One of the Companions, Abū Hurayrah ʿAbd al-Raḥmān ibn Ṣakhr (died 57/676), is reported to have said: 'I have not seen anyone more diligent in consulting his companions than the Prophet ﷺ himself.'[42]

مَا رَأَيْتُ أَحَدًا أَكْثَرَ مَشُورَةٍ لِأَصْحَابِهِ مِنَ النَّبِيِّ صَلَّى اللهُ عَلَيهِ وَسَلَّمَ.

In another *Ḥadīth*, the Prophet ﷺ is reported to have told his two principal advisers, Abū Bakr al-Ṣiddīq and ʿUmar ibn al-Khaṭṭāb, 'If the two of you agree upon a counsel, I shall not oppose you.'[43]

لَوْ اِجْتَمَعْتُمَا فِي مَشُورَةٍ مَا خَالَفْتُكُمَا.

Similarly, on a number of occasions, the Prophet ﷺ, in the context of both private and public affairs, solicited counsel from the Companions, and at times he gave it preference over his own views.[44]

In Arabic usage, the root word from which *shūrā* is derived (i.e. *shāra*) literally means extracting honey from the honeycomb. The juridical meaning of *shūrā* is obviously related to its literal roots in that it consists of extracting an opinion (*ra'y*) on a particular issue.[45] One who deliberates a matter in association with others is often exercising *ijtihād* based on a considered opinion (i.e. *ijtihād fi'l-ra'y*), and as such it may be right or it may be erroneous. But since *shūrā*, unlike *ijtihād* by an individual jurist, consists of a collective opinion (*ra'y*), it is more likely to be right. The strength of *shūrā* also lies in the fact that consultation brings people closer together, and it provides them with an opportunity to voice their views on matters of common concern. In this way, *shūrā* prevents disunity and division among people.[46] But consultation can only be meaningful and effective when the participants enjoy total freedom to express their views. Maḥmūd Shaltūt and al-Sibāʿī merely reiterate this truism when they say that the Qur'ānic principle of consultation takes for granted the freedom of speech and expression for those whose counsel is being solicited.[47] ʿAbd al-Karīm Zaydān is even more emphatic when he writes that 'It would be totally in vain, and would make no sense to say that in Islam the government is bound by the principle of consultation, and yet should have the liberty to deny the participants of *shūrā* the freedom to express an opinion.'[48]

As for the subject-matter of *shūrā*, and whether it should apply to all matters or be implemented on a selective basis, al-Qurṭubī is of the view that consultation has a role to play in both religious and temporal affairs, but he adds that the consultant in religious matters must be well versed in the religious sciences. However, in temporal matters on which counsel is being sought, the consultant need only be wise and capable in order to give sound advice.[49] The jurists have generally held that *shūrā* applies to both religious and temporal affairs on which no clear injunction is found in the text of the Qur'ān or the Sunnah. Should there be guidance available in these sources on a particular issue, consultation would be redundant and it would not be allowed to override textual injunctions. Although the substance of this principle is generally accepted, it would, nevertheless, be less than accurate to say that *shūrā* has no role to play regarding matters which have been regulated in the Qur'ān and Sunnah. For, in such cases, *shūrā* could still operate, in a subsidiary capacity perhaps, in order to facilitate the correct interpretation and understanding of the textual ordinances (*aḥkām*), and to determine proper methods for their enforcement. In this sense, it may be said that *shūrā* has a role to play in all communal affairs both within and outside the textual rulings of the *Sharīʿah.*[50]

Some *ʿulamā'* have attempted to single out certain themes, such as warfare, as the proper or even the exclusive subject-matter to which *shūrā* is applicable; however, this would suggest that *shūrā* is not a requirement in other areas of government.[51] The correct response to such views can be ascertained in the Qur'ānic text (III:159) in which consultation is conveyed in the form of a general command which is not qualified in any way. A general (*ʿāmm*) and absolute (*muṭlaq*) command, according to the rules of Islamic jurisprudence (*uṣūl al-fiqh*), must remain so unless there is evidence to warrant specification (*takhṣīṣ*) or qualification (*taqyīd*) of the original command. There is no compelling reason to specify the subject matter of *shūrā* in any way other than what has already been stated, namely, that *shūrā* must not conflict with the definitive injunctions of the *Sharīʿah.*[52]

In sum, the scope and subject matter of *shūrā* need not be restricted in any way, and as such it entitles every citizen, man, woman, Muslim or non-Muslim to express an opinion on matters of public concern.[53] The government is, in turn, under a duty to solicit such counsel from everyone, especially regarding matters on which there is disagreement within the community. All who are concerned, and who have a view, should be enabled to voice their opinions and the grounds on which they are founded. Action should then be based on that opinion which is closest to the Book of God and the Sunnah of His Messenger ﷺ.[54]

Furthermore, the Qur'ānic provisions on *shūrā* necessitate not only the setting up of one or more representative assemblies as an integral part of government, but also that its consultative decisions are implemented by the head of state. The precise detail as to whether the leader should have powers to veto the decisions of the state consultative assembly (*majlis al-shūrā*), and whether the exercise of such powers should itself be regulated by certain procedures are, as Abū Ḥabīb has aptly observed, matters which remain open to *ijtihād*.[55] This similarly applies to the subject matter of *shūrā*, as to whether or not this should be specified by the provisions of the constitution or other laws to ensure an even distribution of tasks and powers within the various organs of the state. Therefore, the detailed guidelines on these, and other aspects of consultation, may be determined through consultation itself, and through the application of *ijtihād* which derives its inspiration and guidance from the Qur'ān, the Sunnah and the precedent of the Rightly-Guided Caliphs. The participants of *shūrā* must enjoy the freedom to express an opinion to the government, and if necessary to criticise it, for the common good (*maṣlaḥah*) and benefit of the community. Being a principle of the Islamic faith which is described in the Qur'ān as an attribute of the truly Muslim personality, consultation should by no means be confined to government affairs alone. In this capacity, *shūrā* should be seen as a hallmark of Muslim culture, and as a model for its socio-political development.

V. Personal Reasoning (*Ijtihād*)

Literally, *ijtihād* means striving or self-exertion in any activity which entails a measure of hardship. By definition, *ijtihād* is described as the total expenditure of effort by a jurist to deduce, with a degree of probability, the rules of the *Sharīʿah* from the evidence and indications that are found in the sources. The sources of the *Sharīʿah*, namely the Qur'ān and the Sunnah, may expound the rule that is wanting for a particular issue by the direct application of their words, in which case there is no room for deduction by means of *ijtihād*. However, if they provide only indirect indications, it is for the *mujtahid* to interpret the text, and to deduce, by the application of his reasoning and judgement, the necessary solution.[56] *Ijtihād* is validated by the explicit authority of the Sunnah, in particular the well-known *Ḥadīth* reported by the Companion Muʿādh b. Jabal (d. 18/639), and by the implied authority of a number of verses in the Qur'ān.[57] In classical jurisprudence, *ijtihād* is evaluated as a collective obligation (*farḍ kafāʾī*) of the entire community which is fulfilled even if it is exercised by only some of its members. Therefore, it is not merely the right of every knowledgeable individual to carry out *ijtihād*, but also his or her responsibility to do so. What is important is not necessarily the result, but the endeavour itself which, according to the explicit terms of the following *Ḥadīth*, merits a reward even if the result turns out to be erroneous.

> 'When a judge/person making a decision (*ḥākim*) exerts himself and gives a correct decision he will have a double reward, and if he errs in his judgement, he will still merit a reward.'[58]

إِذَا اجْتَهَدَ الْحَاكِمُ فَاصَابَ فَلَهُ أَجْرَانِ وَانْ اَخْطَأَ فَلَهُ أَجْرٌ.

This *Ḥadīth* makes it clear that the efforts of the *mujtahid* may lead to correct results or to erroneous conclusions. In either case, he is entitled to an opinion, despite any opposition or disagreement by other equally qualified *mujtahids* over the same issue. For the truth or falsehood of the results that have been reached may be neither obvious nor immediately ascertainable. The fact that this *Ḥadīth* grants a reward for an attempt at *ijtihād*, would obviously imply that disagreement in *ijtihād* is tolerated, and may even prove beneficial, which is perhaps why it merits a reward.[59] It is further understood from the implied meaning of the same *Ḥadīth* that everyone who is capable of formulating an informed opinion and judgement over an issue is encouraged to do so, and should not withhold their contribution on grounds of mere hesitation over its accuracy or otherwise.[60] This encouragement has, to a large extent, borne fruit which can be seen in the wealth and diversity of opinion in the various spheres of Islamic learning, including Qur'ānic exegesis, the emergence and development of various schools of law, theology, philosophy and Sufism. As al-Bahī points out, the word *ijtihād* in the terminology of *fiqh*, is another term for difference of opinion (*ikhtilāf fi'l-ra'y*).[61] Ever since the time of the Companions, scholars (*ᶜulamā'*) have not ceased to disagree in their opinion and personal reasoning, and this would in turn testify, as Zaydān points out, to the broad consensus that disagreement in *ijtihād* is acceptable.[62]

To ensure propriety in the exercise of *ijtihād*, the scholars of *uṣūl al-fiqh* have laid down certain conditions, such as the qualifications that the *mujtahid* must possess, and a set of rules which are designed to ensure the integrity of *ijtihād*, and to discourage indulgence in arbitrariness or unfounded criticism of others. The theory of *ijtihād* is explicit that the result of *ijtihād* is binding on no one but the *mujtahid* himself. This would clearly suggest that he must be guided only by his true conviction and belief in the conclusion that he has arrived at. For otherwise, as al-Bahī has rightly observed, there would be no point in binding the *mujtahid* to his own *ijtihād*.[63] When *ijtihād* fulfills all of its requirements, then the result it has arrived at is inviolable, and its validity is not affected by opposition and criticism until the truth is established through unanimity and consensus. In the meantime, no one is entitled to attack the integrity of its author. On the contrary, the effort and self-exertion of the *mujtahid* in attaining a true and correct solution to a problem merits commendation and reward. Only in one case does the latter lose its claim to validity, namely, when a decisive consensus of learned opinion (*ijmāᶜ*), declares the *ijtihād* in question invalid, or when the implication of such an *ijmāᶜ* clearly refutes the validity of an individual *ijtihād*. In this case the *ijmāᶜ* itself commands adherence and prevails over individual opinion. But even then, it is only for practical purposes that the individual *ijtihād* loses its merit. Provided that the *mujtahid* has acted in good faith, and in compliance with the requirements of *ijtihād*, his integrity remains intact. The fact that the

Sharīᶜah validates *ijtihād* and defends its integrity, as Mahmassānī points out, is one tangible result of the freedom of expression and belief in Islam.[64] The *mujtahid* who is capable of exercising his own *ijtihād* is not, according to the theory of *ijtihād*, permitted to follow the opinion or *ijtihād* of others unless he agrees with it and is convinced of its veracity and truth.[65] This ruling also requires that judicial decrees must originate in the personal *ijtihād* of the judge (*qāḍī*), and when this is not the case, and the *qāḍī* issues a decision which disagrees with his own judgement, his decision is liable to review. When, for example, the judge conforms to the wishes of another person of influence, or when he adopts the *ijtihād* of another person contrary to his own beliefs, his decision becomes liable to review and may be reversed. For the judge-cum-*mujtahid* must always act upon his true conviction and only issue a decision which he believes to be upright and valid.[66]

The inviolability of *ijtihād* acquires special significance in regard to judicial decisions which are founded on the personal judgement and *ijtihād* of the judge. According to an Islamic legal maxim, *ijtihād* is not reversible by its own equivalent (*lā yunqaḍ al-ijtihād bi-mithlihi*). When a judge renders a decision which is based on his sound reasoning and *ijtihād*, neither the same, nor any other judge is entitled to reverse it by means of fresh *ijtihād*. For the two instances of *ijtihād* are deemed to carry equal force and there is, in theory, no basis for one to justify reversal of the other provided that both are permissible (*sā'igh*) and acceptable (*maqbūl*), in that they are each in accord with the requirements of *ijtihād*. For if one were to be allowed to set aside the other, merely on grounds of a difference of opinion, then there is no reason, as al-ᶜĀmidī expounds, why the second and the third in the series should not be subject to reversal as well. It is obvious that accepting such a proposition would lead to a chain of events (*tasalsul*) that would violate public interest (*maṣlaḥah*), as it would prevent the termination of disputes among people, cause confusion, and undermine public confidence in court decisions.[67] The substance of this argument is equally applicable to the decisions based on *ijtihād*, taken by the head of state and those who represent his authority.

Further evidence as to the reality of the freedom of expression in *ijtihād* comes from the fact that all of the leading imāms of jurisprudence are on record as having discouraged others from imitating their opinion, or *fatwā*,[68] without investigating the grounds on which it founded. This is indicative, as Ghazawī points out, of their deep respect for scholarship and for the right of other *mujtahids*[69] to freedom of expression.[70] Needless to say, without this freedom *ijtihād* would be totally unfeasible.

The development of two different scholastic traditions in the formative stages of Islamic legal history (toward the end of the first century A.H.), namely the *ahl al-ra'y* or partisans of personal opinion, and the *ahl al-Ḥadīth*, or partisans of Tradition as embodied in *Ḥadīth*, is further proof of substantial support, in the ranks of the *ᶜulamā'*, for the use of personal opinion, or *ra'y*, in the development of the *Sharīᶜah*. *Ijtihād bi'l-ra'y*, or *ijtihād* which is founded on considered personal opinion, became the distinctive feature of the *ahl al-ra'y*, especially among the Ḥanafīs who relied extensively on the use of *ra'y*, analogical reasoning (*qiyās*), and juristic preference (*istiḥsān*). These were the more disciplined and regulated methods of *ijtihād* which were developed in order to ensure propriety in the exercise of *ra'y* as a means of developing the *Sharīᶜah*. Despite the initial resistance which it encountered from the partisans of *Ḥadīth*, the basic validity of *qiyās* was generally accepted. This was also the case, to a large extent, with regard to juristic preference (*istiḥsān*), consideration of public interest (*istiṣlāḥ*, or *maṣlaḥah*), and presumption of continuity (*istiṣḥāb*). The essential validity of these, as various manifestations of *ijtihād*, was recognised and as a result, they were all integrated into the legal theory of *uṣūl al-fiqh*. The common ground between these various doctrines is that they are all rationalist in content and rely largely on opinion (*ra'y*). Once again, they all share the basic notion that the ruler, the scholar and the *mujtahid* have not only the right, but the responsibility, to exert themselves for the benefit of the people, and for the fulfilment of the legitimate needs of society in all reasonable ways consonant with the *Sharīᶜah*, even if no specific authority can be found in their support.

Ijtihād may be exercised with regard to subjects that fall under one or the other of the following two categories:

(A) Temporal matters which are not of immediate concern to religion. In this area, as Khallāf has rightly observed, 'the individual enjoys total freedom of expression and may express an opinion as he pleases provided that it does not amount to slander, hostility or sedition.'

(B) In religious and legal matters, the *mujtahid* may express an opinion if the matter in question has not been expressly regulated by a clear text from the Qur'ān or the Sunnah. The only condition that needs to be observed here is that *ijtihād* in juridical matters must not violate the basic principles and objectives of the *Sharīʿah*.[71]

It is commonly observed that, ever since the establishment and crystallisation of the schools of law (*madhāhib*) from the beginning of the fourth to the eleventh century, *ijtihād* has come to a standstill. The closure of the door of *ijtihād* has become a familiar, although somewhat disputed, phrase to describe the end of *ijtihād* and the beginning of indiscriminate imitation (*taqlīd*). A climate of opinion began to prevail in which it was thought that the *Sharīʿah* had been thoroughly explored, all questions had been exhaustively investigated and settled, and consequently thenceforth it was the duty of the subsequent generations of scholars to follow the law as it had been expounded by the leading imāms, and therefore to avoid embarking on fresh *ijtihād*. The claim concerning the so-called 'closure of the door' may be exaggerated, as it is often said that *ijtihād* has never been totally abandoned; but even so, there seems to be little doubt that *ijtihād* has been steadily declining. Was this, then, a voluntary self-restraint that the *ʿulamā'* of the past chose to impose so as to curb the diversity of schools and sects in the vastly expanded territory of the early ʿAbbāsid state?[72] In other words, was the closure of the door of *ijtihād* a circumstantial development in response to a historical situation, or a manifestation of the normative principles of the *Sharīʿah*? The answer is likely to be the first, for, according to one observer, 'after the so-called closure of the door of *ijtihād* whatever limits that were imposed on *ijtihād* were due to a change of circumstances and not a change of principles.'[73] Thus, it would follow that the alleged closure of this gate has no bearing, in principle, on the validity of the freedom of every scholar and *mujtahid* to engage in *ijtihād* in their search for new solutions to new problems.[74]

VI. Freedom to Criticise
(Ḥurriyyat al-Muʿāraḍah)

Under the *Sharīʿah*, people are granted the freedom to criticise and monitor government activity (*ḥurriyyat al-muʿāraḍah*, also known as *ḥurriyyat al-naqd al-ḥākim*), by means of sincere advice, constructive criticism, or even ultimately by a refusal to obey the government if it is guilty of violating the law. This is a corollary of the Qur'anic principle of commanding good and forbidding evil (*al-amr bi'l-maʿrūf wa'l-nahy ʿan al-munkar*) which entitles, indeed commits the individual to criticise, change or rectify transgression and wickedness when he or she witnesses or anticipates its occurrence. '*Muʿāraḍah* is a fundamental principle of the Islamic system of government', writes ʿAfīfī, 'which entitles the individual to tell the truth and expose transgression even when this entails opposing the ruling authorities.'[75] In the Qur'ān and Sunnah the textual authority for this right is the same as can be quoted in support of *al-amr bi'l-maʿrūf wa'l-nahy ʿan al-munkar*, also known as the principle of *ḥisbah*.[76] The Qur'ān, as already discussed in the foregoing section on *ḥisbah*, is so emphatic on the value of this principle that it is elevated into being an integral part, and a requirement of, the Muslim faith. It is the central theme of a number of verses in the Qur'ān, and the Sunnah elaborates it and regulates its detailed implementation. The Qur'ān thus places both men and women on an equal footing with regard to *ḥisbah* and *muʿāraḍah*, and each and every citizen is entitled to disapprove of, and denounce transgression, be it on the part of a government leader, a fellow citizen, or indeed anyone who is engaged in a crime.

Muʿāraḍah is also validated by the Sunnah of the Prophet ﷺ and by the clear precedent of his leading Companions and the orthodox caliphs. Thus, it is reported that, at the signing of the treaty of Ḥudaybiyyah with the Quraysh of Mecca, ʿUmar ibn al-Khaṭṭāb, was critical of some of the clauses of the treaty which he felt were unfavourable to the Muslims. ʿUmar consulted the more senior Companion, Abū Bakr, on the matter but he was still dissatisfied and went on to express his sharply critical view of the treaty to the Prophet ﷺ, who listened to ʿUmar's view and responded to his criticism.[77] Elsewhere we encounter a *Ḥadīth* where the Prophet ﷺ proclaimed, 'The best form of *jihād* is to utter a word of truth to a tyrannical ruler.'[78]

اَفْضَلُ الْجِهَادِ كَلِمَةُ حَقٍّ عِنْدَ سُلْطَانٍ جَائِرٍ.

In his inaugural speech following his election to office, the first caliph, Abū Bakr, is reported to have said: 'O people, I have been entrusted with authority over you, but I am not the best of you.

Help me if I am right and correct me when I am wrong.'[79] This quote is widely considered to invite constructive criticism of the government, and to encourage people to remain vigilant over the activities of their political leaders. As Abū Ḥabīb has observed, the basic attitude which Abū Bakr manifested in this speech, indicates that self-criticism is not only beneficial for healthy growth, but is also a necessary attribute of responsible government.[80]

Numerous instances of *muʿāraḍah* have been recorded in the precedent of the second caliph, ʿUmar b. al-Khaṭṭāb. Following the precedent of the first caliph, Abū Bakr, ʿUmar also asked the people, at his inaugural speech, to 'rectify any aberration' they might see in him. A man from the audience addressed the Caliph saying, 'If we see deviation on your part, we shall rectify it by our swords.' Upon hearing this, the Caliph praised God that there was someone who would, in the cause of righteousness, remedy a wrongful situation.[81] Another report concerns the subject of dowry (*mahr*). Apparently, in a public speech, the Caliph warned the people against exaggerated sums being given as dowry. However, one woman, Faṭimah bint Qays, disagreed and quoted a Qur'ānic text (IV:20) in support of her argument, to which ʿUmar responded with, 'A woman is right, and ʿUmar is mistaken.'[82]

According to another report, a man came to ʿUmar and addressed him somewhat impudently saying, 'Fear God, O ʿUmar.' Someone who was present reminded the man that he was exceeding the limits of propriety in the presence of the Caliph, but ʿUmar responded by saying: 'It would be to no good if they (people) did not remind us so and it would be to no good if we did not listen to them.'[83]

In al-Sibāʿī's assessment, the precedent of Abū Bakr and ʿUmar b. al-Khaṭṭāb indicates clearly that they recognised the citizen's freedom to criticise government leaders. The fact that they listened to such criticism, and often responded to it, is proven by historical evidence.[84] According to another observer, the freedom of speech, opinion, and expression which the Muslims experienced in the earliest stages of their history represents an inspiring example which has hardly been surpassed in the subsequent periods of Islamic government.[85] Based on these and other instances of *muʿāraḍah* which took place during the period of the Rightly-Guided Caliphs (*al-Khulafā' al-Rāshidūn*), it is concluded that 'Islam entitles the citizen to monitor the activities of the head of state and state officials in respect of all that they do, and also all they might neglect doing.'[86] Muḥammad Khiḍr al-Ḥusayn is even more emphatic. He observed that Islam has made it 'an obligation of the community' to monitor the conduct of the head of state and his officials with a view to rectifying those who deviate, and alerting those who might be neglecting the duties with which they are entrusted.[87] 'It is only natural to say', writes al-Qāsimī, 'that *muᶜāraḍah* cannot exist unless there is freedom of speech.' This goes hand in hand with freedom of opinion (*ḥurriyyat al-ra'y*), and it cannot operate in a system of government which does not safeguard constitutional liberties. But whenever there is such freedom, then *muᶜāraḍah* serves as a natural instrument of the freedom of opinion.[88] The right to criticise must not be confused, as Muḥammad al-Ṣādiq ᶜAfīfī points out, with opposition merely for the sake of opposition, nor should it be taken so far as to institutionalise opposition in the form that is known, for example, in present-day political parties.[89] An opposition party is often committed to opposition for its survival, and this fact of contemporary politics tends to encourage criticism that verges on imbalance. This form of opposition is discouraged in Islam on the authority of the *Ḥadīth* which instructs the Muslims as follows: "Be not weak in character (*immaᶜah*) saying: 'If people act rightly we too shall act rightly, and if they act unjustly we too shall do so ...'."[90] Participation in good work is normally encouraged, whether it is self-initiated or by following the example of others; however, if good work is motivated merely by a desire to comply with others, it can have little educational value. An example of *immᶜah*, or weakness of character, is when someone praises or denounces another without reason merely because he sees others doing the same. This is, as Khalīl points out, particularly demeaning and unworthy of the dignity of man, as the motivation does not originate in true conviction and belief. *Immᶜah* also occurs when a person says something he or she does not believe, and believes something but does not say so.[91] The correct approach is to be found in the second portion of the *Ḥadīth* just quoted, which goes on to instruct the believers as follows:

> Rather, make up your minds for yourselves and if people do something good, do it too, but if they do something unjust, do not do it yourselves.

لَا تَكُونُوا اِمَّعَةً تَقُوْلُونَ اِنْ حَسُــنَ النَّاسُ اَحسَــنَّا وإنْ ظَلَمُوا ظَلَمْنَا، ولٰكِن وَطِّنُوا اَنْفُسَكُمْ اِن اَحَسَــنَ النَّاسُ تُحسِــنُوا وَإِنْ اَسَاؤوا فَلَا تَفْعَلُوا.

Consequently, a heightened sense of individual responsibility is of central importance to the proper exercise of *muʿāraḍah*. Indeed, the success of any critique, written or verbal, lies in the sincerity of its author. According to the clear instruction of another *Ḥadīth*, 'every one of you is a shepherd (*rāʿī*) who is responsible for [that which is in his custody].'[92]

كُلُّكُمْ راعٍ وَكُلُّكُمْ مَسْـئُولٌ عَنْ رَعِيَّتِهِ ...

In other words, everyone is accountable, no one is beyond criticism and all criticism should partake of the essence of *naṣīḥah*.

Furthermore, freedom to criticise must not be used as a means to disunite or confuse, nor as a means of self-aggrandisement. In its legitimate use, this freedom should serve as a torchlight by which to find the truth, and to search for the right course of conduct in order to benefit the community as a whole. And lastly, freedom to criticise must not be based on suspicion. Indeed, Muslims are specifically instructed in the Qur'ān and the Sunnah to avoid indulgence in both suspicion and doubt.

There are at least three conditions which need to be met in order to ensure the validity of a given criticism. These are as follows:

(a) It is necessary to establish the facts and ascertain the grounds on which criticism is based. General authority for this requirement is found in the Qur'ān where, in an address to the believers, it is said:

'If a transgressor (*fāsiq*) comes to you with any news, ascertain the truth, lest you harm people unwittingly and then regret what you have done.' (XLIX:6)

يٰاَيُّهَا الَّذِينَ اٰمَنُوآ اِن جَآءَكُمْ فَاسِقٌ بِنَبَاٍ فَتَبَيَّنُوا اَنْ
تُصِيبُوا قَوْمًا بِجَهَالَةٍ فَتُصْبِحُوا على مَا فَعَلْتُمْ نٰدِمِينَ.

Thus, the Qur'ān requires that facts must be investigated first before reaching any conclusion which may otherwise prove to be unfounded and regrettable. The substance of this text is also confirmed a few verses later in the same *sūrah*, where the believers are asked to 'avoid much suspicion (*ẓann*), for some [varieties] of suspicion are sinful'. (XLIX:12)

يٰاَيُّهَا الَّذِينَ اٰمَنُوا اجْتَنِبُوا كَثِيرًا مِّنَ الظَّنِّ اِنَّ بَعْضَ
الظَّنِّ اِثْمٌ.

Therefore, suspicion over the sayings and conduct of others which is not substantiated by evidence should be avoided. Obviously, the text here does not forbid all suspicion, and therefore *ẓann* which is based on proper or reasonable grounds may be sufficient for criticism. This kind of suspicion, which represents a probability of truth, is often referred to as 'permitted speculation' (*al-ẓann al-mubāḥ*).[93]

The conditions for ascertaining the grounds of criticism are further qualified in that they must be within the capacity of the investigator. In this regard, the Qur'ān states, 'God does not burden a person with what is beyond his capacity'. (II:286)

لَا يُكَلِّفُ اللّٰهُ نَفْسًا اِلَّا وُسْعَهَا.

Therefore, when a person has carried out an investigation to the best of his ability and understanding, this is normally sufficient evidence on which to base criticism. This is illustrated in the Qur'ān where we read that the Prophet Moses عليه السلام criticised his teacher, the Prophet al-Khiḍr عليه السلام, for deliberately breaking a barge which belonged to a poor family and was their only means of earning a living. As the Qur'ān records the episode, Moses said to al-Khiḍr, 'Did you break it so as to drown its passengers? Truly a strange thing you have done?' (XVIII:71)

قَالَ أَخَرَقْتَهَا لِتُغْرِقَ أَهْلَهَا لَقَدْ جِئْتَ شَيْئًا إِمْرًا.

But this is said to be a fair criticism based on proper grounds, that is, the observation of an apparent transgression, given Moses's ignorance of the true state of affairs which was known only to al-Khiḍr. The latter then informed Moses of the fact that there was a king who usurped all the barges he could find, so he (al-Khiḍr) had bored a hole in this barge to save it from being seized. In this instance, the whole truth was not known to Moses, yet his criticism was founded on proper grounds.

(b) The critic must be convinced of the moral uprightness of his opinion. For, unless a person believes that what he says is the truth he must not say it, otherwise he is guilty of either hypocrisy or lies - both of which are forbidden. With regard to the first, the Qur'ān declares that 'the hypocrites will be in the lowest reaches of hell' (IV:145) and for the second, the Qur'ān admonishes the believers to 'refrain from telling lies'. (XXII:30)

- إِنَّ الْمُنَافِقِينَ فِي الدَّرْكِ الْأَسْفَلِ مِنَ النَّارِ.

- وَاجْتَنِبُوا قَوْلَ الزُّورِ.

However, if a person believes himself to be right in expressing a critical opinion, and yet the opposite is found to be the case, then he is not to be blamed. Similarly, if a person exerts himself in establishing the grounds pertaining to the object of his critique, but in doing so reaches the wrong conclusion, then he is not to be blamed provided he believed that it was correct. This is the purport of the *Ḥadīth* which declares:

> The person who knowingly argues (for) what is false shall remain afflicted with the wrath of God until he ceases (his false argument) and desists from it.[94]

مَنْ خَاصَمَ فِي بَاطِلٍ وهُوَ يَعْلَمُ لَمْ يَزَل فِي سَخَطِ اللهِ
حَتَّى يَنْزِعَ.

By way of divergent implication (*mafhūm al-mukhālafah*), it is understood from this *Ḥadīth* that a person who did not know that he was engaged in a wrong cause is not to be taken to task.[95]

(c) Criticism must be proportionate to its object. This means that the words used and the manner of criticism should suit the occasion. It must be neither too harsh nor too feeble; however, it must also be courteous and effective. From the quantitative angle, the question arises as to whether a single criticism would suffice, as opposed to repeated and sustained criticism. In principle, perseverance is permitted, especially when the critique is a courteous invitation to what is deemed to be good and beneficial. Indeed, when the critique is aimed at something that comprises aspects contrary to Islamic values (*al-munkar)*, perseverance is recommended until the criticism bears fruit. This is also the purport of the previously cited *Ḥadīth* which concerns the three degrees of *ḥisbah*, namely, that a person who sees evil being committed should change it by his hand, but if he is unable to do that he should change it with his words, and if he is unable to do that he should denounce the evil in his heart, this being the weakest form of faith.[96]

The above *Ḥadīth* encourages persistent effort, even if this means changing the method by which the combating of evil is conducted. The main point of the *Ḥadīth*, however, is that if people have conviction and faith, then they should not turn a blind eye to wrongdoing whenever it is within their capacity to change or prevent it. This *Ḥadīth* also implies that the method, style and intensity of combating something *munkar* should be determined in proportion to what is required in the light of the circumstances. This would naturally involve a prior assessment of the situation, speech or conduct which is to be made the target of criticism. Consequently, the determination of the correct method and style of criticism involves a certain measure of personal judgement on behalf of the critic and his *ijtihād*.

A proper exercise of the right to criticism proceeds upon another principle of the *Sharīʿah*, namely, the principle of validity (*aṣl al-ṣiḥḥah*). Through this principle, which basically aims at giving people the benefit of the doubt, Islam protects peoples' dignity by ensuring that their words and deeds are credited with being true and valid unless there is clear evidence to suggest otherwise. It is to this principle that we now turn.

PRESUMPTION OF VALIDITY (*AṢL AL-ṢIḤḤAH*)

It is presumed that the words and deeds of a Muslim are valid unless the opposite is known to be the case. For example, when a person makes a speech, enters a transaction or performs an act of worship, but doubts arise as to whether these were valid, under the principle of presumption of validity it will be presumed that the words and deeds in question were sound and lawful unless evidence is established to the contrary. Thus, according to the Shāfiʿī jurist, Tāj al-Dīn al-Subkī: 'The norm among us (*al-aṣl ʿindanā*) is to judge as valid an act that manifestly conforms to the *Sharīʿah*. Therefore, no consideration is to be given to suspicion (*al-tuhmah*) in the *aḥkām* of *Sharīʿah*, for this is unreliable and infirm. The *aḥkām* of *Sharīʿah* contemplate obvious causes (*al-asbāb al-jalliyyah*) and they do not refer to hidden meanings (*al-maʿānī al-khafiyyah*). The norm, therefore, is one of validity until the contrary is proven.'[97]

Al-Subkī continues that Imām Abū Ḥanīfah has taken the view that an act which has become the object of suspicion should be deemed invalid on the grounds that this gives rise to a conflict between validity and invalidity (*al-ṣiḥḥah wa'l-fasād*) in which case the latter should prevail.

The Shāfiʿite position is representative of the majority, including the Imāmī Shīʿites: validity prevails over suspicion. The substance of this presumption is also endorsed by another legal maxim, recorded in *The Mejelle* (Art. 74), which provides that 'suspicion commands no credibility' (*lā ʿibrah li'l-tawahhum*). For basic authority on the presumption of validity we refer to the Holy Qur'ān which states that a person should 'avoid much suspicion, for some (varieties) of suspicion are sinful' (XLIX:12). This text clearly forbids indulgence in unfounded suspicion and suspecting the worst of motives behind the acts and words of others. In another passage, the Qur'ān directs the believers as follows: 'And speak well to the people.' (II:83)

وَقُولُوا لِلنَّاسِ حُسْنًا...

This text clearly indicates that the gift of speech, and the freedom to utilise it, should always involve courtesy when dealing with others. The Qur'ān thus addresses the hidden and the manifest aspects of human conduct. Both of these must be positive, and human relations are to be courteous and trustworthy—becoming of the dignity that God Most High has bestowed upon mankind.

Further evidence to support presumption of validity can be found in the *Ḥadīth*, where the Prophet ﷺ has instructed the Muslims as follows, concerning what a fellow Muslim might have said or done:

> When something reaches you from your brother, ascribe to it the best (interpretation) until you can no longer do so.[98]

اذا بَلَغَكَ عَن اَخِيكَ شَيْءٌ فَا حملهُ عَلى اَحْسَنِه حَتّى لَمْ
تَجِدَلَهُ مَحْمَلاً.

ʿAlī b. Abī Ṭālib reiterated the substance of this *Ḥadīth* in one of his sayings when he advised the believers in the following terms:

> Make the best of the affair of your brother until you find evidence that would dissuade you from doing so; suspect not the worst of what your brother might have said while you can still find a way to give it a favourable interpretation.[99]

The presumption of validity is not to be confounded with another presumption of Islamic law, namely that of continuity (*istiṣḥāb*), for the two are different despite their apparent similarity. The principle of *istiṣḥāb* presumes continuity of the *status quo ante* until there is evidence to establish a change. *Istiṣḥāb*, in other words, denotes that facts, rules of law or data which have been proven in the past, are presumed to remain so for lack of evidence required to establish any change.[100] The presumption of validity differs from *istiṣḥāb* in that the former is not concerned with linking the past to the present. In other words, this presumption is concerned simply with validation rather than with maintaining the *status quo*. Moreover, unlike *istiṣḥāb*, which is concerned with linking two situations to each other, the presumption of validity often has no basis on which to operate other than giving the benefit of the doubt as regards validity, and pronouncing an optimistic or favourable judgement in a situation of uncertainty.

Suspicion may also arise regarding whether a person is the lawful owner of a certain object or property which he has in his possession, or whether he has procured it through unlawful means. To answer this type of question, it will be assumed, under the presumption of validity, that it is lawfully owned. In this case, a mere doubt will not be permitted to interfere with the integrity of the character, or the legality of the acts of the individual concerned. Indeed, if doubts and suspicions of this kind were to be given credit, then credibility and confidence in everyday business transactions would be seriously undermined.[101]

To give another example, when a person donates generously to a charitable cause, it is possible that some people may interpret this action adversely and suspect selfish motives, such as a desire for power and fame on the part of the donor. Similarly, when someone opposes a particular idea, or a plan, or simply criticises another person, the critic could be suspected of dishonourable motives, and yet if given a positive interpretation, the criticism could be seen in a favourable light which is precisely what the principle of validity would recommend.[102]

This principle has an important role to play in encouraging social harmony and trust by advising that positive aspects should be emphasised in preference to negative ones. But this is only so when there is no real evidence to suggest that evil motives are at work. Nevertheless, the principle of validity does give the benefit of the doubt to acts and words which may arouse suspicion, but which are actually the result merely of an error of judgement without devious intentions.

Furthermore, the principle of validity advises us not to allow doubt to interfere with the integrity and soundness of acts of devotion. Imām Jaᶜfar al-Ṣādiq has been quoted as having said, 'Surrendering to doubt is a sign of feeble-mindedness.'[103] He is reported to have said this in response to a question concerning a person who kept repeating his ablution and prayers on account of recurring doubts that they were in some way defective. Imām Jaᶜfar al-Ṣādiq attributed the man's suspicions, which merely debilitated his efficiency and alertness, to the work of Satan.[104]

The question still arises as to whether the principle of validity should apply to everyone, including persons of dubious and questionable character. How are we to defend ourselves against the harm of those who hide their evil intentions? In response to this, it is suggested that the principle of validity advocates justice and moderation, and it warns against drawing hasty conclusions which are founded on nothing more than suspicion. The principle of validity does not seek to interfere with sound reasoning, or with indications of context and circumstance. We naturally perceive or expect good and evil in a corroborative context, although we are at times surprised against our expectations since we possess no infallible safeguards against error and miscalculation.[105] The principle of validity advises moderation so that one does not pre-judge, through suspicion and prejudice, the words and acts that one encounters. It also encourages an awareness that there may be hidden aspects to an act or statement and that judgement should not be based only on appearances, but should await the results of investigation. The principle of validity does not necessarily advocate passing a favourable judgement with regard to what we observe, but it does recommend that we avoid passing an unfavourable judgement while there is still the possibility of a favourable verdict. This is precisely the position that the jurists have taken, whereby while a person is not under an obligation to presume beneficence in the words and acts of others, nevertheless a judgement to the contrary should be reserved until doubts, or the possibility of a good interpretation, are eliminated.

This may be illustrated by reference to a situation where a person utters some words while passing by, and the audience cannot make out whether they were an insult or a greeting. The principle of validity in this situation does not support the conclusion that the words uttered were words of insult, nor does it require the addressee to presume them to be a greeting and therefore to return it in kind. All that is advised here is that a negative judgement should be withheld as there is still the possibility, however slight, of a favourable interpretation being sustained. And, finally, the presumption of validity maintains that even when an act or statement appears to be evil, there may be an extenuating explanation, and until that avenue has been explored, one should reserve judgement. It is possible, for example, that a person who utters an apparently objectionable statement actually believes it to be true; in such a case a distinction must be made between the deliberate voicing of wilful error, and harmful speech which originates in an error of judgement. By way of another example, if a man is seen eating during the daytime in Ramaḍān - normally a sinful act - it should be kept in mind that he might be ill or travelling, in which case the obligation of the fast is waived. Hence, before passing judgement, one ought to investigate the possible presence of a lawful justification. In this way, the principle of validity seeks to promote goodwill and trust in society, while also protecting the individual against unfounded suspicion or misinterpretation, and preventing people from reaching hasty, unwarranted conclusions.[106]

VII. Freedom to Express an Opinion *(Ḥurriyyat al-Ra'y)*

Freedom to express an opinion is probably the most important aspect of freedom of speech, since the latter may comprise other distinguishable varieties of expression such as a simple narration of facts, or comedy and fiction. Specifically to express an opinion on a matter implies a level of involvement, commitment and competence which may or may not be the case in a factual narration of an event. This may partly explain why, in the Islamic scholastic tradition, the phrase *ḥurriyyat al-ra'y,* literally 'freedom of opinion' is used to denote 'freedom of speech', in preference to *ḥurriyyat al-qawl,* which is the more precise equivalent. The fact that scholars and jurists have consistently used this phrase for freedom of speech is perhaps indicative of the significance of *ra'y*, or personal opinion, as being the most important aspect of this freedom.

Ra'y has been classified into three main categories: it can be praiseworthy, blameworthy, or doubtful. These categories are further sub-divided into various other types. The principal varieties of the praiseworthy opinion to be discussed here are those which elaborate the Qur'ān, the Sunnah and the opinion of the Companions, *ra'y* which consists of *ijtihād*, and *ra'y* which is arrived at as a result of consultation. The blameworthy opinion is again divided into three types, namely pernicious innovation (*bidᶜah*), caprice (*hawā*) and transgression (*baghy*). Here, I shall address only the recommended or praiseworthy varieties of *ra'y*, as I have discussed the blameworthy forms in a separate section of this work.

Ra'y is defined as an opinion on a matter which has not been regulated by the Qur'ān or the Sunnah. It is a considered opinion arrived at as a result of deep thought and self-exertion by an individual searching for knowledge on a subject regarding which there may be only signs or indications (*amārāt*) of some kind; however the signs that do exist are such that may lead investigators to different conclusions. There is thus an element of arbitrariness attached to *ra'y*, in the sense that it is self-inspired and unrelated to the text of the Qur'ān or the Sunnah, or to definitive consensus of opinion (*ijmāᶜ*). In the usage of the Arabs, *ra'y* is applied to things which are not seen, but are known through the application of reason, intuitive judgement or the light of one's heart. Matters which are regulated by definitive factual or rational knowledge, and matters on which all the signs are bound to concur, such as the number of days in a week, or the virtue of telling the truth, are thus excluded from the scope of *ra'y*. Thus, no one is expected to formulate an opinion on factual or rational matters for these require no deliberation or thought. It is also clear from the foregoing that *ra'y* is specifically founded on given signs and indications. Hence, when a person says something about a matter pertaining to the realm of the unseen about which there is no information, his assertion is not to be regarded as his *ra'y*. In this sense, *ra'y* is preliminary to knowledge, and must take its lead from information open to investigation and rational conclusions.[107]

A person may express an opinion, arbitrary or otherwise, and so long as he does not violate the law concerning blasphemy, sedition and so on, he is free to advance an opinion. Just as the law tolerates an arbitrary opinion, the latter has a role to play in the development of ideas, and in the quest for knowledge and truth. Often, a sound opinion is evoked and stimulated by a weak, provocative or misguided one. The *juris corpus* of *fiqh* is the embodiment of both *ra'y* and authoritative Tradition (the Qur'ān, the Sunnah and *ijmāᶜ*); however only the latter is held to provide criteria by which to judge the propriety of *ra'y*. As already noted, *ra'y* has a limited role vis-à-vis the clear ordinances of divine revelation. But when no such guidance is available in the sources, or when the existing guidance is no more than an indication which is open to interpretation and inference, then the matter is open to *ra'y*. The veracity of *ra'y* is always judged by its proximity to the letter and spirit of the *nuṣūṣ*. Consensus of opinion (*ijmāᶜ*) is the only recognised method for establishing the validity of *ra'y*. Apart from *ijmā*ᶜ, which is usually slow to materialise and retrospective, there is no method for a prompt evaluation of *ra'y* other than *ra'y* itself. In this case, the sound *ra'y* declares the arbitrary *ra'y* as invalid or weak. This process of sifting through the accuracy and veracity of *ra'y* is integral to decision-making and *ijtihād*. Thus, the weak and erroneous opinion has a role to play in the evolution of correct *ijtihād*. Perhaps it was in view of this truism, that the Prophet ﷺ declared in a *Ḥadīth*, already quoted in our discussion of *ijtihād*, that the mere effort of a competent scholar or *mujtahid* at attaining the truth is worthy of reward, whether or not he actually succeeds in his goal.[108]

In the scholastic context of early juristic thought, *ra'y* became increasingly associated with liberality and extrapolation in personal preferences. This was the main charge which the partisans of *Ḥadīth* (*ahl al-Ḥadīth*) laid against their counterparts, the partisans of opinion, or the *ahl al-ra'y*. This somewhat negative connotation of *ra'y*, however, underwent a gradual change due mainly to sustained effort by the *ahl al-ra'y*, the Ḥanafīs in particular, who maintained that Islam never discouraged recourse to reason and personal opinion, provided that these did not violate any of its principles and objectives. To substantiate their efforts, the proponents of *ra'y* devised methodologies and guidelines on the correct use of *ra'y* in the form of analogical reasoning (*qiyās*), juristic preference (*istiḥsān*), blocking recourse to expedients (*sadd al-dharā'i*ᶜ), and presumption of continuity (*istiṣḥāb*). These, and other principles of *uṣūl al-fiqh*, such as the priority given to the opinion of the Companions (*fatwā al-ṣaḥābī*) over that of other *mujtahidūn*, aimed at establishing a closer identity between *ra'y* and the laws and principles of the Qur'ān and Sunnah.[109] Disagreements over the use of *ra'y* between the *ahl al-Ḥadīth* and the *ahl al-ra'y* is a matter of orientation, rather than a total rejection by either side of the basic validity of *ra'y*. The only sectarian movement on record which denies the validity of recourse to *ra'y* is the *Baṭiniyyah* or the *Ta*ᶜ*līmiyyah*.[110] As Abu Ḥāmid Muḥammad al-Ghazālī explains: 'The *Ta*ᶜ*līmiyyah* are called by this name because of their doctrine which forbids personal reasoning and intellectual exercise in the form of *ra'y*. They call instead for total reliance on the instructions of the infallible Imām, as they affirm that the only way to acquire knowledge is through instruction, teaching, and *ta*ᶜ*līm*.'[111]

There is ample evidence in the sources which validates recourse to personal opinion. The Qur'ān (XLII:38) thus authorises consultation (*shūrā*) in public affairs, which essentially consists of the personal opinion of its participants. The Qur'ān also enjoins upon Muslims to refer matters regarding which they disagree to those in authority (*ulū'l-amr*) for a final decision, since they are capable of formulating sound opinions and judgements (IV:59). This is further confirmed in a later verse of the same *sūrah* (IV:83), which validates inference and deduction of the rules of law from the sources, by recource to reasoning and *ra'y*. Furthermore, the *Ḥadīth* of Muʿādh b. Jabal - which reports that when the Prophet ﷺ sent Muʿādh ibn Jabal to Yemen in the position of judge, he questioned him about the sources on which he would rely in making judgements, and Muʿādh's reply ennumerated the Qur'ān, the Sunnah and his own reasoned opinion (*ajtahidu ra'yī),* in that order - provides specific authority for *ra'y* in juridical matters and the settlement of disputes.[112] The Sunnah of the Prophet ﷺ, and the precedent of his Companions, leave no doubt that judges and governors were appointed to distant places with the understanding that they would rely on their personal *ra'y* and *ijtihād* in matters on which they could not find any guidance in the traditional sources.[113]

Furthermore, we note that on numerous occasions the Qur'ān invites people to investigate and explore the world around them, and to draw rational conclusions, not in the manner of blind imitators who follow and accept what others have said, but through intelligent analysis and judgement. Thus, we read in the Qur'ān: 'Thus doth God expound for you the signs that you may think.' (II:266)

كَذٰلِكَ يُبَيِّنُ اللهُ لَكُمُ الْآيٰتِ لَعَلَّكُمْ تَتَفَكَّرُونَ.

Elsewhere in the text we are challenged with the question: 'Do they not examine the realm of the heavens and the earth and whatever God hath created?' (VII:185)

أَوَلَمْ يَنْظُرُوا فِي مَلَكُوتِ السَّمٰوٰتِ وَالْأَرْضِ وَمَا خَلَقَ اللهُ مِن شَيْءٍ.

While commenting on these and other similar passages in the Qur'ān, Abū Zahrah observes that the Qur'ān encourages rational enquiry into the world around us, and that 'this would not be possible without the freedom to express one's opinion and thought'.[114] To this we may add the rider, that the Qur'ān values rational endeavour accompanied by sincerity in the quest for truth and justice. No intellectual enquiry may begin on the premise of denying the fundamental truth of monotheism (*tawḥīd*) and of the clear guidance which is enunciated in the divine revelation.[115] Provided that these values are observed, rational enquiry and the quest for truth must be maintained even in the face of hostility from the masses. For these people may be uninformed, and may themselves be in need of enlightenment. This is the purport of the Qur'ānic verse (VI:116) which proclaims that once clear guidance has been given, a mere conjecture, even if promoted by the masses, should not be allowed to obstruct it.

Notwithstanding the fact that obedience to lawful government is a Qur'ānic obligation, the very text which prescribes this duty (IV:59) goes on to provide, in an address to the believers, that 'Should you dispute over a matter, then refer it to God and to the Messenger.'

فَإِنْ تَنَازَعْتُمْ فِي شَيْءٍ فَرُدُّوهُ إِلَى اللهِ وَالرَّسُولِ.

Obviously, this Qur'ānic text presupposes the possibility of disputes arising between the ruler and his subjects, and it affirms that the duty of obedience does not overrule the right of the citizens to take issue with their leaders and the government.

Disputation, or *jadal*, in its positive sense, is clearly permitted in the Qur'ān. Indeed, it is one of the major Qur'ānic themes which occurs on no less than twenty-five occassions where the sacred text expresses humanity's inclination, as rational beings, towards argumentation.[116] On one such occasion, the Qur'ān refers to the narrative of a woman, Khawlah bint Thaʿlabah, wife of Aws b. Thābit, who complained to the Prophet ﷺ about the abuse and insult she suffered at the hands of her husband. The following Qur'ānic passage was consequently revealed: 'God heard the speech of the woman who disputed with you concerning her husband; she complained to God and God hears your discussion.' (LVIII:1)

قَدْ سَمِعَ اللهُ قَوْلَ الَّتِي تُجَادِلُكَ فِي زَوْجِهَاوَ تَشْتَكِي
إِلَى اللهِ وَاللهُ يَسْمَعُ تَحَاوُرَكُمَا.

Consequently, the woman was granted the right to separate from her husband by a form of separation which is referred to as *ẓihār*. This particular verse recognised the right of the individual, a woman in this case, to argue her problem with the Prophet-cum-head of state and there are words in this verse, such as '*tujādiluka*', 'disputes with you', '*tashtakī*', 'she complains', and '*taḥāwurakumā*', 'your discussion', which suggest that the plaintiff expressed herself forcefully on the occasion. This is perhaps borne out also by the fact that the whole of the *sūrah* which begins with this passage bears the title, '*al-Mujādilah*', 'She that disputeth'.

The root word *jadal* can take two forms: commendable, and reprehensible - the latter meaning I have discussed elsewhere under abuses of the freedom of speech. Commendable *jadal* is normally based on sound reasoning and is intended to rectify an error or violation that one witnesses. Take, for example, the situation when a person hears someone speaking in a manner which distorts the principles of the faith. If the listener attempts to expose the defects of such talk, by recourse to sound argumentation and reasoning, in order to advocate and establish the truth, then this is a commendable act. To remain silent when one has the ability to rectify an aberration is not recommended. However, this is on condition that the argumentation is conducted in accordance with Qur'ānic guidance. It must be in the best form, 'with what is best' (*bi'llatī hiya aḥsan*), and it must comply with the instruction to 'argue not with the followers of the book except in the best way, apart from the unjust/oppressors among them'. (XVI:125; XXIX:46)

- وَجَادِلْهُم بِالَّتِي هِيَ أَحْسَنُ ...
- وَلَا تُجَادِلُوا أَهْلَ الْكِتَابِ إِلَّا بِالَّتِي هِيَ أَحْسَنُ إِلَّا الَّذِينَ ظَلَمُوا مِنْهُمْ.

The Qur'ān, thus, encourages sound and courteous debate when it is likely to be beneficial, but if the audience is so hostile and arrogant that polite reasoning and persuasion is not likely to achieve the purpose, then, according to the latter Qur'ānic text, argumentation should not be attempted and efforts should be made to solve the problem in other more effective directions.[117]

Argumentation with regard to worldly affairs which have no direct bearing on religious principles is also encouraged if it is likely to benefit the people or to prevent possible harm to them. Thus, if a person is indulging in speech which violates public interest, influences people and misleads them, then it is the duty of anyone who knows of the matter to expose its defects by recourse to sound reasoning and disputation. For the protection of the people against harm is the duty of every capable person. Thus, the commendable *jadal* in both of its two varieties aims at rectifying a manifest distortion of the principles of religion, and also to protect the people against any possible harm.[118]

Furthermore, there is a third variety of commendable *jadal*, which is used for the advancement of knowledge, either in the sphere of the religious sciences or in other disciplines such as logic and literature. Discussion and debate, which aim at exploring academic themes, are subject to the same Qur'ānic guidance which applies to other forms of *jadal*. They must be conducted with courtesy and withstraint, and must aim at the discovery of truth, and steer away from exposing the weaknesses of others.

On a more general note, the Qur'ān and Sunnah are replete with moral encouragement and guidance on the proper use of speech. Verbal propriety and courtesy towards others is a central feature of Islamic ethics, often equated with correct guidance (*hidāyah*). The Qur'ān enjoins believers to 'speak to the people in good words' (II:83), and asks them to guide others to be pleasant in speech and lead them to the path of God: '... they are guided unto good speech and are guided unto the path of the Praiseworthy (*al-Ḥamīd*).' (XXII:24)

- وَقُولُوا لِلنَّاسِ حُسْنًا...

- وَهُدُوا إِلى الطَّيِّبِ مِنَ الْقَولِ وَهُدُوا إِلى صِرَاطِ الْحَمِيدِ.

While the Holy Book compares a good word (*kalimah ṭayyibah*) to a tree which is firm and healthy in both foundation and foliage (XIV:24), the Sunnah likens it to charity that every one can afford to give.[119] Moreover, the recurrent Qur'ānic theme which encourages courteous and proper speech (*qawlan maᶜrūfan*) when addressing one's parents (XVII:23), the indigent (IV:8) the ignorant (IV:5), and the people at large (II:83; XVII:53; XVI:125; XXIX:46), all confirm that, if necessary, the law can penalise blatant abuse of the freedom of speech. Nurturing the proper use of this freedom and attaining beauty and goodness in speech is largely a matter of developing good moral and cultural standards. In addition, the Qur'ān calls upon the wisdom and good judgement of the believer when he or she speaks (XXXIII:70). For example, there may be instances where expressing a true opinion or even telling the truth may fail to achieve a good purpose. The speaker is, therefore, urged to be mindful of the end result and the goal that his words are likely to attain.[120] In fact, there are instances where the Sunnah permits silence in regard to the truth or even allows the telling of a white lie if it would serve a higher objective, such as saving a person from imminent danger. Lastly, freedom of opinion and speech is subservient to the general principles of justice, as can be seen from the following text: 'And when you speak, then speak with justice, even if it be against those who are related to you.' (VI:153)

وَإِذَا قُلْتُمْ فَاعْدِلُوا وَلَوْكَانَ ذَاقُرْبى.

The Qur'ānic guidance here applies equally to a witness in the court, to the judge himself, to the head of the family, and to the people at large who are asked to be honest and fair when they speak to, or about, one another.

VARIETIES OF *RA'Y*

Although the nature of *ra'y* and the very diversity of its scope and subject matter defies the idea of a predetermined framework, the *ʿulamāʾ* have nevertheless attempted to divide *ra'y* into the following four types: valid or praiseworthy opinion (*al-ra'y al-ṣaḥīḥ*), void opinion (*al-ra'y al-bāṭil*), blameworthy or objectionable opinion (*al-ra'y al-madhmūm*), and opinion whose validity is in doubt (*al-ra'y fī mawḍiʿ al-ishtibāh*).[121]

Al-ra'y al-ṣaḥīḥ is one which is in accord with authoritative precedent and the approved opinion of past *ʿulamāʾ* who have acted in harmony with such *ra'y*, and accepted it in principle in the formulation of their own *fatwās* and *ijtihād*.[122] In other words, its harmony with the accepted norms of the *Sharīʿah* is not in question. Of necessity, the test here is retrospective, in that past authorities of proven validity are taken as the criteria by which to evaluate a fresh opinion that may well be focusing on a vision of the future. It is to be noted, however, that an opinion of this type may initially be uncertain and doubtful. Only when all doubt as to its propriety is eliminated and resolved, can it be classified as valid. The main process for this form of refinement is known to the classical methodology of Islamic thought as *ijmāʿ* or general consensus; and once an opinion is accepted and supported by this it becomes authoritative and unquestionably valid. *Ijmāʿ*, in other words, puts the final seal of approval on an opinion which might initially have been disputed, but which no longer remains open to question. In modern times, legislation and judicial decisions of higher courts provide for a similar process, in that once a proposal or opinion is adopted by proper legislative or judicial authorities, its validity is, for practical purposes at least, no longer debatable. Collective and consultative resolutions by professional and representative bodies also enhance the authority and weight of an otherwise isolated opinion. Likewise, public opinion and the press may, in contemporary societies, serve the purpose of identifying the direction of a possible consensus in favour of, or against, a doubtful opinion whose validity cannot be readily ascertained by reference to the textual injunctions (*nuṣūṣ*) or general consensus (*ijmāʿ*). On the same subject is this quote from a well-known saying of a leading Companion, ʿAbd Allāh b. Masʿūd (died 32/652): 'What the Muslims deem to be good is good in the sight of God.'[123]

مارآهُ المُسلمونَ حَسَنًا فهو عِنْدَاللهِ حَسَنٌ.

In other words, if there is consultation among experts or with public and representative bodies, and if the resultant opinion incorporates the views of those who are competent in the matter—the community leaders and those who should be consulted (*ahl al-shūrā*)—then this would enhance the weight and authority of that opinion, and would bring it in line with the Qur'ānic principle of consultation.

At the opposite pole of valid opinion stands the void opinion (*al-ra'y al-bāṭil*), which is of no account and carries no authority at all. Ibn Qayyim al-Jawziyyah writes of this on a somewhat retrospective note saying that: 'It is an opinion which is clearly in discord with the approved precedent of the *ʿulamā'* of the past. They would have denounced it in principle and refused to give it any recognition in their juridical decisions and *fatwā*s.'[124]

Ibn Qayyim divides the valid *ra'y* into four types: the *ra'y* of the Companion (*fatwā al-ṣaḥābī*); *ra'y* which interprets and clarifies the *nuṣūṣ* (*al-ra'y al-tafsīrī*); consultative *ra'y*; and *ra'y* which consists of *ijtihād* (*al-ra'y al-ijtihādī*).

The *ʿulamā'* are, on the whole, in agreement on the special status and authority that the *fatwā*s of the Companions of the Prophet Muḥammad ﷺ enjoy in religious and juridical matters. The Companions are generally held in high esteem as they were very knowledgeable about the Qur'ān, and the teachings of the Prophet ﷺ. Opinions that they formulated and advanced are, on the whole, considered to be close, in order of authority, to the Sunnah of the Prophet ﷺ. In support of his own view, Ibn Qayyim quotes Imām al-Shāfiʿī's statement: 'The *ra'y* of the Companions commands greater merit and is preferable to our own opinion.'[125] He then goes on to cite several examples where the *ra'y* of the Companions on certain issues was upheld and corroborated by a revelation of the Qur'ān, 'a blessing and a privilege that is unparalleled and unique'. Thus, the conclusion is drawn that the *fatwā al-ṣaḥābī*, or the opinion of a Companion, is *sui generis* and that any attempt to equate it with that of the generality of the *ʿulamā'* is 'devoid of substance and ill-conceived'.[126]

The second type of valid *ra'y* is one which seeks to interpret the *nuṣūṣ*, clarify their meaning, and facilitate the deduction of legal rules from them. This type of *ra'y* is designed to promote a clearer understanding of the Qur'ān and Sunnah, and seeks to derive guidance from them on matters affecting the life of the community. The hallmark of such an opinion is the sincerity and knowledge of its author, and his devotion to the promotion and understanding of the Qur'ān and Sunnah.[127]

The third variety of valid or praiseworthy opinion is the consultative *ra'y*, which is arrived at, not by a single individual, but through consultation among people, especially those who are competent to give counsel. God Almighty has praised 'this *ummah* (the Muslim community) for their diligence at consultation in community affairs; the Messenger of God ﷺ practised it, and it is one of the best forms of *ra'y*.'[128]

The fourth type of praiseworthy opinion is one which is arrived at through the correct procedures that are characteristic of *ijtihād*. The proper method for anyone who attempts to give an opinion on a matter is to look into the Book of God first. If he fails to find the necessary guidance there, he should look into the Sunnah of the Prophet ﷺ and the precedent of his Companions. But, if he still does not find the guidance he seeks, then he should formulate his own opinion and judgement in the same way as the Companions are known to have done so regarding numerous issues. This is, in fact, the procedure laid down in the *Ḥadīth* of Muᶜādh b. Jabal (see above p. 63-4), which is standard authority on *ijtihād*. An opinion so formulated and expressed may be correct or otherwise, or it may appear at the time to be correct but then be contradicted in the course of time. The principle to apply here is that which is expounded in a letter of the Caliph ᶜUmar b. al-Khaṭṭāb when he was instructing his judges: 'The mere fact that you have made a certain decision must not deter you from changing it, if it becomes clear to you that it was erroneous in the first place. For truth is timeless; nothing must overrule it and it is far better to return to the truth rather than to persist in falsehood.'[129] The principle quoted here would seem to be generally applicable to all decisions, judicial or otherwise, and it clearly rejects the notion which sacrifices truth at the altar of consistency, and of the so-called credibility of judicial office. But the point that is most emphasised in all of this is sincerity and devotion to the cause of truth and justice, for this is the essence of beneficence in any praiseworthy opinion. 'Anyone who exerts himself with the intention of gaining the pleasure of God and to benefit people will be counted as one of the *muḥsinīn*, (persons noted for their piety and good works), as goodwill and sincerity in telling the truth embodies the highest value of *taqwā*.'[130]

As for *ra'y* the validity of which is open to doubt, it is equivalent to a conjecture (*ẓann*). This type of *ra'y* is accepted as a basis of judicial decision and legal opinion (*fatwā*) in cases of emergency, or where no better alternative may be known to exist. Unless it is adopted in a court decision, a doubtful opinon or a conjecture does not bind anyone. The *ᶜulamā'* have neither approved nor denounced it, but have left open the choice of either accepting or rejecting it.[131] But, since we do not always have the necessary knowledge of, nor access to, the truth, a considered opinion which may amount to no more than a probability or a conjecture is sometimes accepted as a basis of decision making. This is done in order to avoid an indefinite delay that the quest for knowledge of the total truth may entail. In the sphere of judicial decisions, however, there are checks and balances, especially with regard to the rules that govern admissibility of evidence, which are designed to minimise the possibility of error. Therefore, decisions and opinions which are formed in conformity with correct procedures are deemed to be valid, even if they comprise a measure of speculation or individual bias of a tolerable sort.

From the viewpoint of its subject matter and relative value, *ra'y* is once again divided into three types. Firstly, there is the *ra'y* on a juridical, or *sharᶜī*, matter which is validated and accepted only on the strength of the *sharᶜī* proof on which it is founded. This is regardless as to whether it is advanced by one person or by a multitude. Secondly, there is the *ra'y* which concerns specialised matters which require technical knowledge. The people at large are not expected to be in a position to form an enlightened opinion on these affairs, and only expert opinion is to be taken into account, and then the value of that opinion is determined on an informed basis. And thirdly, there is the *ra'y* on matters of a practical nature which require public participation and compliance, such as electing the head of state, and opinions on public, constitutional and municipal affairs which concern the community as a whole. On matters of this nature, the preferred opinion is that of the majority of the people whose action and participation is of central importance to the opinion concerned.[132]

VIII. Freedom of Association

The right to peaceful association naturally follows as an integral part of the freedom of speech and expression. The *Sharīʿah* takes an affirmative stand on rights and encourages association in pursuit of lawful objectives. The Holy Qur'ān enjoins mutual assistance and co-operation for valid purposes, but forbids co-operation in transgression and sin.[133]

In our discussion of fundamental rights, we noted that the *ʿulamā'* have not treated these as a separate category from other rights. This is also true of the freedom of association, in that we do not find an exclusive treatment of this in the scholastic works of the *ʿulamā'*. Thus, the *Sharīʿah* evidence on freedom of assembly and association has remained unconsolidated and has to be located under a variety of topics. However, the basic evidence is embodied in the same principles of the Qur'ān and the Sunnah which authorise freedom of speech and expression. Thus, the Qur'ānic principle of *ḥisbah*, that is commanding good and forbidding evil, the principle of *naṣīḥah*, sincere advice, and *shūrā*, consultation, can equally be quoted, *mutatis mutandis*, as the basic authority in the *Sharīʿah* for freedom of association. *Shūrā* is the Islamic equivalent of democracy, but in comparison the latter is individualist in orientation, whereas *shūrā* is more community oriented. For it contemplates consultative judgement and decision, taken as a result of contact and association with those who may have something to say and an opinion to contribute. Moreover, the doctrine of personal reasoning by the qualified jurist (*ijtihād*), as well as the citizen's right to voice a constructive criticism of the conduct of government (*ḥaqq al-muʿāraḍah*) are all premised on recognition in the *Sharīʿah* of the fundamental freedoms of speech, expression and association.

Ḥisbah is by far the broadest of all the principles referred to above. All of them, be it *naṣīḥah*, *muʿāraḍah*, *shūrā* or *ijtihād* may be deemed, each in their respective capacities, to comprise the general concept of promoting good and preventing evil. *Ḥisbah* is, of course, like *naṣīḥah* and *ijtihād*, a collective obligation (*farḍ kafā'ī*) of the community as a whole. These are all matters of common concern, and hence are subjects regarding which members of the community should associate and communicate with one another. We also note that the Qur'ānic principle of *shūrā* can only be implemented as a result of consultation among community members.

Both Muḥammad Asad and ʿAbd Allāh al-ʿArabī have observed that the basic recognition of freedom of speech and opinion in the *Sharīʿah* requires that people must also be accorded the freedom to group together, if they so wish, in pursuit of their common objectives. The *Sharīʿah* thus entitles the people to organise themselves in parties, groups and associations if they deem this to be a more effective way of realising their legitimate interests.[134] ʿAbd al-Ḥamīd al-Anṣārī has observed that in our own time, realisation of the objectives (*al-maqāṣid*) of the *Sharīʿah*, and securing the various benefits (*al-maṣāliḥ*) of the community - be it the essentials (*al-ḍarūriyyāt*) on which the life of the community depends, the complementary benefits (*al-ḥājiyyāt*) which seek to remove hardship, or 'embellishments' (*al-taḥsīniyyāt*), which aim at securing the desirable - all of these require the formation of political parties.[135] To this it may be added that, although the setting up of political parties may be classified under the general category of unrestricted benefits (*al-maṣāliḥ al-mursalah*), it is a benefit which arguably constitutes a means to securing some of the higher categories of *maṣāliḥ*, in which case it would partake of the *sharʿī* value of the latter and, thus, be elevated to a higher category of *maṣlaḥah*.

Some commentators have, however, advanced a view which forbids the formation of political parties in an Islamic state. It is thus suggested that the basis of unity among Muslims is their common allegiance to Islam itself, hence there is no need for further levels of unification and alliance. According to Muṣṭafā Kamāl Waṣfī, 'Islam does not subscribe to any alliance other than unity in faith which is sufficient for the Muslims. When a section of the Muslim community enters a partisan alliance, it is bound to isolate others, and this would consequently lead to disunity.'[136] The soundness of this view may be questioned, however, in that it tends to indulge in a measure of generalisation. Unity in faith does not necessarily forbid differences of opinion on details and matters which need not have a bearing on the essentials of dogma. It is equally possible that people who subscribe to the same principle may differ in the matter of its details and methods of implementation. Surely the correct view should be that only harmful alliances which aim at destroying unity are to be censured, not those which pursue beneficial objectives and aim at rendering service to the community.

The opponents of political parties have also quoted, in support of their position, Qur'ānic passages which emphasise unity, and which warn the believers against divisiveness and separation. Some of the passages thus referred to convey the following:

> And cling to the rope of God all together and do not be divided. (III:103)

وَاعْتَصِمُوا بِحَبْلِ اللهِ جَمِيعًا وَلَا تفَرَّقُوا.

> Those who divide their religion and break up into sects - you are not of them concerning anything. (VI:159)

إِنَّ الَّذِينَ فَرَّقُوادِينَهُمْ وَكَانُوا شِيَعًا لَّسْتَ مِنْهُمْ فِي شَيْءٍ.

> Obey God and His Messenger, and dispute not among yourselves, lest you lose heart and your power departs .... VIII:46)

وَأَطِيعُوا اللهَ وَرَسُولَهُ وَلَاتَنَازَعُوا فَتَفْشَلُوا وَتَذْهَبَ رِيحُكُمْ.

Some Prophetic traditions on the theme of unity, such as 'the hand of God is with the community' are also quoted.

يَدُاللهِ مَعَ الجَمَاعَةِ.

But the relevance of all this to the formation, or otherwise, of political parties is doubtful. It may well be said, for instance, that forming a party which commits itself to enhancing unity among people would derive positive support from the Qur'ān and Sunnah. It is, therefore, avoiding disunity which the Qur'ān primarily advocates. This being the case, the issue is not about the formation of any party as such. Moreover, the proponents of political parties have been able to quote certain other passages in the Qur'ān in support of their position as we shall elaborate later.

Those who are opposed to the formation of political parties have further added that one of the distinctive features of the Islamic state during the lifetime of the Prophet ﷺ and the Rightly-Guided Caliphs, was that the people enjoyed freedom of expression and the liberty to voice opposing opinions. The caliphs were also easily accessible; government leaders consulted the citizens, and together they discussed and deliberated over public affairs. This was done successfully without the need to establish a particular party, either for, or against, the government. Since the opportunity was granted for all members of the community to take part in such discussions, they participated when they had something to say without feeling the need to align themselves into a party.[137] It is further added that references to (political) parties in the Qur'ān, in particular the chapter entitled 'The Parties', (*al-Aḥzāb*), express disapproval of the alliances that were formed in opposition to the Prophet ﷺ; (see also XXXIII:20). It is further suggested that much of the subsequent history of partisan activities has generally been divisive and has brought disunity and conflict among Muslims.[138]

However, this line of argument is by no means conclusive. The reference to parties in *Sūrat al-Aḥzāb*, for example, is, as already indicated, to parties that were formed for the very purpose of challenging the authority of the Prophet ﷺ. Moreover, the early experience of partisan activities, the Shīᶜites and the Khārijites among others, is no proof against the validity, in principle, of forming parties for beneficial purposes.[139] On the other hand, it is suggested by the advocates of freedom of association that Islam validates the formation of political parties and associations; and that many of the general principles of public law in Islam, such as consultation, justice, freedom, equality, and the promotion of good and prevention of evil, are politically orientated and require the formation of political parties that can commit themselves to the enforcement of these principles.[140] Furthermore, some of these principles, such as *shūrā*, can only be effectively implemented if there is a majority opinion either for, or against, a proposition, which has to identified. On the whole, the formation of parties is conducive to this purpose, and it tends to facilitate organisation and discipline. Moreover, in view of the pluralism and complexity of public life in our own time, the sheer size of cities, their inhabitants, and the growth of governmental and non-governmental organisations, it has become exceedingly difficult to know which individuals need to be consulted. Today, public life necessitates organisation, lobbying, pressure groups, and associations, and this means that direct access to government leaders may not be as effective today as it might have been in the early days of Islam.[141]

We need to identify the locus of responsibility and our commitment to a set of objectives, otherwise there is always the risk that consultation may not yield the desired result. Political parties and organisations are, on the whole, more effective in making *shūrā* purposeful; they also tend to have more means at their disposal and are, therefore, more capable in combating a threat to freedom of speech, especially when the speech happens to be critical of the government in power. They can, for example, in the last resort, declare no confidence in a government that persistently ignores sincere advice (*naṣīḥah*), and is entrenched in misguided and authoritarian methods. How can an individual act in conformity with the *Ḥadīth* that says, 'the best form of holy struggle (*jihād*), is to tell a word of truth to a tyrannical ruler', if he has no assurance and support for his safety and the cause which he pursues? Even when the government permits openness and respects freedom of speech, affirmative action, including the formation of political parties, is still necessary to ensure progress in pursuit of valid objectives. Indeed, it is stated that freedom of speech and commanding good (*al-amr bi'l-maʿrūf*), would hold little weight if they did not accede to the people's right to form political parties; and that this, by itself, is a test of a government's respect for freedom of expression.[142]

Furthermore, we find evidence in the Qur'ān to the effect that differences of opinion and disagreements are natural to social life. Note, for example, the text which provides: 'Had thy Lord willed, He would have made mankind one nation, but they never cease to disagree.' (XI:118)

وَلَوْ شَآءَ رَبُّكَ لَجَعَلَ النَّاسَ أُمَّةً وَاحِدَةً وَلَا يَزَالُونَ مُخْتَلِفِينَ.

The Qur'ānic vision here is clearly one of pluralism which, in turn, is premised on the freedom of personal opinion and thought, and the differences of ability and experience among individuals and nations. The message here is further substantiated in another passage which reads:

> 'O mankind, We created you from a male and a female and made you into tribes and nations so that you may know one another. Surely the noblest of you in the sight of God is the most upright and God-fearing among you.' (XLIX:13)

يَٰٓأَيُّهَا النَّاسُ إِنَّا خَلَقْنَٰكُم مِّن ذَكَرٍ وَأُنثَىٰ وَجَعَلْنَٰكُمْ
شُعُوبًا وَقَبَآئِلَ لِتَعَارَفُوٓا إِنَّ أَكْرَمَكُمْ عِندَ اللَّهِ أَتْقَىٰكُمْ.

When people and nations differ in experience and outlook, they can benefit from knowing one another, as this diversity can lead to an enriching and beneficial exchange between them. Yet, the pluralistic vision of life on earth is not meant to detract from the basic unity of the origin and creation of humanity 'from a male and a female'. Pluralism, in reality, means allowing and tolerating differences; for this is a fact of human existence, and it is 'a right therefore of those who differ that no one forbid them, or make them believe in something different'.[143]

In response to a question as to the permissibility, or otherwise, of political parties, Ibn Taymiyyah held the view that parties which invite the people to truth and beneficence (*khayr wa-ḥaqq*), and work for the realisation of benefit to the people, are lawful. He added that this was the proper understanding of the Qur'ānic text which, in reference to the true believers, says, 'They are the party (*ḥizb*) of God and truly the party of God are the successful.' (LVIII:22)[144]

أُولَٰٓئِكَ حِزْبُ اللَّهِ أَلَآ إِنَّ حِزْبَ اللَّهِ هُمُ الْمُفْلِحُونَ.

In contradistinction, the Qur'ān has designated as the 'Party of the Devil' (*ḥizb al-shayṭān*) those who were hostile to God and to His Messenger ﷺ, those who disobeyed the Prophet ﷺ, and those who engaged in conspiracies against him ﷺ. (LVIII:19)

أُولَٰٓئِكَ حِزْبُ الشَّيْطَٰنِ أَلَآ إِنَّ حِزْبَ الشَّيْطَٰنِ هُمُ
الْخَٰسِرُونَ.

As Ibn Taymiyyah added, a party of this kind, or indeed, any party or association that defies the teachings of Islam, falls within the meaning of *ḥizb as-shayṭān* and is, therefore, clearly forbidden.[145] Furthermore, Muḥammad al-Ghazālī stated that Islam permits political parties provided they do not seek to destroy the unity of the *ummah*, but, he added, they are unlawful if they aim at dividing the *ummah* and sowing the seeds of disunity among Muslims.[146]

The history of the scholastic developments of the legal and theological schools (*madhāhib*), is premised on the validity of disagreement and of pluralism in matters which are open to interpretation and *ijtihād*. The Prophet ﷺ declared, as we have seen, that if a person attempts *ijtihād* with the purpose of attaining to the truth, but does not actually achieve this end, his act is still meritorious. But if the truth is realised, then he or she merits a double reward.[147]

In Islamic juridical discourse, *ijtihād* is another name for juristic disagreement and plurality of views on matters which have not been determined by the Qur'ān and the Sunnah. As El-Awa points out, 'the history of Islam from the political and social angle is the history of parties and groups'.[148] Ever since the era of the Companions, factions, parties and sects have never ceased to emerge, and no one has denounced them for the mere fact of being a party. The critics of such partisan developments have always looked at the ideas, activities and objectives of the parties in question, and have evaluated them accordingly. Furthermore, the fact that a distinctive discipline of Islamic learning, namely the science of disagreement (*ʿilm al-ikhtilāf*), has flourished in the midst of the scholastic teachings of the *madhāhib*, is itself testimony to the reality of pluralism and tolerance in the history of Islamic scholarship.

While both the Qur'ān and the Sunnah validate freedom of expression, interpretation and *ijtihād*, they also enjoin co-operation (*taʿāwun*) in good and beneficial works as one of the cardinal teachings of Islam. In order to be effective, co-operation requires unity and organisation and, on this theme, the Qur'ān explicitly addresses the believers to 'co-operate with one another in the pursuit of virtue and piety, but co-operate not in fostering offences and hostility.' (V:2)

وَتَعَاوَنُوا عَلَى الْبِرِّ وَالتَّقْوَى وَلَا تَعَاوَنُوا عَلَى الْإِثْمِ وَالْعُدْوَانِ.

The text here is related to our preceding themes in the sense that co-operation in good work (*al-birr*), like *ḥisbah*, is a broad concept which can apply to all forms of beneficial co-operation, whether in the form of a political party, a professional association, or a workers' union which aims at ensuring fair practices in trade and the equitable treatment of workers.

An instance of illicit co-operation that amounts to transgression and violation of fair trade is when producers of essential commodities stop selling their goods in order to push up the prices. This form of co-operation among producers or suppliers is detrimental, or even hostile, to the public, and the government is therefore within its rights, as Ibn Qayyim al-Jawziyyah points out, to compel the suppliers to offer their goods against a fair market price (*qīmat al-mithl*). The government would, in this case, only be acting in accordance with the dictates of justice which Almighty God has demanded. The same would apply to the suppliers of essential services, such as transport workers, or undertakers, who might decide, in collaboration, to stop their services in pursuit of higher wages or prices. In this case, they also may be compelled by the market controller (*walī al-ḥisbah*) to offer their services at fair market prices.[149]

We also find a specific passage in the Holy Qur'ān which the commentators have quoted as an authority for the formation of political parties. The text at issue is in the form of an address to the believers:

> Let there be among you people *(waltakun minkum ummatun)* that invite others to good *(khayr);* enjoining what is right *(al-maʿrūf)* and forbidding what is wrong *(al-munkar)*. They indeed are the successful. (III:104)

وَلْتَكُنْ مِنْكُمْ اُمَّةٌ يَدْعُونَ الى الْخَيْرِ وَيَأْمُرُونَ بِالمَعْرُوفِ
وَيَنْهَوْنَ عَنِ الْمُنْكَرِ وَاُولَئِكَ هُمُ الْمُفْلِحُونَ.

The text here requires that the community set up one or more parties for the express purpose of conducting *ḥisbah*; and effectively to take upon itself the responsibility of devising ways and means of securing the moral and material benefits of its members. As will be noted, the emphasis in this text is laid on the formation of a party, and not on the execution of *ḥisbah*. Indeed, the passage begins on this note, and this is the only new element which differentiates this quote from a number of other Qur'ānic passages on the subject of *ḥisbah*. The principal theme of the text under consideration is, therefore, that at least one party must be formed among Muslims to take responsibility for the tasks that are spelled out in the subsequent portion of the verse. The word '*ummah*' here means a party, a multitude or *jamāʿah*, and not the larger community of Muslims that the word is normally used for. This distinction in the meaning of *ummah* is once again supported by the wording of the text which explicitly requires that there must be a party of Muslims, not that the Muslims must become a party.[150] Furthermore, the text begins with the phrase '*waltakun*' (let there be) which is a command, therefore creating an obligation, according to the majority of *ʿulamā'*, for the community at large to create such a party.[151]

The party in question needs to be a political party which represents the community and exercises its authority to monitor the government and take its officials to task. By way of elaboration, it is understood that invitation to (good) *khayr*, which is one of the two themes of the text under consideration, can be undertaken by an association, a party, or an organisation, and it need not necessarily be political in character. However, the second theme of the verse, which is to implement *ḥisbah*, implies that the party in question must be a political party. For, one of the most important aspects of *ḥisbah* is to encourage accountability in government. Devious and wicked officials must be taken to task, and this can only be done by a political party.[152]

We also note that the text under discussion does not stipulate whether there should be one party or more. The formation of at least one party is a requirement, but there is no indication in the text against the setting up of more than one political party. This is because the word '*ummah*' occurs in the form of an indeterminate noun, which validates a concept and not a particular number. The grammatical usage here is similar to the *Ḥadīth*, which I quote once again, on the subject of *ḥisbah*. It provides, in an address to the believers: 'Should anyone of you see something evil or wrong, let him set it right with his hand. If he is unable to do that let him set it right with his words. If he is unable to do that then let him denounce it in his heart - but this is the weakest form of faith.'[153] This particular *Ḥadīth* has also evoked many comments which may have a bearing on our discussion, but I shall not go into the details; suffice to say that the word for 'evil or wrong' (*munkar*), occurs in the singular, but its meaning is not confined to a single form of evil. The word '*ummah*' in the Qur'ānic text I quoted likewise applies to any party, one or more, without any qualification. It is, therefore, equally valid to form one party or a number of parties, but the collective duty (*farḍ kafā'ī*) of the community to do so is discharged by the formation of even just one. If one party is formed and there are individuals in the community who wish to set up a second party, in pursuit of valid objectives, no one has the authority to stop them from doing so.[154]

In the Qur'ān, there is further recognition of a multiplicity of parties when it is noted that some people understand and eagerly follow correct guidance when it is given to them, but there are others, as has always been the case, who do just the opposite, and there are still others who might take a middle course:

> Then We caused those of Our servants whom We chose, to inherit the Book. But among them is he who harms his own soul, he who follows a middle course, and he who vies in performing good deeds with God's permission. (XXXV:32)

ثُمَّ اَوْرَثْنَا الْكِتٰبَ الَّذِيْنَ اصْطَفَيْنَا مِنْ عِبَادِنَا فَمِنْهُمْ
ظَالِمٌ لِّنَفْسِهٖ وَمِنْهُمْ مُّقْتَصِدٌ وَمِنْهُمْ سَابِقٌ بِالْخَيْرٰتِ بِاِذْنِ
اللّٰهِ.

It is only natural to expect people to have different abilities and talents, and for their differences of vision and experience to be reflected in their commitments to different causes. Those who are enlightened and devoted are, therefore, in a position to lead others, and they can appeal to the good conscience of the people and also muster their support for the right cause. This is the subject of another Qur'ānic passage which is as follows:

> Why do not [just] a group of people from every company among them go forth to war so that [the rest] may devote themselves to studying the religion and advise and caution their folk when they return to them, that they might guard themselves [against evil]. (IX:122)

فَلَوْ لَانَفَرَ مِنْ كُلِّ فِرْقَةٍ مِّنْهُمْ طَآئِفَةٌ لِّيَتَفَقَّهُوْا فِى الدِّيْنِ
وَلِيُنْذِرُوْا قَوْمَهُمْ اِذَا رَجَعُوْٓا اِلَيْهِمْ لَعَلَّهُمْ يَحْذَرُوْنَ.

As this Qur'ānic quote shows, teaching, warning and reminding is very much the task of those who are devoted to a cause they consider worthwhile and beneficial. To achieve this effectively and to be able to protect the community against harm, they may form groups, committees and associations for the promotion and advancement of religious knowledge, or for other similar beneficial objectives.

After the Prophet's ﷺ migration to Medina, and the formation of the state of Medina, the Qur'ān directed him to consult the community in affairs of common concern (III:159). This shows that *shūrā* was meant to be a general principle of Islamic government, and a requirement with which even the Prophet ﷺ himself had to comply. Since *shūrā* is based on a free exchange of opinion over issues, and because people tend to vary in their views, especially over matters on which no clear injunctions are found in the sources, it is only natural that they should be allowed to marshall themselves behind plans and ideas which they consider beneficial. Issues of constitutional concern, the type of government, its policies and objectives in the socio-economic, educational and cultural spheres and so forth, can be the basis either of unity and success, or of divisiveness and failure; but these all depend on effective organisation, good leadership, and public support. Therefore, to put all of this into just one category, namely, that of religious belief, and say that Muslims are expected to be united in Islam and that hence the idea of party organisation is unacceptable - is definitely to over-simplify matters.[155] If we look at the history of Islam, this type of passive attitude, even in matters of faith, or an attitude which is oblivious of the importance of effective and purposeful leadership, could hardly be supported by the normative example and precedent of Islam.

The Qur'ān encourages openness in associating with others and disapproves of secret conference in matters of public concern. The text quoted below also provides some guidance as to what constitutes the legitimate basis of forming an assembly or association.

> There is no good in most of their secret conferences *(najwāhum)* excepting him who enjoins charity or good, or makes peace between people; whoso does that, seeking the pleasure of God, We shall bestow on him a great reward. (IV:114)

لَاخَيْرَ فِي كَثِيرٍ مِّن نَّجْوٰهُمْ اِلاَّمَنْ اَمَرَ بِصَدَقَةٍ اَوْمَعْرُوفٍ
اَوْاِصْلَاحٍ بَيْنَ النَّاسِ وَمَن يَّفْعَلْ ذٰلِكَ ابْتِغَآءَ مَرْضَاتِ اللهِ
فَسَوْفَ نُؤْتِيهِ اَجْرًا عَظِيمًا.

This text approves of three types of associations, namely those which promote charitable work, secure welfare and develop peaceful relations in society. The Qur'ān commentators elaborate by saying that of the three virtues stated in this passage, it is the last which is highest in order of merit. Therefore, associations that aim at promoting friendly relations among people are highly recommended, especially when a rift which would lead people to improbity is feared to be developing. There are a number of *Ḥadīth*, as Maḥmūd al-Alusī elaborates, which are emphatic on the merit of attempting to bring people closer together at a time when they are moving apart.[156] In turn, the promotion of public welfare applies to associations and societies which promote knowledge in all fields, including the arts and sciences, as well as those which aim at the peaceful settlement of disputes, and the advancement of peace among mankind at any level: private, national or international.[157]

Conspiracies are severely condemned in the Qur'ān; all associations must be for promoting lawful benefits. This is the subject of the following passage, which addresses the believers:

> O ye who believe! When you confer together in private, confer not for the commission of sin, or hostility and disobedience to the Messenger, but confer for the promotion of virtue and piety ... the holding of secret counsels for evil purposes proceeds from Satan. (LVIII:9-10)

يٰاَيُّهَا الَّذِينَ اٰمَنُوآ اِذَاتَنَا جَيْتُمْ فَلَا تَتَنَاجَوا بِالْاِثْمِ
وَالْعُدْوَانِ وَمَعْصِيَتِ الرَّسُولِ وَتَنَاجَوا بِالبِرِّ وَالتَّقْوٰى
وَاتَّقُوا ... اِنَّمَا النَّجْوٰى مِنَ الشَّيْطٰنِ.

Furthermore, when people gather together for a common purpose, they should observe order and discipline. The Qur'ān associates discipline here with faith and knowledge, and elevates to distinction those individuals who are mindful of these principles in public gatherings. This is the subject of the next verse in the same chapter:

> O ye who believe! When you are told to make room in assemblies, then make room. God will make room for you. And when you are told to rise, then rise, [that] God [might] elevate those among you who believe, and those who have been granted knowledge, by degrees. (LVIII:11)

يَاأَيُّهَا الَّذِينَ أَمَنُوا اِذَاقِيلَ لَكُمْ تَفَسَّحُوا فِى الْمَجْلِسِ
فَافْسَحُوا يَفْسَحِ اللهُ لَكُمْ وَإِذَا قِيلَ انْشُزُوا فَانْشُزُوا يَرْفَعِ
اللهُ الَّذِينَ أَمَنُوا مِنْكُمْ وَالَّذِينَ أُوتُوا الْعِلْمَ دَرَجَتٍ.

Participants in public assemblies and associations are, thus, required to respond to reasonable requests made of them in the interests of order and peace. People who use public places must also take care that no undue inconvenience is occasioned to others using the same, nor should anyone be exposed to risk or injury in public assemblies.[158] In a commentary on the preceding Qur'ānic text, it is also stated that even when a great leader comes to an assembly, the participants are not to press forward without discipline, as this would cause inconvenience to him and be detrimental to public order. Nor is it allowed to shut out other people who have an equal right to be in the assembly.[159]

On the basis of yet another Qur'ānic verse, when people are gathered together for a purpose they ought not to depart without the leader's permission:

> But the believers are they who believe in God and in His Messenger, and when they are with him upon a communal matter, do not depart until they have asked for leave ... So when they ask thy leave for any of their affairs, grant them leave ... .(XXIV:62)

إِنَّمَا الْمُؤْمِنُونَ الَّذِينَ آمَنُوا بِاللَّهِ وَرَسُولِهِ وَإِذَا كَانُوا
مَعَهُ عَلَى أَمْرٍ جَامِعٍ لَّمْ يَذْهَبُوا حَتَّى يَسْتَأْذِنُوهُ...

فَإِذَا اسْتَأْذَنُوكَ لِبَعْضِ شَأْنِهِمْ فَأْذَنْ...

Assemblies must, therefore, observe correct discipline from beginning to end. They should be purposeful and terminate only when the purpose is achieved, and it is the leader's responsibility to determine when the meeting should come to an end and when the participants may disperse.

I conclude that the *Sharīʿah* validates the formation of both political parties, and non-political associations that aim at securing benefits for the community. This is perhaps true of all affirmative action in pursuit of such objectives as are upheld in Islam. If the objectives in question comprise accredited interests (*maṣāliḥ muʿtabarah*), which are those that have been clearly recognised by the *Sharīʿah*, then the *sharʿī* value of the means toward their realisation is elevated in order of merit to the same level as that of the values which they pursue. The merit or demerit of a party, association or society is, therefore, to be judged on the basis of the objectives that each of these seeks to realise. If a party or association wants to protect and promote any of the five essential values of the *Sharīʿah* - namely, life, faith, property, intellect and lineage - there should, in principle, be no question of invalidity, and all affirmative action in their pursuit is presumed to be valid. The statement of objectives that a party or association may issue can also be evaluated in the light of the general goals of the *Sharīʿah* (*maqāṣid al-Sharīʿah*), and the unrestricted interests (*al-maṣāliḥ al-mursalah*) of the community. The latter, however, are precisely by definition unrestricted, and cannot be circumscribed in advance as these interests are ascertained in the light of given circumstances, new developments, and issues that need to be considered as, and when, they present themselves.[160]

Any party or association that is established in pursuit of questionable, partisan, or prejudicial objectives which create disunity and conflict is likely to be covered by the legal rules that apply to *fitnah*, sedition. Activities of this nature are deemed to consitute an offence, and would, therefore, fail to meet the *Sharīʿah* criteria of validity.

IX. Freedom of Religion (*Al-Ḥurriyyah al-Dīniyyah*)

One of the manifestations of personal liberty is the freedom of the individual to profess the religion of his or her choice without compulsion. Everyone must also have the freedom to observe and to practise their faith without fear of, or interference from, others. Freedom of religion in its Islamic context implies that non-Muslims are not compelled to convert to Islam, nor are they hindered from practising their own religious rites. Both Muslims and non-Muslims are entitled to propagate the religion of their following, as well as to defend it against attack or seditious provocation (*fitnah*), regardless as to whether such an action is launched by their co-religionists or by others.[161]

Freedom of religion acquires special significance in the *Sharīʿah*, a system of law which recognises no clear division between legal and religious norms. Since the creed of Islam lies at the root of many a doctrine and institution of the *Sharīʿah*, the freedom of whether or not to embrace and practise Islam is the most sensitive and controversial area of all individual liberties.[162] However, this alone should not necessarily change the basic meaning and character of the freedom of belief: it should matter little, therefore, whether one speaks of the freedom of belief in the context of Islam or of any other legal system. For the basic idea of freedom defies impositions of any kind on an individual's personal choice. Freedom of belief, like all other freedoms, operates as a safeguard against the possible menace of oppression from superior sources of power. This is also essentially true of the Islamic concept of this freedom: as Fatḥī ʿUthmān observes, 'No power of any kind in the Islamic state may be employed to compel people to embrace Islam. The basic function of the Islamic state, in this regard, is to monitor and prevent the forces which might seek to deny the people their freedom of belief.'[163]

From a historical perspective it is interesting to note that when the Prophet of Islam ﷺ began his mission among the pagans of Mecca, he invited them into the new faith despite their hostile attitude and response. This situation lends support to the conclusion, as al-ʿĪlī points out, that Islam subscribes to freedom of belief, since Islam itself began by inviting and persuading people to embrace it on the merit of its rationality and truth. In other words, if Islam is to remain true to its own beginnings it can be expected to validate the freedom of belief.[164] This is precisely the stance that the *ʿulamāʾ* have adopted and upheld: 'The doctors of theology and monotheism (*tawḥīd*) are in agreement that confession to the faith (*īmān*) is not valid if it is not voluntary. In the event, therefore, wherever confession to the faith is obtained through compulsion, it is null and void.'[165] On a similar theme, Ibn Qudāmah, the renowned Ḥanbalī jurist/theologian has written:

> It is not permissible to compel a disbeliever into professing Islam. If, for example, a non-Muslim citizen *(dhimmī)* or a person of protected status *(musta'man)* is forced to accept Islam, he is not considered a Muslim unless it is established that his confession is a result of his own choosing. If the person concerned dies before his consent is known, he will be considered a disbeliever . . . The reason for the prohibition of duress here are the words of God Most High that there shall be 'no compulsion in religion'.[166]

The Qur'ānic text that Ibn Qudāmah has referred to in this passage is of central importance to our discussion, and I shall return to it later. At this point, however, I shall proceed with a general characterisation of freedom of religion in the writings of some modern authors. These works, which draw substantially from the evidence in the sources, come to much the same conclusions as are found in earlier writings. The only notable difference between classical and modern works on religious freedom is that some of the earlier writers were persuaded by the argument that many Qur'ānic passages which affirm the freedom of religion have subsequently been abrogated or superseded by other passages of a more restrictive nature. However, modern Muslim opinion on the subject tends to dismiss this rather weak argument. A representative contemporary opinion on the subject of freedom of religion can be found in the following excerpt issued by a recent International Conference on Islamic law, which was held between the leading scholars of Saudi Arabia and Europe. 'The individual is free in regard to the creed he wishes to embrace, and it is unlawful to compel anyone to embrace a religion.' The statement gives as its authority the Qur'ānic text which declares that 'there is no compulsion in religion' (II:256), and also the following Qur'ānic passage which was addressed to the Prophet ﷺ: 'Had thy Lord willed, everyone on earth would have believed. Do you then force people to become believers?' (X: 99)[167]

- لَا إِكْرَاهَ فِى الدِّينِ.
- وَلَوْشَآءَ رَبُّكَ لَاٰمَنَ مَنْ فِى الْاَرْضِ كُلُّهُمْ جَمِيعًا اَفَاَنْتَ تُكْرِهُ النَّاسَ حَتّٰى يَكُوْنُوا مُؤْمِنِينَ.

This latter passage is a Meccan text which was revealed at an early stage in the advent of Islam. This was later followed and confirmed, after the Prophet's ﷺ migration to Medina, by the afore-mentioned verse in *sūrat al-Baqarah* (II:256). Thus, freedom of belief has been consistently enunciated as a norm of the *Sharīʿah* (*aṣl al-tashrīʿ*) regardless of considerations of time and circumstance.[168]

The substance of these Qur'ānic provisions has also been upheld in the 1952 convention of the *ʿulamā'* of Pakistan who drafted a statement entitled 'The Basic Principle of an Islamic State'. This included the following clauses: 'The citizen shall be entitled to all the rights ... he shall be assured within the limits of the law of ... freedom of religion and belief, freedom of worship...'.[169] Similarly, the Universal Islamic Declaration of Human Rights, issued by the Islamic Council of Europe provides: 'Every person has the right to freedom of conscience and worship in accordance with his religious beliefs.' (Art XIII.)[170] Provisions of this kind have now become a regular feature of the constitutions of many contemporary Muslim countries, including Malaysia and Pakistan. The Federal Constitution of Malaysia 1957, which is currently in force, declares the following in Article (II) entitled 'Freedom of Religion':

(1) Every person has the right to profess and practise his religion, and subject to clause (4) to propagate it.

(2) No person shall be compelled to pay any tax the proceeds of which are specially allocated in whole or in part for the purposes of a religion other than his own.

The text goes on to declare, under clause (3) that every religious group is entitled to manage its own religious affairs, to establish religious and charitable institutions, and to acquire and own property for such purposes. Clause (4) provides that a state law, and in respect of the Federal Territories of Kuala Lumpur and Labuan, federal law, may control or restrict the propagation of any religious doctrine or belief among persons professing the religion of Islam.

In the case of 'The Minister of Home Affairs v. Jamaluddin bin Othman',[171] the Supreme Court of Malaysia has upheld its decision to respect the constitutional clause on freedom of religion in its full sense, by dismissing a plea made by the Minister of Home Affairs that conversion to Christianity by a Muslim was a punishable offence. In this case, the respondent, Jamaluddin, was detained under the Internal Security Act 1960, s.8(1), by the Minister of Home Affairs, for what really amounted to apostasy, but was prosecuted for an internal security offence. Originally, the respondent was detained 'for acting in a manner prejudicial to the security of Malaysia',[172] and the allegations that led to Jamaluddin's detention were that he had himself converted from Islam to Christianity and that he was propagating Christianity among the Muslims of Malaysia. It was also alleged that he participated in a work camp and seminar for such a purpose and that, as a result of these activities, he had converted six Malays to Christianity. The defendant pleaded that the Minister did not have the power to order detention without trial. On an application by the respondent for writ of *habeas corpus*, Justice Anuar, the trial judge in the High Court of Kuala Lumpur, took the view that 'the Minister had no power to deprive a person of his right to profess and practise his religion which is guranteed under Art.11 of the Federal Constitution, and, therefore, if the Minister acts to restrict the freedom of a person from professing and practising his religion, his act will be inconsistent with the provision of Art.11 and therefore an order of detention would not be valid'.[173] Consequently, the judge ordered the release of the respondent from detention. The Minister for Home Affairs appealed to the Supreme Court in Kuala Lumpur, but the Criminal Appeal Division dismissed the appeal and stated the grounds of its decision as follows:

> The sum total of the grounds for detention in this case was the supposed involvement of the respondent in a plan or programme for the dissemination of Christianity among the Malays ... We do not think that mere participation in meetings and seminars can make a person a threat to the security of the country. As regards the alleged conversion of six Malays, even if it were true, it cannot by itself, in our opinion be regarded as a threat to the security of the country.[174]

While dismissing the appeal, the court added that the grounds for detention in this case, when read in the proper context, were insufficient; that the guarantee provided by Art.11 of the constitution, namely, the right to freedom of religion, must be given effect, unless the actions of a person go well beyond what can normally be regarded as professing and practising his or her faith.

The 1973 *Constitution of the Islamic Republic of Pakistan*, which is currently in force, proclaims in its section on Fundamental Rights and Liberties that:

> Subject to law, public order and morality: a. every citizen shall have the right to profess, practise and propagate his religion; and b. every religious denomination and every section thereof have the right to establish, maintain and manage its religious institutions. (Art.20)

The constitution of Pakistan also forbids discrimination against religious communities as regards taxation, educational policies, and the allocation of funds and concessions that the state may make to religious communities or institutions. (Arts. 21, 22, 38.)

While quoting some of the Qur'ānic verses on the subject, Mutawallī has characterised the main thrust of the Qur'ānic teaching on religious freedom as follows: religious belief should be founded on conviction and considered choice, not on mere imitation or conformity to the views and beliefs of others. The *Sharīᶜah* forbids compulsion in religion as it is incompatible with the courteous methods of persuasion that the Qur'ān prescribes for the propagation of Islam. While stating the evidence to support his comment, the same author observes, on a historical note, that Muslim rulers and governers have generally exercised tolerance in the treatment of non-Muslim subjects, particularly in the matter of religious beliefs. Mutawallī also agrees with the conclusion which Thomas Arnold came to in his investigations: that the concept that Islam was imposed by the sword is inaccurate and far from the truth. In his book, *The Preaching of Islam*, Thomas Arnold advanced the theme that Christian historians have obscured 'the genuine missionary character of Islam'[175] and have instead laid emphasis on the use of the sword as the principal instrument in its propagation: 'So little is there in the statement that Islam makes progress only by the force of arms'[176] that one can see the opposite of this in the histroy of Islam in Africa, the Middle East and elsewhere. With reference to the spread of Islam in Palestine and Syria, Arnold commented: 'That force was not the determining factor in these conversions may be judged from the amicable relations that existed between the Christian and the Muslim Arabs.'[177] To quote Arnold again:

> From the examples given above of the toleration extended towards the Christian Arabs by the victorious Muslims of the first century of the Hijrah and continued by succeeding generations we may surely infer that those Christsian tribes that did embrace Islam did so of their own choice and free will. The Christian Arabs of the present day, dwelling in the midst of a Muhammadan population are a living testimony of this toleration.[178]

Mutawalli has concluded that any oppression that might have soiled the otherwise tolerant record of Muslim rulers was mainly attributable to political factors which find little support in the principles of Islamic law.[179] The practice of early Islamic leaders, particularly the Rightly-Guided Caliphs, was consistently determined by the Qur'ānic norms which seek to protect the integrity of the individual conscience. Abū Zahrah and Mutawallī, among others, are both explicit on this point. According to the former, 'the early Muslims showed great care and sensitivity not to compel anyone in the matter of religion.' Abū Zahrah also tells of an incident where an elderly Christian woman came as a supplicant to the Caliph ᶜUmar b. al-Khaṭṭāb, who met her request with favour. Afterwards, he invited her to embrace Islam, but she refused. At this the Caliph became anxious, fearing that his invitation might have amounted to compulsion, and he expressed his remorse in these words: 'O my Lord, I did not mean to compel her, as I know that there must be no compulsion in religion ... righteousness has been explained and distinguished from misguidance.' Thus, the Caliph ᶜUmar expressed the point that only God Most High can prevail upon the hearts and minds of people in matters of faith.[180]

The precedent and attitude of the Rightly-Guided Caliphs reflects the correct understanding of the norms of the *Sharīᶜah* which clearly recognise the freedom of religion and proscribe all oppression and violation of the integrity of this freedom.[181]

Notwithstanding the relative clarity of the Qur'ānic proclamations on the freedom of religion, the subject has become controversial. This is due partly to certain other passages in the Qur'ān which have sometimes been interpreted in a manner which casts doubt on the subject. Indeed, some commentators have drawn the drastic conclusion that the Qur'ānic passages which validate holy war (*jihād*) and fighting against disbelievers actually abrogate the Qur'ān's proclamation on tolerance and respect for other religions. The controversy has been exacerbated further by reliance on the provision in the Sunnah which authorises the death penalty for apostasy without due consideration of other evidence in the Sunnah to the effect that punishment by death was meant only for apostasy accompanied by hostility and treason. However, a full enquiry into these issues would fall beyond the scope of this study. Some of these issues have already been treated and investigated at length in books and articles in the English language.[182] I shall, therefore, confine my discussion to some of the conclusions that have been drawn, without paying undue attention to many of the details.

In his monograph, *The Punishment of Apostasy in Islam*, S. A. Rahman looks into the evidence in the Qur'ān and the Sunnah in detail, and draws attention to the fact that the Qur'ān is silent on the question of death as the punishment for apostasy, despite this subject occurring no less than twenty times in the Holy Book. Rahman then traces the chain of transmission of the *Ḥadīth* which proclaims 'kill whoever changes his religion'.

مَنْ بَدَّلَ دِينَهُ فَاقْتُلُوهُ.

As this is a solitary *Ḥadīth* (*āḥād*), Rahman finds some weakness in its transmission (*isnād*). Rahman's conclusion is also supported by other evidence, such as the fact that neither the Prophet ﷺ himself, nor any of his Companions ever compelled anyone to embrace Islam, nor did they sentence anyone to death solely for renunciation of the faith.[183] In the light of this, it is not surprising to find a number of prominent *ᶜulamā'*, across the centuries, subscribing to the view that apostasy is not a punishable offence. Ibrāhīm al-Nakhaᶜī (d. 95/713), a leading jurist and traditionist among the generation succeeding the Companions, and Sufyān al-Thawrī (d. 161/772), who is known as 'the prince of the believers concerning *Ḥadīth*' (*amīr al-mu'minīn fi'l-Ḥadīth*) and is the author of two important compilations of *Ḥadīth*, namely *al-Jāmiᶜ al-Kabīr* and *al-Jāmiᶜ al-Ṣaghīr*, both held that the apostate should be re-invited to Islam, but should never be condemned to death. They maintained the view that the invitation should continue for as long as there is hope that the apostate might change his mind and repent.[184] ᶜAbd al-Wahhāb al-Shaᶜrānī has also cited the views of al-Nakhaᶜī and al-Thawrī and adds that 'the apostate is thus permanently to be invited to repent'.[185] The renowned Ḥanafī jurist, Shams al-Dīn al-Sarakhsi, is rather less explicit but what he writes amounts to saying that apostasy does not qualify for temporal punishment. He begins by stating that apostasy is not an offence for which there is a prescribed punishment (*ḥadd*), because the punishment for it is suspended when the apostate repents:

> The prescribed penalties (*ḥudūd*) are generally not suspended because of repentance, especially when they are reported and become known to the head of state (*imām*). The punishment of highway robbery, for instance, is not suspended because of repentance; it is suspended only by the return of property to the owner prior to arrest ... Renunciation of the faith and conversion to disbelief is admittedly the greatest of offences, yet it is a matter between man and his Creator, and its punishment is postponed to the day of judgement (*fa'l-jazā' ʿalayhā mu'akhkhar ilā dār al-jazā'*). Punishments that are enforced in this life are those which protect the people's interests, such as just retaliation, which is designed to protect life ...[186]

Al-Sarakhsī goes on to recount the punishments for adultery, theft, slanderous accusation, wine-drinking and highway robbery - namely, all the *ḥudūd* punishments - but leaves apostasy out altogether from the list. The Mālikī jurist, al-Bājī (d. 494 A.H.), also observed that apostasy is a sin which carries no prescribed penalty (*ḥadd*), and that such a sin may only be punished under the discretionary punishment of *taʿzīr*.[187] The renowned Ḥanbalī jurist, Ibn Taymiyyah, also categorically agrees on this latter punishment for apostasy.[188]

Among modern scholars, ʿAbd al-Ḥakīm al-ʿĪlī and Ismāʿīl al-Badawī have commented that by al-Nakhaʿī's time, Islam was secure from the hostility of disbelievers and apostates. This, they maintain, indicates that al-Nakhaʿī understood the Prophetic *Ḥadīth* quoted above, which made apostasy punishable by death, to be political in character and aimed at the inveterate enemies of Islam.[189] On a similar note, Maḥmūd Shaltūt analyses the relevant evidence in the Qur'ān and draws the conclusion that apostasy carries no temporal penalty, and that in reference to this particular sin, the Qur'ān speaks only of punishment in the hereafter:

> As for the death penalty for apostasy, the jurists have relied on the *Ḥadīth* reported by Ibn ʿAbbās in which the Prophet has said,'Kill the one who changes his religion' (*man baddala dīnahu faqtulūhu*). This *Ḥadīth* has evoked various responses from the ʿ*ulamā'*, many of whom are in agreement that the prescribed penalties (*ḥudūd*) cannot be established by solitary *Ḥadīth* (*āḥād*), and that unbelief by itself does not call for the death penalty. The key factor which determines the application of this punishment is aggression and hostility against the believers and the [need to] prevent possible sedition (*fitnah*) against religion and state. This conclu-

> sion is sustained by the manifest meaning of many of the passages in the Qur'ān which proscribe compulsion in religion.[190]

Mahmassānī has observed that the death penalty was meant to apply, not to simple acts of apostasy from Islam, but when apostasy was linked to an act of political betrayal of the community. The Prophet ﷺ never killed anyone solely for apostasy. This being the case, the death penalty was not meant to apply to a simple change of faith but to punish acts such as treason, joining forces with the enemy and sedition.[191]

The late Ayatollah Mutahhari highlighted the incompatibility of coercion with the spirit of Islam, and the basic redundancy of punitive measures in the propagation of its message. He wrote that it is impossible to force anyone to acquire the kind of faith that is required by Islam, just as 'it is not possible to spank a child into solving an arithmetical problem. His mind and thought must be left free in order that he may solve it. The Islamic faith is something of this kind.'[192]

Selim el-Awa discusses the issue of apostasy at length, declaring that 'there is an urgent need to reinterpret the principles contained in the Qur'ān and Sunnah'. He cites the fact that the Qur'ān is completely silent on the death penalty for apostasy, and that the evidence in the Sunnah is open to interpretation.[193] El-Awa elaborates that the death penalty in the Sunnah is not designed for apostasy per se but for high treason, or *ḥirābah*, that is, when apostasy is accompanied by hostility and rebellion against the community and its legitimate leadership. The *Ḥadīth* which proclaims 'whoever renounces his religion shall be killed', is a general (*ʿāmm*) command which is in need of specification (*takhṣīṣ*). In its general form, it would apply equally to cases that manifestly fall outside its intention, as it would render this same punishment not only to Muslims but also to Christians who convert to Judaism, and vice versa. Al-Shawkānī adds to the foregoing, that the general purport of this *Ḥadīth* has been restricted in the Qur'ān so as to exclude a person who changes his religion outwardly under duress but remains faithful otherwise.[194] Al-Shawkānī has also criticised the ruling of some Shafiʿī scholars who have followed the literal and general meaning of the *Ḥadīth* in question and erroneously held that the death penalty therein applies equally to a non-Muslim who converts from one religion to another. On this subject, he states that, 'My response to this is that the literal meaning of the *Ḥadīth* has been abandoned in regard to a disbeliever who embraces Islam.'[195] Moreover, the Ḥanafis have countered the general interpretation of this *Ḥadīth* in yet another respect, namely, that a woman apostate is not punished by death but only by imprisonment (since the masculine pronominal suffix alone occurs in the wording). According to the rules of intrepretation, as expounded in *uṣūl al-fiqh*, once a decisive (*qaṭʿī*) ruling of a text has been specified in some respect, the part which remains unspecified becomes speculative (*ẓannī*), and as such, is open to further interpretation and specification (*takhṣīṣ*). It is thus also suggested that the *Ḥadīth* in question may be further qualified, and that the death penalty therein may be reserved only for apostasy which is accompanied by high treason (*ḥirābah*).[196]

The preceding analysis is also extended to the second *Ḥadīth* often quoted in support of the death penalty for apostasy, which is as follows:

> The blood of a Muslim who professes that there is no god but Allāh and that I am His Messenger, is sacrosanct except in three cases: a married adulterer; a person who has killed another human being; and a person who has abandoned his religion, while splitting himself off from the community *(mufāriq li'l-jamāʿah)*.[197]

لايحلُّ دَمُ اِمرِءٍ مُسْلِمٍ يشـهد ان لا اله الاّ الله، وإنّى رسول الله الاّ باحدى ثلاث، الثَّيبُ الزّانِى وَالنَّفْسُ بِالنَّفْسِ، والتَّارِكُ لِدينهِ مُفَارِقٌ لِلجَمَاعة.

As will be noted, this *Ḥadīth* makes clear that the apostate must also boycott the community (*mufāriq li'l-jamāʿah*) and challenge its legitimate leadership, in order to be subjected to the death penalty.[198]

The Qur'ān specifies a three-fold punishment for high treason (*ḥirābah*), culminating in death (V:34). Ibn Taymiyyah, in an attempt to reconcile the terms of the preceding *Ḥadīth* with the Qur'ān, observes that the crime referred to in the *Ḥadīth* under discussion is that of high treason (*ḥirābah*) and not apostasy (*riddah*) as such.[199] This observation is again supported by the fact that the Prophet ﷺ never put anyone to death for apostasy alone. Indeed, there were cases when certain individuals apostasised after professing Islam yet the Prophet ﷺ did not even penalise them, let alone condemn them to death. Affirmative evidence on this point is found in the following incident which appears in the *Ḥadīth* compilations of al-Bukhārī and Muslim:

> A Bedouin came to the Holy Prophet ﷺ and pledged his allegiance to him, professing Islam. The next day he came back, ill with fever and said, 'Return my pledge to me,' but the Prophet ﷺ refused - thrice. Then the Prophet ﷺ said: Medina is like a bellows which rejects its dross and recognises its pure.[200]

عَن جَابِرٍ رَضِيَ اللهِ عَنْهُ: جَاءَ أَعْرَابِيٌّ إِلَى النَّبِي ﷺ فَبَايَعَهُ
عَلَى الاِ سـلاَمِ فَجَاءَ مِنَ الغَدِ مَحْمُوْمًا فَقَالَ: أَقِلْنِي، فَأَبَى
- ثَلاَثَ مِرارٍ فَقَال اَلمَدِينَةُ كَالكِير تَنْفِي خَبَثَها وَيَنْصَعُ
طَيِّبُها.

This was a clear case of apostasy, in which the Prophet ﷺ made no reference to any punishment at all, and the Bedouin, despite his persistent renunciation of Islam was left to go unharmed.[201]

Furthermore, the following Qur'ānic passage is in complete harmony with the purport of the foregoing *Ḥadīth*, and provides, once again, a strong argument against the death penalty for apostasy:

> Those who believe then disbelieve, then believe again, then disbelieve and then increase in their disbelief - God will never forgive them nor guide them to the path. (IV:137)

إِنَّ الَّـذِينَ آمَنُـوا ثُـمَّ كَفَرُوا ثُـمَّ آمَنُـوا ثُـمَّ كَفَرُوا ثُـمَّ ازْدَادُوا
كُفْـرًا لَّـمْ يَكُـنِ اللهُ لِيَغْفِرَلَهُـمْ وَلاَ لِيَهْدِيَهُـمْ سَـبِيلاً.

The implication is unmistakable. The text would hardly entertain the prospect of repeated belief and disbelief if death were to be the prescribed punishment for the initial act. It is also interesting to note that the initial reference to disbelief is followed by further confirmation of disbelief and then 'increase in disbelief'. One might be inclined to think that if the first instance of apostasy did not qualify for capital punishment, the repeated apostasy might have provoked it - had such a punishment ever been intended in the Qur'ān.

The Prophet ﷺ did not treat apostasy as a proscribed offence (*ḥadd*), but, on the contrary, pardoned many individuals who had embraced Islam, then renounced it, and then embraced it again, Included among these was ʿAbd Allāh ibn Abī Sarḥ, the foster brother of ʿUthmān ibn ʿAffān, and one-time scribe of the Prophet ﷺ, whom the Prophet ﷺ forgave when ʿUthmān interceded on his behalf. Other cases included that of al-Ḥārith ibn Suwayd, 'and a group of people from Mecca' who embraced Islam, renounced it afterwards, and then re-embraced it. Their lives too were spared. Ibn Taymiyyah, who has recorded this information, added that 'these episodes and similar other ones are well-known to the scholars of *Ḥadīth*.'[202] Ibn Taymiyyah further added that the Companions reached a consensus (*ijmāʿ*) on this, for when the Prophet ﷺ passed away, most of the Arabs, except for the residents of Mecca, Medina and Ṭa'if, apostasised, including many followers of the self-proclaimed 'prophets', Musaylimah, al-ʿAnasī, and Tulayhah al-Asadī, who renounced Islam and were subsequently fought by Abū Bakr al-Ṣiddīq and other Companions until they returned to the faith again. They were left unharmed and not a single one of them was killed because of their renunciation of Islam. This, Ibn Taymiyyah adds is common knowledge.[203]

In response to the question of whether Islam permits war as a means of propagation, many scholars have reached the conclusion that war is permissible only to protect the freedom of belief and to prevent oppression. The Qur'ān forbids sedition (*fitnah*) in religion, as well as the persecution of people for their religious beliefs. It is this *fitnah*, as Abū Zahrah observes, which the Qur'ān declares to be a menace greater than murder, and thus it permits waging war in order to prevent tyranny and sedition, as the following text shows: 'And fight them until *fitnah* is no more and religion is for God alone. But if they stop then there is to be no hostility except against the oppressors.' (II:193)

وَقَاتِلُوهُمْ حَتَّى لَا تَكُونَ فِتْنَةٌ وَيَكُونَ الدِّينُ كُلُّهُ لِلَّهِ فَإِنِ
انْتَهَوْا فَإِنَّ اللَّهَ بِمَا يَعْمَلُونَ بَصِيرٌ.

From this passage, Abū Zahrah draws the conclusion that 'fighting is only permissible in order to defend the freedom of belief and prevent oppression in religion'.[204] He also quotes another Qur'ānic passage in support of his statement, which declares explicitly:

> Fighting has been permitted for those against whom war has been waged, because they have been wronged - and God is able to give them victory; those who were expelled from their homes for no cause other than saying: "God is our Lord". (XXII:39)

أُذِنَ لِلَّذِينَ يُقَاتَلُونَ بِأَنَّهُمْ ظُلِمُوا وَإِنَّ اللهَ عَلَى نَصْرِهِمْ لَقَدِيرٌ
الَّذِينَ أُخْرِجُوا مِن دِيَارِهِم بِغَيْرِ حَقٍّ إِلاَّ أَن يَقُولُوا رَبُّنَا اللهُ.

Rashīd Riḍā comments on the first of these two passages by saying, 'This verse reaffirms the one which occurs in *Sūrat al-Baqarah* (II:256), and both proscribe compulsion in religion. Both of these passages proclaim and uphold that people are free to pursue religious beliefs of their own choosing. No one is to be compelled to abandon the religion he professes nor must anyone be exposed to punishment and torture for the sake of religion.'[205]

By far the most explicit of Qur'ānic verses on freedom of religion is the following one in *Sūrat al-Baqarah* (II:256):

> There is to be no compulsion in religion. Surely the right direction has been made clear and distinct from error. He who rejects false deities and believes in God has grasped a firm handhold which will never break.

لاَ إِكْرَاهَ فِي الدِّينِ قَدْ تَبَيَّنَ الرُّشْدُ مِنَ الْغَيِّ فَمَن
يَكْفُرْ بِالطَّاغُوتِ وَيُؤمِن بِاللهِ فَقَدِ اسْتَمْسَكَ بِالْعُرْوَةِ
الْوُثْقَى.

This verse was revealed on the occasion when some Companions among the Helpers (*anṣār*) asked the Prophet ﷺ for permission to compel their relatives to profess Islam. However, some of these people had practised Christianity or Judaism since their early childhood, and the Banū Naḍīr, a Jewish tribe of Medina even had children who were related to the Companions, but who were brought up by Jewish parents and were considered Jews. When the Prophet ﷺ issued orders for the Banū Naḍīr to move out of Medina, so as to prevent clashes between them and the Muslims, some Companions sought instead to force their relatives into Islam. It was at this juncture that the preceding verse was revealed, and the Prophet ﷺ ordered his Companions not to compel anyone, but to give them the choice to decide what religion they wished to follow.[206]

Commentators of the Qur'ān, such as Ibn Kathīr and Rashīd Riḍā, have considered this text to be a general proclamation in the sense that it absolutely prohibits compulsion in religion. No one must be compelled to embrace Islam, as it would serve no useful purpose for a person to do so under coercion, while his mind and heart remain closed to enlightenment and guidance. To this Rashīd Riḍā adds that belief (*īmān*), which is the pillar and essence of religion, implies a willing submission of the self which cannot be gained through duress: it must be attained through conviction and reason. Force, therefore, has no place in the matter of belief. The subsequent portion of the text, Riḍā adds, endorses the general message of the verse, namely, in this religion there is guidance and light and the call to the faith should be through explanation. Once people are shown the right path then it is their choice whether to follow it or abandon it. Riḍā continues:

> We are ordered to invite people to the path of God with wisdom and good exhortation ... This would explain the place of holy war (*jihād*) in Islam. *Jihād* is not of the essence of religion nor one of its goals. It is only a protective shield and is resorted to as a matter of political necessity. The common hysteria and its misguided exponents who assume that faith is established by the sword merit no attention whatsoever.[207]

Some commentators have attempted to qualify the general import of the verse under discussion (i.e. II:256) by showing that it was initially in force but was later abrogated when Islam gained victory. S.A. Rahman, the former Chief Justice of Pakistan, responds to this argument as follows:

> There is no warrant for such a conclusion to be found in any Qur'ānic verse, and indeed the ethical plane of such argumentation is too obvious to require comment ... Furthermore, there is no indication in the text that the words are to be understood in a restricted or qualified sense, nor would the *shan-i-nuzūl* reports justify that course.[208]

Rahman characterises *Sūrat al-Baqarah* (II:256) as one of the most important verses in the Qur'ān, and he is perturbed that Muslim scholars have attempted to whittle down its broad humanistic meaning by imposing limitations on its scope dictated by historical theological controversies.[209]

Another aspect of Qur'ānic evidence that relates to our discussion is its explicit recognition of other great religions preceding the advent of Islam. There are a number of verses in the Qur'ān which not only declare the validity and divine provenance of other faiths, but highly compliment their teachings. The Qur'ānic evidence is explicit on the unity of the origin and purpose of all the revealed faiths. Thus, we read in *Sūrat al-Mā'idah* (V:44): 'We revealed the Torah in which there is guidance and light.'

إِنَّآ أَنْزَلْنَا التَّوْرٰىةَ فِيهَا هُدًى وَنُورٌ.

The text then continues to expound and confirm some of the laws of the Torah, in particular, the law of just retaliation, which became an integral part of the *Sharīᶜah* of Islam. A subsequent passage in the same *sūrah* further confirms both the Torah and the New Testament:

> And in their footsteps We sent Jesus the son of Mary confirming the law that was revealed before him; We gave him the Gospel in which there is guidance and light and which confirms the Torah before it, a guidance and admonition to those who fear God. Let the people of the Gospel judge by what God has revealed therein, and whoever refuses to judge by what God has revealed are transgressors. (V:46-48)

وَقَفَّيْنَا عَلَىٰ آثَارِهِم بِعِيسَى ابْنِ مَرْيَمَ مُصَدِّقًا لِّمَا بَيْنَ
يَدَيْهِ مِنَ التَّوْرٰىةِ وَآتَيْنَٰهُ الْإِنْجِيلَ فِيهِ هُدًى وَنُورٌ وَ
مُصَدِّقًا لِّمَا بَيْنَ يَدَيْهِ مِنَ التَّوْرٰىةِ وَهُدًى وَمَوْعِظَةً
لِّلْمُتَّقِينَ وَلْيَحْكُمْ أَهْلُ الْإِنْجِيلِ بِمَآ أَنْزَلَ اللهُ فِيهِ وَمَن
لَّمْ يَحْكُم بِمَآ أَنْزَلَ اللهُ فَأُولَٰئِكَ هُمُ الْفَٰسِقُونَ.

This is followed by a further affirmation which is addressed to the Prophet Muḥammad ﷺ: 'We sent down to you the Book in truth, confirming and safeguarding the Book before It.' (V:48.)

وَأَنْزَلْنَا إِلَيْكَ الْكِتَـٰبَ بِالْحَقِّ مُصَدِّقًا لِّمَا بَيْنَ يَدَيْهِ مِنَ
الْكِتَـٰبِ وَمُهَيْمِنًا عَلَيْهِ.

The Qur'ānic recognition of the truth and essential unity of the revealed faiths is not confined to Christianity and Judaism but extends to all the Prophets preceding Moses ﵇ and Jesus ﵇ and their teachings. Thus, it is stated that belief in all of them is an integral part of the Muslim faith:

> Say: We believe in God and in what has been revealed to us and what was revealed to Abraham, Ishmael, Isaac, Jacob, and the tribes, and in the scriptures that God sent to Moses and Jesus, and the Prophets. We make no distinction between them ... .(III:84)

قُلْ آمَنَّا بِاللهِ وَمَآ أُنْزِلَ عَلَيْنَا وَمَآ أُنْزِلَ على إِبْرٰهِيمَ
وَإِسْمٰعِيلَ وَإِسْحٰقَ وَيَعْقُوبَ وَالأَسْبَاطِ وَمَآ أُوتِيَ
مُوسَىٰ وَعِيسَىٰ وَالنَّبِيُّونَ مِن رَّبِّهِمْ لاَ نُفَرِّقُ بَيْنَ أَحَدٍ
مِّنْهُمْ.

Affirmative references to other revealed religions is one of the major themes of the Qur'ān. These recur in several places in the Book and they consistently confirm that Islam does not deny the followers of other faiths the freedom, both within and outside the territorial domain of Islam, to choose, retain and practise the religion they wish to follow.[210] This is precisely the conclusion that commentators have drawn from the totality of the Qur'ānic evidence. Referring to these verses, Fatḥī ʿUthmān writes that 'Islam rejects compulsion even if it be the only way to Islam itself ... for worshipping God and the enforcement of His law cannot be properly achieved unless man is free from fear ...'.[211]

The Qur'ān is most explicit on the dignity and nobility of man, both individually and collectively, and it repeatedly expresses the theme that a person's dignity is intimately related to his or her freedom - particularly freedom of conscience. In sum, the Qur'ān is consistent in its affirmation of the freedom of belief and it fully supports the conclusion that the objectives of the *Sharīʿah* cannot be properly fulfilled without granting people the freedom of belief, and the liberty to express it.

Another pertinent Qur'ānic theme is the affirmation that religion is a matter of individual conviction and belief, and that persuasion and advice are the only ways through which others may be invited to embrace Islam. The passages that are quoted below also cast light on the function of the Prophet ﷺ, and the methods which he was to follow in his summons to the new faith.

> If they embrace Islam, they are rightly-guided, but if they turn their backs on it, then your only duty is to convey [the message]. (III:20)

فَإِنْ أَسْلَمُوا فَقَدِ اهْتَدَوا وَإِن تَوَلَّوا فَإِنَّمَا عَلَيْكَ الْبَلَٰغُ.

> Remind them, for you are one who reminds; you are not a warden over them. (LXXXVIII:21-22)

فَذَكِّرْ إِنَّمَا أَنتَ مُذَكِّرٌ لَّسْتَ عَلَيْهِم بِمُصَيْطِرٍ.

> And if they turn away, We have not sent you as a guardian over them. Your duty is but to convey the message. (XLII:48)

فَإِنْ أَعْرَضُوا فَمَآ أَرْسَلْنَاكَ عَلَيْهِمْ حَفِيظًا إِنْ عَلَيْكَ إِلَّا الْبَلَٰغُ.

> Obey God and obey the Messenger and beware. But if you turn back then know that Our Messenger's duty is but to proclaim clearly [the message]. (V:92. See also V:99 to the same effect.)

وَأَطِيعُوا اللهَ وَأَطِيعُوا الرَّسُولَ وَاحْذَرُوا فَإِن تَوَلَّيْتُمْ
فَاعْلَمُوا أَنَّمَا عَلَىٰ رَسُولِنَا الْبَلَٰغُ الْمُبِينُ.

Yet another Qur'ānic theme which occurs in a number of passages is that invitation to the faith must be wisely made with courteous advice, and that it must be based on sound reasoning and eloquent persuasion. The message here once again precludes resorting to compulsion in the promotion and propagation of Islam. Moreover, it is to be understood that anything which dilutes the self-evident meaning of the Qur'ān on these points, whether in the name of *jihād* or enlightenment, is unacceptable and should be strongly discouraged. For *jihād* is abused when it is pursued in such a way as to impede the Qur'ānic principle of the freedom of belief.

Both Wafi and ʿAwdah have drawn the conclusion that Islam protects freedom of religion in at least three ways. Firstly, by enacting that no one may be compelled to abandon his religion and embrace Islam, which is clearly proclaimed in *Sūrat al-Baqarah* (II:256). Muslim rulers and conquerors have generally abided by this principle and allowed their subjects to continue practising their own religion, provided they paid the poll-tax (*jizyah*) and obeyed the government in power. They were, on the other hand, exempted from military service and the *jizyah* was a substitute for this. Secondly, Islam validates the freedom of the individual to propagate the religion of his following through sound reasoning and argumentation. Thus, Muslims are required in the Qur'ān to resort to courteous reasoning to attract others to Islam and to permit the practitioners of other religions to employ the same methods. (XXI:46; XVI:125; II:111). Thirdly, the Qur'ān validates the norm that true faith stems from certitude and conviction, and not from imitation and mere adherence to forms. As the following passage shows, this is why the Qur'ān denounced pre-Islamic practices and attitudes which promoted the blind imitation of ancestral precedents at the expense of independent thought and personal conviction.

> When it is said to them: 'Follow what God has revealed', they say: 'Nay we follow the ways of our fathers'; what! even though their fathers understood naught and were not rightly-guided. (II:170)[212]

وَإِذَا قِيلَ لَهُمُ اتَّبِعُوا مَآ أَنْزَلَ اللهُ قَالُوا بَلْ نَتَّبِعُ مَآ
أَلْفَيْنَا عَلَيْهِ آبَآءَنَا أَوَلَوْ كَانَ آبَآؤُهُمْ لَا يَعْقِلُونَ شَيْئًا وَلَا
يَهْتَدُونَ.

Commenting on this Qur'ānic verse, Wafi refers to, and supports the conclusion ᶜAbduh has reached, that 'thoughtless imitation which lacks wisdom and correct guidance is the hallmark of the disbelievers. A man can hardly be called faithful or a believer (*mu'min*) unless he thinks about his faith and satisfies himself as to the veracity of his belief.'[213] ᶜAwdah concurs with ᶜAbduh, but adds that the *Sharīᶜah* also obligates one who is faithful to protect and safeguard his belief. If a person is exposed to intolerable oppression on account of his belief and lacks the means to protect his freedom, then he should migrate to a place where he can safeguard his belief and self-respect. ᶜAwdah concludes by saying that 'if the person is able to migrate and he does not do so, then he would have committed an injustice against himself'. ᶜAwdah's conclusion here is based on the Qur'ānic text (IV:97-98) which denounces the attitude of those who do not exert themselves, if necessary, to migrate, in order to safeguard the integrity and freedom of their consciences.[214]

To sum up, the Qur'ān has explicitly declared freedom of religion a norm and principle of Islam. This declaration, found in *Sūrat al-Baqarah*, (II:256) is consistently endorsed in numerous other verses of the Holy Book. Unfortunately, there are those who have promoted a misleading and politically motivated discourse which declares that Islam denies freedom of religion, and that the Qur'ānic passages which advocate this freedom were subsequently abrogated and overruled by its other provisions on the subject of *jihād*.[215] The proponents of this view have used abrogation, itself a highly controversial issue, as their primary tool in an attempt to whittle away one of the cardinal principles of the Qur'ān.[216] Throughout history, the militant outlook espoused by this group may have had its sympathisers among expansionists and military strategists, but the view has never commanded general acceptance or support. Furthermore, this school of thought lacks sound reasoning and has been less than convincing in its attempts to overshadow the essence of the Qur'ānic message on the freedom of conscience. The unequivocal recognition of this freedom in the constitutions of present-day Muslim nations bears testimony to a decisive movement in favour of the basic rights of the individual, including the freedom to follow the religion of his or her choice. As a result, there appears to be a consensus of opinion emerging among the Muslims of the twentieth century in support of the universal validity of the freedom of religion in the *Sharīᶜah* and contemporary constitutional law.

CONCLUSION

The evidence that I have looked at in the various areas of the Qur'ān and Sunnah is clearly affirmative of the fundamental right to freedom of speech. Nevertheless, only the Qur'ānic principle of *ḥisbah* is broad enough in scope to include freedom of speech and expression in most of its material manifestations. There are, as previously noted, numerous passages on *ḥisbah* in the Qur'ān, and although the Qur'ānic directives on *ḥisbah* are mainly addressed to the believers, this does not preclude their application to non-Muslims. For the latter enjoy the same rights in respect of speech and constructive criticism as do their fellow Muslim citizens. *Ḥisbah*, in the specific sense of duty, does not exclude the non-Muslim either, although there may be instances where necessary exceptions have to be made. For example, to attempt to save the life of a drowning person - whether a Muslim or non-Muslim - is an obligation of everyone who witnesses the incident, regardless of their faith. But, preventing another person from drinking wine is not expected from an individual in whose religion the consumption of alcoholic beverages is not forbidden.

On a similar note, the Qur'ānic principle of consultation, although primarily addressed to the Muslims, does not exclude the non-Muslim citizen from the scope of its application, nor indeed from the ranks of the consultative assembly (*majlis al-shūrā*). Thus, the non-Muslim may be elected to the consultative assembly, and may represent his or her own community. The following Qur'ānic text authorises non-Muslim participation in consultation pertaining to community affairs outside the scope of religion.

'And ask the people of renown if you yourselves do not know'. (XVI:43)

فَسْئَلُوا أَهْلَ الذِّكْرِ إِنْ كُنْتُمْ لَا تَعْلَمُونَ.

The right to criticise government leaders and express an opinion, critical or otherwise, in public affairs, or indeed to formulate a response to a statement or opinion expressed by another individual is, once again, the right of every citizen, Muslim and non-Muslim alike. There is nothing in the *Sharīʿah* which reserves the *ḥaqq al-*

muʿāraḍah for Muslims alone. However, a general observation which should be made here is that in matters which pertain to the dogma of Islam, or those which are regulated by the direct authority of the Qur'ān or Sunnah, criticism, either from Muslims or non-Muslims, will not be entertained, as personal or public opinion does not command authority in such matters. Islam is basically a religion of authority, and the values of good and evil, or rights and duties are not determined by reference to public opinion, or popular vote, although these too have a certain role to play in the determination of the *aḥkām* (such as in *ijmāʿ* and *maṣlaḥah*). But, this need not diminish in any material sense the substance of the freedom of expression that the individual must enjoy under the *Sharīʿah*.

The history of legal development in almost all the major systems of law reflects the realities and experiences of the world's different nations and societies, and Islamic law is no exception to this. There may be instances, however, in some of the detailed formulations of the established schools of law, which may not serve the ideals of harmony and cohesion in the pluralistic and multi-religious societies of our own time. In such instances, recourse to the broad principles of justice in the Qur'ān and the Sunnah, and a fresh look at the principal objectives of the *Sharīʿah* (*maqāṣid al-Sharīʿah*), could be recommended. This may be done in accordance with the true spirit of unfettered *ijtihād* in order to effect changes that reflect a more considered approach to the Qur'ānic standards of equality and justice.

NOTES

1. *'Fiqh'* is often used synonymously with *'Sharīʿah'*, both of which refer to the general body of Islamic law, although there is a difference between them in that *'fiqh'* consists largely of juristic interpretation whereas *'Sharīʿah'* bears a closer affinity with divine revelation.

2. Al-Ghazālī, *Iḥyā' ʿUlūm al-Dīn* (al-Maktabah al-Tijāriyyah edn.) II, 310.

3. Ibn Qayyim, *al-Ṭuruq al-Ḥukmiyyah fi'l-Siyāsah al-Sharʿiyyah*, (Al-Mu'assasah al-ʿArabiyyah, 1961 edn.), p. 278.

4. The early *ʿulamā'* have raised and discussed in detail the question as to whether *ḥisbah* is a collective duty (*farḍ kafā'ī*), or an individual obligation (*farḍ ʿaynī*) which should be performed by every Muslim, like the canonical prayer (*ṣalāh*) and other obligatory duties. For further detail see Ḥammād, *Ḥurriyyah*, p. 221 ff.

5. Azzam, ed., *Universal Islamic Declaration of Human Rights,* p. 8.

6. Ḥammād, *Ḥurriyyah*, p. 221.

7. Zaydān, *Majmū*ʿ*at Buḥūth Fiqhiyyah*, p. 128

8. Al-Sibāʿī, *Ishtirākiyyat al-Islām*, p. 52.

9. Al-Ghazālī, *Iḥyā'*, (al-Maktabah al-Tijāriyyah edn.) II, 304.

10. For '*Ḥadīth*' see either note 14 of Part One or the glossary.

11. Muslim, *Mukhtaṣar Ṣaḥīḥ Muslim*, p. 16, *Ḥadīth* no. 34.

12. Cf. Ḥammād, *Ḥurriyyah*, p. 221.

13. Al-Maqdisī, *al-Ādāb al-Sharʿiyyah wa'l-Minaḥ al-Marʿiyyah*, I, 94.

14. Breaking the instruments of gambling or spilling away the wine are more illustrations that al-Ghazālī gives of the use of force in *ḥisbah*. For details see *Ihyā'* II, 329-33.

15. Al-Maqdisī, *al-Ādāb*, I, 94.

16. Al-Ghazālī, *Ihyā'*, II, 324.

17. Al-Qarafi, *Kitāb al-Furūq*, IV, 255.

18. Hans Wehr, *Arabic-English Dictionary*, p. 970.

19. Al-Ghazālī, *Kitāb Ādāb al-Ṣuḥbah wa'l-Muʿāsharah maʿ Aṣnāf al-Khalq*, p. 270.

20. Al-Maqdisī, *al-Ādāb*, I, 328.

21. Cf. Ḥammād, *Ḥurriyyah*, p. 207.

22. Al-Bukhārī, *Ṣaḥīḥ*, Kitāb al-Īmān, I, 23; Muslim, *Ṣaḥīḥ Muslim*, Kitāb al-Īmān, Bāb al-Dīn al-Naṣīḥah. Ibn Mājah quotes this *Ḥadīth* and repeats the first clause therein three times, while al-Nasā'ī quotes the first clause with a slight variation, that is *innamā al-dīn al-naṣīḥah*.

23. Al-Nawawī, *Riyāḍ al-Ṣāliḥīn*, p. 113, *Ḥadīth* no. 186.

24. Cf. Naḥwī, *Malāmiḥ al-Shūrā fi'l-Daʿwah al-Islāmiyyah*, p. 703.

25. Al-Nawawī, *Riyāḍ al-Ṣāliḥīn*, p. 113, *Ḥadīth* no. 187.

26. Al-Maqdisī, *al-Ādāb*, I, 327, records this *Ḥadīth*:

'An amīr who is in charge of the affairs of the Muslims and fails to exert himself for their benefit and give them sincere advice shall not enter Paradise with them.'

مَا مِن امير يَلِي أَمْرَ الْمُسلمين ثُمَّ لاَ يَجْتَهِدُ لَهُمْ الا
لَمْ يَدْخُلِ الْجَنَّةَ مَعَهُمْ

27. Ibid., I, 327.

28. Al-Khulafā' *al-Rāshidūn*, literally, the Rightly-Guided Caliphs, refers to the first four caliphs who took office following the demise of the Prophet Muḥammad ﷺ, namely Abū Bakr al-Ṣiddīq (died 12 A.H./634 A.D.), ʿUmar ibn al-Khaṭṭāb (d. 23/643), ʿUthmān ibnʿAffān (d. 35/656) and ʿAlī ibn Abī Ṭālib, (d.40/661). The period of their rule lasted forty years.

29. Cf. Abū Ḥabīb, *Dirāsah fī Minhāj al-Islām al-Siyāsī*, p. 337.
30. Al-Nawawī, *Riyāḍ al-Ṣāliḥīn*, pp. 103-107.
31. Ibid.
32. Zaydān, *Majmūʿah*, p. 128; Abū Ḥabīb, *Darāsah*, p. 334.
33. This is unanimously reported *(muttafiqun ʿalayhi)* and recorded as such by Al-Nawawī, *Riyāḍ al-Ṣāliḥīn*, p. 113, *Ḥadīth* no. 188; al-Maqdisī, *al-Ādāb*, I, 327-28.
34. Abū Ḥabīb, *Darāsah*, p. 336.
35. Ibn Ḥanbal, *Fihris Aḥādīth Musnad al-Imām Aḥmad b. Ḥanbal*, II, 162; al-Suyūṭī, *al-Jāmiʿ al-Ṣaghīr*, I, 41.
36. Ibn Mājah, *Sunan Ibn Mājah*, Kitāb al-Fitan, Bāb al-amr bi'l-maʿrūf wa'l-nahy ʿan al-munkar.
37. Al-Bahī, *al-Dīn wa'l-Dawlah min Tawjīhāt al-Qur'ān al-Karīm*, p. 389.
38. Al-Ṭabarī, *Tafsīr al-Ṭabarī*, IV, 152.
39. Ibn Taymiyyah, *al-Siyāsah al-Sharʿiyyah fī Iṣlāḥ al-Rāʿī wa'l-Raʿiyyah*, p. 169.
40. Riḍā, *Ta'rīkh al-Ustādh al-Imām Muḥammad ʿAbduh*, II, 207; Abū Ḥabīb, Darāsah, p. 642.
41. Asad, *Principles of State and Government in Islam*, p. 57; Zaydān, *al-Farḍ wa'l-Dawlah fi'l-Sharīʿah al-Islāmiyyah*, p. 37; al-Bahī, *al-Dīn wa'l-Dawlah*, p. 387; see also Abū Ḥabīb, *Darāsah*, p. 642, where he quotes Abū al-Aʿlā Mawdūdī and ʿAbd al-Qādir ʿAwdah to the effect that *shūrā* is a Qur'ānic obligation.
42. Al-Tirmidhī, *Sunan al-Tirmidhī*, IV, 213.
43. Ibn Ḥanbal, *Musnad*, IV, 277.
44. For details see al-Khālidī, *Qawāʿid Niẓām al-Ḥukm fi'l-Islām*, p. 145 ff.
45. Cf. al-Khālidī, *Qawāʿid*, pp. 141-42.
46. Al-Bahī, *al-Dīn wa'l-Dawlah*, p. 388.
47. Shaltūt, *al-Islām ʿAqīdah wa-Sharīʿah*, p. 556; al-Sibāʿī, Ishtirākiyyah, p. 5.
48. Zaydān, *Majmūʿah*, p. 128.
49. Al-Qurṭubī, *al-Jāmiʿ li-Aḥkām al-Qur'ān* (known as *Tafsīr al-Qurṭubī*), IV, 250-51.
50. Cf. al-Khālidī, *Qawāʿid*, pp. 155; El-Awa, *On the Political System of the Islamic State*, p. 90.
51. Ibid., p. 155.
52. Ibid., p. 157.
53. For details on the *ahl al-shūrā* and the participation of women and non-Muslims therein see al-Khālidī, *Qawāʿid*, pp. 176, 185; Abū Ḥabīb, *Darāsah*, p. 661 ff; and al-Nabhānī, *Muqaddimat al-Dustūr*, pp. 114-117.
54. Ibn Taymiyyah, *al-Siyāsah*, p. 169.
55. Abū Ḥabīb, *Darāsah*, pp. 681-82.
56. Al-Āmidī, *al-Iḥkām fī Uṣūl al-Aḥkām*, IV, 162; al-Shawkānī, *Irshād al-Fuḥūl min Taḥqīq al-Ḥaqq ilā ʿIlm al-Uṣūl*, p. 250.
57. For details on the textual authority of *ijtihād* see my *Principles of Islamic Jurisprudence*, pp. 470-73.

58. Abū Dāwūd, *Sunan*, Eng. trans. Aḥmad Ḥasan, III, 1013, *Ḥadīth* no. 3567.

59. Cf. Zaydān, *Majmūʿah*, p. 288.

60. Cf. Ghazawī, *al-Ḥurriyyah al-ʿĀmmah fi'l-Islām*, p. 60.

61. Al-Bahī, *al-Dīn wa'l-Dawlah*, p. 415.

62. Zaydān, *Majmūʿah*, p. 288; al-Sibāʿī, *Ishtirākiyyah*, p. 48; Munayminah, *Mushkilat al-Ḥurriyyah fi'l-Islām*, p. 15.

63. Al-Bahī, *al-Dīn wa'l-Dawlah*, p. 415.

64. Mahmassanī, *Arkān*, p. 143.

65. Al-Kāsānī, *Badā'iʿ al-Ṣanā'i*, VII 4; Ibn Qudāmah, *al-Mughnī*, IX, 40-41.

66. Madkūr, *al-Qaḍā' fi'l-Islām*, p. 63.

67. Al-Āmidī, *Iḥkām*, III, 232; al-Qarāfī, *al-Furūq*, IV, 43; Ibn Qudāmah, *al-Mughnī*, IX, 57.

68. '*Fatwā*' is often used synonymously with '*ijtihad*'; it means a considered opinion by a qualified person on a legal or religious issue—often given in response to a particular question.

69. *Mujtahid* (pl. *mujtahidūn*), one who is qualified to carry out *ijtihād*, usually by direct recourse to original sources.

70. See for details Ghazawī, *al-Ḥurriyyah*, p. 60.

71. Khallāf, *al-Siyasah al-Sharʿiyyah*, p. 136; Mutawallī, *Mabādi'*, p. 281; Ramadan, *Islamic Law: Its Scope and Equity*, p. 78.

72. For details on how freedom of expression in this period exceeded its limits in debates on the matter of the Essence and the Attributes of God, the createdness or uncreatedness of the Qur'ān etc., see al-Bahī, *al-Dīn wa'l-Dawlah*, p. 552 ff.

73. Mutawallī, *Mabādi'*, p. 282.

74. For further details see the chapter on *ijtihād* in my *Principles of Islamic Jurisprudence*, especially p. 484 ff, and my article 'The Approved and Disapproved Varieties of Ra'y (Personal Opinion) in Islam' in the *American Journal of Islamic Social Sciences*, vol. 7, No. 1, 1990, 39-64.

75. ʿAfīfī, *al-Mujtamaʿ al-Islāmī wa-Uṣūl al-Ḥukm*, p. 93; see also al-Sibāʿī, *Ishtirākiyyah*, p. 50.

76. Al-Qāsimī, *Niẓām al-Ḥukm fi'l-Sharīʿah wa'l-Ta'rīkh*, p. 101.

77. The clause to which ʿUmar protested stated that if a member of the Quraysh tribe went to the Prophet ﷺ without the permission of his guardian *(walī)*, then he was to be returned to his tribe. But, if a member of Quraysh from the side of the Prophet ﷺ went back to his kin-folk, it was not obligatory on the latter to return him to the Prophet ﷺ. The conversation between ʿUmar and the Holy Prophet ﷺ is recorded as follows: "'Are you not the Messenger of God?' asked ʿUmar. 'I am', said the Prophet ﷺ. 'Then why are we being denigrated because of our faith?' questioned ʿUmar. To this the Prophet ﷺ said, 'I am the servant and messenger of God, I shall not disobey Him and He shall not let me be the loser'." (Ibn Hishām, *al-Sīrah al-Nabawiyyah*, III, 331).

78. Ibn Mājah, *Sunan*, Kitāb al-Fitan, Bāb al-amr bi'l-maʿrūf wa'l-nahy ʿan al-munkar, *Ḥadīth* no. 4011.
79. Ibn Hishām, *al-Sīrah*, IV, 262; Abū Ḥabīb, Darāsah, p. 725; al-Qāsimī, *Niẓām al-Ḥukm*, p. 106.
80. Abū Ḥabīb, *Darāsah*, p. 727.
81. Abū Zahrah, *al-Jarīmah wa'l-ʿUqūbah fi'l-Fiqh al-Islāmī*, p. 160; al-Sibāʿī, *Ishtirākiyyah*, p. 50; al-Nabhān, *Niẓām al-Ḥukm*, p. 250.
82. Al-Khudarī, *Muḥāḍarāt fī Ta'rīkh al-Umam al-Islāmiyyah*, II 17-18; al-Nabhān, *Niẓām al-Hukm*, p. 240; Abū Ḥabīb, *Darāsah*, p. 743.
83. Abū Yūsuf, *Kitāb al-Kharāj*, p. 13.
84. Al-Sibāʿī, *Ishtirākiyyah*, p. 50.
85. Khalīl, *Fi'l-Naqd al-Islāmī al-Muʿāṣir*, p. 35.
86. Abū Ḥabīb, *Darāsah*, p. 743.
87. Ḥusayn, *Naqd Kitāb al-Islām wa Uṣūl al-Ḥukm*, p. 89.
88. Al-Qāsimī, *Niẓām al-Ḥukm*, p. 100.
89. ʿAfīfī, Al-Mujtamaʿ al-Islāmī, p. 94.
90. *Ḥadīth* reported by al-Tirmidhī in al-Tabrīzī, *Mishkāt al-Maṣābīḥ*, III, 1418, *Ḥadīth* no, 5129.
91. Khalīl, *al-Naqd*, pp. 33-34.
92. Al-Bukhārī, *Jawāhir Ṣaḥīḥ al-Bukhārī*, Kitāb al-Jumʿah, Bāb al-Jumʿah fi'l-qurrā wa'l-mudun.
93. Cf. Ḥammād, *Ḥurriyyah*, p. 416.
94. Ibn Ḥanbal, *Musnad*, II, 70.
95. Cf. Ḥammād, *Ḥurriyyah*, p. 416.
96. Muslim, *Mukhtaṣar Ṣaḥīḥ Muslim*, p. 16, *Ḥadīth* no. 34.
97. Al-Subkī, *al-Ashbāh wa'l-Naẓā'ir*, I, 275; Tuffāḥah, *Maṣādir al-Tashrīʿ al-Islāmī wa-Qawāʿid al-Sulūk al-ʿĀmmah*, p. 46.
98. Al-Maqdisī, *al-Ādāb*, I, 340; Tuffāḥah, *Maṣādir*, p. 46.
99. Tuffāḥah, *Maṣādir*, p. 47.
100. For details on *istiṣḥāb* see my *Principles of Islamic Jurisprudence*, p. 377 ff.
101. Abū Sulaymān, *'al-Naẓariyyāt wa'l-Qawāʿid fi'l-Fiqh al-Islāmī'*, in *Majjalat Jāmiʿat al-Malik ʿAbd al-ʿAzīz*, no. 2, Jamāda al-Thānī 1398/May 1978, p. 56; Tuffāḥah, Maṣādir, p. 89.
102. Tuffāḥah, *Maṣādir*, p. 87.
103. Imām *Jaʿfar al-Ṣādiq*, a descendant of the Prophet ﷺ and the sixth of the Shiʿī Imāms, is greatly respected by both Sunnis and Shiʿīs. In addition to his outstanding spiritual qualities he was a man of great learning in theology, jurisprudence and the science of *Ḥadīth*. One of the oldest extant Qur'ān commentaries is attributed to him. He died in the year 148/765.
104. Tuffāḥah, *Maṣādir*, p. 88.
105. Al-Subkī, *al-Ashbāh wa'l-Naẓā'ir*, I, 275; Tuffāḥah, *Maṣādir*, pp. 88-92.

106. Tuffāḥah, *Maṣādir*, pp. 93-95.

107. Cf. Ibn Qayyim al-Jawziyyah, *Iʿlām*, I, 55.

108. Abū Dāwūd, *Sunan*, III, 1013, *Ḥadīth* no, 3567.

109. The reader might be interested to know that a chapter is devoted to each of these topics in my *Principles of Islamic Jurisprudence.*

110. Al-Ghazalī uses the name '*Taʿlīmiyyah*' as a synonym of '*Bāṭiniyyah*', literally 'esoterists' - a term which can be used quite loosely; for example, Ibn Taymiyyah uses it for certain Sufis and philosophers in addition to its conventional application. The latter is in respect of the *Ismāʿīliyyah*, and refers to their distinctive emphasis on the non-literal interpretation of the Qur'ān *(ta'wīl)*, specifically involving reading it in terms of their own sectarian doctrines, a hermeneutic which was hierarchically and secretly imparted. The *Ismāʿīliyyah* are complicatedly ramified eg. the *Qarmatiyyah*, the *Fāṭimids* proper (ie the great *Shīʿite* counter-caliphate ruling from Egypt from 358/969 for two centuries), the *Nizārī's* and the Musta'līan *Ismāʿīliyyah*. In general, the *Ismāʿīliyyah* are a branch of the *Shīʿah* - the 'partisans of *ʿAlī ibn Abi Ṭālib*' who believed that politico-religious authority after the Prophet's ﷺ death should by rights fall exclusively to the Prophet's son-in-law, ʿAlī, and thence to his descendants through *Fāṭimah*, the daughter of the Prophet ﷺ. Unlike the *Ithnā ʿAshariyyah* branch, for whom the *Imāmate* is in 'occultation', the *Ismāʿīliyyah Shīʿites* tend to see the *Imāmate* as continuous and living, and historically show themselves in consequence of this understanding of religious authority to be more prone to the view that the religious law can be modified and even overturned - famously exemplified amongst the Assassins by the declaration in 1164 A.D. by Ḥasan, fourth lord of the secret stronghold of Alamut, of the 'Resurrection' - interpreted by them as the end of exoteric religion. [Editor's note.]

111. Al-Ghazālī, *al-Munqidh min al-Ḍalāl* (MacCarthy's translation), pp. 122 and 183.

112. Abū Dāwūd, *Sunan*, III, 1019, *Ḥadīth* no. 3585.

113. Cf. Shaltūt, *al-Islām*, p. 555.

114. Abū Zahrah, *Tanẓīm al-Islām li'l-Mujtamaʿ*, p. 194.

115. Cf. al-Bahī, *al-Dīn wa'l-Dawlah*, p. 376.

116. ʿĀ'ishah ʿAbd al-Raḥmān, *al-Qur'ān wa Qaḍāyā'l-Insān*, p. 116.

117. Cf. Fikrī, *al-Muʿāmalāt al-Māddiyyah wa'l-Adabiyyah*, pp. 84-85.

118. Ibid., p. 87.

119. Thus we read in a *Ḥadīth* that 'A good word *(al-kalimah al-ṭayyibah)* is a form of charity'. See al-Nawawī, *Riyāḍ al-Ṣāliḥīn*, 2nd ed., p. 284, *Ḥadīth* no. 699.

اَلْكَلِمَةُ الطَّيِّبَةُ صَدَقَةٌ.

120. *The Holy Qur'ān*, Text, Translation and Commentary by ʿAbdullah Yusuf ʿAli, footnote No. 3775.

121. Cf. Ibn Qayyim, *Iʿlām*, I, 55.

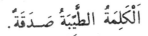

122. Ibid.

123. This is often quoted as a Ḥadīth of the Prophet ﷺ. Both al-Āmidī (*al-Iḥkām*, I, 214) and al-Shāṭibī, *al-I'tiṣām*, II, 319) refer to it as such. It is, however, more likely to be a saying of the famous Companion, 'Abd Allāh Ibn Mas'ūd (Cf. Aḥmad Ḥasan, The *Doctrine of Ijmā' in Islam*, p. 37).

124. Ibn Qayyim, *I'lām*, I, 55.

125. Ibid., I. 67.

126. Ibid., I. 68.

127. Ibid., I. 69.

128. Ibid., I, 70.

129. Ibid., I. 72.

130. Ibid., II, 120.

131. Ibid., I, 55.

132. Cf. al-Khālidī, *al-Shūrā*, p. 91.

133. Cf. *The Holy Qur'ān*, V:2.

134. Cf. Asad, *Principles*, p. 6; al-'Arabī, *Niẓām al-Ḥukm fi'l-Islām*,p. 92.

135. Cf. al-Anṣārī, *al-Shūrā wa-Āthāruhā fi'l-Dimuqrāṭiyyah*, p. 432.

136. Waṣfī, *al-Niẓām al-Dustūrī fi'l-Islām Muqārinan bi'l-Nuẓum al-'Aṣriyyah*, p. 76.

137. Maudūdī, *al-Ḥukūmah al-Islāmiyyah*, p. 217.

138. 'Abd Allāh, *Naẓariyyat al-Dawlah fi'l-Islām*, p. 153.

139. As mentioned above the Shī'ites are literally 'the partisans of 'Alī ibn Abī Ṭālib' *('Shī'at 'Alī')*, who believed that politico-religious authority after the Prophet's ﷺ death should by rights fall exclusively to the Prophet's son-in-law, 'Alī, and thence to his descendants through Fāṭimah, the daughter of the Prophet ﷺ, thereby excluding the first three of the Rightly-Guided Caliphs.

The Khārijites, literally 'seceders', were a very early group of extremists who rebelled against Caliph 'Alī, when he agreed to arbitration in his dispute (over the matter of bringing to justice the assasinators of Caliph 'Uthmān) with Mu'āwiyah (who eventually became the first 'Umayyad caliph). Although 'Alī defeated the Khārijites, he was murdered by one of them in revenge. The Khārijites went on to terrorise the Muslims, in that they held that the status of being a believer is actually anulled by major sins, and for the Khārijites it was a major sin to oppose their point of view. In practice this meant that they declared licit the blood of countless Muslim opponents, whom they held to be effectively pagans.

For the author's discussion of this group, see the section below on 'Historical Examples' under 'Sedition *(Fitnah)*' of Part Four. For further details of the Shī'ite and Khārijite political and theological beliefs please refer to the relevant sections of the *Encyclopaedia of Islam*, new edition, Leiden: Brill 1978. [Ed. note.]

140. Cf. al-Anṣārī, *al-Shūrā*, p. 429.

141. Thus, according to El-Awa, 'The people's interest at the present time can only be served by allowing political parties so that the differing opinions on the ummah's

affairs can be (ascertained) and expressed.' (cf. conference report on 'Pluralism in Islam', *The American Journal of Islamic Social Sciences,* 8 (1991) at p. 353.)

142. Anṣārī, *al-Shūrā,* p. 431.

143. El-Awa, 'Pluralism in Islam', *The American Journal of Islamic Social Sciences,* 8 (1991) n. 130 at p. 431.

144. Ibn Taymiyyah, *Majmūʿat al-Rasā'il wa'l-Masā'il,* I,141.

145. Ibid.

146. Muḥammad al-Ghazālī, quoted in a conference report by IIIT, Cairo on 'Pluralism in Islam', *American Journal of Islamic Social Sciences,* 8 (1991), p. 353.

147. Abū Dāwūd, *Sunan,* Ḥasan's Trans., III, 1013, *Ḥadīth* no. 3567.

148. El-Awa, 'Pluralism in Islam', *The American Journal of Islamic Social Sciences,* 8 (1991) n. 130 at p. 353. See also Idem, *Fi'l-Niẓām al-Siyāsī,* pp. 83-84.

149. Ibn Qayyim al- Jawziyyah, *al-Ṭuruq al-Ḥukmiyyah fi'l-Siyāsah al-Sharʿiyyah,* pp. 286-289.

150. Cf. al-Khālidī, *Qawāʿid,* p. 205.

151. Al-Ghazālī, *Al-Mustaṣfā min ʿIlm al-Uṣūl,* I, 17.

152. Al-Nabhānī, *Muqaddimat al-Dustūr,* p. 101.

153. Muslim, *Mukhtaṣar Ṣaḥīḥ Muslim, Ḥadīth* no. 34.

154. Al-Nabhānī, *Muqaddimat,* p. 104; see also al-Khālidī, *Qawāʿid,* p. 290.

155. Note, for example, Ṣaī al-Raḥmān al-Mubārakfūrī's booklet, *al-Aḥzāb al-Siyāsiyyah fi'l-Islām,* al-Jāmiʿah al-Salafiyyah, India, 1407/1987, whose whole discussion focuses on unity in Islam, and is almost totally oblivious of the application of party organisation to political and economic development matters.

156. Al-Alusī, *Rūḥ al-Maʿānī fi Tafsīr al-Qur'ān al-ʿAẓīm,* V, 144.

157. Khan, *Human Rights,* p. 45.

158. Ibid., p. 46.

159. Yusuf Ali, *The Holy Qur'ān,* note 5347.

160. For further details on *maṣlaḥah mursalah* see my article 'Have We Neglected the Sharīʿah Law Doctrine of Maṣlaḥah?', *Islamic Studies,* 27 (1988), pp. 287-304.

161. cf. Abū Zahrah, *Tanẓīm al-Islām li'l-Mujtamaʿ,* p.190; al-ʿĪlī, *al-Ḥurriyyah al-ʿĀmmah,* p. 330.

162. cf. Fatḥī ʿUthmān, *Ḥuqūq al-Insān Bayn al-Sharīʿah al-Islāmiyyah wa'l-Fikr al-Qānūnī al-Gharbī,* p. 97.

163. Ibid., p. 91.

164. Al-ʿĪlī, *al-Ḥurriyyah,* p. 330.

165. Ibid., p. 356 (quoting Rashīd Riḍā's *Tafsīr al-Manār* XI, 484).

166. Ibn Qudāmah, *al-Mughnī,* VIII, 144.

167. *Nadwat al-Riyāḍ,* p. 33.

168. Cf. ʿAbd al-Raḥmān, *al-Qur'ān wa Qaḍāyā'l-Insān* p. 96.

169. The full statement of this convention appears in Maudūdī, *Islamic Law and Constitution,* p. 333 ff.

170. Azzam. ed., *Universal Islamic Declaration*, p. 11, The Islamic Council of Europe, 1981.
171. *Malayan Law Journal*, (1989) I, pp. 368-70, 418-20.
172. *Malayan Law Journal*, (1989) I, p. 368.
173. *Malayan Law Journal*, (1989) I, p. 369.
174. *Malayan Law Journal*, (1989) I, p. 419.
175. Arnold, *The Preaching of Islam*, p. 46.
176. Ibid.
177. Ibid. pp. 47-48.
178. Ibid. pp. 51-2.
179. Mutawallī, *Mabādi'*, p. 287.
180. Abū Zahrah, *Tanẓīm*, p. 192.
181. Mutawallī, *Mabādi'*, p. 287 ff.
182. Note e.g. S.A. Rahman, *The Punishment of Apostasy in Islam*, Abdul Hamid Abu Sulayman, *The Islamic Theory of International Relations: New Directions for Islamic Methodology and Thought*; El-Awa, *Punishment in Islamic Law*.
183. Rahman, *The Punishment of Apostasy*, pp. 63-64; al-ʿĪlī, *al-Ḥurriyyah*, p. 339.
184. Ibn Taymiyyah, *al-Ṣārim al-Maslūl ʿalā Shātim al-Rasūl*, p. 321; al-Shawkānī, Nayl al-Awṭār, VII, p. 230.
185. Al-Shaʿrānī, *Kitāb al-Mīzān*, II, p. 152.
186. Al-Sarakhsī, *al-Mabsūṭ*, X, p. 110.
187. Ibn Taymiyyah, *al-Ṣārim al-Maslūl ʿalā Shātim al-Rasūl*, p. 318; *al-Shaʿrānī, Kitāb al-Mīzān*, II, 134; El-Awa, *Punishment*, p. 55.
188. Ibn Taymiyyah, *al-Siyāsah*, p. 124.
189. Al-ʿĪlī, *al-Ḥurriyyah*, p. 426; Badawī, *Daʿā'im al-Ḥukm*, p.166.
190. Shaltūt, *al-Islām ʿAqīdah wa-Sharīʿah*, pp. 292-93; al-Samara'ī, *Aḥkām al-Murtadd fī al-Sharīʿah al-Islāmiyyah*, p. 114 ff.
191. Mahmassanī, *Arkān*, pp. 123-24.
192. Mutahhari, *'Islam and the Freedom of Thought and Belief'*, Al-Tawḥīd, p.154.
193. El-Awa, *Punishment*, p. 55.
194. Al-Shawkānī, *Nayl al-Awṭār: Sharḥ Muntaqā al-Akhbār*, VII, 218.
195. Ibid., VII, 219.
196. Ibid., VII, 219; El-Awa, *Punishment*, p. 55.
197. Muslim, *Mukhtaṣar Ṣaḥīḥ Muslim*, p. 271, *Ḥadīth* no. 1023.
198. El-Awa, *Punishment*, p. 52.
199. Ibn Taymiyyah, *al-Ṣārim al-Maslūl*, p. 52,
200. Al-Bukhārī, *Jawāhir Ṣaḥīḥ al-Bukhārī*, p. 150, *Ḥadīth* no. 229.
201. Cf. El-Awa, *Punishment*, p. 54.
202. Ibn Taymiyyah, *al-Ṣārim*, p. 318.
203. Ibid. For similar information and additional names of apostates whom the Prophet ﷺ pardoned after the conquest of Mecca, see Ibn Hishām, *Sīrah*, IV, 23.

204. Abū Zahrah, *Tanẓīm*, p. 192.

205. Rashīd Riḍā, *Tafsīr al-Manār*, IX, 665, Beirut: *Dār al-Maʿrifah*, 1324.

206. Ibid., III, 37; al-ʿĪlī, *al-Ḥurriyyah*, pp. 333-34.

207. Ibn Kathīr, *Tafsīr*, I, 310; Riḍā, *Tafsīr*, III, 37-39.

208. S.A. Rahman, *The Punishment of Apostasy*, p. 21. *Shan-i nuzūl*, the Persian and Urdu equivalent of the Arabic *asbāb al-nuzūl*, means the historical context of the revelations of the Qur'ānic verses.

209. Ibid., p. 16.

210. Note *Qur'ān* II:91 & 97; IV:46; XXXV:31 and XLVI:30.

211. ʿUthmān, *al-Farḍ*, pp. 27-28; note also Ghazawī, *al-Ḥurriyyah*, p. 69, and ʿĀ'ishah ʿAbd al-Raḥmān, *al-Qur'ān wa Qaḍāyā'l-Insān*, p. 97 ff.

212. Wafī, *Ḥuqūq al-Insān*, pp. 122-23.

213. Ibid., p. 124.

214. ʿAwdah, *al-Tashrīʿ al-Jinā'ī*, pp. 31-33.

215. For a discussion as to how military and political interests have influenced the writings of medieval Muslim jurists on the subject of *jihād*, see Abū Sulaymān, *The Islamic Theory of International Relations*.

216. For a discussion of the theory of abrogation *(naskh)* and its impact on Islamic law see my *Principles of Islamic Jurisprudence*, ch. 7.

PART THREE: MORAL RESTRAINTS

I. General Themes

1. INTRODUCTORY REMARKS

Some of the violations of freedom of speech that the *Sharīᶜah* has specified are expounded in positive legal terms which require enforcement by government authorities. Slanderous accusation (*qadhf*), for example, is an offence for which the Qur'ān specifies a particular punishment (*ḥadd*). Similarly, blasphemy, sedition and insult are punishable offences under the law. Beyond these specific violations which shall be discussed later, the bulk of the guidelines that the *Sharīᶜah* provides on the subject are of a moral import and are, by and large, addressed to the conscience of the believer, and so may or may not be justiciable. The moral violations of freedom of speech include a variety of reprehensible utterances such as telling lies, backbiting, ridiculing others and calling them by offensive names. There is a wealth of instruction on all of these in the Qur'ān and Sunnah, as well as in the teachings of the *ᶜulamā'* across the centuries. Notwithstanding the emphatic tone of the Qur'ānic language on many of these violations, they have not been translated into practical rules of Islamic law. However, this is not an unfamiliar feature of the Qur'ān, which is largely devoted to establishing basic values and fundamental norms of conduct, and these are best conveyed in the form of broad and comprehensive guidelines. From this basic framework it is then possible for the government, and those who are in charge of community affairs (i.e. the *ulū'l-amr*), to convert these moral teachings of Islam into legal ordinances if they deem this to be in the interests of the community and for protection against evil.

2. BACKBITING, DEFAMATION AND DERISION

These are some of the varieties of abusive speech which receive much attention in the Qur'ān and the Sunnah of the Prophet ﷺ. The Qur'ān specifies, in a number of passages, the varieties of evil speech which violate the dignity of others and seek to expose their weaknesses. In the following text the believers are instructed on this theme:

> O believers, let not people ridicule other people, perchance the latter may be better than the former, nor let women ridicule other women, perchance the latter may be better than the former. Neither find fault with each other, nor insult one another with derisive nicknames ... (XLIX:11)

يَاَيُّهَا الَّذِينَ اٰمَنُوا لاَيَسْخَرْ قَوْمٌ مِّن قَوْمٍ عَسَىٰ أَن
يَكُونُوا خَيْرًا مِّنْهُمْ وَلاَ نِسَاءٌ مِّن نِّسَآءٍ عَسَىٰ أَن يَكُنَّ
خَيْرًا مِّنْهُنَّ وَلاَ تَلْمِزُوا أَنْفُسَكُمْ وَلاَ تَنَابَزُوا بِالأَلْقَابِ.

This is immediately followed by another passage which singles out backbiting (*ghībah*) and depicts its enormity in particularly striking terms:

> Spy not and defame not others behind their backs. Would any of you like to eat the flesh of his dead brother? [Surely] you would abhor it. (XLIX:12)

وَلاَ تَجَسَّسُوا وَلاَ يَغْتَبْ بَّعْضُكُم بَعْضًا أَيُحِبُّ أَحَدُكُمْ أَنْ
تَأْكُلَ لَحْمَ أَخِيهِ مَيْتًا فَكَرِهْتُمُوهُ.

Elsewhere in the Qur'ān is the *sūrah* bearing the title 'The Slanderer' (*al-Humazah*). It begins with a clarion denunciation of 'every slandering defamer' (CIV:1), and indeed, the whole of this *sūrah* is devoted to a rigorous condemnation of backbiting.

The Prophet ﷺ often warned the believers against *ghībah*. In a particular *Ḥadīth*, the Prophet ﷺ is reported to have asked his Companions the following question: 'Do you know what *ghībah* is?'

To this they replied, 'God and His Messenger know best.' Then the Prophet ﷺ said, 'It is to mention your brother in a way that he would dislike.' A Companion then asked: 'What if that which I say concerning my brother is true?' The Prophet ﷺ replied saying, 'If what you say is true then you have defamed him [by *ghībah*], and if he is innocent of what you say, then you have slandered him.'[1]

وَعَن أَبِى هُرَيْرَه رض قال رسول الله ﷺ: أَتَدْرُونَ ماالغيبه؟
قَالُوا اللهُ وَرَسُولُهُ أَعْلَم، قَالَ ذِكْر أَخَاكَ بِمَايَكْرَه. قِيلَ أَفَرَ
أَيْتَ إِن كَانَ فِي أَخِى مَا أَقُول؟ قَالَ إِن كَانَ فِيه مَا تَقُولُ
فَقَد إِغْتَبْتَهُ وإِن لَم يَكن فيه مَا تَقُول فَقَدْ بَهَتَّهُ.

Al-Ghazālī reiterated the purport of this *Ḥadīth* when he stated that 'The hallmark of *ghībah* is to mention your fellow Muslim in a way that would displease him if he heard you, even if you are telling the truth.' *Ghībah* can be committed, al-Ghazālī adds, by word of mouth, by signs, by betraying secrets, or by any form of expression that comprises the basic concept of defaming others.[2]

In a commentary on the same *Ḥadīth*, al-Nawawī, the author of *Riyāḍ al-Ṣāliḥīn*, points out: 'It is permitted, however, to tell the truth even if it technically amounts to *ghībah*, as a matter of necessity, in order to prevent an evil. Similarly, a witness, a petitioner, or a pleader who reveals the oppressive conduct of another, may speak about the character of a person if this would help the course of justice.'[3] Thus, it is evident that *ghībah* is permitted only if it serves the cause of justice and the uncovering of truth. However, when no higher objective is being served, the mere truthfulness of the content of *ghībah* does not justify it. *Ghībah* is generally held to be one of the major sins (*al-kabā'ir*), although some *ʿulamā'* have reached the conclusion that it is one of the *ṣaghā'ir*, or minor sins. While quoting the above verse (i.e. XLIX:12) on *ghībah*, Muḥammad Khiḍr al-Ḥusayn points out that exceptions concerning the utterance of *ghībah*, or criticising others in their absence, are made on grounds of necessity (*ḍarūrah*). The concession granted here is in the nature of tolerating a lesser evil, that is, *ghībah* against a particular individual, in order to secure a higher interest (*maṣlaḥah ʿāliyah*) which often consists of serving the cause of justice, protecting the essential values, and preventing harm to society.[4]

The following instances of permissible *ghībah* have been recorded in the writings of the *ᶜulamā'*:[5]

(a) The impugning of witnesses (*jarḥ al-shuhūd*): The law requires that judicial decisions be based on reliable evidence, which is why the *Sharīᶜah* makes it a duty of the judge to ascertain the reliability and just character of witnesses. This may, in turn, necessitate enquiry into the character and personality of the witnesses and entail revealing their weaknesses, even at the expense of indulging in *ghībah*.

(b) Another area where the *ᶜulamā'* have found it necessary to engage in the character analysis of individuals is in the transmission of *Ḥadīth* and the attribution of statements to the Messenger of God ﷺ. The scholars of *Ḥadīth* have thus enquired at length into the personality and character of the transmitters of *Ḥadīth* so as to expose any weakness that might have a bearing on their trustworthiness.

(c) *Ghībah* is permitted with regard to a person who is actively engaged in crime, and who openly declares his sinful activities to others without any attempt at concealing his wrongdoing. For an individual who indulges in speech that recommends lawlessness and sin transgresses the teachings of the *Sharīᶜah* and shows his or her contempt of them; his personal dignity is therefore no longer immune from the explicit disapproval of others. According to a statement attributed to the founder of the Ḥanbalite school of law, Imām Aḥmad b. Ḥanbal, which is endorsed by his disciple, Ibn Taymiyyah, and also the Mālikī jurist, Ibn ᶜAbd al-Barr, there is no *ghībah* regarding a person who publicises his sinful conduct (*mujāhir bi'l-maᶜāṣī*). However, a number of other *ᶜulamā'* have drawn the conclusion, once again from the source materials in the Sunnah, that *ghībah* is absolutely forbidden, with only one exception, namely, when a person is himself actively engaged in harming others by word or deed.[6]

(d) According to the express terms of the Qur'ān, 'God loves not the public utterance of evil speech except by one who has been wronged.' (IV:148.)

لَا يُحِبُّ اللّٰهُ الْجَهْرَ بِالسُّوءِ مِنَ الْقَوْلِ إِلَّا مَنْ ظُلِمَ.

This verse will be discussed later in detail, but suffice it to say that the exception granted in this text entitles the victim of an act of injustice to expose the facts of his case and to denounce, if need be, the oppressor (*ẓālim*) and seek help against him. The Qur'ānic proclamation here makes it clear that a firm stand against oppression can hardly be taken without granting the victim the right to speak out.

(e) *Ghībah* is once again permissible if it constitutes an integral part of sincere counsel, or *naṣīḥah*. For example, it is allowable when someone consults another person as to the character of a prospective spouse, or when an individual proposes a trade partnership with someone and seeks advice about the latter's character. Provided that the counsellor is impartial, he is permitted to give advice which may involve exposing a weakness of character, or a bad record of the person in question. But this may be done only if it is believed that a greater evil is likely to occur unless the advice is given.

(f) *Ghībah* is also permitted if it is intended to deter its victim from crime and evil. For example, when we know someone who steals or commits other crimes but manages to keep it all hidden, and we know that he will not be deterred unless the matter is given publicity, then *ghībah* is not only permitted but is an integral part of the Qur'ānic principle of *ḥisbah*, that is, commanding good and preventing evil. As such, it is the duty of everyone to prevent wickedness by whatever means they may have at their disposal, provided that the attempt at prevention is not likely to lead to a greater evil.

(g) If a person is convinced of an impending harm (*ḍarar*) which may threaten the safety and integrity of religion or the state unless a particular person is criticised and denounced in his absence, then the former is permitted to do so, but only when he deems this to be a lesser evil than the one which is anticipated.

(h) If a person's own life is endangered, then *ghībah* is permissible if the danger cannot be averted unless someone's weakness of character is exposed and he is openly criticised for it.

(i) Lastly, the *Sharīʿah* permits criticism of the views and opinions of others in pursuit of establishing righteousness and truth, even if this involves exposing a fault in the thought or character of the people concerned. A mistake or misunderstanding may thus be corrected if this is deemed necessary for the preservation of truth or for the elimination of falsehood.

In his discussion of the 'calamities of speech' (*āfāt al-lisān*), al-Ghazālī specifies five: lying, backbiting, acrimony (*mumārāt*), sycophancy (*madḥ*) and unrestricted jocularity. The author then elaborates: 'Lying is forbidden in all things except when it is absolutely necessary. It must, therefore, be avoided at all times even in one's imagination and self-suggestion. One ought to make a deliberate effort not to sow the seeds of falsehood in one's thoughts, and to try to avoid it at all times.' To substantiate his statement further, al-Ghazālī quotes the following *Ḥadīth* of the Prophet ﷺ:

> For so long as a person lies or justifies a lie, his (or her) name is recorded before God as one of the liars.[7]

لَا يَزَالُ العَبْدُ يَكْذِبُ وَيَتَحَرَّى الكَذِبَ حَتَّى يُكْتَبَ عِنْدَ اللهِ كَذَّابًا.

Among the instances when telling a lie may be necessary, is when it helps to save an innocent life. For example, if someone is trying to capture and kill an innocent person and asks another of his whereabouts, the respondent may tell a lie in order to prevent bloodshed. In the sayings of the Prophet ﷺ, three other instances when lying is permissible are noted: firstly, when it helps to remove hostility and create harmony between two parties; secondly, when it is done in order to mislead the enemy in warfare; and lastly, a man is allowed to praise and encourage his wife in order to please her, even if the speech so uttered is not literally true.[8] The Shīʿī doctrine of dissimulation or expedient concealment (*taqiyyah*), furthermore, permits telling a lie if it would repel an imminent danger or an act of aggression against one's life, honour or property. While protecting property by means of *taqiyyah* is in principle permitted, many Shīʿī *ʿulamā'* have discouraged recourse to *taqiyyah* and the concealment of truth for the sake of merely a small amount (*al-māl al-yasīr*).[9] This subject will be dealt with later.

While enumerating the calamities of speech, al-Ghazālī goes on to say that people usually praise the powerful and the rich in their presence and when they attend special gatherings. However, sycophancy often consists of lying and hypocrisy (*kidhb wa riyā'*) on the part of the flatterer and of self-gratification (*iʿjāb*) on the part of those who are being praised. Therefore, both should avoid this type of behaviour.

Other forms of expression which al-Ghazālī has listed under the calamities of speech are undisciplined anger, excessive jocularity, and acrimonious contention (*mumārāt*). The author goes on to elaborate that anger (*ghaḍab*) usually leads to abusive speech and to exposure of the victim's weak points. Anger in its disciplined and defensive form, such as when fighting aggression and evil, is not forbidden, however; it is disallowed only when it exceeds the limits of propriety. The sources of such discipline are the *Sharīʿah*, human reason, and concern for the promotion of the moral qualities of gentleness (*ḥilm*) and good character (*ḥusn al-khulq*).[10]

Acrimonious contention (*mumārāt*) consists of objecting to the speech of another person simply for the sake of establishing one's own superiority over others. (*Mumārāt* is further discussed in a separate section below.)

Al-Ghazālī commented that 'excessive indulgence in jokes extinguishes the light of one's heart and leads to loss of dignity'.[11] Jokes are permissible in principle, especially those which please people of sound nature, provided they are tasteful and truthful (*yāsiran ṣādiqan*). The Prophet ﷺ used to be humourous (he was known to be kind to children and enjoyed joking with them), but his humour did not involve distortions. Excessive indulgence in jokes is discouraged, as it is likely to include some distortion and disrespect.[12]

To this list we may add excessive questioning (*kathrat al-su'āl*), which is generally discouraged in the Qur'ān and receives much attention in the teachings of the Prophet ﷺ. Questioning is discouraged only when there is no need for it; it is permitted in the pursuit of knowledge and in the search for truth.[13]

3. EXPOSING THE WEAKNESSES OF OTHERS

Avoiding harm to others and concealing the weaknesses of one's fellow human beings is a prominent theme of the moral teachings of the Qur'ān and Sunnah. The message here is conveyed in a variety of forms, contexts and ideas, all of which are indicative of Islam's emphasis on the honour and dignity of the individual, and of his or her right to privacy safe from the encroachment of others. Thus, according to a *Ḥadīth*, 'If a person conceals [the weakness of] another in this world, God will conceal their [weakness] in the Hereafter.'[14]

لاَ يَسْتُرُ عَبدٌ عَبدًا فِى الدُّنيَا اِلاَّ سَتَرَهُ اللهُ يَوْمَ القِيَامَةِ.

A variant version of the same message is reported in another *Ḥadīth* which provides: 'Whoever protects the honour of his brother, will have God protect his countenance from the Fire on the Day of Judgement.'[15]

مَن رَدَّ عَن عِرضِ اَخِيه رَدَّاللهُ عَن وَجهِهِ النَّار يَومَ القِيَامة.

In yet another *Ḥadīth* we read: 'Do not harm Muslims, and do not revile them, nor pursue their imperfections. For verily, whosoever pursues the imperfections of his brother shall have his own imperfections pursued by God.'[16]

لاَ تُؤذُو المُسلِمِينَ ولا تَعيرُوا، وَلاَ تَتَّبِعُوا عَورا تِهِم. فَانَّ
مَن يَتَّبِعُ عَورَةَ اَخِيهِ المُسلِم يَتَّبِعُ اللهُ عَورَتَهُ.

Concealing the faults, and respecting the privacy of others is again the theme of the following *Ḥadīth*:

> The Muslim who helps another when the latter's honour and dignity are under attack, shall be helped by God - Glorious and Sublime is He! - at a time when he would wish for God's help. But he who forsakes a Muslim whose dignity is under attack, shall have God forsake him at a time when he would wish for God's help.[17]

مَا مِن اِمرِءٍ مُسلِم يَنصُرُ مُسلِمًا فِى مَوْضِعٍ ينتهكُ فِيهِ مِن عِرضِه وَتَسْتَحِلُ حُرْمَتَهُ اِلاّ نَصَرَهُ اللهُ عَزَّ وَجَلَّ فِى مَوطِنٍ يُحبُّ فِيهِ نَصْرَهُ وَمَا مِن اِمرِءٍ خَذَل مُسلِمًا فِى مَوطِنٍ تنتَهكَ فِيهِ حُرمَتَهُ اِلاَّ خَذَلَهُ اللهُ فِى مَوْضِعٍ يُحِبُّ فِيهِ نَصرَتَهُ.

It is reported that one night when the second caliph ʿUmar b. al-Khaṭṭāb was patrolling Medina, he saw a man and a woman committing adultery. The following day the caliph informed other Companions and asked them whether he should enforce the prescribed penalty (*ḥadd*) for *zinā'* on the basis of his own observation. To this ʿAlī b. Abī Ṭālib replied that the law of God stated clearly that four witnesses were required to prove *zinā'* and that this provision was to be applied equally to the caliph. Other Companions are also reported to have concurred with ʿAlī's opinion. While quoting this report, al-Ghazālī observes that 'this is strong evidence that the *Sharīʿah* demands the concealment of sins (*satr al-fawāḥish*); it also discourages spying on or reporting the private affairs of others.'[18]

It will be noted, however, that concealment (*satr*) is recommended (*mandūb*) only with regard to persons who are not generally known to engage in corrupt and harmful activities. As for those who are notorious, it is recommended that their evil is not concealed and that the matter is reported to the authorities. For *satr* in such cases will only encourage further corruption and lawlessness.

All of this is relevant to concealing sins (*maʿṣiyah*) that occurred in the past. As for *maʿṣiyah* which takes place before one's eyes, one must personally attempt, to the extent of one's ability, to prevent or denounce it without delay.

In addition to the faults of narrators of *Ḥadīth* and of witnesses in judicial disputes, it is also permissible to report the wrongdoings of trustees of charities and orphans. This is allowable whenever it is deemed necessary, and no *satr* is required when the trustees in question are seen to be doing something which violates the proper terms of their duties.[19]

Exposing the faults of others by casting aspersions, or spying on them, is particularly reprehensible. Thus, according to a *Ḥadīth*, people are warned:

> Beware of suspicion. For suspicion is the most untrue form of speech; and do not spy upon one another and do not revile each other.[20]

إِيَّاكُمْ والظن فَإِنَّ الظن أَكْذَبُ الحَديثِ وَلاَ تَجَسَّسُوا ولاَ تَعيرُوا.

Imām Aḥmad b. Ḥanbal was once asked about the correct meaning of the following *Ḥadīth*: 'When you hear something from or about your brother, ascribe to it the best interpretation until you can no longer do so.' This presumably refers to something a fellow Muslim might have said or done.

إذَا بَلَغك شَيءٌ عَنْ أَخيكَ فَاحْمِلْهُ على أَحْسَنِه حَتّى لاَتَجِدَ لَهُ مَحْمَلاً.

To this the Imām replied: 'Find an excuse for him by saying "maybe he said this, or maybe he meant such and such".'[21] It is further reported in another *Ḥadīth:* 'Whoever is offered an apology from a fellow Muslim should accept it unless he knows that the person apologising is being dishonest.'[22]

مَن اِعتَذر اِلَيهِ أَخُوهُ المُسلمُ فَلْيَقْبَل عُذرَهُ مَا لَمْ يَعْلَمْ كذبَهُ.

While commenting on these *Ḥadīths*, Tuffāḥah has rightly observed that, despite the occurrence of the word brother (*akh*) therein, they are of general import, and their scope need not be confined to Muslims, the reason being that in Islam justice and benevolence (*ʿadl wa iḥsān*) are not confined to Muslims alone. The question of the way people treat their fellow citizens in society, their brothers and sisters in humanity, is closely linked with the Qur'ānic concepts of *ʿadl* and *iḥsān*, and these do not admit of any restriction that would compromise their objective application.[23] This indeed, is the main point of the following Qur'ānic text: 'And let not the hatred of a people harm [degrade] you into being unjust. Be just, for it is closest to piety (*taqwā*).' (V:8)

وَلَا يَجْرِمَنَّكُمْ شَنَآنُ قَوْمٍ على الَّا تَعْدِلُوا اعدِلُوا
هُوَ اَقْرَبُ لِلتَّقْوٰى.

Furthermore, Ḥasan the son of ʿAlī ibn Abī Ṭālib is reported to have said, 'If a man abuses me in [one] ear and then apologises to me in the other, I shall accept his apology.'[24]

Thus, it is evident that silence takes priority over speech when it comes to exposing the faults and weaknesses of others. 'One should not talk about the defects of others even if one is asked about them. One must try to avoid prying and asking personal questions about the private lives of others.'[25] For tolerance and forgiveness are necessary in order to encourage an atmosphere of fraternity in the community.

4. RECOMMENDED SILENCE

Another theme which has acquired prominence in the Sunnah of the Prophet ﷺ is the relative value of silence, especially when speech would serve no useful purpose. There are numerous *Ḥadīth*s on this subject, including the following:

> Whoever believes in God and the Last Day, let him utter what is good or remain silent.[26]

مَن كَانَ يُؤْمِنُ بِاللهِ وَالْيومِ الآخِرِ فَلْيَقُلْ خَيْرًا او لِيَصْمُتْ.

To speak only when there is occasion for speech, or when one has a purpose in doing so, is a sign of piety as the following *Ḥadīth* declares:

Part of the beauty of a person's Islam is that they remain silent about that which does not concern them.[27]

مِن حُسنِ إِسلَامِ المَرْءِ أَن يَسْكُتَ فِيمَا لاَ يَعْنِيهِ.

According to a report attributed to Ibn 'Abbās,[28] people are warned to beware of indulging in talk on matters that are of no concern to them, or when there is no occasion for them to speak. For a person who speaks out of place has indulged in excess. Ibn 'Abbās continues: 'Engage yourself not in bitter speech either with the learned or the fool. For the former is likely to defeat you, and the latter is likely to abuse you. Mention your brother favourably in his absence, not in a way that would displease him were he to hear you.'[29]

The best form of speech is that in which a little removes the need to say more, and the meaning is self-evident in the words.[30] A person ought to be reserved in speech, and to speak only when there is some benefit to be achieved by it. In the event of there being any doubt about the benefit of talking, one ought to remain silent.[31]

The Qur'ān encourages believers to speak out, but only if this serves a worthy purpose. Indeed, to remain silent on such an occasion is reprehensible. This Qur'ānic guidance is found in numerous places in the text, including the following: 'O you who believe! Fear God and [always] speak apposite words.' (XXXIII:70)

يَأَيُّهَا الَّذِينَ أَمَنُوا اتَّقُوا اللهَ وَقُولُوا قَوْلاً سَدِيدًا.

In another passage, God Most High gives the following instruction to the Prophet ﷺ, regarding courtesy to others: 'Tell my servants to say what is best. For Satan sows dissension among them; verily Satan is to man an evident enemy.' (XVII:53)

وَقُل لِّعِبَادِي يَقُولُوا الَّتِي هِيَ أَحْسَنُ إِنَّ الشَّيْطَنَ يَنزَغُ بَيْنَهُمْ إِنَّ الشَّيْطَنَ كَانَ لِلإِنسَانِ عَدُوًّا مُّبِينًا.

Commentators have elaborated on these Qur'ānic passages, saying that in them the believers are asked: to speak fairly, even if they are addressing their foes or manifest transgressors of God's law; not to entertain suspicions concerning others; and to speak courteously to others according to the best standards of discourse. For an inaccurate or discourteous utterance could easily destroy the result of one's efforts at strengthening the bonds of fraternity.[32]

Furthermore, the Holy Qur'ān instructed the Prophet ﷺ not to reciprocate wicked speech:

> Nor are the good deed and the evil deed equal. Repel evil with what is better; then will he between whom and thee was hatred, become, as it were, thy friend and intimate. (XLI:34)

وَلَا تَسْتَوِي الْحَسَنَةُ وَلَا السَّيِّئَةُ ادْفَعْ بِالَّتِي هِيَ
أَحْسَنُ فَإِذَا الَّذِي بَيْنَكَ وَبَيْنَهُ عَدَاوَةٌ كَأَنَّهُ وَلِيٌّ حَمِيمٌ.

The message in this verse is that wickedness must not be allowed to perpetuate itself; if evil is reciprocated with evil, then this will be the necessary outcome. To avoid this, the Qur'ān enjoins the Prophet ﷺ to repel evil with what is better and, by doing so, to turn potential hatred into friendship.[33] Another point to be noted here is that God Most High has granted no one, not even the Prophet ﷺ, absolute freedom of speech. For the Prophet ﷺ is given specific guidance as to the way he must propagate his call and communicate with people through good advice and courteous methods of persuasion.[34]

The believers are also encouraged to be thoughtful and to speak only with discretion and forethought as to the likely effects of the words they utter. For those who do so, the following *Ḥadīth* promises a great spiritual reward:

> When a servant of God says that which is clear and correct (ie having given thought to whether it is beneficial or not), through (his words) he is distanced from the Fire by a distance greater than what is between sunrise and sunset.

إِنَّ الْعَبْدَ ان يَتَكَلَّمَ بِالْكَلِمَةِ مَا يَتَبَيَّنُ فِيهَا (اَى يُفَكِّرُ أَنَّـهَا خَيْرٌ اَمْ لا) يَزِلُّ بِهَا مِنَ النَّارِ اَبْعَدُ مِـمَّا بَيْنَ الْمَشْـرِقِ وَالْمَغْرِبِ (متفق عليه).

When quoting this *Ḥadīth*, al-Nawawī makes the following observation: although talk that is not for the sake of a benefit is generally frowned upon, conversation with one's guests, discussion in pursuit of knowledge and remembering the virtues of upright men of piety (*ṣāliḥīn*), are not discouraged.[35]

Speech can take the form of a considered opinion (*ra'y*), sincere advice (*naṣīḥah*), or consultation (*shūrā*); it can be righteous (*kalimah ṭayyibah*) or evil (*kalimah khabīthah*); or it may be foolish talk (*laghw*). The Qur'ān and Sunnah explicitly encourage the first four, discourage evil speech, and advise the believers to ignore the last and remain silent in response. The Holy Qur'ān thus praises 'Those who do not give false testimony and when they encounter foolish talk (*laghw*) pass by it with dignity'. (XXV:72)

وَالَّذِينَ لاَيَشْـهَدُونَ الـزُّورَ وَاِذَا مَـرُّوا بِالـلَّغْـوِ مَـرُّوا كِـرَامًا.

5. ABUSES OF PERSONAL OPINION *(RA'Y)*

In a previous section on freedom of opinion (*ḥurriyyat al-ra'y*) I addressed the approved or praiseworthy varieties of *ra'y*. The present section addresses the disapproved or blameworthy opinion and its sub-varieties such as pernicious innovation (*bidᶜah*), transgression (*baghy*), caprice (*hawā*), and dissension (*ikhtilāf*). The blameworthy opinion (*al-ra'y al-madhmūm*) is a type of *ra'y* which is neither completely false nor totally invalid, and yet is misguided and reprehensible. It may occur in the form of *bidᶜah*, *baghy*, or *hawā*. There is yet a fourth variety of reprehensible *ra'y* which is referred to as 'ignorance' (*jahl*), as it is deemed to be no more than an unfounded extrapolation that stems from ignorance. All of these varieties fall under restrictions on freedom of speech primarily because the right to free speech and expression does not extend to these areas. The term 'restrictions' here does not necessarily mean prohibition. For, as this section shall show, the whole of this field is governed, not by legal prohibitions as such, but by moral sanctions, sincere and persuasive advice. Although the precise legal position is not always clear on some forms of *bidʿah* and *hawā*, these are, broadly speaking, non-justiciable violations of the freedom of speech.

However, it should be borne in mind, that the whole of this classification overlaps somewhat; scholars have sometimes used these terms almost interchangeably, presumably because the concepts of, for example, ignorance or transgression, are often present in some measure in the case of a capricious opinion (*hawā*), and of a pernicious innovation (*bidʿah*). The main difference between the last two would be that *hawā* consists of a strong element of selfishness, and the pursuit of one's desire in disregard of clear guidance, whilst *bidʿah*, on the other hand, is distinguished by an attempt to distort the principles of Islam, or to interpret them as one wishes. That is to say that *hawā* involves a disregard of the law and *bidʿah* a 'manipulation' of it. The word '*bidʿah*' is generally used in contradistinction with 'Sunnah', that is, the normative and familiar practice. In this sense, *bidʿah* signifies a deviation from, or superimposition on, the Sunnah of the Prophet ﷺ. An opinion which amounts to *bidʿah* may, or may not, be motivated by self-seeking interest, and as such, it is not always distinguishable from *hawā*. Note, for example, the distinction between the two forms of divorce (*ṭalāq*) in Islamic law, known as *ṭalāq al-sunnah* and *ṭalāq al-bidʿah* respectively. The former signifies the type of divorce which conforms with the law and established precedent, while the latter is labelled as *ṭalāq al-bidʿah* primarily because it departs from the legal norm which requires that the maximum of three pronouncements of the divorce are each uttered during the women's period of ritual purity (*ṭuhr*), that is, the period between two menstruations. *Ṭalāq al-bidʿah* ignores this, and combines the three pronouncements of *ṭalāq*, so that they may be pronounced all together in one go. As for the question of whether this form of *ṭalāq* also comprises a measure of selfish desire (*hawā*) on the part of the husband, the answer is not always clear, but is likely to be in the affirmative. Hence, the distinction between the concepts under discussion is expected to be broad in outline and is not necessarily exclusive.

Baghy may be distinguished from both *bidʿah* and *hawā* in that it indulges in self-righteousness and attempts to impose a person's own opinion on others, often acompanied by a denouncement of all those who oppose it. Beyond these shades of differences, however, the concepts under discussion have much in common, and are often used interchangeably. The Qur'ān uses the term *hawā* in a somewhat generic sense which could include both *bidʿah* and *baghy*. We also find that many scholars have used the term '*bidʿah*' so widely as to include all varieties of reprehensible opinion. Furthermore, none of these are confined to the realm of opinion alone, but apply equally to acts which may fit the attendant description and attributes of each.

1. INNOVATION AND CAPRICE *(BIDʿAH* AND *HAWĀ)*

Literally, *bidʿah* means either an innovation which cannot be vindicated by authoritative precedent, or a pernicious innovation which is far removed from normal and established practice.[36] *Bidʿah* is defined as an innovation in religion which resembles what the *Sharīʿah* has expressly approved of and, as such, is intended to fulfil the proclaimed objectives of the *Sharīʿah*.[37] However, the resemblance between *bidʿah* and the established norms of the *Sharīʿah* mentioned in this definition is merely nominal, for in reality *bidʿah* violates the established standards of the *Sharīʿah*. The definition also indicates that the intention behind *bidʿah* does not deviate from the norm in the sense that the rules of the *Sharīʿah* are generally intended to achieve benefits (*maṣāliḥ*), and this is precisely what the innovator intends to do. However, the good intentions behind *bidʿah* are of no account, as Abū Isḥāq Ibrāhīm al-Shāṭibī explains, because the innovator arrogates to himself the authority of the Lawgiver in such a manner that the objectives of the law are frustrated.[38] *Bidʿah* is divided into two types; namely genuine *bidʿah* (*al-bidʿah al-ḥaqīqiyyah*), for which no justification or support, neither wholly nor in part, can be found in the Qur'ān, the Sunnah, or *ijmāʿ*, nor in any precedent or learned opinion. In other words, it is an innovation in the true sense of the word.

The second type of *bidʿah* is known as *al-bidʿah al-iḍāfiyyah*, or partial innovation, which has two facets. One of these is identical with substantial *bidʿah* in that it is unprecedented and indefensible, but, there is another side to this second type of *bidʿah*, for which support can be found in the established norms. In other words, *al-bidʿah al-iḍāfiyyah* is an ambivalent innovation which can be either accepted as part of the authoritative Sunnah or completely rejected, depending on how it is viewed.[39]

There are two further categories of *bidʿah*, namely *al-bidʿah al-*

tarkiyyah which consists of abandoning something, such as, for example, when a person abandons, or advises others to forsake, something which is lawful under the rules of the *Sharīʿah*. The opposite of this is *al-bidʿah ghayr al-tarkiyyah*, that is, innovation which does not consist of abandoning anything, but rather, involves changing something of the *Sharīʿah*, or advancing a different perspective on it; which amounts to innovation, but not abandonment.[40]

The hallmark of *bidʿah* is the pursuit of capricious and whimsical opinion (*hawā*) in preference to divine guidance. Thus we read in the Qur'ān in an address to the prophet-king David ﷵ:

> O David, We have made you a vicegerent on earth, so judge between people in truth and follow not [the dictates of] *hawā* which would lead you astray from the path of God. (XXXVIII:26)

يٰدَاوُدُ اِنَّا جَعَلْنٰكَ خَلِيفَةً فِى الْاَرْضِ فَاحْكُمْ بَيْنَ النَّاسِ
بِالْحَقِّ وَلَا تَتَّبِعِ الْهَوٰى فَيُضِلَّكَ عَنْ سَبِيلِ اللهِ

And in this verse:

> And who is more misguided than one who follows his own *hawā*, without guidance from God? (XXVIII:50)

وَمَنْ اَضَلُّ مِمَّنِ اتَّبَعَ هَوٰنهُ بِغَيْرِ هُدًى مِّنَ اللهِ.

In addition, a person who chooses to follow the vagaries of *hawā* is not to be obeyed by others, as the Qur'ān proclaims:

> Obey not the one whose heart We have closed to Our remembrance (*ʿan dhikrinā*), and who follows his *hawā*, and is excessesive [in his affairs]. (XVIII:28)

وَلَا تُطِعْ مَنْ اَغْفَلْنَا قَلْبَهُ عَنْ ذِكْرِنَا وَاتَّبَعَ هَوٰنهُ وَكَانَ
اَمْرُهُ فُرُطًا.

When quoting the foregoing passages, al-Shāṭibī points out that in all three verses the matter is confined to a choice between following one of two things: guidance (*hudā, dhikr*), or caprice (*hawā*). The innovator (*mubtadiʿ*) has chosen the latter; hence, while he is utterly misguided he himself thinks otherwise. Al-Shāṭibī also quotes another Qur'ānic passage which denounces those who attempt to confuse the meaning of the Qur'ān through misguided and self-styled interpretation:

> He it is who has sent down to thee the Book. In it are verses which are perspicuous; they are the foundation of the Book: Others are allegorical. But those in whose hearts is perversity follow the part which is allegorical, seeking discord *(fitnah)* and searching for its hidden meaning. (III:7)

هُوَ الَّذِي أَنْزَلَ عَلَيْكَ الْكِتَبَ مِنْهُ ءَايَتٌ مُّحْكَمَتٌ هُنَّ
أُمُّ الْكِتَبِ وَأُخَرُ مُتَشَبِهَتٌ فَأَمَّا الَّذِينَ فِي قُلُوبِهِمْ زَيْغٌ
فَيَتَّبِعُونَ مَاتَشَابَهَ مِنْهُ ابْتِغَاءَ الْفِتْنَةِ وَابْتِغَاءَ تَأْوِيلِهِ.

It is reported from the Prophet's ﷺ wife ʿĀ'ishah, that he read this verse and then said: 'When you see those who argue and dispute about the Qur'ān, these are the ones that God has meant, and they should be shunned.' Al-Shāṭibī adds to this: 'The disputation to which the Prophet ﷺ has referred concerns the pursuit of the ambiguous passages (*mutashābihāt)* in the Qur'ān.' Disputation of this kind leads to disunity and deviation from the guidance of the Qur'ān, as the following passage shows:

> This is My way, leading straight, so follow it and follow not the paths which would scatter you away from it. (VI:153)

وَأَنَّ هَذَا صِرَاطِي مُسْتَقِيمًا فَاتَّبِعُوهُ وَلَا تَتَّبِعُوا السُّبُلَ
فَتَفَرَّقَ بِكُمْ عَن سَبِيلِهِ.

According to Qur'ān commentators, the phrase 'follow not the paths' refers to the ways of those who have deviated from the straight path, namely, the innovators and sceptics (*ahl al-bidʿah wa'l-shubhāt*).[41]

Elaborating on some of these statements, al-Shāṭibī adds: 'The innovators distort the *Sharīʿah* in various ways, such as by upholding the literal meanings (*ẓawāhir*)of the Qur'ān without looking into the objectives and intentions of the Lawgiver.' In a reference to the Khārijites,[42] al-Shāṭibī wrote that they: upheld the ambiguous portions (*mutashābihāt*) of the Qur'ān in preference to the perspicuous (*muḥkamāt*); declared most of the Companions of the Prophet ﷺ to be infidels; held the view that in the event of the imām becoming an infidel, all of his subjects automatically become infidels; and held that the adulterer is not liable to the punishment of stoning to death (*rajm*). The Khārijites also maintained that the prescribed punishment of slanderous accusation (*qadhf*) applies to those who accuse women of unchastity, but not to those who charge men of similar conduct; that ignorance of the detailed rules of *fiqh* (*furūʿ*) is an [acceptable legal] excuse; that God will send a prophet from among the *ʿajam* (i.e. non-Arabs) who will bring a book and the *Sharīʿah* of Prophet Muḥammad ﷺ will then be abandoned; and that *Sūrat Yūsuf* (i.e. chapter XII of the standard text) is not a part of the Qur'ān, and so on. All these views which the Khārijites advocated are contrary to the principles and established tenets of Islam.[43]

Commenting on the subject of the ambiguous verses of the Qur'ān, Ibn Qayyim al-Jawziyyah wrote: 'A particular form of *hawā* in connection with the Qur'ān is to uphold the ambiguous in preference to the perspicuous so as to advance and substantiate a particular point of view. An even more hideous practice is that when the morbid attempt to find a *mutashābih* with which to reject the *muḥkam* fails, attempts are then made to find some weakness in the latter and thereby downgrade it to the level of *mutashābih* and in this way, to suspend the definitive importance of the *muḥkam*.' References are made, at this point, to the Jahmiyyah and Qadariyyah (sub-divisions of the Muʿtazilah) and their views on the meaning of certain portions of the Qur'ān.[44] The author concludes his discussion by saying that the correct approach, which the Companions and leading jurists and scholars adopted, is precisely the opposite: The *mutashābih* must be read in the light of the *muḥkam*, and not vice versa, so as to maintain internal harmony and consistency in interpreting the Qur'ān.[45]

References are also made in this context to the views and beliefs of the *Bāṭiniyyah* (also known as *Ismāʿīliyyah*),[46] and in particular, to the meanings they have given to some of the key concepts of the Qur'ān, such as the canonical prayer (*ṣalāh*), legal alms (*zakāh*), fasting (*ṣawm*), - meanings that are very different from the understanding that the majority of the *ʿulamāʾ* have of these terms. The Bāṭiniyyah have thus interpreted *ṣalāh* as referring to the Prophet ﷺ, for example, in the Qur'ānic verse 'Surely *ṣalāh* keeps one away from indecency and evil' (XXIX:44). In their view it is the Prophet ﷺ who staves off evil, not the prayer as such. Similarly, according to the Bāṭiniyyah, *zakāh* means 'purification of the soul', *ṣawm* means 'abstaining from evil'; paradise (*jannah*) is held to mean 'the sweet smell of the human body'; the ablution (*wuḍūʾ*) is said to mean 'following the awaited Imām'. *Tayammum*, which is the ritual ablution performed with clean earth in the absence of water, is held by the Bāṭiniyyah to mean 'obedience to the deputy of the Imām in the absence of the Imām himself'; and they interpret the full bath (*ghusl*) to mean 'the renewal of one's pledge of allegiance to the Imām'.[47] It is, perhaps, due to these and similar remote and allegorical interpretations they have given to the Qur'ān, that the Bāṭiniyyah have derived their name.

A more recent form of *bidʿah*, embraced by some Muslims, is to deny the authority of the Sunnah with the view that the Qur'ān, being self-contained, authentic and comprehensive, is the only source of the *Sharīʿah*. This is the view taken by a faction calling itself *al-Firqah al-Qur'āniyyah*, or partisans of the Qur'ān, whose views are known to have found adherents in Egypt, Libya,[48] Pakistan, Malaysia and elsewhere.

Whereas some scholars, notably the Imām al-Shāfiʿī, have accepted the notion of a good innovation (*bidʿah ḥasanah*), Ibn Taymiyyah rejects the division of *bidʿah* into good (*ḥasanah*) and evil (*qabīḥah*) maintaining that all *bidʿah* is evil. The former group hold that when a *bidʿah ḥasanah* is accepted and generally approved by the community of believers it is no longer pernicious innovation. Ibn Taymiyyah refutes this, saying that these views came into being only after the third century A.H. (tenth century A.D.), that all *bidʿah* is evil and that the Sunnah is completely clear on this point. The author then quotes the following three *Ḥadīths*: 'All innovation (*bidʿah*) is misguided - *kulli bidʿatin ḍalālah*'; 'Every novelty is an innovation - *kulli muḥdathatin bidʿah*'; and 'The worst of things are the novel among them—*inna sharr al-umūr muḥdathātuhā*'. The examples which Ibn Taymiyyah has given of *bidʿah* in this context pertain mainly to rituals of the faith, such as fasting on certain days of the year, unauthorised prayer (*al-ṣalāt al-muḥdathah*), and festive celebrations other than those which are commonly recognised.[49]

The view that some *bidʿah* is good has its origin in the precedent of ʿUmar b. al-Khaṭṭāb who is reported to have welcomed the *ṣalāt al-tarāwīḥ* during Ramaḍān and said of it: '*niʿma'l-bidʿah*' - 'what an excellent *bidʿah*'. To this, Ibn Taymiyyah responds that *tarāwīḥ* was not an innovation at all but rather originated in the Sunnah of the Prophet ﷺ: he and the Companions used to perform the prayer but, after a while, the Prophet ﷺ ceased to perform it regularly lest people thought it was obligatory. Hence, what ʿUmar b. al-Khaṭṭāb is quoted to have said does not contradict the *Ḥadīth* that states: 'All *bidʿah* is misguided'. Ibn Taymiyyah concludes that ʿUmar must have used the word '*bidʿah*' in its linguistic sense, that is 'welcoming something which was forgotten'; and that he did not use the word in the sense of an innovation in matters pertaining to the *Sharīʿah* (*bidʿah sharʿiyyah*).[50]

Imām al-Shāfiʿī, on the other hand, acknowledged that innovations are of two kinds, one of which violates the Qur'ān, the Sunnah, the precedent of the Companions and *ijmāʿ*, and the other comprising some benefit. The first of these is misguided innovation (*al-bidʿah al-ḍalālah*), but the second is not. The Shāfiʿī jurist, ʿIzz al-Dīn ʿAbd al-Salām has taken this analysis one step further by stating that the beneficial *bidʿah* may consist of an obligation, such as establishing courses to teach the Arabic language, or of something which is recommendable (*mandūb*), such as opening a school for general education. The misguided *bidʿah* can also vary in the degree of its enormity from being merely reprehensible (*makrūh*), such as the excessive adornment and decoration of a mosque, to that which is totally forbidden (*ḥarām*), such as reciting the Qur'ān in such a way that its words and meaning are distorted. And finally, a *bidʿah* may be neutral (*mubāḥ*), such as the use of colouring in food. Those who advocate the idea of a good *bidʿah* have interpreted the prophetic *Ḥadīth*, 'all *bidʿah* is misguided', in such a way that the word *bidʿah* therein refers only to innovations which violate the Qur'ān and Sunnah.[51] Imām Mālik, on the other hand, totally rejected the notion of a good *bidʿah*. He maintained that reading such a meaning into the words of the *Ḥadīth* amounted to an outright distortion which must be avoided.[52]

Those who take a totally negative view of *bidʿah*, hold that the latter may consist of: an innovation in religion which is invalid *ab initio*, such as performing additional prayers at certain times of the year (in the month of Rajab and during ʿĀshūrā, for example); or of an addition to something which is basically valid, for example chanting or reciting prayer-words accompanied by dance or rhythmical movement (where chanting or reciting words of prayer is valid, while dance and rhythmical movement is considered to be *bidᶜah)*; or, conversely, of a detraction from the due measure of something, such as 'monologic' prayer, that is, chanting the name of Allāh in isolation from His other Names (such as, the Almighty, the Beneficent, the Merciful etc.); or lastly, of reversing the correct order of something, such as giving the sermon of the ᶜĪd prayer prior to the actual prayer - instead of it being given thereafter.

Some of the worst forms of *bidᶜah* that Khiḍr al-Ḥusayn has noted are ones which entail loss of property and life, such as placing food and valuables by the graves of the dead, or worse still, sacrificing and slaughtering animals in order to seek the pleasure of the dead and thereby seek protection from misfortune and evil.

However, the findings of a qualified scholar (*mujtahid*) are precluded from all of this is. They may not be labelled as *bidᶜah* even if his conclusions happen to be innovative and conflict with the majority opinion. An opinion or *ijtihād* of this kind may not command authority, and is considered to be no more than a weak opinion, but it would not be correct to apply the term *bidᶜah* to a ruling of *ijtihād*.[53]

Al-Shāṭibī has also discussed the notion of a good *bidᶜah* and whether this is a concept that is substantially concurrent with considerations of public interest (*maṣlaḥah mursalah*) and *istiḥsān*. Although al-Shāṭibī advances the argument almost to the point of proving that these are all parallel concepts, he stops short of drawing this conclusion. He tells us, for instance, that many people have in fact considered *maṣlaḥah mursalah* to be essentially a form of beneficial *bidᶜah* (*bidᶜah mustaḥsanah*), and if *maṣlaḥah* were to be accepted as a valid principle, then there would be no reason to deny the idea of a good *bidᶜah*, for the two concepts are essentially the same. Both of these are founded on the notion of what is proper under the circumstances (i.e. *al-iᶜtibār al-munāsib*) for which no specific evidence can be found in the *Sharīᶜah*. If *maṣlaḥah mursalah* commands any credibility, then that should also be the case with regard to the *bidᶜah mustaḥsanah*.[54] Al-Shāṭibī goes on to point out that Imām Mālik and most Ḥanafī scholars have validated *maṣlaḥah mursalah* and *istiḥsān*. But, at this point he abandons the discourse, and seems to return to the position that *maṣlaḥah mursalah* and *istiḥsān* have nothing to do with *bidᶜah*, that a *bidᶜah* may not be equated with either of these, that all *bidᶜah* is misguided, and that there is no such thing as a good *bidᶜah*.

The logical conclusion, however, would be to say that *maṣlaḥah mursalah* and *bidᶜah ḥasanah* are truly parallel concepts and it would seem inconsistent to accept one and reject the other. If there is evidence in the *Sharīᶜah* that validates *maṣlaḥah mursalah*, then that should also be the case with regard to *bidᶜah ḥasanah*. In my opinion, Imām al-Shāfiᶜī's affirmative stand with regard to accepting the notion of *bidᶜah ḥasanah* is more consistent and logical. It also stands to reason to understand the text of the *Ḥadīth* in question, as meaning that the Holy Prophet ﷺ denounced only pernicious *bidᶜah* which violates the established norms and principles of the *Sharīᶜah*.

Al-Ghazālī divides the innovator (*mubtadiᶜ*) into two types: one who invites others to *bidᶜah*, and the other who remains silent out of fear or personal choice. The first type of *mubtadiᶜ* may be propagating something which does not amount to infidelity (*kufr*), in which case the matter rests between him and God (*fa-amruhu baynahu wa bayn Allāh*). But if he invites people to what may amount to *kufr*, he can be even more harmful than the *kāfir ab initio*. For the evil of the latter is not as influential, in the sense that he is known as a non-believer and, as such, believers are not likely to pay attention to him. But the *mubtadiᶜ* who actively propagates *bidᶜah* has a claim to righteousness and tries to spread corruption under the guise of truth; and this type of evil is contagious. This second type of *mubtadiᶜ* must be denounced and his wickedness exposed. People should openly show their disapproval of him; they should shun him, refuse to respond to his greeting (*salām*) in public, and should avoid helping, or co-operating with, him.

As for the commoner who indulges in *bidᶜah* (*al-mubtadiᶜ al-ᶜāmmī*), but is unable to persuade others and is unlikely to command any following, then he should be given good counsel (*naṣīḥah*) and kind advice instead of stern treatment and humiliation. But if *naṣīḥah* proves futile and shunning (*iᶜrāḍ*) is called for, then this should be done. For if *bidᶜah* is not denounced it is likely to spread and give rise to undesirable tendencies in society.[55]

Al-Shāṭibī advises reticence in relation to the *bidᶜah* of which the truth or falsehood is not known, saying: 'We are commanded not to disseminate such views until the truth emerges.'[56] In response to the suggestion by some *ᶜulamā'* that innovators who propagate *bidᶜah* should be severely punished, al-Shāṭibī observes that they should be treated in accordance with the seriousness of their misconduct. If the *bidᶜah* is a minor one, they should be punished lightly, but if it amounts to a grave violation, the punishment should be proportionately increased. The author then concludes that *bid*ᶜ*ah* is not a monolithic concept, nor is it a singular offence; that each *bid*ᶜ*ah* should be viewed and evaluated individually; and that the treatment or reprimand accorded to its perpetrator must be determined strictly on this basis.[57]

In concluding this discussion I will now refer to a response that Imām al-Ghazālī gave to the question of whether one should avoid discussing *bid*ᶜ*ah* in any capacity, even if only to refute it.

In his work *al-Munqidh min al-Ḍalāl*, al-Ghazālī addresses the question of the incidental dissemination of *bid*ᶜ*ah*. Referring to his own writings in refutation of the beliefs and doctrines of the Bāṭiniyyah, al-Ghazālī points out that 'the result was that one of the Sunnites found fault with me for overstating the arguments and viewpoints of the Bāṭiniyyah'. The point of the criticism was that had it not been for al-Ghazālī pinpointing and marshalling the Bāṭiniyyah's arguments, they would have been unable to articulate and defend their own doctrine. Al-Ghazālī, accepted the criticism but then referred to the case when Aḥmad b. Ḥanbal found fault with al-Ḥārith al-Muḥāsibī for the latter's writings in refutation of the Muᶜtazilah. Al-Muḥāsibī replied that 'refuting innovation is a duty'; to which Aḥmad b. Ḥanbal replied: 'Yes, but you have first reported their specious argument and then responded to it. It is possible that a man might read only the [first] part, or that only that part may stick in his mind!' Al-Ghazālī commented that Aḥmad b. Ḥanbal's remark was valid, but that it had concerned a specious argument that had not become widespread and notorious. However, once such an argument does become widespread, a response to it becomes imperative, and that is possible only after setting forth the argument.[58]

Although in its literal sense, *hawā* can mean a passing whim, an inclination, or a desire, without necessarily leading to either the formulation or the expression of an opinion, the *ᶜulamā'* have nevertheless used it to imply an opinion which originates in these impulses. This usage, which is basically a metaphor that identifies the effect by the cause, is probably motivated by the frequent recurrence of the word *hawā*, and its derivatives, in the Qur'ān. *Hawā* has been defined as 'the pleasure-seeking inclination of the soul (*nafs*) towards that which is not permitted by the *Sharī*ᶜ*ah*'.[59]

As already indicated, the Qur'ān refers to *hawā* in contradistinction to guidance (*hudā, dhikr*), and identifies it with deviation from the truth which the Qur'ān itself has expounded. It is in this sense that the Qur'ān warns the believers, on no less than twenty-five occasions, against the dangers and temptations of *hawā* and the hold that it can have on the hearts and minds of people.[60] The phrase 'capricious people' (*ahl al-hawā*) typically refers to those who say what they please, and who violate the truth by indulging in corrupt and distorted interpretations which are unacceptable to the believer. For, whenever opinion is allowed to follow personal prejudice and desire, it leads to divergence from the truth and even to outright falsehood.

The personal desire to be the winner at all costs, regardless of the merit of one's case, and without concern for the well-being of others, is an instance of *hawā*. One of the worst forms of *hawā* is when personal craving for superiority and power masquerades under specious reasoning and plausible argumentation in the name of justice, piety, and truth. The hold that *hawā* can have on the minds and lives of people is depicted in the Qur'ānic text where the believers are asked the question, 'Do you see the one who took as his god his own vain desire (*hawā*) and [consequently] God left him to stray?' (XLV:23)

أَفَرَءَيْتَ مَنِ اتَّخَذَ إِلَٰهَهُ هَوَىٰهُ وَأَضَلَّهُ اللَّهُ.

Hawā also occurs in the Qur'ān in contradistinction to the *Sharīᶜah*, as is shown in the following passage:

> Thus We have set you upon a path (*sharīᶜah*) of [Our] command, so follow it, and follow not the desires (*ahwā'*) of those who know not. (XLV:18)

ثُمَّ جَعَلْنَٰكَ عَلَىٰ شَرِيعَةٍ مِّنَ الْأَمْرِ فَاتَّبِعْهَا وَلَا تَتَّبِعْ
أَهْوَآءَ الَّذِينَ لَا يَعْلَمُونَ.

The Qur'ān commentator, al-Zamakhsharī (d. 538/1143) elaborates on the meaning of this verse thus: follow the *Sharīᶜah* which is founded on proofs and evidences, and let yourself not be tempted by the views and arguments of the ignorant which are founded on caprice and pernicious innovation (*hawā wa-bidᶜah*).[61] Furthermore, the Prophet ﷺ is reported to have addressed his followers with the words: 'None of you can be a [true] believer until your desire (*hawā*) is made subservient to [the guidance] I have brought forth.'

لا يُومِن اَحَدَكُم حَتّى يكونَ هَواهُ تَبَعًا لماجِئْتُ بِهِ.

According to another *Ḥadīth*: 'Of all 'gods' worshipped under the heavens none is more odious to God than *hawā*.'[62]

مَاعُبِدَ تَحْتَ السَّمَاءِ اِلٰهٌ اَبْغَضُ اِلَى اللهِ مِنَ الهوىٰ.

Another instance of clearly forbidden *hawā* is when a person believes in the legality or prohibition of something and then ignores this when it applies to himself or his friends. For example, a person may demand his right of pre-emption (*shufᶜ*) believing in its validity, but when someone else demands the same right of him, he ignores it, claiming that it is unproven and advancing an opinion to that effect.[63] Similarly, a person may denounce another for a certain activity such as listening to music, but when his friends do the same, he claims that the prohibition is not proven, and that the subject remains open to *ijtihād*.[64]

The jurists have not specified any punitive measures for *hawā*, and no particular punishment for the perpetrator of *bidᶜah* either, except for a form of social boycott (*al-hajr*, also referred to as *iᶜrāḍ*) which is signified by refusing to greet the perpetrator, or speak to him, or approve of his views. The *ᶜulamā'* have spoken of *hajr* as a moral obligation of the community, regardless of whether the perpetrator of *bidᶜah* is a relative, a neighbour or a stranger, and especially when the *bidᶜah* concerns the community at large, and violates what is referred to as the Right of God (*Ḥaqq Allāh*).[65] But if the *bidᶜah* relates to private rights, and consists, for example, of a form of slander or libel, then the greeting is permitted and *hajr* is not required. There is no maximum limit on the duration of *hajr* and it continues until the person repents and corrects himself. The community is under a moral obligation to denounce the *bidᶜah*, and those individuals who are able to produce evidence for its refutation or who are in possession of authority and able to put an end to it, must do so.[66]

The *ᶜulamā'* have held that it is a duty of the head of state to prevent *bidᶜah* and *hawā* in the government. This is part of the general obligation of a nation's leader to facilitate the transmission and dissemination of knowledge whenever necessary, or when it is in the interest (*maṣlaḥah*) of the community. These duties of the head of state comprise the following: propagation of the faith by defending it against doubts and *bidᶜah*, and offering an adequate response to the promoters of *bidᶜah* and *hawā*; inviting the disbelievers and the misguided to righteousness and truth; investigating and bringing together the various views concerning *bidᶜah* and *hawā*, and trying to resolve disputes over them by validating or authorising the view that seems best. Whenever the imām exercises this form of *ijtihād*, or when he selects the *ijtihād* of others for the purpose of general practice, even if that *ijtihād* is of disputed validity, it nevertheless becomes authoritative and action upon it becomes obligatory.[67]

2. TRANSGRESSION AND DISSENSION *(BAGHY* AND *IKHTILĀF)*

Baghy means lawlessness, refusing to acknowledge the truth, and exceeding behavioural limits with a corrupt intention, dishonesty and arrogance.[68] *Baghy* also means disobedience to lawful government. In this sense, *baghy* is defined as a refusal to obey the lawful imām who is not indulging in sin (*maᶜṣiyah*), whether or not such disobedience is based on an interpretation or a particular point of view which the perpetrator believes to be the truth.[69]

An instance of *baghy* which is frequently encountered is when a person, or a group of persons are engaged in a lawful pursuit but are denounced for wrongdoing by their opponents. The followers of different legal schools observe certain religious rituals, such as the call to prayer (*ādhān*), standing to prayer (*iqāmah*), and even part of the contents of the canonical prayer, with slight variations. Basically, all the variations are permissible, as they all subscribe to the tenet of *ᶜibādah*; and a mere difference of form does not justify any claim to superiority or preference of one over the other. And yet, owing to *baghy*, the followers of some legal schools have denounced and abused their counterparts in the other schools for not performing the rituals as they themselves specify. This behaviour is not confined to issues of ritual alone. We know, for example, that the mystic has often criticised the jurist for the latter's zeal in the exoteric aspect of religion. The jurist has, in turn, criticised the mystic for his esoteric approach to the rules and doctrines of the *Sharīᶜah*. When each denounces the other, in disregard of their respective merits, the views of both mystic and jurist partake of 'transgression' as they indulge in self-righteousness and an unwarranted denunciation of the opposing view. The correct approach in such cases would be for both sides to assess the merit and demerit of each view, and then to acknowledge them accordingly, without transgression and prejudice. All other considerations which are extraneous to the essence of the matter, such as the desire to expose the ignorance of one's opponent, or to establish one's own superiority and power, etc., must be excluded from the quest for truth and in the assessment or criticism of other opinions.[70]

Dissension (*ikhtilāf*) over the details of formal worship, including variations in the forms of the call to and 'setting up' of the canonical prayer (*ādhān*, and *iqāmah*); the 'Īd prayer; prayer at times of fear for one's safety (*ṣalāt al-khawf*); and other such rituals which vary in form but are the same in essence are, according to Ibn Taymiyyah, a type of *ikhtilāf al-tanawwuʿ*, that is, an insubstantial difference of opinion. As opposed to *ikhtilāf al-taḍādd* (a substantial difference of opinion amounting to contradiction), *ikhtilāf al-tanawwuʿ* consists of a preference of one of two or more equally valid views, over the others, which should be presented and evaluated as such. The essence of preference (*tarjīḥ*), according to Ibn Taymiyyah, lies in the recognition of the basic validity of two views, one of which may be recommended, while the other is neither denounced nor rejected as false.[71] The author then quotes the following relevant *Ḥadīth*, reported by ʿAbd Allāh b. Masʿūd:

'I heard a man reciting a verse of the Qur'ān which I had heard the Prophet ﷺ recite differently. So I took him by the hand and led him to the Prophet ﷺ and mentioned the matter to him. Then I noticed (a look of) displeasure appear on the Prophet's ﷺ face and he said: 'Both of you are right (*kilākumā muḥsin*) [so] do not disagree [over this]. For those who came before you disagreed [over trivialities], and consequently perished.[72]

سَمِعْتُ رَجُلاً قَرَأَ آيَةً سَمِعْتُ النَّبِيَّ ﷺ يَقْرَأُ خِلاَ فَهَا،

فَأَخَذْتُ بِيَدِهِ فَانْطَلَقْتُ بِهِ إِلَى النَّبِيِّ ﷺ فَذَكَرْتُ ذَلِكَ لهِ،

فَعَرَفْتُ فِى وَجْهِهِ الكَرَاهِيَّةَ وَقَالَ: كَلاَ كُمَا مُحْسِنٌ، ولا

تَخْتَلِفُوا ، فَإِنَّ مِنْ كَانَ قَبْلَكُمْ اخْتَلَفُوا فَهَلَكُوا.

Ibn Taymiyyah continues by saying that the Prophet ﷺ forbade disagreement which consists of *juḥd*, that is, denial of the truth and veracity of the opinion or conduct of the other party. This was the case in the foregoing *Ḥadīth*, where the Prophet ﷺ drew the attention of the parties to the fact that disagreement over insubstantial matters is basically destructive. The parties were both reciting the Qur'ān but with different dialectical variants, which was why the Prophet ﷺ declared them both to be *muḥsin* (doing something good and proper), but corrected them for questioning the validity of their different opinions on something non-essential - the variant readings.[73]

As for *ikhtilāf al-taḍādd*, which amounts to contradiction, the two views at issue are diametrically opposed to one another in regard to either essentials or subsidiary details or both. The majority opinion on this type of disagreement is that only one of the opposing views can be right and declared as such, but not both. Examples of this type of *ikhtilāf* among scholars are found: over the issue of free-will and determinism; regarding the attributes of the Companions; and concerning the views and beliefs of different factions of jurists (*fuqahā'*) and mystics/Sufis (*mutaṣawwifah*). The matter is different in *ikhtilāf al-tanawwuᶜ*, where each of the two parties is undoubtedly right, but where blame befalls the one who exceeds limits and resorts to *baghy* with regard to the other.[74] In Ibn Taymiyyah's assessment, by far the greatest differences of opinion among the Muslim community fall into the latter category. These differences usually consist of mere variations and amount to nothing more than a different perspective on truths held in common, and yet they still lead to conflict. This is because neither of the disputing parties acknowledges the merit in the views of their opponents and each persists in self-righteously claiming superiority over the other.[75]

Religious and sectarian fanaticism of the type that lays exclusive claim to righteousness is, as one observer explains, a deviation from the valid precedent of the Companions and a form of *bidᶜah/baghy* which is found among the followers of different legal schools. For example, the generators of such transgression among the Ḥanafis are often people who lay claim to piety and knowledge, and yet propagate fanaticism to such an extent that they proclaim invalid the *ṣalāh* of one who performs it behind a non-Ḥanafī imām. They also vehemently denounce the raising of hands during the ritual prayer prior to the bowing, which is a normal practice among the Shāfiᶜīs. There are, in fact, fanatics of this type in every *madhhab*, including the

Shāfiʿī, Mālikī, and Ḥanbalī schools - people who see the truth as the prerogative of the school of their own following. Even outside the sphere of formal worship, for example in matrimonial matters, these fanatics engage in transgression and innovation when they forbid their daughters from marrying a Muslim who is not a follower of their own *madhhab*.[76] They are, indeed, deviating from the consensus of all the leading imāms who have urged their followers to adhere to the teachings of the Qur'ān and the Sunnah, and to abandon individualistic and scholastic opinions which do not conform to the authority of these sources.

Al-Shahristānī has held that *istibdād bi'l-ra'y*, or the arbitrary imposition of one's own opinion on others without clear authority, is a transgression and innovation which contradicts the precedent of the pious and upright *ʿulamā'* of the past. The same author adds that *istibdād bi'l-ra'y* is not a *bidʿah* when it is founded on knowledge and reason; it is only so when views of doubtful provenance and validity are inflicted on others.[77]

One of the manifestations of *istibdād bi'l-ra'y*, which often comprises transgression and ignorance, is the assumption that one's own knowledge, opinion and belief is all that counts; that everyone must follow it; and that anyone who differs from it should be denounced. The type of person who persists in such an attitude has little regard for objective knowledge and the truth, and tends to ignore the merit and reason in other people's opinions. This behaviour leads only to hostility, and as a result, no benefit is to be expected therefrom.[78]

And, finally, Ibn Qayyim al-Jawziyyah includes, under the category of reprehensible opinion, over-indulgence in personal preference (*istiḥsān*), and the advancement of analogies and speculative argumentation which verge on *hawā* and seek to circumvent the *Sharīʿah*. He reflects that this kind of *ra'y* pays little attention to the origin and proper causes of the principles (*aḥkām*) of the *Sharīʿah* and often deviates from their objectives. Over-indulgence in this type of *ra'y* leads to 'suspension of the Sunnah, ignorance and confusion regarding the correct meaning of the Book of God, and to their ultimate neglect'.[79] The author includes in this category, argumentation and opinions which originate in excessive questioning, and highly theoretical issues which have little bearing on reality and practical experience. He also points out that there is evidence in the Qur'ān and Sunnah which discourages over-indulgence in such questions. Ibn Qayyim then quotes the relevant evidence and draws his conclusion that Islam shuns over-indulgence in opinions and questions that are the result of a libertine attitude toward the authority of divine revelation. This is borne out, Ibn Qayyim adds, by the accepted principles of *uṣūl al-fiqh*, on which the various schools are in agreement: Even a weak *Ḥadīth* is to be given priority over both *ra'y* and *qiyās*. But this only refers, Ibn Qayyim hastens to observe, to 'that type of *ra'y* and *qiyās* which the generality of *ʿulamā'* have discouraged because they diverge from the Qur'ān and Sunnah'. As for the type of *ra'y* whose conformity to, or divergence from the latter are not known, it may be adopted as the basis for action only when necessary, but carries no binding authority on anyone.[80]

I conclude this chapter by informing the reader that under the heading '*Bidʿah* and False Doctrine Under Malaysian Law' I have surveyed provisions of the state enactments of Selangor, Perak, Terengganu, and Kedah on the teaching and propagation of 'false doctrine'. This information appears under Appendix II at the end of this volume.

II: Special Subjects

There is evidence in the sources which restricts freedom of speech with reference to particular subjects. Three of these which have been singled out in the *Ḥadīth* literature, are the Self or Essence of God, free-will and predestination, and acrimonious contention (*mirā'*, or *mumārāt*, also referred to as *jadal*). In this category of subjects, I have also discussed dissimulation (*taqiyyah*) as the Sunnī *ʿulamā'* have discouraged 'freedom of speech' on this matter except on grounds of necessity.

Historical evidence suggests that the first two of these themes became the focus of controversy among theological sects and factions during the period of the Companions and the Umayyads, and have remained so ever since. The Khārijites were probably the first of the sectarian movements whose ideas and doctrines marked a departure from the mainstream of the theological thought and belief-structure of Islam. Then there were a number of other movements such as the Muʿtazilah, the Jahmiyyah, the Qadariyyah and others who became immersed in controversy and eventually lost their ground. One of the reasons given for their failure was their indulgence in aggressive polemics in debating subjects on which the Sunnah of the Prophet ﷺ has advised restraint.[81]

1. THE ESSENCE OF GOD *(DHĀT ALLĀH)*

God has made Himself known to mankind by His Most Beautiful Names, *al-Asmā' al-Ḥusnā*, which are all revealed in the Qur'ān, and it is through these that the believer must seek knowledge of God, His attributes and His creation. Because of the exclusive validity and all-pervasive character of the Most Beautiful Names of God, the believer is forbidden from coining new names and attributes for God. The reason for this prohibition is that the believers have no direct knowledge of God beyond what was revealed through the Qur'ān. There are ninety-nine Exalted Names of God, all of which are attributes that describe His being. The Names also manifest qualities that mankind needs to strive to conform to, and even mirror in some sense. To negate or reject any of these attributes not only destroys the foundation of belief but also amounts to a renunciation of the ideals of Islamic spiritual and cultural values. The Exalted Names of God are not listed in any particular section of the Qur'ān, but appear in different places throughout the Holy Book.[82] With regard to these Names, the Qur'ān instructs the believers as follows:

> To God belong the Most Beautiful Names, so call upon Him with them and leave those who profane His Names. (VII:180)

وَلِلَّهِ الْأَسْمَآءُ الْحُسْنَىٰ فَادْعُوهُ بِهَا وَذَرُوا الَّذِينَ يُلْحِدُونَ فِي أَسْمَآئِهِ.

> Say: Call upon Allāh or call upon al-Raḥmān, by whichever Name you call, to Him belong the Most Beautiful Names. (XVII:110)

قُلِ ادْعُوا اللَّهَ أَوِ ادْعُوا الرَّحْمَٰنَ أَيًّا مَّا تَدْعُوا فَلَهُ الْأَسْمَآءُ الْحُسْنَىٰ.

Having given the attributes of God, the Qur'ān then discourages any attempt at personifying God or drawing any resemblance concerning Him that would reduce Him to, or define Him in any particular form: 'Sight cannot perceive Him but He encompasses sight and He is the Subtle, the Aware (*al-Laṭīf al-Khabīr*).' (VI:103)

لَا تُدْرِكُهُ الْأَبْصَارُ وَهُوَ يُدْرِكُ الْأَبْصَارَ وَهُوَ اللَّطِيفُ الْخَبِيرُ.

The last two words in this text are two of the Exalted Names of God. As this text shows, it is not granted to anyone, not even the Prophet Muḥammad ﷺ, to actually see God. However, an attempt was made by the Prophet Moses ﷺ, as the Qur'ān tells us, when he requested an actual encounter with God Most High. Moses ﷺ was told, 'You shall not see Me, but look at the mountain; if you find the mountain stable in its place, then you shall see Me ... '

لَنْ تَرَانِي وَلَكِنِ انْظُرْ إِلَى الْجَبَلِ فَإِنِ اسْتَقَرَّ مَكَانَهُ فَسَوْفَ تَرَانِي...

The story goes on to say that God showed Himself upon the mountain, and [by looking in that direction] Moses ﷺ lost consciousness. When he recovered, He praised God and repented and testified to his faith in Him (VII:143).

Thus, the Qur'ānic evidence draws attention to the transcendence of God - He is utterly beyond the human, and cannot be defined by man. Any attempt to do so is bound to involve speculation; therefore, the *Sharīʿah* discourages expatiation on the subject of the Essence of God in order to prevent errors in the conception of His Absolute Being.

The Most Beautiful Names of God are to be taken for what they are, and they may only be attributed to Him according to their revealed literal meanings. Consequently, the few anthropomorphisms that occur in the Qur'ān (the Eyes of God as in XI:37; His Face as in LV:27, and so forth) have become the object of controversy in scholastic theology. The central point in the debates advanced by the Ashʿariyyah, the Muʿtazilah and the Māturīdīyyah is the question of the reality of the attributes and their relationship to the Essence of God.[83]

One of the controversial sects that invoked strong condemnation from the *ʿulamā'* was the Jahmiyyah, supposedly an offshoot of the Muʿtazilah, which is named after its leading figure, Jahm b. Ṣafwān. Originally from Khurāsān, Jahm resided in Kūfa and served as chief scribe (*kātib*) to the Umayyad governor, al-Ḥārith b. Shurayḥ - both of whom were eventually executed for rebellion in 128 A.H. Jahm acquired fame for his controversial views concerning the Essence of God. He denied that God had any attributes (*ṣifāt*) and maintained that those which are mentioned in the Qur'ān are not to be understood according to their literal meanings, as they are all allegorical (*mu'awwal*). Jahm held that if the literal were to be upheld, it would amount to anthropomorphism, that is, making God resemble His creatures, hence, it is necessary to discover the allegorical meanings of the attributes. As a corollary to this line of thought, Jahm further observed that the Qur'ān was created like the rest of God's creation. Since God does not speak, in the ordinary sense of the word, the Qur'ān is not His speech in the ordinary sense of the word. We merely call it so as a figure of speech, that is, by way of allegorical explanation (*ta'wīl*).[84]

Across the centuries, the *ʿulamā'* have denounced and refuted these views in the strongest terms and have maintained that the Qur'ānic attributes of God must be understood literally, and that any remote or allegorical interpretation of them must be avoided. Thus, according to al-Ghazālī, the right course to follow is to refrain entirely from changing the literal meaning and to be wary of introducing any interpretation which was not sanctioned by the Companions. Al-Ghazālī maintains the same view with regard to all the ambiguous or mysterious expressions that are found in the Qur'ān (i.e. the *mutashābihāt*).[85]

There is a clear instruction in the Sunnah regarding the approach that the believers must take on this issue. Thus, according to a *Ḥadīth*, the believers are asked to 'ponder upon the creation of God, but not on God. For you will never be able to do Him justice.'[86]

تَفَكَّرُوا فِي خَلْقِ اللهِ وَلَا تَتَفَكَّرُوا فِي اللهِ فَإِنَّكُمْ لَنْ تَقْدِرُوا قَدْرَه.

The restriction is obviously based on the premise that the human mind is not endowed with the capacity to define its Creator, although it may explore and explain His attributes in relation to those aspects of His creation which are known or can be known by it. In this way, our knowledge of God is directly related, as the

Qur'ān indicates, to our knowledge of His creation. The Qur'ān, on numerous occasions (II:219; VII:117, etc.), invites attention to the signs in the creation of God which testify to His omniscience and omnipresence. We are, thus, encouraged to investigate the world around us, to acquire knowledge of the mysteries of creation, and through it also to increase our understanding of the attributes and Exalted Names of God.

Since human knowledge of the universe is incomplete, knowledge of the Creator of the universe must also be an on-going process, and one which is unlikely to attain perfection. Attempting to 'investigate' the Essence of God is, as ʿAbduh points out, an idle and dangerous exercise (*ʿabath wa muhlikah*) which seeks to fathom the unfathomable, something beyond human capacity. It is dangerous as it leads to error in belief. To attempt to specify the Essence of God is to try to limit the limitless, which is, in turn, tantamount to an attempt at reducing God Most High.[87]

2. FREE-WILL AND PREDESTINATION *(AL-QAḌĀ' WA'L-QADAR)*[88]

The question as to whether people are free agents who cause and determine their own acts, and the consequences that these acts generate, or whether all this is predetermined in accordance with the foreknowledge and will of God, is clearly related to the understanding of God and His attributes. God has, as the Qur'ān proclaims, 'created every thing and measured it in due proportions' (XXV:2); thus every single incident and phenomenon which takes place anywhere in the universe is known to God:

> No leaf falls but He knows it; nor (is there any) seed in the darknesses of the earth, nor tender plant, nor dry one, but is in a clear Book. (VI:59)

- وَخَلَقَ كُلَّ شَيْءٍ فَقَدَّرَهُ تَقْدِيرًا.

- مَا تَسْقُطُ مِن وَرَقَةٍ إِلَّا يَعْلَمُهَا وَلَا حَبَّةٍ فِي ظُلُمَٰتِ الْأَرْضِ وَلَا رَطْبٍ وَلَا يَابِسٍ إِلَّا فِي كِتَٰبٍ مُّبِينٍ.

It is suggested that this measurement (*taqdīr*) - mentioned in the first of the two citations above - means that God specified the nature of all things, and determined their place in, and relationship to the other parts of His creation. In consequence, this is the order of His creation, for God has subjugated all things to the laws of causality and purpose, and nothing in His creation is a complete void or accident.[89]

The subject of the Divine attributes and the interaction between the human will and the Divine will and knowledge has aroused speculation and controversy in the various theological schools: the Muᶜtazilah maintained a rationalist stance in favour of free-will, the Ashᶜariyyah advocated predestination; while the Māturīdīyyah attempted a compromise between the two positions.[90]

3. ACRIMONIOUS CONTENTION, DISPUTATION AND ARGUMENTATION *(MIRĀ', JADAL* AND *KHUṢŪMAH)*

The word *mirā'*, or *mumārāt*, sometimes used synonymously with the word for disputation, *jadal*, means an indulgence in soul-destroying arguments which serve no worthy purpose and mar the climate of fraternity and peace. *Mirā'* often consists in objecting to the speech of another person in order to show its defects either explicitly or by implication. The motive is usually self-commendation and the attribution of ignorance to others. The hallmark of *mirā'* is that it humiliates its victim, and leads to embitterment and hostility.[91]

Jadal, too, consists of raising objections to the speech of another in an attempt to expose its defects, be it in regard to the words uttered, or their purport, or the intention of the speaker. *Jadal* and *mirā'* are interchangeable in this sense, and yet, the latter may differ from the former in that the purpose of *mirā'* is to humiliate another person by exposing his ignorance and establishing one's own superiority over him; whereas *jadal*, depending on the intention behind it, may have a positive aspect, and could apply to argumentation which seeks to explore differences of opinion for a legitimate purpose.[92] If the underlying intention is good, it would be *jadal* in its positive sense, otherwise it would be the reprehensible form of *jadal*, which resembles *mirā'*.

As for argumentation (*khuṣūmah*), it may be said to consist of disputation and of raising, rightly or wrongly, objections to the speech of another in pursuit of material gain. *Khuṣūmah* may be in response to someone else's speech, or it may itself be the initiation of an argument, whereas *mirā'* normally consists only of an objection to the speech of another person. The hallmark of *khuṣūmah* is excessive indulgence in speech in order to vanquish the opponent and attain one's own purpose. It may occur in any of the following three varieties:

1) *Khuṣūmah* without intent of malice or harm in order to establish a right which is denied by the opponent. This type of *khuṣūmah* is permissible as the *Sharīʿah* entitles the individual to defend his right in all peaceful ways.

2) *Khuṣūmah* accompanied by a violation of the right of another and comprising discourteous and hostile speech. This form of argumentation is undoubtedly reprehensible and must be avoided. The enormity of such *khuṣūmah* is accentuated in the *Ḥadīth* which proclaims, 'The most disliked of men before God Most High is one who is most stubborn in *khuṣūmah*.'[93]

أَبْغَضُ الرِّجَالِ الى الله تعالى اَلْاَلَدُّ الخَصِمْ.

This *Ḥadīth* primarily applies to those who engage in disputes either in pursuit of falsehood, or over matters of which they have little knowledge. For example, the disputant may be a lawyer who has not studied a case, or has studied it and knows his side is in the wrong but still chooses to fight for it. Also included in this category are people who deliberately defend false views and beliefs in order to influence the feeble-minded.

An individual who disputes on behalf of a good cause, and yet exceeds the limits of propriety by engaging in abusive language, is also blameworthy, although to a lesser degree than the one who argues in pursuit of falsehood.[94]

3) *Khuṣūmah* not in violation of another person's rights, but merely for the sake of arguing even when the objective could be attained without engaging in *khuṣūmah*. This is once again reprehensible conduct, although to a lesser degree than the second variety, quoted above. According to a *Ḥadīth*, reported by Jābir b. ʿAbd Allāh al-Anṣārī (d. 78/697), the Prophet ﷺ said, 'May the mercy of God be on one who is kind and forbearing when he sells, kind and forbearing when he buys, and kind and forbearing when he makes a demand.'[95]

رَحِمَ اللهُ عَبْدًا سَمْحًا اِذَا بَاعَ، سَمْحًا اِذَا اِشْتَرَى، سَمْحًا اِذَا اِقْتَضَى.

Mirā' is the most reprehensible of all three varieties of abusive speech under discussion. It is often referred to as the opposite of *ḥusn al-khulq* - good and pleasant character. The leading *ʿulamā'* have cautioned against *mirā'* so much so that they have even discouraged the asking of questions which might mar the atmosphere of fraternity and good relations.[96] This attitude of the *ʿulamā'* to *mirā'* reflects the overall message of the Sunnah which accentuates the moral enormity of *mirā'* to such an extent that it is held to interfere with the integrity of the faith of the believing perpetrator. Thus, according to one *Ḥadīth*:

> Perfection in faith *(al-īmān)* cannot be accomplished unless the believer abandons distortion in the jokes he makes, and abandons acrimonious contention *(al-mirā')*, even if what he is saying is true.[97]

لاَيُؤمِنُ العَبدُ الايمانَ كُلَّه حَتَّى يَتْرُكَ الكِذْبَ فى الْمَزَاح وَيتْرُكَ المِراءَ وَلَوْ كانَ صَادِقًا.

The relevance of *mirā'* to personal piety is seen in the following *Ḥadīth* which promises distinction and a great reward for those who avoid it.

> A dwelling shall be built in the highest [echelons] of Paradise for him who refrains from *mirā'* even though he be in the right; and for him who is in the wrong but refrains from *mirā'*, a dwelling shall be built in the outer realms of Paradise.[98]

مَن تَرَكَ المِراءَ وَهوَ مُحِقٌّ بُنِىَ لَه البَيت فِى أَعْلَى الجَنَّةِ وَمَن تَرَكَ المِراءَ وَهُوَ مُبْطِلٌ بُنِىَ لَهُ البَيت فى ربض الجنة.

In both of these *Ḥadīths*, the message is clear: telling the truth should not justify engaging in acrimonious arguments; *mirā'* is to be avoided at all times. The proper manner of engaging in argumentation, as specified in the Qur'ān and the Sunnah, is with courtesy and tact - when dealing with Muslims and non-Muslims alike. *Mirā'* is in direct opposition to this behaviour, and, according to al-Ghazālī, it is obligatory (*wājib*) upon every Muslim to avoid *mirā'* if he knows that he is in the wrong.[99] This statement is backed up by a *Ḥadīth*, which ʿAlī b. Abī Ṭālib has reported from the Prophet ﷺ:

> He who knowingly argues for what is wrong remains under God's wrath for as long as he argues ... .[100]

مَنْ خَاصَمَ فِى بَاطِلٍ وَهُوَ يَعْلَمُ لَمْ يَزَلْ فِى سَخَطِ اللهِ حَتَّى يَنزِعَ.

This *Ḥadīth*, as one observer comments, clearly forbids a person from engaging in deliberate distortion, and from undermining the validity of a correct opinion with an opinion that is known to be erroneous.[101]

Al-Ghazālī also quotes another *Ḥadīth* in which the following was reported:

> The Messenger of God ﷺ came out to us while we were arguing (*natamārā*). He became angry and said: 'Abandon *mirā'* since there is little good in it; abandon *mirā'* for it is of little benefit and causes hostility among brothers.'[102]

عَنْ أبى أُمامه البَاهِلى قال: خَرَجَ عَلَيْنَا رسول الله ﷺ ونحن نَتَمَارَى فغضب فقال: ذَرُو المِرَاءَ لِقلّةِ خيره، ذروا المراءَ فَإنّ نَفْعَهُ قَلِيلٌ وَإنَّهُ يُهَيِّجُ العَدَاوَةَ بين الاخوَانِ.

Thus, it appears from the preceding *Ḥadīths* that *mirā'* is a defect of morality and faith, and that it is a subject which cannot properly be addressed and regulated by legislation. Perhaps this is why the *Sharīʿah* has no punitive provisions for *mirā'* other than giving moral advice and exhortation. But when this proves ineffective, then the social boycott (*hajr*) is recommended. The following *Ḥadīth* is instructive as to the enormity of *mirā'*, and how it compares with other offensive behaviour, such as ridiculing others, and breach of promises. Of these three, the *Ḥadīth* refers to *mirā'* first: 'Do not contend (*lā tumār*) with your brother, nor ridicule him, nor make him a promise which you do not honour.'[103]

لاَ تُمارِ أخاكَ وَلاَ تُمازِحْهُ وَلاَ تَعِدْهُ مَوْعِدًا فَتُخْلِفَهُ.

Imām Aḥmad Ibn Ḥanbal is reported to have said that it is characteristic of the followers of the Sunnah (*ahl al-Sunnah*) to avoid acrimonious contention. The following conversation took place between him and the interlocuter, one ʿAbbās b. Ghālib al-Warrāq: 'I asked Aḥmad b. Ḥanbal whether I should repudiate any *bidʿah* I might hear if I were at a meeting where the participants were ignorant of the Sunnah and I was the only one (present) who knew it.' The Imām advised him not to engage in such an exchange: 'Say what you know of the Sunnah and avoid any hostile exchange (*mukhāṣamah*). If you refute his speech you would be engaging in *mukhāṣamah*. If he does not accept it from you, then you should remain silent.' ʿAbbās also relates that in this conversation Imām Mālik is reported to have given the same advice.[104]

On a similar note, al-Awzāʿī made the following statement: 'When God Most High intends to inflict calamity upon a people, He opens the door of disputation (*jidāl*) to them and closes the door of action (*ʿamal*) upon them. Imām Mālik has said that *mukhāṣamah* is not a part of religion. Imām Shāfiʿī has likewise said that *mirā'*, even in pursuit of knowledge, blackens the heart and sows the seeds of hatred.'[105]

4. DISSIMULATION *(TAQIYYAH)*

Literally, *taqiyyah* means guarding or protecting a person and refers to measures that may be taken to protect the individual against harm on account of holding a particular belief or opinion which is opposed to the views of the majority. *Taqiyyah*, as such, is validated by Shīʿī law and it is generally treated as an integral part of Shīʿī theological doctrine.[106] Thus, Shīʿī Islam allows its followers to conceal their true beliefs, opinions and criticisms if this proves to be expedient and safe. Therefore, a person who is permitted to hide his true beliefs in order to protect himself against hostility should, by the same token, be able to make statements which are contrary to his true conviction either to mislead others, or to please them by approving in his words that which he believes to be untrue.

The Sunnī *ʿulamā'* have, in principle, proscribed *taqiyyah*, but this basic prohibition may be set aside in the event of dire necessity, that is, when recourse to *taqiyyah* would repel an imminent danger to a person's life, honour or property, or to ensure the prevention of grave bodily harm. However, in the absence of such fears, recourse to *taqiyyah* is prohibited.[107]

The following three Qur'ān verses are quoted in support of this doctrine:

> Let not the believers take unbelievers rather than believers for friends - whosoever does that is not of God in anything - except if you are guarding yourselves against them, for protection. And God cautions you (of) Himself, and with Him is the final end. (III:28)

لَا يَتَّخِذِ الْمُؤْمِنُونَ الْكٰفِرِينَ أَوْلِيَآءَ مِن دُونِ الْمُؤْمِنِينَ
وَمَن يَفْعَلْ ذٰلِكَ فَلَيْسَ مِنَ اللهِ فِي شَيْءٍ إِلَّا أَن تَتَّقُوا
مِنْهُمْ تُقٰةً وَيُحَذِّرُكُمُ اللهُ نَفْسَهُ وَإِلَى اللهِ الْمَصِيرُ.

The second verse begins by denouncing those who utter words of disbelief but makes an exception for those who do so under duress:

> Whosoever disbelieves in God after believing in Him, excepting he who is compelled while his heart remains steadfast in the faith, but he who opens his breast to disbelief - on such is the wrath of God, and for them is a grievous chastisement. (XVI:106)

مَن كَفَرَ بِاللهِ مِن بَعْدِ إِيمَانِهِ إِلَّا مَنْ أُكْرِهَ وَقَلْبُهُ مُطْمَئِنٌّ
بِالْإِيمَانِ وَلٰكِن مَّن شَرَحَ بِالْكُفْرِ صَدْرًا فَعَلَيْهِمْ غَضَبٌ
مِّنَ اللهِ وَلَهُمْ عَذَابٌ عَظِيمٌ.

The third verse begins by recounting the story that when Pharaoh, Haman and Kora ordered Moses's followers to be killed, a man who was a believer but kept his faith concealed, questioned the wisdom of the proposed killing:

> And a believing man of Pharaoh's people, who hid his faith, said: Will you slay a man because he says 'My Lord is God', and indeed he has brought you clear evidence from your Lord … . (XL:28)

وَقَالَ رَجُلٌ مُّؤْمِنٌ مِّنْ آلِ فِرْعَوْنَ يَكْتُمُ إِيمَانَهُ أَتَقْتُلُونَ
رَجُلًا أَن يَقُولَ رَبِّيَ اللَّهُ وَقَدْ جَاءَكُم بِالْبَيِّنَاتِ مِن رَّبِّكُمْ...

Thus, a man who himself pretended to lack faith, or dissimulated, spoke in defence of a believer who was exposed to imminent danger. Furthermore, it is reported that the sixth Imām of Shīʿism, Jaʿfar al-Ṣādiq, affirmed *taqiyyah* as a necessary component of the faith, and an integral part of religion by saying: 'He who has no *taqiyyah* has no religion. *Taqiyyah* is [a mark of] my religion and that of my forefathers.'[108]

The Ḥanafī jurist, al-Sarakhsī, defines *taqiyyah* as dissimulation by a person when he says something which is contrary to his inner belief in order to protect himself against danger.[109] The Sunnī *ʿulamā'* refer to the same Qur'ānic passages as are quoted by their Shīʿī counterparts in support of the basic notion of *taqiyyah*, but they differ widely in their interpretations of the textual evidence. The fundamental difference between them is that *taqiyyah* has no part as such in the Sunnī theological belief-system; it is a totally subsidiary matter in Sunnī Islam, and is virtually forbidden. In addition, *taqiyyah* may be practised only in cases of necessity, but not for purposes of expediency and opportunism. In Shīʿī Islam, on the other hand, *taqiyyah* is a requirement and, as such, it occupies a far more prominent place. Shīʿī beliefs in fact encourage *taqiyyah* generally and do not confine its application to any particular situation, whereas the Sunnī *ʿulamā'* have attempted to minimise recourse to *taqiyyah*. This can be seen from the following four conditions that the latter have laid down in order to validate recourse to *taqiyyah*: Firstly, there must be such fear of danger as would necessitate recourse to *taqiyyah*. The absence of this condition would consequently make *taqiyyah* unlawful. Thus, if a person speaks an untruth merely to please others, or if he expresses support for the oppressive acts of a tyrant while he could have avoided the danger in question simply through silence, he would have committed a transgression. Secondly, a person who resorts to *taqiyyah* and utters, for example, words of disbelief, may do so only in the knowledge that dissimulation would actually save him from danger. Thirdly, if there is no other escape from danger except by recourse to *taqiyyah*. Fourthly, that the danger so feared involves intolerable harm, whether to the person himself or to someone else, or to the honour or properties of the parties involved. Thus, small hardships such as slight hunger, detention or beating would not justify recourse to *taqiyyah*.[110]

The critics of *taqiyyah* have held that it conflicts with the principles of *ḥisbah* and *naṣīḥah*, and, most of all, with the commitment of all believers to the values of truth and justice which are integral to Islam. A Shīʿī writer, Hamid Enayat, tends to concede the substance of this critique and even goes on to state that *taqiyyah* is also in conflict with the true character of Shīʿī Islam. Thus, in Enayat's phrase 'If Shiʿism is to retrieve its pristine character as a creed of militancy, then it must go on the offensive in all areas of social and political life and this makes *amr bi'l-maʿrūf*, commanding good, the strongest sanction of its campaign for the total regeneration of the community.'[111]

The Sunnīs have elaborated the *Sharīʿah* doctrine of *ḥisbah* as having, to some extent, accommodated the basic notion of *taqiyyah*. The evidence for this comes from the *Ḥadīth* already cited which specifies three levels of response that a Muslim may give to an evil which he or she witnesses: To change it by one's act, or by one's words or through silent denunciation - this last response being referred to as the weakest form of faith. The *Ḥadīth*, which I have just paraphrased, leaves no doubt that taking positive steps, physical or verbal, in the fulfilment of *ḥisbah* merits a greater reward than mere silence. In other words, it permits a limited form of *taqiyyah* by validating silent disapproval within the scope of *ḥisbah*, but it is obviously not recommended. The Sunnī *ʿulamā'*, who have spoken at length about *taqiyyah*, have concluded that if everyone, especially the learned members of the community, adopted silence in the face of transgressions and distortions of religion, then heresy and corruption would proliferate, and the truth would be defaced in the eyes of the people. On the same theme, Imām Aḥmad b. Ḥanbal has been quoted as having said that it is not permissible for one who is learned (*ʿālim*) to speak for, or condone, falsehood in his words while he knows that the *Sharīʿah* grants him no such concession by way of *taqiyyah*. He continues: When learned persons indulge in dissimulation of this kind, the ignorant will not find guidance in their words, as they would be likely to confuse the truth with statements that are made in *taqiyyah*.[112]

It is interesting to note, however, the role that *taqiyyah* might have played in endorsing the Shīʿī creed of militancy toward an unjust government. It has been argued that, in the interests of political stability, scholars like al-Ghazālī and others demanded obedience to an unjust government which was in possession of military force. On the other hand, the Shīʿī jurists, by recourse to *taqiyyah*, were able to co-operate, for specific purposes, with those in power, while refusing to accept in principle any responsibility for the existence of an unjust government. The result of both the Sunnī and Shīʿī practices was political quietism, but while the Sunnī *ʿulamā'* openly attempted to validate the exercise of power in the interests of stability, the Shīʿī *ʿulamā'* refused to take part in validating an unjust government, and were able to maintain that attitude by recourse to *taqiyyah*.[113]

NOTES

1. Muslim, *Mukhtaṣar Ṣaḥīḥ Muslim*, Kitāb al-birr wa'l-ṣilah, Bāb al-nahy ʿan al-ghībah, *Ḥadīth* no. 1806; al-Nawawī, *Riyāḍ al-Ṣāliḥīn*. The *Ḥadīth* is self-evident on the difference between *ghībah* and *buhtān*, ie defamation and slander.
2. Al-Ghazālī, *Kitāb Ādāb al-Ṣuḥbah*, p. 129.
3. Al-Nawawī, *Riyāḍ al-Ṣāliḥīn*, pp. 489-90.
4. Al-Ḥusayn, Khiḍr, *al-Ḥurriyyah fi'l-Islām*, p. 55.
5. Al-Maqdisī, *al-Ādāb al-Sharʿiyyah*, I, p. 7 & pp. 276-77; Tuffāḥah, *Maṣādir*, pp. 109-113; al-Ḥusayn, Khiḍr, *al-Ḥurriyyah*, p. 55.
6. Al-Maqdisī, ibid.
7. Ibn Ḥanbal, *Fihris Aḥādīth*, I, 440; al-Ghazālī, *Kitāb Ādāb al-Ṣuḥbah*, p. 128.
8. Al-Maqdisī, *al-Ādāb*, I, 13,14 & 23.
9. For detail see Tuffāḥah, *Maṣādir*, p. 123.
10. Al-Ghazālī, *Kitāb Ādāb*, p. 129.
11. Al-Ghazālī, ibid.
12. Al-Ghazālī, ibid., pp. 128-131.
13. See e.g. *Ṣaḥīḥ Muslim* which has a chapter devoted to the subject entitled 'Chapter on the Prohibition of Unnecessary Excessive Questioning' under Kitāb al-

Aqḍiyah.

14. Al-Nawawī, *Riyāḍ al-Ṣāliḥīn*, p. 135, *Ḥadīth* no. 245; al-Ghazālī, *Kitāb Ādāb*, p. 344. Muslim and Abū Dāwūd also record a similar *Ḥadīth*, albeit with minor differences of wording. 'God will conceal, both in this world and the Hereafter, the fault of he who conceals (the fault of a Muslim).'

15. Al-Nawawī, *Riyāḍ al-Ṣāliḥīn*, p. 488, *Ḥadīth* no. 1530.

16. Al-Tirmidhī, *Sunan*. Translation quoted from Muhammad Asad, *Principles of State and Government in Islam*, p. 85.

17. Al-Ghazālī, *Iḥyā' ʿUlūm al-Dīn*, 2nd edn., Cairo: Dār al-Fikr, 1400/1980 VI, 26; Idem., *Kitāb Ādāb al-Ṣuḥbah*, p. 369.

18. Ibid., VI, 15-16. See also al-Ghazālī, *Kitāb Ādāb*, p. 345-46.

19. Al-Maqdisī, *al-Ādāb*, I, 266.

20. *Ṣaḥīḥ Muslim*, Kitāb al-birr wa'l-ṣilah, Bāb al-nahy ʿan al-tajassus.

21. Al-Maqdisī, *al-Ādāb*, I, 340.

22. Al-Tabrīzī, *Mishkāt*, Vol. III, *Ḥadīth* no. 5052.

23. Tuffāḥah, *Maṣādir*, pp. 89-90.

24. Al-Maqdisī, *al-Ādāb* I, 341.

25. Al-Ghazālī, *Kitāb Ādāb*, pp. 242-43.

26. Muslim, *Mukhtaṣar Ṣaḥīḥ Muslim*, *Ḥadīth* no. 844; al-Maqdisī, *al-Ādāb*, I, 41.

27. Al-Tabrīzī, *Mishkāt*, Vol. III, Ḥadīth no. 4839.

28. ʿAbd Allāh ibn ʿAbbās (d. 68/686-8) is called 'The Sea' (*al-Baḥr*) on account of his great learning. He was one of the foremost scholars, if not the foremost, among the first generation of Muslims, particularly famous for his knowledge of Qur'ān interpretation. He belonged to the Hāshimite tribe of the Prophet ﷺ.

29. Al-Maqdisī, *al-Ādāb*, I, 43.

30. Ibid.

31. Al-Nawawī, *Riyāḍ al-Ṣāliḥīn*, p. 483.

32. Abdullah Yusuf Ali, *The Holy Qur'ān, Text, Translation and Commentary*, f.n. 2238.

33. Ibid., f.n. 4504.

34. Cf. Ghazawī, *al-Ḥurriyyah*, pp. 56-57.

35. Al-Nawawī, *Riyāḍ al-Ṣāliḥīn*, p. 483.

36. Cf. Nieuenhuijze, *The Lifestyles of Islam*, p. 155.

37. Al-Shāṭibī, *al-Iʿtiṣām*, I, 29. The Arabic definition of *bidʿah* reads as follows: *Al-bidʿah ṭarīqah fi'l-dīn mukhtaraʿah tuḍāhī al-sharīʿah yuqṣad bi'l-sulūk ʿalayhā mā yuqṣad bi'l-ṭarīqah al-sharʿiyyah.*

38. Ibid., I, 50.

39. Ibid., I, 54.

40. Ibid., I. 38.

41. Ibid., II, 54.

42. For the Khārijites, see page 114 note 139 of the previous section.

43. Al-Shāṭibī, *al-Iʿtiṣām*, I, 240-80.

44. There is some uncertainty as to whether 'Qadariyyah' is just another name for the Muʿtazilah. Evidence suggests that the Qadariyyah were the ancient Muʿtazilah before Wāsil ibn ʿAṭā' separated himself from the teachings of al-Ḥasan al-Baṣrī. Subsequently, the Muʿtazilah are said to have refused to be known as the Qadariyyah. For example, when Aḥmad ibn Ḥanbal wrote a book in refutation of the Qadariyyah and Jahmiyyah, referring to them both as al-Muʿtazilah, Bishr ibn al-Muʿtamir, a leading Muʿtazilite, protested, denying any association with either. (Cf. Aḥmad Amīn, *Fajr al-Islām*, pp. 287-8; Hughes, *Dictionary*, note 22 at p. 478; and Goldziher, *Introduction*, p. 82 ff, where the Muʿtazilah and the Qadariyyah are treated as two separate movements.) Nevertheless, it seems clear, as can be seen below, that on the subject of man's accountability for his conduct, the two maintained similar positions.

The Muʿtazilah were the earliest formal theological school in Islam, before Ashʿarism. The original two centres of Muʿtazilism were Baṣrah and Baghdād. The doctrines associated with the Muʿtazilah were ultimately absorbed into Shīʿism, once Ashʿarism took hold in the Sunni world. However, it would be too facile to say that Muʿtazilism is intrinsically incompatible with Sunnism, and one of the last great Muʿtazilite theologians, the Qāḍī ʿAbd al-Jabbār (d. 415/1025), was a Shāfiʿite Sunni judge. Muʿtazilism characteristically emphasises: negative theology (the Baghdādī position negating the divine attributes, the Baṣran position of Abū Hāshim al-Jubbāʿī viewing the divine attributes as modes (*aḥwāl*) of the Essence); the createdness of the Qur'ān; free-will; and finally, the absoluity of the Judgement - there is no intercession with God.

The Qadariyyah were proponents of free-will, a term used only by their opponents in this sense. In the early period, in Syria in particular, the Qadariyyah were associated with political activism - and this is understandable given the emphasis here on the idea that people are individually free to produce their own destiny. While the Qadariyyah are referred to in *Ḥadīth* as the 'Magians' of the Muslim community, there is strong evience that many profoundly orthodox voices of the early period viewed free-will as the correct interpretation of revealed statements on this subject. For example, the famous al-Ḥasan al-Baṣrī (d. 110/728) propounds this view in his *Risālah* to the ʿUmayyad caliph ʿAbd al-Mālik. The outstanding ʿUmayyad caliph, ʿUmar ibn ʿAbd al-ʿAzīz, affirms in a treatise preserved by Abū Nuʿaym, that this type of moderate Qadarite was orthodox, i.e. belonged to the 'people of the Sunnah'. However, two decades after al-Baṣrī's *Risālah*, an extremist Qadariyyah movement known as the Shahibiyyah emerged in ʿIrāq, asserting that the deeds of men are not even foreknown by God, and denying the revealed doctrine of God's guidance (*hudā*) and leading astray (*iḍlāl*) - i.e. with human acquiesence - a far cry from the moderate Qadarism of al-Baṣrī.

The Jahmiyyah were a nebulous grouping associated with the name of Jahm ibn Safwān (d. 128/746). The combination of views pigeon-holed as 'Jahmite' included, on the one hand, latitudinarianism, i.e. 'Murjiʿism', which comprises the view that the status of believer is attained by the merest verbal declaration, and on the other hand, an extreme form of determinism, i.e. 'Jabarism', such that humans were held to 'act' in a purely metaphorical sense, as we might describe the sun as 'acting' in setting. The result of such doctrines is a virtual antinomianism. For more information on Jahm's views see the section on 'The Essence of God' under 'Special Subjects' above. [Ed. note.]

45. Ibn Qayyim, *Iʿlām*, II, 230. The author discusses the sectarian views of the Jahmiyyah, Qadariyyah etc., and their interpretations of the Qur'ān in some detail at pp. 220-31.

46. For the Bāṭiniyyah, see page 113, note 110.

47. Al-Banʿalī, *Taḥdhīr al-Muslimīn ʿan al-Ibtidāʿ wa'l-Bidaʿ fi'l-Dīn*, pp. 38-8.

48. Ibid., p. 41.

49. Ibn Taymiyyah, *Iqtiḍā' al-Ṣirāṭ al-Mustaqīm li-Mukhālafat Aṣḥāb al-Jaḥīm*, I, 55.

50. Ibid., I, 56; Idem., *Majmūʿat al-Rasā'il wa'l-Masā'il*, X, 371.

51. Al-Ḥusayn, Khiḍr, *Rasā'il*, II, 169.

52. Ibid.

53. Ibid., II, 171.

54. Al-Shāṭibī, *al-Iʿtṣām*, II, p. 111 ff.

55. Al-Ghazālī, *Kitāb Ādāb*, pp. 201-4.

56. Al-Shāṭibī, *al-Muwāfaqāt*, IV, 104.

57. Ibid.

58. Al-Ghazālī, *al-Munqidh* (MacCarthy's trans.: *Freedom and Fulfilment*), p. 82.

59. Al-Miṣrī, *al-Kulliyyāt: Muʿjam fi'l-Muṣṭalaḥāt wa'l-Furūq al-Lughawiyyah*, V, 38.

60. Abū Ḥabīb, *Darāsah*, p. 454.

61. Al-Zamakhsharī, *al-Kashshāf ʿan Ḥaqā'iq al-Tanzīl*, III, 511.

62. Both *Ḥadīths* are quoted by Qurṭubī in his *Tafsīr al-Qurṭubī*, XVI, 167.

63. Zaydān, *Majmūʿah*, p. 298; al-Sibāʿī, Ishtirākiyyah, p. 54.

64. Al-Maqdisī, *al-Ādāb*, I, 183.

65. '*Ḥaqq Allāh*', 'the right of God', is generally used in reference to public or community rights, that is in contradistinction to '*al-ḥaqq al-ādamī*', 'the right of man', or private rights.

66. Al-Maqdisī, *al-Ādāb*, I, pp. 237, 269.

67. Ismāʿīl, *Manhaj al-Sunnah fi'l-ʿIlāqah bayn al-Ḥākim wa'l-Maḥkūm*, pp. 330-32.

68. Zaydān, *Majmūʿah*, p. 295.

69. While the Ḥanbalī definition of *baghy* includes disobedience to an unjust ruler, the Ḥanafīs define it as disobedience to a just or lawful imām only. See Ibn ʿĀbidīn, *Ḥāshiyat al-Radd al-Mukhtār ʿalā al-Durr al-Mukhtār* (known as *Ḥāshiyat Ibn ʿĀbidīn*), 2nd edition, Cairo: Maṭbaʿat al-Bābī al-Ḥalabī, 1386/1966, III, 426; Ismāʿīl, *Manhaj al-Sunnah*, p. 147.

70. Cf. Zaydān, *Majmūʿah*, pp. 277, 295.

71. Ibn Taymiyyah, *Iqtiḍā'*, p. 130.

72. Ibid., p. 123; al-Tabrīzī, *Mishkāt*, ed. Albanī, I, 677, *Ḥadīth* no. 2212.

73. Ibn Taymiyyah, *Iqtiḍā'*, pp. 124-5.

74. Ibid., pp. 130-1.

75. Ibid., p. 134.

76. Al-Banᶜalī, *Taḥdhīr*, p. 61.

77. Al-Shahristānī, *al-Milal wa'l-Niḥal*, p. 1045; Ismāᶜīl, Yaḥyā, *Manhaj al-Sunnah*, p. 106.

78. Ibn Taymiyyah, *Iqtiḍā'*, p. 127; Zaydān, *Majmūᶜah*, p. 299.

79. Ibn Qayyim, *Iᶜlām*, I, 57.

80. Ibid., I, 64.

81. For details on sectarian movements see Ibn Qayyim, *Iᶜlām*, I, 57 ff.; Aḥmad Amīn, *Fajr al-Islām*, pp. 252-307; Fazlur Rahman, *Islam*, pp. 167 ff. and Goldziher, *Introduction to Islamic Theology and Law*, pp. 167 ff. See also note 42 above and note 139 at page 114 above.

82. Shaltūt, *al-Islām*, p. 330; Sardar, *The Future of Muslim Civilization*, p. 28.

83. For further detail see Louis Gardet, 'God in Islam', *The Encyclopedia of Religion*, VI, 29 ff.

84. Cf. Aḥmad Amīn, *Fajr al-Islām*, p. 287. See also note 44.

85. Al-Ghazālī, *al-Munqidh*, p. 158.

86. Al-Suyūṭī, *al-Jāmiᶜ al-Ṣaghīr*, I, 227.

87. ᶜAbduh, *Risālat al-Tawḥīd*, p. 51.

88. *Al-Qaḍā' wa'l-Qadar*, literally means, 'The Divine Decree and Fate/ Destiny'. However, since it is the exact equivalent of the debate on free-will and predestination, we have preferred not to use the literal translation. [Ed. note.]

89. Cf. al-Maᶜhad al-ᶜĀlamī li'l-Fikr al-Islāmī, *Islāmiyyat al-Maᶜrifah*, p. 84.

90. Ashᶜarism is the mainstream theological perspective of Sunni Islam - in the specific sense that it was established as a self-conscious attempt to spell out the theological doctrines implicit in the Qur'ān and Sunnah. The school begins with the disaffection of its founder Abū'l-Ḥasan al-Ashᶜarī (d. 324/935) with the views of his Muᶜtazilite teacher, Abū ᶜAlī al-Jubbāᶜī in Baṣrah. Al-Ashᶜarī's conversion from Muᶜtazilism is dated to Ramaḍān, 300/912, and was heralded by admonitary dreams of the Prophet ﷺ. Al-Ashᶜarī gave revealed knowledge absolute primacy; this was decisively represented by a rejection of the Muᶜtazilite doctrine that the Qur'ān is created in favour of the doctrine that it is uncreated. Al-Ashᶜarī was furthermore opposed to any presumptious interpretation of the Qur'ān. Specifically, descriptions of God by God were to be accepted without reduction, 'without [asking] why' (*bilā kayf*). However, al-Ashᶜarī evaded the anthropomorphism (*tajsīm* = corporealism) that would result from an acceptance of only the literal meaning of the descriptions, by making these very descriptions subject to the '*via negativa*', thus carefully preserving the transcendence of God alongside the integrity of Qur'ānic descriptions. So, for example, God is seeing, but not as we are; He hears, but not as we do, etc. Ashᶜarism is strongly inclined towards determinism, ultimately denying any secondary causes (occasionalism); thus God pre-determines everything and all acts belong to God who is the sole agent, but

man is answerable for the acts that are perpetrated through him - the merit or demerit of which he acquires (*iktisāb*). To mitigate the awkward implication of injustice herein, Ashʿarism emphasises Prophetic intercession (*shafāʿah*). While the Muʿtazilites also referred their doctrines to revealed texts (*nuṣūṣ*), the Ashʿarite claim to being the normative perspective is somewhat born out by the contemporary emergence of an almost identical theology elsewhere in the Islamic world in the shape of Māturīdism. [Ed. note.]

91. Al-Ghazālī, *Kitāb Ādāb*, p. 129; Ḥammād, *Ḥurriyyah*, p. 124.
92. Fikrī, *al-Muʿāmalāt al-Māddiyyah wa'l-Adabiyyah*, p. 84.
93. Al-Tirmidhī, *Sunan, Ḥadīth* no. 2976.
94. Ibid., p. 90.
95. Al-ʿAsqalānī, *Jawāhir Ṣaḥīḥ al-Bukhārī, Ḥadīth* no. 275.
96. Al-Ghazālī, *Kitāb Ādāb*, p. 261.
97. Al-Maqdisī, *al-Ādāb*, I, 21.
98. Al-Tirmidhī, *Sunan, Ḥadīth* no. 1993; al-Ghazālī, *Kitāb Ādāb*, p. 258; idem., *Iḥyā'*, V, 179.
99. Al-Ghazālī, *Kitāb Ādāb*, p. 258.
100. Ibn Ḥanbal, *Fihris Aḥādīth Musnad*, II 70.
101. Ḥammād, *Ḥurriyyah*, p. 124.
102. Al-Ghazālī, *Kitāb Ādāb*, p. 259; Ibn Qudāmah, *al-Mughnī*, II, 16.
103. Al-Tabrīzī, *Mishkāt*, vol. III, *Ḥadīth* no. 4892.
104. Al-Maqdisī, *al-Ādāb*, I, 226, 323.
105. Ibid., I, 227.
106. Cf. Enayat, *Modern Islamic Political Thought*, p. 175.
107. *Al-Mawsūʿah al-Fiqhiyyah* (of Kuwait), V, 185.
108. Quoted in Enayat, *Political Thought*, p. 176.
109. Al-Sarakhsī, *al-Mabsūṭ*, XXIV, 48.
110. *Al-Mawsūʿah al-Fiqhiyyah* (of Kuwait) V, 191 ff.
111. Enayat, *Political Thought*, p. 179.
112. *Al-Mawsūʿah al-Fiqhiyyah* (of Kuwait) V, 199.
113. Cf. Lambton, *State and Government in Medieval Islam*, p. 263.

PART FOUR: LEGAL RESTRAINTS

I. Introductory Remarks

Freedom of expression is, broadly speaking, subject to the same general restrictions which apply to other rights and liberties. The most important of these is avoiding harm to others, therefore freedom of speech must not be hurtful to others nor encroach on their rights or dignity. Similarly, it falls beyond the scope of the valid exercise of this freedom for it to be used as a means to promote chaos, violence or social strife.[1] Furthermore, freedom of speech, like other liberties, is subservient to the 'essential interests' (*maṣāliḥ ḍarūriyyah*)[2] and values which are needed to maintain a stable socio-political order.[3] Therefore, the exercise of this freedom must not jeopardise the five essential values of life, faith, intellect, lineage and property. As a general rule, the underlying intention of an utterance, the purpose that motivates it, plays a significant role in determining its legality. Has the right of free speech been exercised in order to discover the truth? To attract some benefit? To fulfil a legitimate need; or to injure others? These are among the questions that frequently arise in judicial disputes over the abuse of this freedom. The question of the intention behind words rightly commands attention; however, there may be instances when the freedom of speech is violated but only the words uttered are of consequence, the question of intention being rendered insignificant - such as in the case of a person being abused or insulted.

Under the *Sharīᶜah*, violations of the freedom of speech occur either in the form of particular offences - such as slanderous accusation (*qadhf*), blasphemy, sedition (*fitnah*), insult (*sabb)* and cursing *(laᶜn*), attribution of lies or calumny (*iftirā')*, and the labelling of others as disbelievers (*takfīr*) - or they may take the form of a contempt for, or a denial of, the accepted norms and principles of Islam, which may fall under the general headings of infidelity or disbelief *(kufr)*, and heresy *(bidʿah)*. Some of these are criminal offences and carry specific penalties, whereas others are not so well defined and tend to evoke moral condemnation only. This chapter examines each of these violations in the light of the evidence found in the valid sources and the juristic formulations of the *fuqahā'*.

II. Public Utterance of Hurtful Speech

The title of this section is a direct translation of the Qur'ānic phrase '*al-jahr bi'l-sū' min al-qawl*', perhaps one of the most far-reaching of the Qur'ānic enactments which offer guidelines on the restrictions that may be imposed on freedom of speech. The passage where this phrase occurs is as follows:

> God loves not the public utterance of evil speech *(al-jahr bi'l-sū' min al-qawl)* except by one who has been wronged. God is ever Hearer and All-knowing. If you disclose good or keep it secret, or forgive evil, verily, God is forgiving, omnipotent. (IV:148–149)

لَايُحِبُّ اللهُ الْجَهْرَ بِالسُّوءِ مِنَ الْقَوْلِ اِلاَّ مَنْ ظُلِمَ
وَكَانَ اللهُ سَمِيعًا عَلِيمًا اِن تُبْدُوا خَيْرًا اَوْ تُخْفُوهُ اَوْ تَعْفُوا
عَنْ سُوءٍ فَاِنَّ اللهَ كَانَ عَفُوًّا قَدِيرًا.

Al-jahr literally means broadcasting or publicising, whereas *sū'* denotes something evil, or hurtful, hence 'the publicising of evil' - *al-jahr bi'l-sū'*. Words uttered in public which hurt another person by violating his honour or causing him physical harm or loss of property, whether directly or indirectly (such as by abusing his close relatives or homeland), are all covered by this verse. Hurtful speech, in this text, comprises that which is addressed to an individual, to more than one person, or to the community at large. Furthermore, the text is broad enough to comprehend all modern methods and facilities which are used for publicity and broadcasting.[4]

In their commentaries on this verse, the commentators (*mufassirūn*) indicate that the text here denounces the utterance of offensive speech absolutely, that is, regardless of the end it may serve or the context in which it may occur. The text does not, for instance, draw any distinction as to whether the speech so uttered consists of truth or falsehood, or whether it contemplates any kind of benefit. With only one exception, which is specified in the text itself, all varieties of hurtful speech made in public are proscribed. The only exception here is made for a person who has been wronged, and his cry for justice must be granted a hearing even at the expense of it being hurtful. Public utterance of evil speech may consist of speaking ill of others and finding faults in their character, or of attributing misdeeds to individuals and their families. It may also consist of self-indulgent speech concerning misdeeds committed by oneself, such as adultery, wine-drinking, gambling, or designs with these in mind. Also forbidden is the publication and display of obscene literature, and any other forms of misleading advertising which are all different manifestations of *al-jahr bi'l-sū'*. The only exception that the Qur'ān has granted aims at encouraging the quest for justice, which is given priority over the prevention of evil speech. However, even then *al-jahr bi'l-sū'* must be limited to only that which is deemed necessary in the circumstances.[5]

Public utterance of evil speech has, thus, been permitted only in order to fight oppression or *ẓulm*, consequently *al-jahr bi'l-sū'* is illegitimate in the absence of *ẓulm*. For a society in which evil speech is unchecked can expect the decline and ultimate destruction of its moral and cultural values.[6] As already indicated, the scope of the verse under discussion is also broad enough to include virtually all the specific violations of freedom of speech, including slander, insult, cursing, sedition, and so forth. The one exception which is made to the general meaning of the text indicates that the Qur'ān attaches a higher value to justice than to the prevention of evil speech. Yet, while granting the oppressed party recourse to unrestricted freedom of speech, the succeeding portion of the same verse urges everyone concerned, especially the victim of the abuse, to be forgiving and forbearing - privately or in public - in anticipation of God Most High's mercy and reward. Thus, while justice must be served and oppressed persons granted the opportunity to express their grievances, there may be instances, as the Qur'ān reminds us, when maintaining peaceful communal relations merits greater attention. To this end, it is forgiveness and tolerance that often take priority over a persistent demand for retributive justice. As indicated in the following text, the Qur'ān repeatedly stresses the value of forgiveness: '... and those who swallow their anger and forgive others' are elevated to the rank of the virtuous (*muḥsinīn*). And in yet another text we read '... and he who exercises patience and forgiveness - verily that is a matter to be resolved upon'. (III:134, XLII:43)

- الَّذِينَ يُنْفِقُونَ فِى السَّرَّآءِ وَالضَّرَّآءِ وَالْكَاظِمِينَ الْغَيْظَ وَالْعَافِينَ عَنِ النَّاسِ وَاللّٰهُ يُحِبُّ الْمُحْسِنِينَ.

- وَلَمَن صَبَرَ وَغَفَرَ اِنَّ ذٰلِكَ لَمِنْ عَزْمِ الْاُمُوْرِ.

As for people who persist in defaming others, who disseminate evil and expose the weaknesses of others, this Qur'ānic passage warns them of the bitter consequences of their conduct:

> Those who love to circulate scandal among [or about] the believers will have a grievous punishment in this life and (in) the Hereafter; God knows and you know not. (XXIV:19)

اِنَّ الَّذِينَ يُحِبُّونَ اَن تَشِيعَ الْفَاحِشَةُ فِى الَّذِينَ اٰمَنُوا لَهُمْ عَذَابٌ اَلِيمٌ فِى الدُّنْيَا وَالْاٰخِرَةِ وَاللّٰهُ يَعْلَمُ وَاَنْتُمْ لَا تَعْلَمُونَ.

The emphasis here is obviously not on forgiveness but on punishment, as the text refers only to *ʿadhāb*, punishment, followed by the sober expression: 'God knows and you know not.' Sternness is obviously recommended when there is no room for leniency and forgiveness.

The guidance that the Sunnah provides is not only to avoid the utterance of hurtful speech, but also to contribute positively to fraternity and peace in society. This is the purport of this *Ḥadīth*: 'A Muslim is one from whose tongue and hand other Muslims are safe.'[7]

المُسلِم مَن سَلِمَ المُسلِمُونَ مِن لِسَانِهِ وَيَدِهِ.

Although the text refers to Muslims, the message in it is, however, not confined to believers alone. As one observer notes, the *Ḥadīth* specifies Muslims, 'because it is with one's own community that one has largely to deal. But the aim is to lay down the foundation of a world-wide brotherhood in which everyone should feel safe.'[8] To maintain peace and order in society and to promote fraternity among Muslims is indeed the ultimate goal of the restrictions that the *Sharīʿah* imposes on freedom of expression.[9]

The *Sharīʿah*, however, does not propose any punishment for, nor even lay blame on, a person who tells the truth and speaks-up about things as they are. Hence, no punishment is envisaged for someone who calls an adulterer 'adulterer', provided that this statement is proved to be a fact. It is also permissible and justified under the principle of promoting good and preventing evil (*ḥisbah*) to point out the misdeeds and shortcomings of government employees, people's representatives in national assemblies, and anyone engaged in public service, provided that the charges so made can be established by evidence.

Furthermore, the *Sharīʿah* does not grant special privileges to individuals or groups in regard to statements made by them, nor does it recognise any special status for a member of parliament, or even for the head of state, in regard to what they say. The same unitarian approach to justice and truth that is so characteristic of Islam and its philosophy of *tawḥīd* is reflected in the organisation of the *Sharīʿah* law courts which, under normal rules, do not allow the setting up of specialised tribunals for civil servants or those who hold high offices of state. Everyone is answerable for their abuse of rights before the same courts, and the unitary standards of justice and propriety in speech and conduct apply to everyone alike.

III. Slanderous Accusation *(Qadhf)*

Indicative of the serious view that Islam takes when the honour and good name of a law-abiding individual is attacked, the Qur'ān prescribes a mandatory punishment for slanderous accusation, besides a handful of other offences - collectively known as the *ḥudūd*. Furthermore, even when the slanderer is duly tried and punished for the offence, he is liable to yet another supplementary punishment, which is to bar him permanently from being a witness in a court of law. For slander, once committed, tarnishes the good name of its victim, who may well have suffered irreparable damage to his reputation.[10]

Literally, *qadhf* means 'throwing' words of abuse at others. In this general sense, *qadhf* could comprise all forms of abusive words including slander, libel, insult, cursing etc.[11] However, the Qur'ānic offence of *qadhf* is a more specific concept which consists of either accusing another person of committing the act of adultery (*zinā'*), or denying the legitimacy of his or her child. In the former case, if the accuser can produce four witnesses to testify to the truth of his or her accusation, then the charge is proven and the accused becomes liable to the punishment of *zinā'*. If the accuser fails to provide evidence, then he becomes liable to the punishment of *qadhf*. All other types of allegation, such as accusing another person of bribery or other offences, are liable to the discretionary punishment of *taʿzīr*.[12]

The accuser may be a Muslim or non-Muslim, but the person accused of *qadhf* must be a *muḥṣan*, that is, a married Muslim of upright character who has not committed adultery (*zinā')* or apostasy (*riddah*) prior to the accusation. However, it is not necessary for the accused to be clear of all criminal acts. The prescribed penalty for *qadhf* is applied only if the victim (*maqdhūf*) demands it, and the accuser fails to prove the accusation. The slanderer is liable to the same punishment if the victim is a deceased person, in which case the heirs may demand that the accuser be punished. The offence of *qadhf* must in all cases be proven by the normal means of proof, including the testimony of two just witnesses, and confession.[13]

Qadhf may be divided into two types: one is *qadhf* proper, consisting of the accusation of adultery as discussed above, which carries the prescribed punishment of eighty lashes. The second type of *qadhf* may consist, as already mentioned, of any abusive speech such as insult, libel, or the accusation of criminal conduct. The victim thus need not be a *muḥṣan*, that is a married Muslim of upright character. The subject-matter of the accusation may be any criminal act, such as theft, homicide or fraud, or on the other hand it may consist simply of an insult (*sabb*), which is somewhat different from slanderous accusation proper. *Sabb* requires no proof of its veracity, as the mere utterance of insulting words is enough for the offence to have occurred, regardless of whether they are truthful or not. If, for example, one person calls another an ass, this is naturally not amenable to proof. *Qadhf* proper however, is open to affirmation or denial, as it is usually possible to prove a slander to be either true or false. An insult, however, is assumed to be untrue and the meaning it conveys cannot generally be proven by evidence.[14]

Sabb also differs from *qadhf* in that the latter does not take place without attributing a specific charge to another person, whereas *sabb* can be a general attribution which humiliates the person to whom it is addressed. When, for example, a person calls another a thief or a drunkard, these are specific charges which are also recognised offences under the law and are amenable to proof. However, a general attribution, such as calling another person 'immoral' is in the nature of an insult, but does not qualify as *qadhf* proper. In some events the distinction between the two may be unclear, in which case the court may have to determine the exact nature of the offence.[15] In its assessment, the court will refer to popular custom as this is the main indicator with regard to words and expressions which are not self-evident in meaning or connotation. Only in the case of the Qur'ānic offence of *qadhf*, which carries a prescribed penalty, is it necessary that the words uttered leave no doubt as to their meaning. If there are doubts, however insignificant, the prescribed punishment would not apply, but the judge may still sentence the offender to a lesser punishment under *taʿzīr*.[16]

The leading imāms of jurisprudence are in agreement that repeated slanderous accusations addressed to the same person, whether uttered on one or several occasions prior to sentencing, invoke only one punishment. In addition, the prescribed penalty of eighty lashes is equally applicable to cases where the slanderous accusation is addressed to more than one person. With regard to the latter scenario, however, there is a difference of opinion as to whether the offender should be punished for one or for several offences of *qadhf.* Abū Ḥanīfah, Mālik, Ibn Ḥanbal and al-Thawrī have held that the offender may be punished only once, whereas, according to al-Shāfiʿī, the slanderer is to be punished as many times as the number of individuals in the group slandered. According to a third opinion, if a group of people are all accused in a single instance, for example if they are addressed 'O adulterers', this would be punishable as a single offence, but if each member of the group is individually addressed, then a separate offence would have been committed in respect of each. This ruling is based on the analysis that the violation of a person's rights does not in principle admit of amalgamation (*tadākhul*); hence, every instance of *qadhf* addressed to different individuals is treated as a separate offence. *Qadhf*, in this respect, differs from other *ḥadd* offences which consist mainly of the violation of the right of God, and as such several instances of the violation carry only one punishment.[17]

There is some disagreement among legal schools as to whether the punishment of *qadhf* can be dropped if the accused forgives the offender. The Ḥanafīs are of the view that *qadhf*, like the other *ḥadd* offences, is a violation of the right of God, and that pardon by the victim may not obstruct enforcement of the prescribed punishment. On the other hand, the Shāfiʿīs and Ḥanbalīs have held that *qadhf* is a violation against the 'right of man' (*ḥaqq al-ʿabd*), therefore, the victim is entitled to grant a pardon, in which case no penalty would apply. The Mālikīs concur with this view but with the proviso that the victim may pardon the offender prior to the commencement of judicial proceedings. The Shāfiʿīs and Ḥanbalīs, on the other hand, allow the pardon to be granted either before or after the commencement of judicial proceedings, and this is considered to be the preferred view.[18]

It is not necessary for *qadhf* to be uttered in public, as it can be committed in both public places or in private dwellings; in the presence of other people or away from public sight. This ruling is founded on the analysis that dignity is an inherent attribute of a person which does not vary with changing circumstances.[19] Moreover, the Qur'ān invites believers to 'abandon (both) the visible sin and the secret one'. (VI:120)

وَذَرُوا ظَاهِرَ الإِثْمِ وَبَاطِنَهُ.

As already discussed, there is another Qur'ānic text which declares that 'God loves not the public utterance of hurtful speech except by one who has been wronged.' (IV:148) Although this verse suggests public utterance to be the criterion of assessing the offensive character of a particular pronouncement, the passage itself does not lay this down as a condition. The text may be said to be referring to the worse of the two ways in which *qadhf* is committed, but the circumstances in which it is pronounced does not necessarily change the substance of the speech in question. As a general rule, the prescribed punishments (*ḥudūd*) are enforced only when they are proven beyond doubt. Thus, only explicit instances of *qadhf*, namely, the unequivocal attribution of *zinā'* to an upright person, would evoke the penalty of eighty lashes. All other varieties of implicit slander would fail to qualify for this penalty but may still be punished by a lesser penalty under *taʿzīr*. Certain situations are not totally clear, such as if someone says to another: 'I have not committed adultery, nor have my parents. Can you say the same about yourself?' Statements of this kind, often referred to as *al-tarʿīḍ bi'l-qadhf* (attempted *qadhf*), are not free of doubt and are likely to fall within the purview of the *Ḥadīth* which provides 'Drop the *ḥudūd* in instances of doubt.'[20]

إدرأ والحُدُود بالشبهات.

Finally, the rules of the *Sharīʿah* pertaining to *qadhf* apply to men and women alike, despite the contrary impression one may obtain from the wording of the Qur'ānic text. There is, however, a gender bias in the nature of this offence, as the *ʿulamā'* have often pointed out, in that women tend to be the more likely victims of *qadhf*. For example, the Qur'ānic text in *Sūrat al-Nūr* (XXIV:4) begins with '*walladhīna yarmūn al-muḥṣanāt*', 'and those who accuse chaste women ...'. Here, the pronoun *walladhīna*, being in the masculine form, refers to men. Similarly, the word *al-muḥṣanāt* is in the feminine plural and therefore refers only to women. But, scholars across the legal schools have maintained the view that this Qur'ānic text is still applicable to men and women alike. Thus, it makes little difference, in so far as the application of this text is concerned, whether the offence is committed by a man or a woman, and whether the victim is male or female. Both sides may belong to the same gender, or may differ in any combination; none of this affects the general import of the text under discussion. Indeed, it is not unusual that the Qur'ān, as is also the case in other legal texts, uses masculine pronouns to include the feminine gender. The Qur'ān has referred to the perpetrators of *qadhf* in the masculine plural simply because this is the more common variant; it is not meant to preclude women from the ranks of potential perpetrators.[21]

IV. Libel *(Iftirā')*

Iftirā' means the attribution of lies to another person, maliciously accusing another person of criminal acts, or inventing something false about an individual. In its Qur'ānic usage, *iftirā'* is synonymous with lying (*kidhb*),[22] and in the juristic manuals of *fiqh*, *iftirā'* (also referred to as *firyah*) is treated as a sub-category of slanderous accusation, *qadhf*, and the rules that apply to *qadhf* are also applicable to *iftirā'*.

The maximum penalty for *iftirā'* is the same as that for *qadhf*, namely, eighty lashes. All other varieties of false accusation, whether of adultery or other offences, which do not amount to *qadhf* may amount to criminal libel and invoke a deterrent punishment of *taʿzīr*.[23] Ibn Taymiyyah explains:

> Slander normally consists of accusation that cannot be retaliated to in kind, hence, the rules of just retaliation *(qiṣāṣ)* cannot be invoked in regard to this offence. Accordingly, if someone accuses a chaste woman of adultery, and fails to prove the charge by the testimony of four witnesses, then the accuser is liable to a punishment of eighty lashes. Similarly, if a man accuses a chaste man of either adultery or sodomy, and fails to prove it, he is liable to the same punishment. However, if the slanderous accusation is other than these, then the accuser would be liable to lashes under *taʿzīr*, and furthermore, if the accused person chooses to forgive the accuser, no punishment will be imposed. For, according to the majority of jurists, in all cases of retaliation, as well as in the misappropriation of property, the personal rights of the defendant and the owner, respectively, take priority over the Right of God.[24]

The judge may also exercise discretion as to whether or not to grant a hearing to claims which seem unfounded or which comprise the abuse of a right (*sū' istiʿmāl al-ḥaqq*). Admittedly, every individual has the right to seek judicial relief, and initiate a lawsuit in a court of justice, but if a claim by all indications seems false, and aims at inflicting harm on the good name and reputation of another person, then the judge may deny it a hearing, and may punish the claimant if the falsity of the claim is supported by circumstantial evidence (*al-qarā'in*). For example, according to the jurists of the Mālikī school, if a poor and needy person brings claims against dignitaries with the sole intention of tarnishing their reputation and making them appear in court, the court may deny such claims to a hearing and even punish the accuser. For this type of action is an abuse of the right to seek judicial relief.[25]

Iftirā' differs from a simple lie (*kidhb*) in that the former is normally coupled with malice - that is, the intention to defame another person - whereas this is not always the case with regard to lying.[26] The test of *iftirā'* is not whether the charge it contains amounts to a crime, but whether it qualifies under the Qur'ānic criterion of 'evil speech' - in any form including written words, signs and pictures.[27] For a speech to qualify as 'evil and hurtful', it must violate the personal honour and dignity of the individual(s) concerned. Speech which does not fulfil this criterion would, therefore, not amount to libel and must be tolerated.

Libel, lies and false accusation are abuses of the freedom of speech which are not amenable to just retaliation (*qiṣāṣ*). If *qiṣāṣ* can be applied, then it is in principle applicable. But this is usually not so, in which case the punishment of libel is determined under the principle of *taʿzīr*,[28] which may consist of disciplinary and punitive measures to be determined by the judge. Alternatively, the punishment may consist of *taʿzīr bi'l-māl*, or damages for the plaintiff, which must be commensurate with the harm caused, the social status of the plaintiff, and the prevailing custom of the community.[29]

In order to execute the punishment, whether in slander or libel, the plaintiff must request it, failing which the penalty cannot be enforced. If the victim in either *qadhf* or *iftirā'* is notorious for their corruption and is known to be a person of compromised integrity, the accuser is not liable to any punishment. Furthermore, if the libellous speech is injurious to the community, and threatens its moral and religious values, then the 'right of God' takes priority. The offender must, consequently, be punished and no one would be entitled to grant him a pardon.[30] In determining the nature and quantum of the *ta*ʿ*zīr* punishment in this case, the judge, or the head of state, considers the interest (*maṣlaḥah*) of the community, the nature of the conduct, and the conditions of the offender. For offences pertaining to speech *ta*ʿ*zīr* should, in principle, not exceed the *ḥadd* (prescribed punishment) for slanderous accusation (*qadhf*). There are, however, differences of opinion on this point. Jurists who maintain that the *ta*ʿ*zīr* penalty should be commensurate with the nature of the offence and the interests of community, do not overrule the possibility of *ta*ʿ*zīr* exceeding the *ḥadd* of *qadhf*, and furthermore, they maintain that the judge or the imām has the discretion to sentence the offender to a heavier punishment, whether this consists of lashes or other punitive and disciplinary measures.[31]

In all cases of criminal libel, the subject of the accusation or the conduct which it refers to is, in principle, open to enquiry and proof. When someone is accused, for instance, of a criminal act such as theft or murder, and so on, and the accused person is, by all appearances, not likely to have committed the offence, the claim may still be investigated, and when the claimant fails to prove his accusation, the accused person may wish to restore his good reputation by suing the accuser for *iftirā'*. However, the latter may be punished for the offence only if he had clearly intended to harm the plaintiff or to damage his personal honour and reputation.[32]

V. Insult
(Sabb; Shatm)

Any word, expression, or gesture which attacks the dignity of the person to whom it is addressed, and which humiliates the latter in the eyes of his or her compatriots may be termed 'insult'. No legal authority provides an exhaustive list of words and expressions that may be classified as *sabb*. Instead, the law refers to the prevailing social customs which are adopted as the principal indicators by which to assess the abuse. While certain words and expressions are generally known to be insulting, there may be instances where their precise significance needs to be measured in the light of prevailing circumstances, such as the social status of the victim, and the context in which the words were expressed. As Ibn Taymiyyah has observed, a word may amount to *sabb* in certain circumstances but not in others, and that without reference to circumstances, neither the language nor the law may be expected to provide definitive guidelines.

To be insulting, words must be hurtful, but they need not be uttered in public in order to qualify as *sabb*. Similarly, the intention behind the words uttered is not of great significance, especially when the words in question are common words of insult whose purport can be objectively ascertained.[33]

Insult to all persons must be proven by the normal methods; however, the offence does not carry a fixed penalty but may evoke a deterrent punishment under *ta'zīr*. Then it is up to the court to determine the type and quantum of the punishment, bearing in mind the nature of the offence and the circumstances in which it was committed. Only when the insult is addressed to God and the recognised Prophets does it amount to the more serious offence of blasphemy which the *'ulamā'* have unanimously treated as a separate offence which invokes a heavier punishment than the common offence of insult. As I have discussed blasphemy in a separate section, suffice it to say that in almost all cases of insult, regardless of whether they are addressed to Muslims or non-Muslims, men or women, the offence is punishable under *ta'zīr*. It is interesting to note that the only Qur'ānic verse (see following) which specifies the prohibition of *sabb* is actually concerned with insult to non-Muslims, although obviously this does not mean that insulting a Muslim is not an offence.

> Revile not *(lā tasubbū)* those who call upon [deities] other than God, lest, exceeding the limits, they abuse God in ignorance. (VI:108)

وَلَا تَسُبُّوا۟ الَّذِينَ يَدْعُونَ مِن دُونِ اللهِ فَيَسُبُّوا۟ اللهَ عَدْوًا بِغَيْرِ عِلْمٍ.

Commentators on the Qur'ān have concluded that this verse forbids any insults that are likely to invoke hostility and abuse in response - which shows that the religious affiliation of the person to whom the insult is addressed is immaterial, although the text refers explicitly only to disbelievers and makes no reference to believers.

Nevertheless, the conclusion is drawn that if it is forbidden to insult the followers of revealed scriptures, specifically Jews and Christians (*ahl-al-Kitāb*), the non-Muslim citizens of a Muslim state (*dhimmī*), and virtually all non-Muslims, then by a process of deduction known as the 'analogy of the superior' (*qiyās al-awlā*), insulting a Muslim is all the more forbidden.[34] Similarly, the Qur'ān provides clear instructions (see XVI:125 and XXIX:46) to the effect that invitation to the faith must be through persuasion and sound reasoning, and must at no time be allowed to involve insult and abuse.

In similar vein, insult and slander may not be used even as a means of preventing wickedness. A person who attempts to prevent something *munkar* is only permitted to use, if necessary, harsh words which are free of lies, insults and abuse. It is only permitted to use words such as 'ignorant' (*jāhil*), 'foolish' (*aḥmaq*), or 'transgressor' (*fāsiq*), for it is understood that every sinner tends to partake of these attributes.[35] The question may arise as to whether it is allowable to curse or insult a person, whether Muslim or non-Muslim, who is in fact notorious for criminal and evil behaviour. Moreover, might it not be permissible to curse and abuse sinners and profligates non-specifically i.e. in general, for their corruption? The answer to both of these queries is in the negative, precisely because insulting such persons may lead to reciprocal abuse. Similarly, according to a *Ḥadīth* reported by both al-Bukhārī and Muslim, the Prophet ﷺ said: 'One of the major sins a man can commit is to insult his parents.' [This statement evoked a question from] the Companions [who] asked, 'O Messenger of God! Does a man ever insult his own parents?' The Prophet ﷺ replied '[Yes] when he insults another man's father or mother and this is reciprocated in turn.'[36]

مِنَ الكَبَائِر شَتْمُ الرَّجُلِ والِدَيْه، قالوا يا رسُولَ الله وَهَلْ يَشْتُمُ الرَّجلُ والديه، قال يَسُبُّ ابا الرجل فيسبُّ أبَاهُ ويَسُبُّ أمّه فَيَسُبُّ أمّه.

In its typically broad and comprehensive style, the Qur'ān lays down the principle when it enjoins the believers: 'Do not find fault with one another (*anfusakum*) nor insult one another with bad names'. (XLIX:11)

وَلاَ تَلْمِزُو اَنْفُسَكُمْ وَلاَ تَنَابَزُوا بِالاَ لْقَابِ.

'Finding fault' and 'bad names' are concepts broad enough to embrace almost all varieties of abuse and insult. Commenting on this text, al-Maqdisī points out that, although certain expressions may appear to attribute a fault to another person, they may not fall within the purview of the text. Thus, if a person is described in such terms as 'deaf' or 'lame', merely with the intention to identify him without any wish to insult, then this is neither backbiting nor calling bad names.[37] The preceding portion of the same Qur'ānic passage forbids ridiculing and backbiting others, but as al-Bahī points out, these are interrelated terms in the sense that ridiculing another person may at times amount to insulting him, and backbiting may amount to false accusation and libel, and that all of these, in turn, stem from discourtesy and arrogance.[38] Therefore, it is for the judge to determine the specific import of the words and conduct of the accused in the light of the general guidelines that are provided in the sources.

The Qur'ān forbids all forms of transgression (*taᶜaddī*, or *iᶜtidā'*) against others (II:190), and insult is clearly a form of transgression. Futhermore, it is stated in a *Ḥadīth* that 'insulting a Muslim is an iniquity (*fusūq*) and fighting him (*qitāluhu*) is disbelief (*kufr*)'.[39]

– وَلاَ تَعْتَدُوا اِنَّ اللهَ لاَ يُحِبُّ الْمُعْتَدِينَ.

– سِبَابُ الْمُسلِمِ فُسوق وقِتالُه كُفرٌ.

Clearly, this suggests that insult can lead to fighting, and that fighting is even uglier than insult. The word *kufr* in this *Ḥadīth* is used metaphorically in order to accentuate the enormity of the conduct.

Insulting a deceased person falls under the same prohibitive rules as are applied to the living. The Prophet ﷺ has strongly recommended that the dead should be remembered only for their virtues and not for their failings. The seriousness of this type of insult is emphasised by the fact that the dead are unable to defend themselves against attacks on their personal integrity and good name. The Prophet ﷺ has thus instructed the Muslims to 'mention only the virtues of your deceased ones and avoid talking about their misdeeds'.[40]

أُذْكُروا مَحَاسِنَ موتاكم وكفوا عن مساويهم.

In yet another *Ḥadīth* he directs the believers to 'avoid reviling the dead as, by doing so, you hurt the feelings of their living relatives'.[41]

لَا تَسُبُّوا الاَمْوَاتَ فَتُؤْذُوا بِهِ الاَحْيَاءَ.

To relate all this to the moral character of the believer, the Prophet ﷺ has elsewhere declared that the avoidance of insulting others is indicative of the strength of one's character and faith. 'The believer is not abusive, nor is he a slanderer, nor does he curse.'[42]

لَيْسَ المُؤمِنُ بالسَبَّابِ وَلَا بِالطَّعانِ وَلَا بِاللَّعَّانِ.

With reference to the Companions, it is noted that the Prophet ﷺ held them in affection and esteem. This is substantiated not only by the overall tone and tenor of *Ḥadīth* literature in general, but more specifically, as in the following quote, where the believers are instructed to refrain from reviling the Companions.

> Revile not my Companions, revile not my Companions! By the One in whose hand my life reposes, should one of you happen (to have) the like of Mount Uḥud in gold, he would still not match in worth any of (my Companions), not even by half.[43]

لَا تَسُبُّوا اَصْحَابِى لَا تَسُبُّوا اَصْحَابِى. فوَ الَّذِى نَفْسِى بِيَدِهِ
لَوْاَنَّ اَحَدَكُمْ اِنْفَقَ مِثْلَ اُحُدٍ ذَهَبًا مَابَلَغَ مُدَّ اَحَدِهِم وَلَا نِصْفَه.

The emphasis that the Prophet ﷺ has laid on the dignified status of his Companions has led the *ʿulamāʾ* to treat insult to the Companions (*sabb al-ṣaḥābī*) as a separate offence, which is next in order of gravity to the capital offence of blasphemy. Notwithstanding this, however, according to the majority of the *ʿulamāʾ*, the offence carries an unspecified deterrent (*taʿzīr*) punishment. The penalty so accorded reflects the enormity of reviling a

Companion, which is a far more serious crime than the common offence of *sabb*. Imām Mālik's attitude, in this regard, reflects the general stance the *ᶜulamā'* have taken over this issue. He strongly recommended that a Muslim should move away and abandon a town wherein the Companions of the Prophet ﷺ are frequently reviled.[44]

When a person insults another in several utterances which are commonly known to be abusive, the question of whether he should be punished for one or for several offences arises, just as it did for *qadhf* above. The Ḥanafī jurist Ibn ᶜĀbidīn ruled that each insult is punishable separately under *taᶜzīr*, the reason being that insult is an offence against the right of man and that rights of this kind are not amenable to amalgamation (*tadākhul*). This is unlike the offences for which there are prescribed penalties (*ḥudūd*), which consist of the right of God, and as such, are held to be amenable to amalgamation. But if a deterrent punishment of *taᶜzīr* is imposed on account of a violation of the right of man, for example when the prescribed punishment of the *qadhf* is reduced to *taᶜzīr* because of a deficiency in proof, then, if the accused has committed several such offences, they all become liable to amalgamation and may be penalised as one.[45]

When the object of insult is the religion (*dīn*) of a Muslim, the question arises as to whether an insult of this kind amounts to disbelief (*kufr*). The dominant view is that it does not, as it would remain susceptible of the interpretation, however remote, that the object of insult was the personal character of the victim and not necessarily his religion.[46]

VI. Cursing *(Laᶜn)*

Cursing (*laᶜn* or *laᶜnah*) normally consists of an expression of disapproval or displeasure and an invocation of malediction upon the object of the curse. Curses are often uttered by calling the curse and wrath of God upon someone, or by an invocation in the passive voice where the agent is not always specified, for example: may God's curse be upon him; may he be cursed.[47] An incident of cursing in the history of Islam occured when one of the Prophet's ﷺ Companions called Khubayb, who had been captured and condemned to death by the disbelievers in Mecca, called out just before he was executed, 'O God, count their number and slay them one by one, and let none of them remain alive'.[48]

Instances of cursing are also found in the Qur'ān and the Sunnah, for example: '... those who lie about their Lord; verily, the curse of God is upon the unjust' (XI:18); 'those who annoy God and His Messenger, God has cursed them in this world and in the hereafter, and He has prepared for them a painful punishment' (XXXIII:57); '... and [those who] spread mischief on earth, those are they on whom is the curse and for them is the ill abode'. (XIII:25)

- الَّذِينَ كَذَبُوا عَلَىٰ رَبِّهِمْ أَلَا لَعْنَةُ اللهِ عَلَى الظَّٰلِمِينَ.

- إِنَّ الَّذِينَ يُؤْذُونَ اللهَ وَرَسُولَهُ لَعَنَهُمُ اللهُ فِي الدُّنْيَا وَالْآخِرَةِ وَأَعَدَّ لَهُمْ عَذَابًا مُّهِينًا.

- وَيُفْسِدُونَ فِي الْأَرْضِ أُولَٰئِكَ لَهُمُ اللَّعْنَةُ وَلَهُمْ سُوءُ الدَّارِ.

The general rule that the *ʿulamā'* have upheld, which is founded on the authority of the Qur'ān, and the Sunnah, is that no one, including parents and relatives, whether alive or dead, may be abused by cursing. The evidence also sustains the conclusion that cursing is permissible on those who have been cursed in the Qur'ān and the Sunnah but that 'there is no sin in abandoning such'.[49] While stating this, al-Maqdisī hastens to add that according to a *Ḥadīth* reported by Muslim, someone asked the Prophet ﷺ to call the curse of God upon the polytheists (*mushrikūn*), to which the Prophet ﷺ replied, 'I have not been sent to curse. I have been sent only as a mercy.'[50]

إِنِّي لَمْ أُبْعَثْ لَعَّانًا، إِنَّمَا بُعِثْتُ رَحْمَةً.

Al-Maqdisī then quotes Abu'l-Ḥusayn al-Baṣrī (author of *al-Muʿtamad fī Uṣūl al-Fiqh*) as having held that cursing is forbidden whether the victim is a particular person or a group of people. It is further reported that when Imām Aḥmad Ibn Ḥanbal was asked about the permissibility of cursing transgressors such as adulterers, thieves, murderers and wine-drinkers, he advised silence.[51]

Cursing particular individuals is 'a dangerous violation', except when this is specified, for example, in the Qur'ān where God has cursed individuals such as the Pharaoh and Abū Jahl.[52] Apart from cases like this, it is unlawful to curse a particular person by name, partly because it is just possible that the person concerned, if a non-Muslim or a sinner, might have become a Muslim, or might have repented. 'If cursing a disbeliever is unlawful, then it is all the more so with regard to a transgressor (*fāsiq*) and heretic (*mubtadiʿ*).'[53] It is thus concluded that cursing a particular individual, even a disbeliever, is unlawful and must be avoided. The *ʿulamā'* have, however, differed as to the permissibility of cursing Yazīd b. Muʿāwiyah, who is the chief culprit of the carnage at Karbala in which the Prophet's ﷺ grandson Ḥusayn and his supporters were martyred. While some have held this to be permissible, Imām Ibn Ḥanbal, his disciple Ibn Qayyim al-Jawziyyah, and many others have advised silence on the issue of cursing Yazīd.[54]

During the lifetime of the Prophet ﷺ there was a Muslim known as Nuʿaymān (his real name is reported as being ʿAbd Allāh) who used to drink wine and was known for his comic nature. There are reports that he was punished for the wine-drinking more than once and, knowing of this, one of the Companions denounced Nuʿaymān's conduct and cursed him saying, 'May the curse of God be upon him for his frequent deviations.' This evoked the following response from the Prophet ﷺ, who obviously ignored Nuʿaymān's failing on account of his other virtues:

> Do not become an ally of Satan against your brother. Do not say this [i.e do not curse Nuʿaymān] for he loves God and His Messenger.[55]

لَا تَكُنْ عَوْنًا لِلشَّيْطَانِ على اَخِيكَ، لَاتَقُل هٰذَا فَاِنَّهُ يُحِبُّ
اللهَ وَرَسُولَهُ.

According to another report the last portion of this *Ḥadīth* reads, 'I have known only that he loves God and His Messenger.' Thus, in both of its reported versions the *Ḥadīth* clearly substantiates the principle that no one, not even an offender, may be cursed or insulted, regardless of whether or not the person in question is guilty of misconduct.[56] The *ᶜulamā'* have generally even upheld the ruling that offensive and sinful acts committed by wrongdoers should only be denounced by citing the attributes of the misconduct and not by specific naming.[57]

Cursing is discouraged even when it is not addressed to a person, when it is uttered in vain, or when it is addressed to objects and natural phenomena. It is reported from Ibn ᶜAbbās that when a man cursed the wind in the presence of the Prophet ﷺ he was told 'curse not the wind for it is ordained [to take its course]. When a person inappropriately curses something, the curse returns to him.'[58]

لاَ تَلْعَنِ الرِّيحَ فَإِنَّـهَا مَأْمُورَةٌ وإِنَّـهُ مَن لَعنَ شَيْـئًا لَيْسَ لَـهُ بِأَهلٍ رَجَعَتِ اللَّعْنَةُ عَلَيْـهِ.

And lastly, if an insult or a curse is reciprocated on the spur of the moment, then it must be within the limits of moderation. This is aptly illustrated by the *Ḥadīth*, reported by both al-Bukhārī and Muslim, concerning a group of Jews who came to visit the Prophet ﷺ. When they addressed him with the distorted phrase 'may death be upon you (*al-sām ᶜalaykum*)' instead of the familiar Islamic greeting, 'peace be upon you (*al-salām ᶜalaykum*)', the Prophet's ﷺ wife, ᶜĀ'ishah replied with these words, 'may death and curse be upon you (*al-sām ᶜalaykum wa'l-laᶜnah*)'. Upon hearing this, the Prophet ﷺ told his wife; 'O ᶜĀ'ishah, God Most High loves gentleness', to which she replied, 'Did you not hear what they said?' And the Prophet ﷺ said, 'Yes, but you could have just said "and upon you (*wa ᶜalaykum*)".'[59]

Gentleness (*al-rifq*) and moderation are among the most desirable features of the Islamic ethos which God and His Messenger ﷺ have repeatedly recommended. These attributes are the real antidote to cursing and insult; they adorn everything to which they are applied, and beautify every occasion. Islam sets no bounds on gentleness and moderation.

VII. Attribution of Disbelief to a Muslim (*Takfīr al-Muslim*)

The *Sharīʿah* forbids the attribution of disbelief, blasphemy or heresy to a Muslim. This is a normative principle which is applied even to cases where one suspects another of disbelief (*kufr*). Thus, if a believer observes a fellow Muslim uttering words or indulging in acts which might be suggestive of disbelief, he must give him the benefit of the doubt, and avoid charging him with disbelief in all cases which fall short of self-evident proof. Even in the latter event, it is strongly recommended, for reasons that I shall presently elaborate, that people should avoid charging others with infidelity and disbelief. Apart from the emphatic tone of a large number of prohibitive *Ḥadīth*s on this subject, the issue is so sensitive and complex that only a judge or a jurisconsult (*muftī*) who is well-versed in theological sciences is authorised to determine what exactly amounts to disbelief.

A Muslim may not be declared a disbeliever or an apostate when he says or does something which carries only the probability of disbelief. According to Imām Abū Ḥanīfah, if the utterance in question consists ninety-nine percent of disbelief but one percent of belief (*īmān*), it would still not amount to *kufr*. While recording this view, Abū Zahrah elaborates that there may be extenuating circumstances for an utterance that seems to consist of disbelief; for instance, the context in which it was spoken, or the point of view in which it originates - thus it may be susceptible of an intepretation that precludes *kufr*. All such cases should be given the benefit of the doubt. There were instances, for example, during the rule of the fourth caliph, ʿAlī b. Abī Ṭālib, when the Khārijites went to excess and levelled accusations of disbelief on even the leading figures among the Companions. Although the Khārijites were regarded as transgressors, on no occasion did the Caliph declare any of them to be an infidel (*kāfir*); instead he said that a person who seeks the truth but makes an error is never the same as a person who seeks falsehood, and then proceeds to commit it.[60]

Ibn Ḥazm has stated the principle clearly as follows: anyone who has uttered the testimonial of faith (*kalimat al-shahādah*), and declared his or her faith in the mission and guidance of the Prophet Muḥammad ﷺ, is a Muslim and this bond with Islam cannot be severed by allegations of any kind unless his or her disbelief is proven by indisputable evidence.[61]

By the same token, once a person is known to have embraced Islam, he or she is presumed to retain that status indefinitely. The fact that a person is known to be a born Muslim, or is known to have embraced Islam, creates a status which, according to the legal maxim that certainty may not be overruled by doubt, is then presumed to continue indefinitely. From this point onwards, no amount of doubt, suspicion or allegation is allowed to interfere or overrule the continued validity of a person's faith.[62]

The *ʿulamā'* and the leading imāms of jurisprudence agree that it is unlawful to attribute disbelief to anyone merely on grounds of differences of opinion. Similarly, no one may be declared a *kāfir* specifically by name. 'For this is', as al-Bahnasāwī rightly points out, 'a matter only for the competent judge. It is therefore impermissible for a layman to declare another as infidel.' In support of this, the following report is cited: During the time of the second caliph, ʿUmar b. al-Khaṭṭāb, a person known as Ibn Mazʿūn made a statement that wine-drinking was permissible in Islam. However, the Caliph did not declare him a *kāfir*, saying that it was a matter requiring evidence and proof in order to ascertain and establish the facts of the case before any judgement was passed on it.[63]

With regard to the nature of the evidence that needs to be produced, the general rule is that determining the faith or disbelief of a person is to be based entirely on obvious and explicit evidence without any reference to the hidden thoughts and feelings of people, which are known only to God. This is the purport of the Qur'ānic text which instructs the believers: 'Say not to those who greet you with peace (*al-salām*): "you are not a believer".' (IV:94)

وَلَا تَقُولُوا لِمَنْ أَلْقَىٰ إِلَيْكُمُ السَّلَامَ لَسْتَ مُؤْمِنًا.

If just the utterance of the *salām* is evidence enough to establish a presumption in favour of a person being a believer, then it is obvious that the Qur'ān does not permit inquisitions of any kind to establish the Islamic status of individuals. The Qur'ānic principle here established is further elaborated in a *Ḥadīth* which states:

'Whoever prays our prayer, facing the *qiblah* that we face and eats what we have slaughtered, is a Muslim. He shall have the same rights and obligations as we have.'[64]

مَن صَلّى صَلاَتُنا وَاِسْتَقبَل قِبْلَتُنا وأكَل ذَبيحَتُنا فَهُو المُسلِمُ، لَهُ مَالَنا وعليه ما عَلَيْنا.

Since unity in faith is the very foundation of the Islamic fraternity, the Prophet ﷺ has warned the believers to avoid accusing one another of disbelief. Thus, according to a *Ḥadīth* reported by ʿAbd Allāh Ibn ʿUmar, 'When a man calls his brother "*kāfir*" one of them is afflicted with the charge. Either it is as he says or [if the accusation is not true], it befalls the person who uttered.'[65]

إذا قَالَ الرَّجل لِاخيه يَا كَافِر فَقَدْ بَاءَبِه اَحَدُهُمَا فَإن كَان كَمَا قَالَ وَإلاَّ رَجَعَتْ عَلَيْه.

According to yet another *Ḥadīth*, reported by Abū Dharr al-Ghaffārī: 'Whoever charges another person with disbelief, or calls him an "enemy of God", while this is not so, will have the charge redound upon himself.'[66]

مَن دَعَا رَجُلا بِالْكُفْرِ او قال: عَدُوّ الله، وَلَيْسَ كَذلِكَ الاَّ حَارَ عليه (اَيْ رَجَعَ عَليه).

The message in the preceding *Ḥadīths* is not confined to the prohibition of *takfīr*, but extends also to transgression or sin (*fisq*) and the unfounded attribution of crime and sin to others. A Muslim is thus forbidden from charging others with *fisq*. This is the purport of another *Ḥadīth* which declares in the broadest of terms: 'No man accuses another of transgression (*fisq*) or disbelief (*kufr*) without partaking of it himself if the accused is not what the accusation claims he is.'[67]

لَا يَرْمِى رَجُلٌ رَجُلاً بِالْفِسْقِ أَوِ الكُفر اِلاَّ اِرْتَدَّتْ عَلَيْهِ اِن لَمْ يَكُنْ صَاحبه كَذلِكَ.

Commenting on these *Ḥadīths*, Abū Zahrah draws the conclusion that no one may accuse another of blasphemy, apostasy, disbelief and transgression without manifest evidence, and anyone who does so partakes of the accusation himself. This obviously means, as Abū Zahrah points out, that 'if the accuser is lying, he becomes a disbeliever himself.'[68]

Takfīr is a grave sin and an offence under Islam. Hence, anyone who accuses another of *kufr* in explicit words, or charges him with attributions that imply *kufr,* is liable to a deterrent *taʿzir* punishment which is to be determined by a competent judge.[69]

In a statement published in the Egyptian newspaper, al-Aḥrām, (8.12.1981, p.3), the Muftī of Egypt was reported to have held the following opinion concerning the attribution of disbelief to a Muslim.

(a) It is unlawful to attribute disbelief to a Muslim for a sin he might have committed, even if it be a major sin; and

(b) Declaring someone a *kāfir* or *fāsiq* may only be attempted by a learned person who specialises in the religious sciences (*ʿulūm al-dīn*).[70]

In view of the complexity of the issue and the exceedingly diverse rulings and statements that jurists and theologians have recorded on the subject, Abū Zahrah has proposed the creation of a separate judicial post, within the ranks of the regular judiciary, with specialised jurisdiction to adjudicate issues pertaining to apostasy, blasphemy and disbelief. The court so created would be entrusted with the task, *inter alia,* of determining exactly what utterances and conduct amount to disbelief, blasphemy, or apostasy as the case may be. The individual must, therefore, try to avoid passing hasty judgements in matters involving the attribution of disbelief to others.[71]

All that a person may do when he suspects that disbelief, heresy or apostasy is being committed by another is to give him good advice in the true spirit of the Qur'ānic principle of *ḥisbah.* A person who witnesses the incidence of heresy and disbelief would have fulfilled his duty if he provided the necessary evidence to establish the truth, and then left the matter in the hands of the authorities. Al-

Bahnasāwī sums up the position when he writes 'no one may be subjected to adversity and harm on the basis of a mere suspicion or allegation of disbelief, blasphemy or apostasy without the necessary proof and adjudication of competent authorities.[72]

VIII. Sedition *(Fitnah)*

1. MEANING AND DEFINITION

Dictionaries record various meanings for *fitnah*, including temptation, trial, misguidance, enticement, fascination, commotion, sedition, affliction, torture, and strife.[73] This polysemy might have contributed to a certain ambiguity that is also observed in the juridical meaning of the word. *Fitnah* and its derivatives feature prominently in the Qur'ān where they occur in no less than sixty places. The *Ṣaḥīḥ al-Bukhārī* records eighty-six *Ḥadīth*s in its chapter entitled Kitāb al-Fitan. But *fitnah* occurs, both in the Qur'ān and *Ḥadīth*, in a variety of contexts, and denotes meanings which converge and overlap. Among the juridical meanings of *fitnah*, one example which concerns us most in the context of freedom of expression, is seditious speech which attacks the legitimacy of a lawful government. An equally important meaning of *fitnah*, the one which tends to be most dominant in the Qur'ān, is to deny the faithful the right to practise their faith.[74] As the discussion proceeds, I shall address both of these two meanings of *fitnah* in detail; however, at this point, I propose to outline briefly some of the other meanings of *fitnah*.

As a dominantly moral concept, *fitnah* occurs in the Holy Qur'ān in the sense of temptation or enticement. Note, for example, the following: 'Know that your possessions and your offspring are but a trial (*fitnah*) and that with God lies an immense reward.' (VIII:28; LXIV:15.)

– وَاعْلَمُوا أَنَّمَا أَمْوَالُكُمْ وَأَوْلَادُكُمْ فِتْنَةٌ وَأَنَّ اللَّهَ عِنْدَهُ أَجْرٌ عَظِيمٌ.

– إِنَّمَا أَمْوَالُكُمْ وَأَوْلَادُكُمْ فِتْنَةٌ وَاللَّهُ عِنْدَهُ أَجْرٌ عَظِيمٌ.

Here, man is cautioned that love of property and children may entice a person to indulge in sinful conduct for their sake.[75]

Fitnah also occurs in the Qur'ān to denote the testing of someone in regard to something he or she finds difficult to accept or deny. *Fitnah* in this sense entails exposure to hardship with a view to forcing someone to accomplish or abandon an act, statement or belief. As an example, God Most High tests believers and unbelievers in order to reward or punish them in proportion to the *fitnah* they have undergone: We put to test (*laqad fatannā*) those who preceded them [the believers]; thus God knows the truthful and He knows those who lie. (XXIX:3; see also IX:49 and XLIV:17)[76]

Another meaning of *fitnah* in the Qur'ān, one which the commentators interpret diversely, is *shirk*, or the association of other deities with God, such as in the following passage: 'And fight them [the disbelievers] until *fitnah* is no more, and religion is entirely for God.' (VIII:39)

وَقَاتِلُوهُمْ حَتَّى لَا تَكُونَ فِتْنَةٌ وَيَكُونَ الدِّينُ كُلُّهُ لِلَّهِ.

According to a commentary attributed to Ibn ʿAbbās, and upheld by Ibn Kathīr and the majority of the leading commentators, *fitnah* in this passage means disbelief (*shirk*). In this sense, the text would thus be held to mean: 'fight the disbelievers until *shirk* and all false religion is eliminated, and Islam is established.' Al-Alusī, however, has differed from this reading as he maintains that the correct meaning of *fitnah* in this passage is aggression which aims at eliminating the freedom of belief.[77] Commenting on the same verse, Ibn Qayyim al-Jawziyyah points out that *fitnah* occurs here in contradistinction to 'the whole of religion' (*dīn kulluh*), a phrase which appears in the latter part of the sentence. It is thus implied that *fitnah* destroys religion, which may explain why commentators have interpreted *fitnah* as denoting disbelief.[78]

Among the various usages of *fitnah* in the Qur'ān, the most typical is the one which denotes such aggression, whether verbal or actual, against the believers as denies them the right to pursue and practise their faith. Note, for example, this Qur'ānic verse: 'And expel them from where they have expelled you. For oppression (*fitnah*) is worse than killing.' (II:191)

وَاقْتُلُوهُمْ حَيْثُ ثَقِفْتُمُوهُمْ وَأَخْرِجُوهُمْ مِنْ حَيْثُ أَخْرَجُوكُمْ وَالْفِتْنَةُ أَشَدُّ مِنَ الْقَتْلِ.

The subject-matter of this verse is described as *fitnah* in religion (*fitnah fi'l-dīn),* that is, *fitnah* which destroys the freedom of religion. In the early days of Islam the disbelievers obstructed the Muslims from observing their faith, using hostile means including persecution, expulsion and the expropriation of property.[79] ʿAbd Allāh b. ʿUmar described '*fitnah*' when he said: 'And there were very few Muslims, so a man used to be persecuted on account of his religion. They either murdered him or subjected him to torture; [this was the state of affairs] until Islam became predominant.'[80]

On a slightly different note, Rashīd Riḍā points out that the hypocrites (*munāfiqūn*) sought to promote *fitnah* by asking people, during the battles of Uḥud and Tābūk, not to participate in the holy war (*jihād*). In the case of Uḥud, about one-third of the Muslim forces were persuaded, by Ubayy b. Sallūl, to stay behind. As to the incidence of this type of *fitnah* in modern times, Rashīd Riḍā observes further that it is *fitnah* when disbelievers propagate their beliefs among Muslims, especially among those who are weak of mind and ignorant, and try to tempt them away from Islam and toward disbelief.[81] In *Ḥadīth* literature, the word *fitnah* (pl. *fitan*) is typically used in reference to war and general social commotion but is also used for the tumult that precedes the Resurrection. Thus, we expect to find a chapter bearing the title '*al-fitan*' in many major collections of *Ḥadīth. Fitnah* in this sense springs from oppression by misguided rulers which can lead to chaos and a confusion over values.

Capricious challenges to the authority of lawful government, and the calamity that afflicts the community in the form of rampant corruption, are among the other modes of *fitnah* that feature prominently in *Ḥadīth* literature. If a total sense of insecurity afflicts the believers, the best course they are advised to take is to dissociate themselves from the sources of chaos, and to isolate themselves until the truth emerges.[82]

Freedom of expression does not permit subjugating the faithful to corrupt influences which violate the principles of Islam. Offensive speech and conduct of this kind may be penalised, but the precedent of the first four caliphs of Islam suggests that the punishment should not be severe unless the conduct in question amounts to blatant disbelief (*kufr ṣarīḥ*). While Islam forbids its own followers from the use of coercive methods in propagating ther faith, it also takes measures to protect them against aggression which denies them their own freedom. *Fitnah* in this sense is the antithesis of freedom of religion, and can claim no validity under any of the legitimate concepts and varieties of freedom.[83]

Seditious *fitnah*, that is *fitnah* in its political sense, is an abuse of freedom of expression which threatens the legitimacy of lawful government, and which could lead to the collapse of normal order in society. The practical consequences of this seemingly uncontroversial theoretical characterisation of sedition can be problematic; for instance, defining the scope of *fitnah*, and establishing a correct balance among conflicting values is often difficult. It was noted, for instance, that sedition undermines the authority of lawful government, but the legitimacy of a government is not always self-evident. Many instances can be given of self-styled leaders and regimes who came to power by illegal means, for example, the former, Soviet-installed, President Najibullah of Afghanistan,[84] whose government imprisoned and persecuted others on charges of sedition and other crimes against the state. Moreover, words and acts constitute *fitnah* only when they succeed, or are likely to succeed, in posing a threat to normal order. An isolated act or opinion which remains ineffective and does not incite opposition to lawful government would therefore fail to qualify as *fitnah*.

Statutory restrictions on freedom of speech and expression are commonplace in the legislation of both Muslim and non-Muslim countries. The main areas of concern tend to differ from country to country, although a broad division could be ascertained between advanced and developing countries. Sedition which threatens the security of the state tends to occur more frequently in developing nations than it does in industrialised nations with longer experience in democracy. On the other hand, the latter are faced with problems of obscenity and vice, perhaps on a larger scale than is the case in the developing countries.

Seditious *fitnah* also applies to words and acts which incite dissension among people, with the effect that right and wrong can no longer be distinguished from one another. This clouds the understanding, and confounds the minds of people to such an extent that they are no longer able to advocate the truth.[85]

The Sunnah emphasises solidarity within the just community (*ahl al-ᶜadl*), and the citizen's duty of obedience to the lawfully elected head of state. Succession to the rule is an event that is particularly susceptible to seditious *fitnah*. When a leader is duly elected and confirmed through the community's pledge of allegiance (*bayᶜah*), any attempt to overthrow him or incite disobedience and strife against him is liable, according to the declared terms of a *Ḥadīth*, to the capital punishment of death.[86] However, entering into further detail on this subject at this point would lead us away from the main theme of the discussion at hand, namely, the bearing of *fitnah* on freedom of speech.

2. HISTORICAL EXAMPLES

A total separation between the religious and political aspects of *fitnah* is unfeasible in the context of an Islamic polity. For in Islam the state is closely associated with religion, which exceeds, in order of significance, all other considerations of race, language, geography and culture. Hence, when the religious principles of Muslim society are made the target of subversion and attack, the threat is automatically directed at the very foundations of the Islamic society and state.[87] Abū Zahrah illustrates this by reference to the Khārijites,[88] and states that when the latter spread pernicious views and doctrines against Islam, they were not exercising legitimate freedom of expression in pursuit of either truth or knowledge, 'but were bent on destruction and abuse; their activities threatened the community with disintegration'. The Khārijites acted in concert and had enough power with which to jeopardise the security of the nascent Islamic state.[89] I shall have occasion to discuss the Khārijites in further detail, but here I refer to some relatively minor instances of *fitnah* which preceded that of the Khārijites. In an incident of theft in which the caliph ᶜUmar b. al-Khaṭṭāb was adjudicating, he asked the thief, 'why did you commit the offence?' The thief replied, 'It was God's will.' The Caliph is reported to have ordered an additional number of lashes to be added to the prescribed penalty of theft on account of the misguided remark, referred to by Abū Zahrah, as ill-conceived interpretation (*sū' al-ta'wīl*). According to a similar report, Caliph ʿUmar flogged a group of wine-drinkers, in punishment for their *sū' al-ta'wīl* in the course of the investigation of their case. The accused were confronted with the question as to why they drank, and they had replied by reciting a passage from the Qur'ān which is of general import, and is couched in language that could plausibly be interpreted so as to validate unrestricted eating and drinking (V:93). The text in question refers to pious believers who may eat and drink as they wish, so long as they remain steadfast in righteousness. The culprits attempted to apply the general terms of this passage to their case, in preference to the specific prohibition that occurs elsewhere in the Qur'ān on wine-drinking (V:90). The Caliph responded tersely, 'If you were pious, you would have avoided drinking.' Reports indicate that the Caliph punished these instances of *fitnah* only lightly, as they were incidental and were offered in excuse for offences, and not, so to speak, by way of inciting the public to challenge the accepted meaning of the Qur'ān.[90]

In the context of *fitnah*, writers have also discussed the incident in which the prominent companion, Abū Dharr al-Ghaffārī, preached and urged the people to avoid accumulating gold and silver. Abū Dharr was critical of the conduct of government officials under the caliph ʿUthmān and charged them with conduct repugnant to accepted norms and precedents - *bidʿah* - for accumulating wealth and for indulging in an ostentatious show of affluence. According to Abū Dharr, the acquisition of wealth beyond one's needs extinguished the light of faith in one's heart and was clearly indefensible. Abū Dharr was initially exiled by Muʿāwiyah, then Governor of Syria, to Medīna, and later by the Caliph, from Medīna to one of its suburbs, in order to prevent *fitnah*.[91]

There is no substance, in my opinion, to the claim that this case constituted a *fitnah* or even a potential *fitnah*. It would appear that the fragility of the political climate during the caliphate of ʿUthmān played a part in labelling Abū Dharr's views as seditious, but the substance of his views are so eminently in conformity with the teachings of Islam that they could hardly be refuted, let alone branded as *fitnah*. For in support of his views, Abū Dharr quoted the Qur'ānic verse, 'Those who hoard gold and silver and spend it not in the way of God, are to be given news of a painful chastisement'. (IX:34)

وَالَّذِينَ يَكْنِزُونَ الذَّهَبَ وَالْفِضَّةَ وَلَا يُنْفِقُونَهَا فِي سَبِيلِ اللهِ فَبَشِّرْهُم بِعَذَابٍ أَلِيمٍ.

Another *fitnah*, which occurred during the caliphate of ʿAlī b. Abī Ṭālib, was that of ʿAbd Allāh b. Sabā and his followers, who elevated ʿAlī to the rank of a deity, claiming that he partook of the essence of God. Al-Sibāʿī writes that Ibn Sabā 'was intent on destroying Islam and spreading corruption among its followers'. This is borne out by the fact that ʿAlī himself equated Ibn Sabā's assertions with apostasy (*riddah*) and a total renunciation of Islam.[92] On the other hand, the Caliph did not punish anyone for such views as they expressed on predestination and free-will (*al-jabr wa'l-ikhtiyār*), or speculations as to whether man is a free, and consequently responsible, agent in regard to his own conduct or an automaton who conforms to a predetermined programme and cannot be held responsible for his actions. Reports further indicate that the Caliph did not take to task anyone for holding the view, as many of the Khārijites did, that a person who committed a major sin automatically renounced Islam and became a *kāfir.*[93] The Caliph considered these to be matters which fell within the purview of the Qur'ānic principle that argumentation should be conducted with courtesy and tolerance (XVI:125). The authors and propagators of such opinions were to be given sincere advice (*naṣīḥah*) and be persuaded to change their views through correct guidance.[94]

A historically renowned instance of *fitnah*, also referred to as an inquisiton (*miḥnah*), occurred under the ʿAbbāsid Caliph al-Ma'mūn (c. 833 A.D) over the nature of divine revelation: whether the Qur'ān is the created or uncreated speech of God. Al-Ma'mūn adopted the controversial view of the Muʿtazilah on this issue: that the Qur'ān is the created speech of God, that God does not speak like men, that the attribution of speech to Him is a form of anthropomorphism, and that He created the Qur'ān as He does His other creatures. Many *ʿulamā'*, on the other hand, embraced the view that the Qur'ān is the uncreated speech of God which is essentially eternal, but which was communicated to the Prophet Muḥammad ﷺ at a certain point in time. The ʿAbbāsid caliph held an inquisition on the issue and went so far as to imprison and persecute members of the *ʿulamā'* who opposed the officially adopted doctrine. Al-Ma'mūn also directed, among other things, that only people who were both trustworthy and believed in this doctrine of the createdness of the Qur'ān were to be admitted as witnesses.[95] This is, however, seen to be a somewhat isolated albeit startling exception to the otherwise tolerant picture of the history of academic freedom in Islam. Comparing the medieval university professor in Christendom to the jurist and *mujtahid* of Islam, George Makdisi has concluded that 'the professors did not achieve that complete autonomy enjoyed by their colleagues in Islam'.[96]

The turmoil which followed the assassination of Caliph ʿUthmān, the dispute between Caliph ʿAlī and Muʿāwiyah, and the ensuing emergence of the Khārijites, is by far the most widely debated instance of *fitnah* in the history of Islam. The Khārijites (literally 'seceders') were so called because they separated themselves from the community as a result of the attempted arbitration between ʿAlī and Muʿāwiyah.[97] Having been followers of ʿAlī, they became his (and also Muʿāwiyah's) opponents. They maintained the view that arbitration should never have been proposed and that arbitration in the face of aggression (in this case Muʿāwiyah's agression) was against the dictates of the Qur'ān. Some of the Khārijites also held the view that the presence of an imām was not necessary and did not constitute a religious obligation. They felt that the community could administer its own affairs through mutual advice and consultation, but that an imām might be elected if this was deemed necessary by the community itself. The Khārijites also held the view that the perpetrator of a major sin became an infidel, and it was on this basis that they charged many of the leading Companions with disbelief for their approval of the proposed arbitration. And lastly, they maintained that leadership was not a prerogative of the tribe of Quraysh and that any Muslim, Arab or non-Arab, who was competent could be elected as imām.[98]

The Khārijites challenged the legitimacy of the caliphate of ʿAlī because he acceded to arbitration. The nature of the proceedings in which arbitration was conducted, and their outcome, have been variously reported and interpreted; nevertheless, the Khārijites denounced the arbitration, and maintained that fighting should have continued until the matter was determined on the grounds of true principles. In support of this they quoted the Qur'ān, in particular, the passage which authorises fighting rebels and outlaws who deviate from the path of God (XLIX:9). The Khārijites also quoted another Qur'ānic passage: 'The [prerogative of] command belongs to none but God' (VI:57).

إِنِ الْحُكْمُ إِلاَّ لِلَّهِ.

However, the Caliph considered this last assertion as 'a word of truth which was given a false meaning': he concluded that although judgement belongs to God Most High, to interpret these passages so as to mean that there was no need for a leader to administer community affairs was a total fallacy.[99] Reports also indicate that about eight thousand Khārijites came out to protest ʿAlī's decision over the arbitration. But ʿAlī did not resort to the use of force, but instead sent the renowned Companion, Ibn ʿAbbās, to discuss their differences amicably. About four thousand of the Khārijites were persuaded to return. Then the Caliph asked the rest to return too, but they refused. He then sent them this message: 'You may stay as you wish and we shall not wage war on you so long as you avoid bloodshed, highway robbery, and acts of injustice and corruption. But if you commit any of these, we shall fight you.'[100]

Discussing this issue, Abū Zahrah voices the view, like many others, that: "ʿAlī, may God be pleased with him, was confronted with rebellion and aggression, but he did not fight the Khārijites until they embarked on violence by killing [one of his governors,] Khabbāb b. al-Art'. Accordingly, Abū Zahrah has concluded that it is not lawful for the imām to fight rebels (*ahl al-baghy*) solely on grounds of differences of opinion, unless they break the peace and embark on violence.[101] According to yet another report, while Caliph ʿAlī was delivering a Friday sermon, one of the Khārijites interrupted and criticised him. The Caliph responded to his criticism, and then said, 'We shall not prohibit you from entering our mosques to mention God's Name and we shall not deny your share in the spoils of war (*fay'*) so long as you join hands with us and fight on our side, nor shall we fight you until you attack us.' Then he resumed the Friday sermon.[102]

Furthermore, we read in a report from Kathīr b. Tamār al-Ḥaḍramī who said: 'I entered the mosque of Kūfa ... where I met five men cursing the caliph ʿAlī. One of them, dressed in a *burnus*, said, "I have made a convenant with God that I shall kill him". I then took this man to ʿAlī and reported to him what I had heard. "Bring him nearer", said ʿAlī and added, "Woe to you. Who are you?" "I am Sawwār al-Manqūrī", replied the man. "Let him go", said the Caliph, to which al-Ḥaḍramī responded, "Should I let him go even though he has made a convenant with God to kill you?" "Shall I kill him even though he has not killed me?" replied ʿAlī. "He has cursed you", said I. "You should then curse him or leave him," said ʿAlī.'[103]

The Khārijites declared many of the leading Companions, including ʿUthmān, ʿAlī, Ṭalḥah and Zubayr, to be infidels, and validated aggression against the lives and properties of Muslims who refused to join their ranks.[104] The majority of jurists declared the Khārijites a rebel faction (*bughghāt*) and applied to them the same rules that they applied to rebels, which meant that they were to be fought. This is the view of Abū Ḥanīfah, al-Shāfiʿī, Ibn Ḥanbal, and most of the jurists (*fuqahā'*) and traditionists (*ahl al-Ḥadīth*). However, Imām Mālik has held that they should be asked to repent, and if they refuse to do so, they should be killed, not for disbelief (*kufr*) but for causing corruption in the land (*fasād fi'l-arḍ*). A group of the *ahl al-Ḥadīth* have held, on the other hand, that rebels, like the Khārijites, are to be treated in the same way as apostates (*murtaddūn*).[105]

According to Imām Abū Ḥanīfah's disciple, al-Shaybānī, those who depart from truth and justice or from the generally accepted Sunnah, and follow a heterodox creed, are to be regarded as rebels and dissenters. If they do not renounce the authority of the imām, they are not to be denied residence in the territory of Islam; but if they renounce the authority of the imām and take up arms against the community, they are liable to *jihād* and may be killed. In support of this ruling, al-Shaybānī refers to those of the Khārijites who took up arms against Caliph ʿAlī and were consequently fought and defeated in the battle of Nahrawān.[106]

ʿAbd al-Qādir ʿAwdah defines rebels (*al-bughghāt*) as political criminals, with followers as well as power at their disposal,[107] who renounce the authority of the imām, and confront him while maintaining a viewpoint based on an allowable interpretation (*ta'wīl sā'igh*). To distingush them from common criminals, the rebels must therefore have a viewpoint which opposes the accepted beliefs of the community at large. Their action is attributed to rebellion only when it is accompanied by force which challenges the authority of the imām. Thus, it appears that *fitnah* and *baghy* (rebellion) resemble one another and can have a common origin, the only distinction between them being the access to power, and the threat of using it in a challenge against the authority of the imām, which would transform *fitnah* into *baghy*. It is on grounds of such circumstances that al-Mawardī has, in the following quote, drawn a parallel between sedition and rebellion.

> When a group of Muslims opposes the view of the community *(ra'y al-jamāʿah)* and follows a course or a *madhhab* which they have innovated, no war is to be waged on them so long as they do not all congregate en masse. Provided they act as individuals who can be reached by the government, no war should be waged on them, but they are, nevertheless, subject to the rules of law *(aḥkām al-ʿadl)* which applies to the community at large. Should the rebellious faction congregate in a given locality where they are out of reach but cannot spread corruption, then provided they do not obstruct justice, nor embark on active mutiny, no war is to be waged on them. However, like the rest of the community, they still remain subject to the rule of law. If the rebels mix with the law-abiding community *(ahl al-ʿadl)* and try to spread corruption and commit acts of injustice, then the *imām* is within his rights to punish them with a deterrent punishment of *taʿzīr*. The punishment in this case must, however, neither be death nor exceed any of the prescribed penalties of the *ḥudūd*.[108]

ʿAbd al-Qādir ʿAwdah concurs substantially with this, especially where he outlines the rights and duties of persons who may have views opposing those of the community and the lawful government. The opposition is within its right to propagate its views through peaceful means and enjoys the liberty, within the limits of the *Sharīʿah*, to say what it wishes, just as the law-abiding community has the right to refute such views and expose the evil and corruption in them. If anyone, from either side, violates the injunctions of the *Sharīʿah* pertaining, for example, to blasphemy or slander, in speech or in other methods of propagation, the perpetrator is liable to punishment under the normal rules of law, and the offence is treated as an ordinary offence. The opposition is also entitled to hold assemblies, and, provided that they do not renounce obedience to the imām nor obstruct nor violate the rights of others, no one has the authority to ban their assemblies. This conforms to the precedent of ʿAlī b. Abī Ṭālib and the treatment he accorded to the Khārijites. The Khārijites isolated themselves from the rest of the community in Nahrawān, but they still obeyed the regional governor appointed by the Caliph. The Caliph fought the Khārijites only when they killed his governor, Khabbāb b. al-Art. Following this incident, the Caliph asked the Khārijites to surrender the murderer to justice. But they refused to comply and replied that it was a communal act, committed by all of them in concert. Thus, they refused to obey the Caliph and openly challenged his authority at which point the Caliph declared war against them.[109]

For the Imāms Mālik, al-Shāfiʿī and Ibn Ḥanbal, it is a prerequisite that the rebels initiate agression against the law-abiding community first, and only then is the latter entitled to wage war on them, in which case their lives are no longer protected under the law. Only Imām Abū Ḥanīfah has validated waging war on the rebels before they embark on actual violence, that is, when they bring together their supporters in such a way as presents a threat to normal order in the community.[110]

3. TYPES OF *FITNAH*

Fitnah is divided into two main types, namely *fitnah* pertaining to doubts (*fitnat al-shubuhāt*), and *fitnah* pertaining to sensuality (*fitnat al-shahawāt*). The former is by far the more extensive in scope and significance, in the works of the early *ʿulamāʾ* at least, by comparison with the latter. *Fitnat al-shahawāt* is concerned mainly with obscenity and corruption both in word and deed, and would appear to be no less significant and, if anything, more intractable in our own times. But the *ʿulamāʾ* have not paid the same degree of attention to this second type of *fitnah* as they have to the first. This may partly be due to the heavy penalty for illicit sex in the *Sharīʿah* which ensures that open indulgence in illegitimate sexuality has been checked.

The two types of *fitnah* may occur separately or together in one or many individuals. In Ibn Qayyim's assessment, the *fitnah* which consist of doubts stems from the weakness of knowledge and vision, and its enormity is intensified when it is attended by ill-intent and the pursuit of passion (*hawā*).[111] The doubt in question confuses truth with falsehood, and the lawful (*ḥalāl*) with the forbidden (*ḥarām*) in such a way that neither side is supported by proof. The *shubhah*, or doubt may also arise when there are conflicting indications which remain unresolved and result in confusion. Ibn Qayyim goes on to quote two *Ḥadīth*s in which the Prophet ﷺ has instructed the believers to 'abandon doubt in favour of that which is not doubtful'; and 'whoever abandons the *shubuhāt* (pl. of *shubhah*) purifies his faith and his honour'.[112]

- دَعْ مَا يُرِيبُكَ إلى مَالاَ يُرِيبُك.
- من تَرَكَ الشُبهاتَ فقد استبرأ لِدينه وعرضِه.

Ibn Qayyim lays emphasis on ill-intent (*fasād al-qaṣd*) which, in combination with ignorance, leads to the greatest of evils. The result is disbelief and hypocrisy (*kufr wa nifāq*), the kind of *fitnah* that befell the hypocrites (*munāfiqūn*) and inventors of heresy (*ahl al-bid*ᶜ*ah*). 'All of these indulged in *fitnah* which originated in doubt that clouded the truth in their eyes and confounded it with falsehood and misguidance (*ḍalāl*).' The *fitnah* in question may consist of a misconception (*fahm fāsid*), false narration (*naql kādhib*), prejudice or the pursuit of passion, accompanied by a blindness to the truth and a corrupt intention.[113]

It is exceedingly difficult to demarcate the often overlapping concepts of *fitnah* of the mind, or *fitnat al-shubuhāt*, from outright heresy and disbelief (*kufr*). The subject-matter of *fitnah* can, of course, be something which may not have a direct bearing on faith or adherence to a creed, in which case no difficulty would be expected to arise in distinguishing the *fitnah* from *kufr*.[114] I will return to this subject later. At this point, I refer simply to an example given by Ibn Qayyim of the *fitnah* of doubt. It relates to distorting the meaning of the Qur'ān by reading into its words the kind of interpretation which is in total contradiction with the rest of its teachings. The phrase in question appears in more than one place in the Qur'ān side by side with a reference to the lawfully wedded wife with whom sexual intercourse is legitimate. Thus, while validating conjugal relations between spouses the text then continues 'and those whom your right hands possess', '*aw mā malakat aymānukum*' (XXIII:6; LXX:30). This last phrase is taken by some to mean, as Ibn Qayyim points out, that sodomy is lawful with one's male slave. However, he then hastens to write that 'anyone who embraces this view is an infidel (*kāfir*) by virtue of the unanimous agreement of the entire *ummah* (*bi ittifāq al-ummah*).'[115]

This is a striking and, perhaps, also a typical example of what *fitnat al-shubuhāt* is supposed to mean. Given the severe condemnation of sodomy in the Qur'ān in the story of the Prophet Lot ﷺ - God sent his angels to destroy Sodom and Gomorah totally for their perverse homosexual practices - there is clearly a corrupt intention behind interpretations like the one cited above, since they stand in stark contrast to the moral teachings, and indeed to both the letter and the spirit of the Qur'ān.[116] This element of ill-intent (*fasād al-qaṣd*), which Ibn Qayyim has himself specified, is also a useful indicator by which to draw a distinction between the *fitnah* of doubt and some of the instances of heresy or *bidᶜah* which I have discussed elsewhere. For *bidᶜah* is by definition an honest but misguided attempt on the part of its author at making a contribution to the development of a legal or religious theme. This is clearly not the case in *fitnat al-shubuhāt*. Moreover *bidᶜah* is closely related to personal opinion (*ra'y*), albeit a misguided one, and tends to have an intellectual content, whereas *fitnah*, in its simpler varieties at least, can be an utterance or an act without an intellectual overtone. Seditious *fitnah* can nevertheless be distinguished from both *bidᶜah* and *kufr* on grounds of their respective political and religious contents. Whereas seditious *fitnah* is predominantly a political concept, *bidᶜah* and *kufr* tend to have specifically religious overtones. Opposition to the government, and pursuit of political power, often constitute the key ingredients of sedition, whereas these may or may not be relevant to heresy and disbelief. Having said this, however, circumstantial factors tend to play a crucial role in transforming *bidᶜah* and *kufr* into *fitnah* and the latter into rebellion (*baghy*).

The second type of *fitnah* to be discussed here is speech or forms of expression which promote obscenity, sensuality, and lust, which are obviously implied in the phrase *fitnat al-shahawāt*. This type of 'sedition' consists of sinful deeds (*fisq al-aᶜmāl*), for instance, when people indulge in prurience which perverts their thinking and behaviour, especially if they are weak or ignorant. *Fitnah* of this type often originates in lust and corrupts the mind, faith and character of both perpetrator and victim. The result is either an active adherence to falsehood, or indulgence in corrupt activity, or both.[117]

Obscenity is value-laden and broad in its meanings, which is why it does not lend itself to a clear definition. Part of the difficulty concerning this type of *fitnah* lies in the changeable character of public opinion conerning what it regards as acceptable and decent, as opposed to what it considers lascivious and obscene. Notwithstanding the difficulty over the definition and understanding of *fitnat al-shahawāt*, a reasonable case can be made for imposing limits on freedom of expression in the interests of public decency, and to protect vulnerable members of society against provocative expressions that appeal to their baser passions.

According to Ibn Qayyim, the root and origin of all *fitnah* is traceable to the attitude which gives priority to personal opinion (*ra'y*) over the legal (*sharʿ*), and to caprice (*hawā*), over reason (*ʿaql*). It thus appears that sedition may originate in any, or all, of the allied concepts of caprice (*hawā*), pernicious innovation (*bidʿah*), distorted interpretation (*sū' al-ta'wīl*), and inimical doubt (*shubhah*). These become *fitnah* when they are expressed or propagated in ways that challenge the legitimacy of lawful government, or if they disrupt peace and order, or pervert and corrupt the minds of ignorant and vulnerable individuals.[118]

Fitnah pertaining to doubt is prevented, as Ibn Qayyim observes, by certitude (*al-yaqīn*), and *fitnah* pertaining to lust is prevented through patience (*al-ṣabr*).[119] The Qur'ān provides the necessary guidance when it exhorts the believers to uphold the truth, which protects them against doubt, and to exercise patience, which is their principal defence against corruption (CI:3). Ibn Taymiyyah has quoted al-Shāfiʿī in support of his own view concerning this *sūrah*, that 'If everybody were to meditate on *Sūrat al-ʿAṣr* (CI:3), they would find it sufficient.' He goes on to say that God Most High has informed us in this *sūrah*, that all men are at a loss except for those who stand for truth, [act righteously] and exhort each other to it and to patience. Ibn Taymiyyah then adds that patience here includes patience in bearing hurt and in regard to things that are said, patience in adversity and patience against temptation. But then, he adds that patience of this calibre is unfeasible unless there is something from which a person can gain reassurance and comfort, and this can be gained through the certainty of firm conviction. As the Prophet ﷺ said in a *Ḥadīth*, narrated by Abū Bakr al-Ṣiddīq: 'People! Ask God for certitude and good health, for after certitude no gift of His is better than good health, so ask God for both.'[120]

The *Sharīʿah* does not specify any penalty for sedition. The precedent of the Rightly-Guided Caliphs indicates that they penalised the *fitnah* of doubt with a light deterrent punishment, being careful not to impose unduly on the dignity and freedom of the individual. Instead, the Caliphs applied persuasive methods of giving correct guidance to those who engaged in minor instances of *fitnah*. However, this climate of constructive tolerance and restraint was short-lived, and radical changes soon took place after the emergence and proliferation of sectarian movements and their indulgence in speculative discourse, when confusing and polemical ideas became commonplace. There were also conspiracies against the state by individuals and groups, which prompted the jurists to authorise heavier penalties for subversive conduct and sedition. Imām Mālik, and many of the Ḥanbalites, went so far as to validate the death penalty for propagators of heresy (*zanādiqah*) and for the instigators of *fitnah*. The jurists apparently resolved on this for fear of mischief spreading in the land, and not out of a desire for retribution. Ibn Taymiyyah maintained the same attitude, adding that it is not always necessary to wait until the *fitnah* actually occurs, but that preventive action can be taken. Ibn Taymiyyah also maintained that when the offender possesses force, i.e. the means by which to act on his dissenting opinions, as in the case of the Khārijites and the *zanādiqah*, then punishment is justified and need not be delayed until after the incidence of the *fitnah*.[121]

Imām Abū Ḥanīfah has, on the other hand, ruled out the death penalty for instigators of heresy and sedition. They are, instead, he maintains, to be given a deterrent punishment of *taᶜzīr* which does not amount to death, and yet is severe enough to deter evil. The death penalty, he adds, is permitted only when the offenders take up arms, in which case they become treasonous rebels (*bughghāt muḥāribūn*), and must be fought.

While referring to Caliph ᶜAlī's attitude toward the Khārijites, the Ḥanafī jurist, al-Sarakhsī, observes that the imām may neither kill nor imprison those who differ from the majority and challenge their leadership. According to him, only when the dissenters muster their forces and embark on violence against the just community (*ahl al-ᶜadl*), does it become lawful to resort to the use of force.[122] From his enquiry into the views of the legal schools (*madhāhib*) on this issue, Abū Zahrah has reached the following conclusion: 'We are inclined toward the opinion of Abū Ḥanīfah and his disciples. For death is the ultimate punishment and it must be avoided for as long as there is an alternative course of action that can be taken.'[123]

While affirming that both procreation and enjoyment are the legitimate functions of sex and marriage, al-Ghazālī hastens to add that sex is also one of the greatest incentives to *fitnah*, and that to resist the powerful urge of this instinct requires strong faith and determination. In the following two verses of the Qur'ān, the believers are advised to invoke God's help against 'the evil of darkness when it prevails' and against a 'burden which we do not have the capacity to bear'. (CXIII:3 and II:286)

– وَمِن شَرِّ غَاسِقٍ إِذَا وَقَبَ.

– رَبَّنَا وَلَا تُحَمِّلْنَا مَا لَا طَاقَةَ لَنَا بِهِ.

In both of these, it is said that the reference is in fact to sexual urges which 'darken' the intellect when they prevail and can overwhelm a person's capacity of resistance.[124] To prevent such *fitnah*, both the Qur'ān and the Sunnah forbid men and women from looking at length at each other, unless they be man and wife (XXIV:30). According to one *Ḥadīth* 'the look is a poisonous arrow that belongs to the devil ... '.

اَلنَّظْرَةُ سَهْمٌ مَسْمُومٌ مِن سِهَامِ ابليس.

In another *Ḥadīth*, it says that the first (inadvertent) glance at a woman is forgiven but not the second deliberate one.[125]

لَكَ الأُولى والأُخْرى عَلَيْك.

Commenting on this second *Ḥadīth*, al-Sarakhsī observes that the repeated look here means one which is motivated by lust (*shahwah*).[126] This would obviously preclude looking at a woman for a legitimate purpose or on the grounds of necessity.

The Sunnah also warns against illicit proximity, intimacy or privacy (*al-khalwah*) with members of the opposite sex. For the *fitnah* of lust does not fail to arise in such situations. A sense of self-discipline and restraint is to be cultivated in all encounters between men and women. 'The adultery (*zinā'*) of the eyes', writes al-Ghazālī 'is the greatest of the minor sins as it leads to *zinā'* itself, and one who is unable to control his eyes is also unlikely to be able to control his body.'[127] These rules are generally relaxed when the fear of *fitnah* is absent such as in meetings between elderly people or in other situations where the nature of the circumstances overrules the possibility of *fitnah*.[128] When an unmarried person feels overwhelmed by sexual urges, he is advised to seek marriage, and if he cannot afford that, he is advised to fast in order to break the tide of lust. There are, thus, three things, as al-Ghazālī points out, that an unmarried person can do: fasting, lowering the gaze, and busying himself with an occupation that requires concentration and so takes his mind off his carnal urges. But, if all of these prove ineffective, then marriage remains the only possible cure.[129]

On the positive side, a person who has the means to obtain illicit sexual gratification and still avoids it is counted, according to one *Ḥadīth,* among the 'seven whom God Most High will safeguard under His shade on the day of resurrection ...'. And a person who dies in such a state, that is, of 'silent abstinence', is ranked in another *Ḥadīth* as a martyr.[130] However, such praise for the abstinent should not be taken to imply that a temperate attitude is anything but normative in the circumstances. The Prophet ﷺ is thus also reported to have said that 'obscenity and indulgence in it (*al-faḥsh wa'l-tafaḥḥush*) have nothing to do with Islam. The best among Muslims are those who are best in character.' This is reaffirmed in another *Ḥadīth* which exhorts Muslims to 'avoid obscenity (*al-faḥsh*) as God Most High loves not indecency and corruption'.

– إِنَّ الْفَحْشَ وَالتَّفَحُّشَ لَيْسَا مِنَ الاسلامِ فِي شَيْءٍ، وَإِنَّ أَحْسَنَ النَّاسِ إِسلَامًا أَحَاسِنُهُمْ أَخْلَاقًا.

– إِيَّاكُمْ وَالْفَحْشَ فَإِنَّ اللهَ تعالى لَا يُحِبُّ الفحشَ وَالتَّفَحُّشَ.

Al-Ghazālī comments that *faḥsh* in the above *Ḥadīth*s is envisaged as obscene and indecent speech or conduct, mostly relating to sexual perversity, engaged in by those who are morally corrupt (*ahl al-fasād*). The morally corrupt, thus, speak of sex in explicitly repugnant and abusive language, which is either reprehensible (*makrūh*) or forbidden (*maḥẓūr*), depending to some extent on the linguistic usage of the people and the prevailing local custom.[131]

As for *tashbīb*, that is, extolling the physical and moral beauty of women, this is, in principle, not forbidden, neither in poetry nor prose, especially when it is not related to a particular person. However, *tashbīb* may comprise some transgression (*ma*ᶜ*ṣiyah*) if it is attributed to a particular person other than one's own spouse.[132] And as far as singing, dancing, playing of musical instruments, or being an audience for such, is concerned, despite an opinion to the contrary which al-Ghazālī acknowledges, the latter nevertheless maintains that they are permissible - for men or women - provided that they are not utilised as the means to sensuality and *fitnah*.[133] Thus if dancing and singing take place as art forms for general pleasure and entertainment they are permissible, but not if they are used as a means and temptation to sexual corruption.

In all of this, it is well to bear in mind that the *Sharīᶜah* validates 'blocking the means' (*sadd al-dharāʾiᶜ*) to criminal and evil conduct, which is why it forbids drinking even a small amount of wine since this could lead to imbibing larger quantities - which is physically, socially, and morally dangerous. Similarly, *khalwah* is forbidden as it could lead to *zināʾ*. The rule here is that the means and incentives to what is forbidden (*ḥarām*) become themselves *ḥarām*.[134]

As for the punishment of those who become the agents of immorality, the jurists do not specify any particular punishment, but suggest that this is a matter to be determined under the discretionary powers of the imām and the judge, known as *al-siyāsah al-sharᶜiyyah*, or '*Sharīᶜah*-oriented policy'. In order to combat immorality, the judge may order a deterrent punishment of *taᶜzir*, which is an instrument of *siyāsah sharᶜiyyah* in the matter of sentencing, and which provides the authorities with the flexibility to tailor the sentence to the particular circumstances of each case.[135] The principle of *siyāsah* also authorises the ruler and the judge to take all necessary measures to prevent corruption. Ibn Qayyim has quoted Imām Mālik, in support of his own view, that the government and those in charge of community affairs (*ulū'l-amr*) should take action to restrict the free intermingling of men with women in the market-place, recreation areas or other places which are frequented by men. Women, he adds, should be discouraged from sitting for longer than necessary in the shops of craftsmen and manufacturers. But these restrictions may be relaxed, it is added, in respect of elderly women.[136]

While discussing the application of *siyāsah* and *taᶜzīr* to immorality and *fitnah*, the Ḥanafī jurist, Ibn ᶜĀbidīn, refers to the precedent of the caliph ᶜUmar b. al-Khaṭṭāb which validates banishment (*taghrīb*), and the destruction of the tools of immorality and corruption, where this is likely to be effective. Indeed, there is general agreement that a house of corruption, and a dwelling belonging to one who is known for vice, is no longer given the immunity that the *Sharīᶜah* generally grants to private homes. Therefore, it is permitted to raid such a place and destroy any alcohol found as well as the vessels in which it is made or stored, any gambling apparatus etc, if this would deter evil and protect the community against harm. But this may be done only by the authorities, not by the general public. In response to a question as to what should be done to a sinner whose house has become a den for drinking and vice, Imām Mālik said that he should be expelled, and that the house should be rented out. The house should not be sold, Mālik added, because of the possibility that the owner might repent, and in such a case, he should be able to return to it. The Imām further added that prior to expelling the owner from his house, he should be warned two or three times.[137] On the other hand, Ibn ʿĀbidīn also discusses the case of Rabīʿah b. Ummayah who was banned from Medina by Caliph ʿUmar and exiled to Khaybar because of his indulgence in wine-drinking. Ibn Ummayah fled from Khaybar and embraced Christianity. When the Caliph learned of this, he declared, 'I will never sentence a Muslim to exile again.' It is, therefore, suggested that imprisonment is preferable to banishment, since the purpose of punishment in such cases is to prevent corruption, whereas banishment precisely leaves open the possibility of this recurring. Furthermore, when the suspect is sentenced to exile, he is no longer exposed to the same social pressure that he would encounter were he to live in his own community. This may explain why Ibn ʿĀbidīn has observed that 'banishment tends to open the door to corruption'.[138]

Turning to pornographic and indecent literature, and books which distort the truth or propagate pernicious views and doctrines - these may be destroyed. For 'the harm that emanates from these is greater than wine vessels or musical instruments, and there is no liability for financial loss.' There is basically no objection to the publication of books which oppose a prevailing view or doctrine, or which challenge and refute certain positions. However, they may be judged and evaluated on merit and a decision as to whether they should be destroyed may be taken on that basis.[139] There is some disagreement as to whether this ruling is also applicable to non-Muslims, and, according to a minority opinion, no distinction is to be made on grounds of the religious affiliation of the individual concerned. The majority of jurists, however, have held that non-Muslims are entitled to compensation unless the imām rules otherwise.

Broadly speaking, *fitnah* in all of its varieties falls under the purview of *ḥisbah*, that is, commanding good and forbidding evil, which is both a right and duty accorded by the Qur'ān to every individual. Unlike the prescribed punishments *(ḥudūd)*, retaliation *(qiṣāṣ)*, and most of the *taʿzīr* offences, which require adjudication prior to enforcement, *ḥisbah* is not dependant on the prior decision of government authorities. Thus, when a person witnessess any vice being committed, he or she is entitled to intervene and change it to the extent of his or her ability, as the circumstances permit. The question of compensation for loss may then arise and be considered. If *ḥisbah* is attempted within its stipulated limits, no compensation would be payable either by the person who has attempted it or by the state.[140] The imām has authority to entrust the task of *ḥisbah* to a special government body, such as the market inspector (*muḥtasib*), or the police, by statutory legislation and the ordinance of the *ulū'l-amr*, as indeed has been done in most Muslim countries. The imām may do this if he deems it to be of benefit to the community, and if it is in harmony with the objectives of *siyāsah sharʿiyyah*. But the government does not have the authority to overrule altogether the citizen's right to involvement in the promotion of good and the prevention of evil, which is based, as stated above, on the Qur'ān.

Likewise, the principle in regard to the application of the discretionary punishment of *taʿzīr* is not unrestricted: the judge and the imām may order it only upon the perpetration and proof of a clear offence or *maʿṣiyah*. The Muslim judge has, therefore, no open-ended authority to penalise acts which the *Sharīʿah* has neither proscribed nor discouraged.[141] In the light of the overriding concern for government under the rule of law, I have ascertained elsewhere some of the limitations on the powers of the *qāḍī* in regard to *taʿzīr*.[142] One of the basic purposes of flexibility in the application of *taʿzīr* is to facilitate the protection of the moral standards of the Muslim community. In response to the question of whether the judge may impose a penalty under *taʿzīr* without there being an actual violation through *maʿṣiyah*, Ibn ʿĀbidīn has observed that the basic approach in the application of *taʿzīr* is to confine it to its proper grounds (*ḥaṣr asbāb al-taʿzīr*). Nevertheless, the *ʿulamā'* have validated *taʿzīr* for illicit privacy (*khalwah)*, because it might lead to *zinā'*; consequently, the punishment of *khalwah* is permissible in order to pre-empt *zinā'*. Many jurists across the legal schools, and in particular of the Mālikī school, have validated the detention of individuals who are suspected of having committed an offence, prior to adjudication and proof, as a form of *taʿzīr*.[143] This is also the case with regard to persons who are suspected of immorality, if they are found in suspicious circumstances. Lastly, the judge and the imām have authority to combine *taʿzīr* with the prescribed punishment when the circumstances call for it. For instance, a poet by the name of

Najāshī was brought before the Caliph ʿAlī in a state of drunkenness during the daytime in the holy month of fasting, Ramaḍān. The Caliph punished him with the prescribed eighty lashes for drinking, and then twenty lashes again on the following day, and told him that 'the twenty lashes were on account of the disrespect you have shown to the holy month of Ramaḍān'.[144]

4. CONCLUSION

Ever since the rise of the nation-state in Muslim societies, legislation has abounded on how to protect the state against the threat of sedition, conspiracy and rebellion. But the nation-states in Muslim societies were generally unable to make a proportionate effort to balance their overriding concern for security with measures that would safeguard the basic rights of their citizens. Both of these are essential to the viability and success of national governments and neither should be neglected at the expense of the other. It is almost certain that success in securing and protecting the basic rights of citizens improves the prospects of national security. The two objectives are therefore complementary and should be seen and pursued as such. We need to ensure security as well as to protect and enhance the basic rights of the individual. The question of legitimacy and recognition of the lawful authority of the nation-state lies at the root of what has become one of the most dangerous forms of *fitnah* this century, namely the military *coup d'état*. There can be little support, let alone genuine loyalty, for a government that has acceded to power through coercion in the first place, and who then holds on to it through oppressive methods. For a legitimate government must manifest popular representation, and have a clear commitment to the fundamental rights and liberties of its citizens.

One of the many ways in which the government in Muslim societies could enhance popular support for, and loyalty to the state, would be through forging a closer identity with their own heritage, the *Sharīʿah* of Islam. The *Sharīʿah* provides guidelines which preserve human dignity and safeguard individual rights; they protect the individual and inspire latitude, and can be utilised to enhance the Islamic content of statutory law pertaining to *fitnah*, and other related themes such as *ḥisbah*, and *shūrā*. To a large extent, all the following modes of *fitnah* can be regulated under the umbrella of *siyāsah sharʿiyyah*: sedition and incitement to mutiny; violation of the freedom of religion; distorted interpretation; and indulgence in immorality and corruption. But a sound and judicious policy can only be expected of a government which is confident of its own integrity and the loyalty of its citizens. The soundness and propriety of a government is directly related to its concern for the moral standards of society, and to the diligence that it shows in protecting the family unit, youth and vulnerable individuals against corrupt influences. The seditious *fitnah* of our time is closely related to the consultative capacity of the government, the degree to which it can involve citizens in decision-making processes, and the extent to which it can offer inspiration and moral leadership to its people. The oppressive *fitnah* of our time, and the violation of the religious freedom of believers which is its consequence, is a major issue in minority Muslim communities who live under the sovereignty of non-Muslim governments. The challenges that they face are, however, mostly beyond the scope of this discussion. *Fitnah*, in the sense of distortion accompanied by compromised integrity or the outright intention to corrupt, can be diminished simply by encouraging good standards of morality in the family, the educational system, government departments, and, most of all, by taking care to nurture well-balanced and integrated individuals who are not prepared to compromise their conscience by a non-altruistic and unqualified pursuit of materialism. To be sure, no society has ever been totally free of *fitnah*, but when *fitnah* overtakes the leaders of the community and, worse still, when concern on the part of the community itself to combat *fitnah* fades into insignificance in a world where people have lost sight of their values - that is when despair sets in and the ship of society is truly adrift.

IX. Blasphemy
(Sabb Allāh wa Sabb al-Rasūl)

I. INTRODUCTORY REMARKS

I begin my presentation here with a general statement that classical Islamic law penalises both blasphemy and apostasy with death - the juristic manuals of *fiqh* across the *madhāhib* leave one in little doubt that this is the stand of the law. Yet, despite the remarkable consistency that one finds on this point, the issue of punishment by death for apostasy is controversial, and various opinions have been recorded on the matter ever since the early days of Islam. My own presentation of this issue is, however, founded on the basic premise that the death penalty for apostasy is anomalous and conflicts with the explicit Qur'ānic declaration on the freedom of religion. I believe that one way to resolve this conflict is to distinguish apostasy from blasphemy, on the one hand, and then to isolate the political aspect of apostasy - this latter aspect having been the main reason for the capital nature of the punishment in the early period - from the religious aspect thereof, which is a matter entirely of individual conscience. This shall be elaborated in the following pages; at this point, some basic issues need to be addressed.

The first issue that arises concerning blasphemy is over the definition and scope of this offence. Blasphemy has always remained a somewhat open and difficult concept to define. This is to a large extent true not only of Islam but also of Christianity and Judaism. Part of the difficulty over the absence of a specific definition for blasphemy in the works of *fiqh* is due to the fact that blasphemy in these works has generally been subsumed under apostasy and treated as a part thereof. The hallmark of blasphemy is, of course, a contemptuous and hostile attack on the fundamentals of religion, which offends the sensibilities of its adherents. It is on this basis that blasphemy can be distinguished from apostasy, for the latter can take place without any contemptuous attack or sacrilege being committed. The *ʿulamā'* have generally subsumed blasphemy under apostasy with the view that one who blasphemes the essentials of the faith cannot fail, at the same time, to renounce it. This is, of course, true, but a separate definition for blasphemy is still wanting, especially with reference to non-Muslims who can only commit the one but not the other. In the initial section of this chapter, I have explained the nature of the issue of the definition and scope of blasphemy and its differences from or overlap with apostasy (*riddah*), disbelief (*kufr*), and heresy (*zandaqah*). The discussion then proceeds to expound the works of the *ʿulamā'* of the major schools on what may, or may not, amount to blasphemy; whether blasphemy consists primarily of a violation of the right of God or of the right of man, and the consequences, if any, of drawing such distinctions. The chapter continues to set forth the scholastic rulings of the *madhāhib* concerning the admissibility, or otherwise, of repentance for blasphemy, and the issue of blasphemy by a non-Muslim. The reader may thus expect the two major themes of this chapter to be an exposition of the rules and doctrines of the leading schools on the subject of blasphemy, and an attempt at a contemporary re-evaluation of issues that may warrant analysis. This is to a large extent a corollary of my attempt at separating blasphemy from its allied concepts of apostasy, heresy and disbelief.

In Appendix IV, which appears at the end of this volume, I have presented a brief account of the law of blasphemy in Malaysia, Indonesia, Pakistan and Egypt. A section has also been devoted in Appendix V, to Salman Rushdie's novel, *The Satanic Verses*, where I have reviewed some of the opinions and responses proffered by contemporary jurists and commentators.

This enquiry does not aim to be a comprehensive treatment of blasphemy, as many of the juristic details concerning the punishment of this offence etc. fall properly within the scope of criminal law. Therefore, I have presented a brief discussion of such details, concerning myself primarily with the main subject as outlined above.

2. DEFINITION AND SCOPE

The linguistic origin of the word 'blasphemy' is traceable to the Greek '*blapto*' (to harm) and '*pheme*' (speech), simply meaning to defame or insult. According to the *Encyclopedia of Religion and Ethics* (II, 672), blasphemy in Islam is a very broad concept which comprises 'all utterances expressive of contempt for God, for His Names, attributes, laws, commands and prohibitions ... such is the case for instance if a Muslim declares that it is impossible for Allah to see and hear everything, or that Allah cannot endure to all eternity, or that He is not one (*wāḥid*) ... All scoffing at Muhammad or any other prophets of Allah is also to be regarded in Islam as blasphemy.'

It is noted that blasphemy in this passage is so broadly defined as to be capable of application to a wide variety of concepts. No clear distinction has been made between blasphemy and its allied concepts such as apostasy (*riddah*), heresy (*zandaqah*), and denial of Islam (*kufr*). It is interesting to note, perhaps, that Judaism attempts to confine the scope of blasphemy so that it does not include a simple renunciation of the faith. Similarly, blasphemy as an offence in contemporary western law does not include the simple renunciation of faith. In Islamic law, too, prominent scholars like Ibn Taymiyyah and others have attempted to distinguish blasphemy from apostasy, but the majority of jurists, as stated earlier, subsume blasphemy under apostasy. There is, in other words, a tendency to treat blasphemy, apostasy, and infidelity as substantially coterminus and interchangeable. It is, perhaps, true to say that during the lifetime of the Prophet ﷺ almost all the instances of apostasy were accompanied by hostility against and abuse of the Prophet ﷺ, and, as such, it became difficult to separate apostasy from blasphemy. In that era, the 'repudiation of Islam', rather than 'insulting the Prophet ﷺ', was seen to be the more fitting charge to be laid against the renegades and enemies of Islam.

The principal offence of blasphemy in Islam, which I shall address in the following pages, is the reviling of God and the Prophet Muḥammad ﷺ, and a contemptuous rejection of their injunctions. The *ʿulamā'* of the various schools have expounded on the words, acts and expressions which amount to a renunciation of the faith. These include insults to God Most High and to the Prophet ﷺ, irreverent and contemptuous statements that outrage the religious sensibilities of believers, acts such as throwing the Holy Qur'ān on a heap of rubbish, giving the lie to the fundamentals of law and religion, and so on. These have all been identified as words and acts that at one and the same time amount to apostasy, disbelief, heresy, and blasphemy.[145]

Al-Samarā'ī has quoted twelve definitions of apostasy (*riddah*), all of which identify *riddah* as the renunciation or abandonment of Islam by one who professes the Islamic faith. They differ only in regard to certain additional elements, for while some of these definitions specify that renunciation can take place either by word or deed, others add that it can occur not only by means of deliberate speech but also in jest. Most of these definitions are, however, silent on the point of whether apostasy also subsumes blasphemy. But the one definition that al-Samarā'ī has singled out as being most comprehensive is that given by the Shāfiʿī jurist, al-Qalyūbī, since it comprises, as al-Samarā'ī points out, all the varieties of *riddah* - both verbal and physical - and all conduct that denotes a rejection of the [Islamic] religious doctrine. This definition includes expressions which are contemptuous and hostile, as well as those which consist of a simple renunciation of the faith. Al-Qalyūbī's definition is as follows: '*Riddah* is severing one's ties with Islam, with the intention of converting to disbelief (*kufr*), by words or acts that are indicative of *kufr,* regardless of whether they emanate from contempt, hostility, or just disbelief.'[146]

It is thus clear that neither al-Qalyūbī nor al-Samarā'ī have attempted to draw a distinction between disbelief on its own and disbelief which is accompanied by hostility and contempt. Al-Qalyūbi's definition of *riddah* is considered comprehensive precisely because it applies equally to all varieties of disbelief. However, I submit this to be a point of weakness in this definition. For it combines fundamentally different concepts. Simple disbelief is not the same as disbelief which is contemptuous and hostile to the belief-structure of Islam and the sensibilities of its followers. Moreover, the attempt to combine blasphemy with apostasy and disbelief is indicative of weakness on yet other grounds. For instance, it would be difficult to implement the principle of the Qur'ānic proclamation 'there is no compulsion in religion' (II:256), if blasphemy and apostasy were treated as a unified concept.

لَا إِكْرَاهَ فِي الدِّينِ.

I have, therefore, attempted to separate blasphemy from apostasy and disbelief, and to confine my discussion to the treatment of blasphemy alone. Any references which are made to the allied concepts of apostasy, heresy and disbelief are intended only to serve as aids to the elaboration of the main theme of this discussion.

Without entering into detail, it will briefly be noted that the Qur'ānic verses on the subject of disbelief have, on the whole, been conveyed in broad and general terms which enable two possible approaches to be taken toward them. One would be a generic approach that would seek to apply the broad concept of *kufr* to all acts and utterances that amount to a denial of faith and its principles. Such an approach would tend to blur the dividing lines between blasphemy and a variety of other concepts. The alternative approach that may be taken to these Qur'ānic verses would be to distinguish blasphemy from other forms of disbelief in the light of the terms and references that are found in the Holy Book itself. Thus, we find three distinctive terms in the relevant Qur'ānic passages that relate to blasphemy, namely, hostile opposition (*muḥādadah*) as in *Sūrat al-Tawbah* (IX:63), splitting off and militant separation (*mushāqaqah*) as in *Sūrat al-Anfāl* (VIII:13) and 'annoyance' (*adhā*) as in *Sūrat al-Aḥzāb* (XXXIII:57), all of which signify hostility towards God Most High and His Messenger ﷺ expressed through vilification or militancy.[147] Now, if we apply the name of blasphemy to only the hostile and contemptuous varieties of *kufr*, we would effectively be separating blasphemy from the other varieties of disbelief in which these elements are absent.

The attempt to treat blasphemy as a distinct offence is justified, as already noted, firstly, on the grounds that it consists of insult and contempt which may not be the case with regard to other varieties of *kufr*, and secondly, in that it offends the religious sensibilities of the community of believers. It would appear that blasphemy, for the most part, subsumes apostasy, whereas the latter may not amount to blasphemy, especially when apostasy consists of a simple rejection of the faith but does not involve sacrilege. This must be qualified by saying, however, that blasphemy only subsumes apostasy with reference to Muslims, since a non-Muslim by definition could not commit the Islamic offence of apostasy. Blasphemy can, on the other hand, be committed by Muslims and non-Muslims alike. However, words and acts must be explicitly hostile and offensive to the religious sensibilities of Muslims if they are to qualify as blasphemous. A non-Muslim would not be committing blasphemy merely by professing a religious doctrine which conflicts with the belief-structure of Islam. The Christian belief, for example, that Jesus ﷵ is the son of God may be deemed blasphemous by the Muslim faith as it explicitly contradicts the clear text of the Qur'ān wherein God Most High denies having any offspring (CXII:3). But since Christians normally profess this belief, not so as to offend Muslim sensibilities but as an article of their own faith, they are not committing blasphemy. By contrast when a Muslim commits blasphemy, he or she automatically renounces Islam, for as Ibn Taymiyyah points out, the blasphemer (*al-sābbāb*) 'insults, ridicules and denigrates God, or His Prophets, and the enormity of this is greater than any type of disbelief.'[148] This is the view of the vast majority of *ʿulamā'* and some have even claimed a consensus (*ijmāʿ*) in its support.[149] But, there is a minority opinion, attributed to some jurists of Iraq, that utterances which consist of insult and abuse amount to blasphemy only when the perpetrator considers what he says to be permissible in principle (*in kāna mustaḥillan*), but not if he does not make such a claim, in which case he would be guilty of a transgression (*fisq*), but not of *kufr*.[150] This opinion would preclude from the purview of blasphemy, expressions that the perpetrator may have uttered in attenuating circumstances which do not reflect balanced judgement or his normal state of mind.

The juristic manuals I have consulted exhibit a remarkable consistency in the themes that they discuss in their chapters devoted to apostasy. Thus, we find that the juristic expositions of the *ʿulamāʾ* of the four leading legal schools on apostasy differ only on certain points, when they discuss issues such as whether the apostate/blasphemer should, or should not, be offered an opportunity to repent; whether his repentance is at all acceptable; whether he automatically relinquishes some of his rights, including the property that he owned prior to recantation; and whether, in the event of repentance, his devotional acts, such as prayer and fasting performed prior to apostasy remain intact. Other issues that are typically addressed by the jurists include the question as to whether or not the non-Muslim (*dhimmī*) should be treated differently from the Muslim in the matter of blasphemy; whether the female apostate is liable to the same punishment as the male; and whether insulting the Prophet's ﷺ wives and Companions is to be treated on the same footing as insulting the Prophet ﷺ himself. The jurists also discuss the question as to whether a distinction should be made between insult to God (*sabb Allāh*) and insult to the Prophet Muḥammad ﷺ, and also whether insulting other recognised Prophets and the Angels amounts to blasphemy. These issues, addressed in the juristic manuals, receive fairly consistent responses. Expositions of these issues have the advantage of identifying the positions that the *ʿulamāʾ* have taken with regard to them fairly clearly, even in the absence of clear definitions. The relative absence of disagreement over issues pertaining to apostasy also tends to impress upon the reader the high level of sensitivity and caution that the *ʿulamāʾ* have exhibited in the treatment of this subject. Certain issues have, nevertheless, remained unresolved and controversial, one of these being the actual definition of disbelief (*kufr*), which has meant different things to different individuals and sects.

3. DISBELIEF *(KUFR)*

The juristic literature on *kufr* is primarily concerned with the question as to what may, or may not, amount to *kufr*, a broad term which comprises almost every variety of disbelief, polytheism (*shirk*), blasphemy, and apostasy. In the Qur'ān and Sunnah, as well as in the juristic works of the *ʿulamā'*, *kufr* occurs with two different meanings, namely, the greater *kufr* (*al-kufr al-akbar*), which is the explicit and unequivocal renunciation of the faith, and the lesser *kufr* (*al-kufr dūn al-kufr*) which is a degree below the former. *Kufr* in the latter sense does not involve outright disbelief, and it is used metaphorically in order to accentuate the gravity of conduct which actually amounts to transgression (*fisq*).[151] What is of interest here is that the word *kufr* has been applied in a generic sense to concepts which do not necessarily amount to disbelief. Readers who are familiar with the sectarian literature of Islam will also note the somewhat facile manner in which accusations of *kufr* were made by the different sects and factions against one another, so much so that it often becomes difficult to distinguish between the greater and the lesser *kufr*. Thus, it is not always easy to differentiate the infidel (*kāfir*) from the transgressor (*fāsiq*) or from the hypocrite (*munāfiq*) respectively.

In his *al-Fiṣal fi'l-Milal wa'l-Ahwā' wa'l-Niḥal,* Ibn Ḥazm has a chapter entitled 'Who is an infidel and who not?' where he opens the discussion with the following comments:

> There is disagreement on the question of what amounts to disbelief and what exactly distinguishes belief from disbelief. There are groups and sects, on the one hand, who maintain that anyone who rejects their own respective views and doctrines on the articles of the faith becomes a *kāfir* ... others have held that rejection of their own doctrines by their opponents amounts to *kufr* only in regard to the attributes of God but that it amounts to transgression *(fisq)* in all other areas. According to yet another view: a Muslim may not be charged with *kufr* or *fisq* for an opinion regarding either dogmatic or juridical issues *(iʿtiqād aw fatwā)*; and opinions of this kind may [in fact] consist of *ijtihād* which merits a reward.[152]

On the same page, Ibn Ḥazm notes that the *ʿulamā'* disagreed on whether a person who abandons the obligatory canonical prayers (*ṣalāh*), legal alms (*zakāh*), fasting (*ṣiyām*), and the pilgramage (*ḥajj*) also becomes a *kāfir.* He then continues to expound the views and doctrines of the Khārijiyyah, the Qadariyyah, the Bāṭiniyyah, and the Murjiʿah, their accusations and counter-accusations against one another, and debates, taking each case, whether they amount to a mere transgression or to outright disbelief.

It is not my purpose to enter into the details of such polemics and even less so to ascertain, justify or refute the charges of disbelief that have often been laid by individuals and sects against one another. I only submit here that many of these accusations tend to be at odds with the letter and spirit of the guidance that is found in the revelatory sources. It is also due partly to the absence of consensus on the definition of *kufr* that the different sects and factions have found it possible to level charges of disbelief against one another. Furthermore, the concept and definition of *kufr* would appear to have widened so much in scope that it became possible to label as '*kufr*' almost any deviation, or even a mere disagreement. Surely, though, the correct approach would lie in the opposite direction, for instead of allowing an expansion in the definition of the concept of *kufr*, it should have been narrowed down, specified, and isolated from its allied concepts. This would have been possible, for instance, through distinguishing and specifying the various types of *kufr*, and those of its components which would merit such isolation. There is evidence to suggest that such an approach would be more in harmony with the Sunnah of the Prophet ﷺ.

The basic guideline that is conveyed in a number of *Ḥadīth*s (some of which I have quoted in an earlier chapter on freedom of religion) has been summarised by Abū Zahrah as follows: 'no one may accuse another of disbelief, blasphemy or apostasy without manifest evidence, and anyone who does so partakes of the charge himself.'[153] This view finds support in al-Ghazālī who is critical of the peremptory manner in which a number of sectarian scholars have accused opposing sects of infidelity and disbelief. Note, for example, the following statement in al-Ghazālī's *al-Munqidh min al-Ḍalāl*:

> The Ḥanbalites tax the Ashᶜarites with unbelief regarding the affirmation of God Most High 'being firmly seated on the throne ... ' The Ashᶜarites accuse the Muᶜtazilah with unbelief claiming that the latter tax the Apostle with lying regarding the 'possiblity of the ocular vision of God Most High'.[154]

In a subsequent passage, al-Ghazālī expresses his disapproval of these accusations:

> Speculative matters are of two sorts, one which touches on the roots of belief, and one which touches on the branches. Now, the roots of belief are three: belief in God, and in His Apostle, and in the Last Day. All other things are branches. Know too, that there can in no wise be any taxing with unbelief regarding the branches ...'.[155]

It thus appears that the precise meaning of the references in the sources to the ocular vision of God, and of God's 'being firmly seated on the throne' (see for example LVII:4) are not known, for these issues are decidedly speculative, and to base accusations of unbelief on them is totally unjustified. These phrases are also included in the parts of the Qur'ān which are known as 'obscure' (*mutashābihāt)* whose precise meaning is known only to God Most High. Engaging in speculative discourse and polemics over such issues is clearly discouraged by evidence found in the Sunnah, and any claim to certainty concerning them is an excess in itself, let alone a basis for a charge of disbelief.

In addition to al-Ghazālī, Ibn ʿĀbidīn also made a similar comment concerning this subject. He admits that there are many unfounded accusations of disbelief in the works of the followers of the *madhāhib*, but hastens to add that none of the prominent *mujtahidūn* engaged in such, and that those who made such charges were mainly writers of a lesser calibre whose works do not command a high degree of credibility.[156]

4. HERESY *(ZANDAQAH)*

This is a parallel concept which is frequently encountered in the literature on the subject of *kufr*. Broadly speaking the term 'heretics' (*zanādiqah*) refers to persons who ostensibly profess Islam but who, like the hypocrites (*munāfiqūn*) during the lifetime of the Prophet ﷺ, conceal their inner disbelief and pretend to believe, the while disseminating falsehood among the believers.[157] The precise meaning and definition of *zandaqah* has remained somewhat uncertain. However, due to a variety of considerations, including the implication of conspiracy against the ruling authorities, the *ʿulamā'* have taken an unmistakably vigorous stand on the punishment of *zandaqah*.

Many different meanings of '*zandaqah*' and '*zanādiqah*' have been recorded, for example: expressing impudence and disdain (*al-tahattuk wa'l-istihtār*) towards the established religious values of Islam; or adherence to Magian and Manichean beliefs, and agnosticism. Evidence suggests that the word has most frequently been applied to persons who professed the beliefs of Mani and Mazdak in private, but who claimed to be Muslim in public. This was the early usage of the word '*zandaqah*', the other meanings gradually being added during the latter half of the second century A.H. 'The word was loosely used to describe people who believed in their older religions, but who ostensibly professed Islam for self-aggrandisement and material gain.'[158] *Zanādiqah* was also used to describe people who doubted the veracity of the established religion and who professed the supremacy of reason in all spheres; it also included persons who propagated disbelief, and indulged in wine-drinking and immoral activities, and those who ridiculed the whole idea of religion. Furthermore, those who believed in the permanence of the temporal world (*dawām al-dahr*) were also called *zanādiqah*. Originally, they were the followers of Disan, Mani and Mazdak, who believed that light and darkness were the essence of creation and that the universe originated from them. Mazdak also propagated the view that women and land were the common property of all.[159]

This uncertainty in defining *zandaqah, kufr, sabb Allāh wa'l-Rasūl* ﷺ and *riddah*, and the absence of clear distinctions between them, can be seen, once again, in the following quote from *The Encyclopedia of Religion*:

> From the viewpoint of Islamic law, blasphemy may be defined as any verbal expression that gives grounds for suspicion of apostasy *(riddah)*. In theological terms, blasphemy often overlaps with infidelity *(kufr)* which is the deliberate rejection of God and revelation. In this sense, expressing religious opinions at variance with standard Islamic views could easily be looked upon as blasphemous. Blasphemy can also be seen as the equivalent of heresy *(zandaqah)* ... Thus, in describing the Islamic concept of blasphemy, it is necessary to include not only insulting language directed to God, the Prophet, and the revelation, but also theological positions and even mystical aphorisms that have come under suspicion.[160]

Some jurists have taken a particularly rigorous stand on *zandaqah*, especially the Ḥanafīs of Iraq who treated the heretic (*zindīq*) even more severely than the apostate. While punishment by death was assigned for both, the latter was to be given an opportunity to repent and to be acquitted as a result. But the Ḥanafīs, and also Imām Mālik, ruled that repentance in the case of a *zindīq* was of no avail and did nothing to relieve him of the mandatory death penalty. On the other hand, the majority, including the Shāfiʿīs, have held that the heretic was to be treated like the apostate and should likewise be given the opportunity to repent.[161]

5. BLASPHEMOUS EXPRESSIONS AND THE QUESTION OF INTENT

The first issue to be discussed here is the state of mind of the blasphemer and the relevance of his intention regarding the words or expressions he might have uttered. To what extent is it true, for instance, to say that blasphemy is a strict liability offence? Does the law require proof that the words uttered must be representative of the state of mind of the offender? A second issue would be to ascertain the criteria by which to evaluate the meaning and import of words. In this context, I shall review some words and expressions that the *ʿulamā'* have identified as being typically blasphemous.

In response to the question of whether a person who reviles God becomes a *kāfir* solely on the basis of the words he or she uttered, Ibn Ḥazm writes that no one on the face of the earth would disgree that *sabb Allāh* amounts to *kufr*, except for the Jahmiyyah and the Ashʿariyyah who have held that insult to God Most High and declaration of *kufr* is not necessarily *kufr*, but only an indication that the perpetrator has ceased to believe in God. Ibn Ḥazm hastens to add that this view is premised on a corrupt foundation far removed from the consensus of the followers of Islam. For they (the Jahmiyyah and Ashʿariyyah) maintain that faith (*īmān*) consists only of inner affirmation (*taṣdīq bi'l-qalb*) and that words and statements are of little significance by comparison. In their view, a man may utter words of disbelief and yet still be a believer. Once again Ibn Ḥazm rejects this line of argument and regards it as undiluted disbelief (*kufr mujarrad*), as it is contrary to the consensus (*ijmāʿ*) of the *ummah* and violates the commands of God Most High and His Messenger ﷺ. He continues by saying that all those who believe that the Qur'ān is the speech of God which was revealed to us by the Prophet Muḥammad ﷺ will agree that our judgement of the belief and disbelief of others must be based on what they say. In addition, he adds that there is ample evidence in the Qur'ān to prove that this is the case. At this point, Ibn Ḥazm cites two Qur'ānic passages in support of his statement:

(a)- Verily those who say that God is the Messiah, the son of Mary, have disbelieved. (V:17)

لَقَدْ كَفَرَ الَّذِينَ قَالُوا إِنَّ اللهَ هُوَ الْمَسِيحُ ابْنُ مَرِيم.

(b)- And they uttered the word of *kufr* and so disbelieved after their [profession of] Islām. (IX:74)

وَلَقَدْ قَالُوا كَلِمَةَ الْكُفْرِ وَكَفَرُوا بَعْدَ إِسلامِهِمْ.

Thus, it is clear from the foregoing that the belief or disbelief of individuals is determined on the basis of their words, unless it is known that they were uttered under duress. Similarly, as Ibn Ḥazm points out, evidence can be found in the Qur'ān, with reference to conduct being a sufficient means of establishing a person's belief or otherwise. For example, God Most High declared Satan a disbeliever when the latter was ordered to prostrate to Prophet Adam ﷺ, but refused (II:34). It is suggested that the declaration was on account of Satan's conduct, despite his professed belief in God as his creator - manifest in his statement that God created him from fire and Adam from clay. Ibn Ḥazm also adds that faith is a hidden phenomenon which is known only to God Most High, but that our judgement of it has to be based on the words and conduct of people. Ibn Ḥazm concludes, that reviling God and the Prophet ﷺ amounts to *kufr*, regardless of the possibility that its perpetrator may not have meant to renounce Islam.[162]

There is general agreement on the point that declaring a Muslim an infidel (*takfīr al-Muslim*), whether for blasphemy or apostasy, is for the most part a matter which is determined on the basis of obvious facts, that is, speech and conduct which can be supported by evidence. Words of disbelief may be explicit, such as reviling God and the Prophet ﷺ by expressions which are commonly known to be abusive and which convey mockery, hostility or contempt. In the case of such words, the question of motive and intention is immaterial, provided that the perpetrator is in full possession of his faculties. There is no denial that faith is essentially a state of mind, and the jurists are in agreement that a person who conceals his disbelief is still an infidel in the eyes of God, but that the rules of the *Sharīᶜah* concerning blasphemy and apostasy do not apply to him unless his state of mind is expressed in words and deeds. Words that are uttered under duress while the speaker remains a believer or words spoken in a state of permissible intoxication are of no account. However, with regard to intoxication which is forbidden in the first place, the Mālikīs, Shāfiᶜīs and Ḥanbalīs have held that this is not an excuse and that one who commits blasphemy or apostasy in such a state is accountable for it. Only the Ḥanafīs have held, according to the preferred view of this school, that an intoxicated person may not be declared *kāfir*, regardless of the type or the grounds of his intoxication.[163]

There is a circumstantial aspect to blasphemy which tends to vary with reference to its context, the prevailing custom, and public opinion. The meaning of words is often determined in the light of the context in which they are uttered, as well as the nuances they may have acquired through customary usage. But, neither the words nor their customary usage are always clear, and a certain amount of ambiguity arises with regard to words of abuse that are implicit and allusive. Furthermore, words and expressions may convey an insult according to their customary usage, even if they are not offensive in the dictionary sense, and it is usually the former which carries the greater weight in such an evaluation. Since custom varies with reference to time and place, it would follow that insulting words may amount to an insult in certain circumstances but not necessarily in others. It is for this reason, as Ibn Taymiyyah points out, that insult or *sabb* cannot be defined either on linguistic or juridical grounds alone, and that the basic criterion to which reference must be made is popular custom. The import of abusive words is thus to be ascertained on this ground, and anything which the people regard as insulting will be deemed as such.[164] Ibn Taymiyyah elaborates that verbal insult occurs in two forms, namely, maledictions or abuse. The former would include such statements as 'may God disgrace so and so', or 'may God's curse be upon so and so', or 'death to so and so'. With reference to the Prophet ﷺ, maledictions of this kind include expressions such as 'may no peace and blessing of God be upon him,' or 'may he be disgraced', etc. These are said to amount to insult when they are explicit, but not if they are couched in terms that are obvious only to some people and not to others. For instance, according to reports, on more than one occasion the Prophet ﷺ was addressed by the Jews with the phrase 'death be upon you (*al-sām ʿalaykum*)' instead of the common greeting 'peace be upon you (*al-salām ʿalaykum*)'. The question arose as to whether this and similar other expressions amounted to blasphemy at all. There are two views on this: firstly, that they do indeed amount to blasphemy, and secondly, that they do not since the insulting words are not conveyed in explicit and unequivocal terms. An insult, in other words, which is hidden behind a greeting is not explicit. The reports also suggest that the Prophet ﷺ did not himself penalise such offences. Moreover, he ﷺ instructed the Muslims that 'when the Jews greet you with the phrase 'death be upon you (*al-sām ʿalaykum)*', then you should simply say 'and upon you (*wa ʿalaykum)*'.[165]

قَالَ النَّبِيُّ ﷺ: إِنَّ اليهودَ اذا اَسْلَمُوا فانّـما يَقـولُ اَحَدُهُم
السَّام عليكم فَقُولوا وعليكم.

There is a view concerning these incidents, however, which maintains that in principle the insult in question would be sufficient for the death penalty to be applied to the Jews, and the fact that the Prophet ﷺ pardoned the offenders was due to the weakness of Islam at that time. Having recorded this view, though, Ibn Taymiyyah goes on to observe that it is no more than an arbitrary and presumptive elaboration. For, had it been an insult that incurred capital punishment, the Prophet ﷺ would have ordered it; or if it called for some penalty but not capital punishment, he would have ordered a lesser punishment. But the fact that the Prophet ﷺ did not do so indicates that a punishment was not warranted.[166] Ibn Ḥazm makes a hypothetical observation on this point, saying that if the Jew in question had been a Muslim, then his saying *al-sām ʿalaykum*, to the Prophet ﷺ would have rendered him an infidel (*kāfir*).[167]

Another type of insult known in Arabic is *taʿrīḍ bi'l-adhā*, or an attempt to annoy, and it consists of an ill-wish or malediction the contents of which are ultimately true. When someone says, for example, that 'death is incumbent upon so and so', the question arises as to whether a malediction of this sort really amounts to an insult. According to one opinion, such utterances fall short of an insult on the analysis that they consist of something which is obviously true. But Ibn Taymiyyah refutes this as being no more than a weak opinion, and adds that any invocation of death upon the Prophet ﷺ amounts to an insult as it would also with reference to other individuals.[168]

The second form of insult under discussion consists of words of abuse such as 'ass', 'dog', 'fraud', and other similar names and adjectives which are straightforwardly insulting in the customary usage of most peoples. While affirming that all of these are typical words of insult in the custom of the Arabs, Ibn Taymiyyah observes that it matters little whether the insult is conveyed in poetry or prose. He adds that satirical poetry is even more offensive as it tends to arouse emotions more effectively than does prose; he then adds a very lengthy list of abusive and insulting expressions which cannot be exhaustive as they are virtually endless in any language. Reference must, therefore, be made to the prevailing customs of society, and the circumstances in which such expressions are uttered.[169]

In addition, in contrast to libel and slander, words of insult usually attribute a defect (*ᶜayb*) to someone in a manner that compromises their personal honour in the eyes of others. The factual content of such an attribution is of no relevance. This is, as I have elsewhere explained, a point of distinction between insult and libel, for the latter normally implies the factuality of the charge being made.[170]

Expressions which convey a state of mind, or else an attitude of one person towards another, without the intent to offend, normally do not amount to insult. Thus, when someone makes a statement such as 'I do not believe so and so', or 'I do not follow so and so', or 'I do not like so and so', then expressions of this kind amount neither to insult nor to explicit accusation and denial (*takdhīb ṣarīḥ*). For lack of affection and belief may be due to a variety of factors, including ignorance, envy and arrogance. However, with reference to the Prophet ﷺ, an explicit denial (*takdhīb ṣarīḥ*) such as saying that 'he was neither a Messenger nor a Prophet', or that 'nothing was revealed to him', and so forth, amounts only to disbelief (*kufr*) but not insult (*sabb*).

Although these are explicit denials which are equivalent to saying that 'he was a liar', there is, nevertheless, a difference between a simple denial and calling someone a liar. Often, the same meaning can be conveyed in different words, some of which may amount to *sabb*, but not all. Notwithstanding this, Imām Aḥmad b. Ḥanbal held the opinion - and he seems to be alone in this - that a person who says to the muezzin, with regard to the call to prayer, 'you lied' (*kadhabta*), is a blasphemer, for his statement denies the Muslim affirmation of and belief in the Oneness of God and the truth of the prophethood of Muḥammad ﷺ (which is explicitly stated in the call); it is also an insult to the community of believers.[171]

Insulting a person (*sabb*) and attributing a lie to them (*takdhīb*) are, however, two different concepts and this can be seen clearly in the following *Ḥadīth Qudsī*[172] where God Most High states upon the tongue of the Prophet ﷺ:

> The son of Adam insulted Me *(shatamanī ibn Ādam)* and it was unbecoming of him to do so; he also attributed a lie to Me *(khadhdhabanī)* and

it was unbecoming of him to do that. As for his insult to Me, it was his saying that I took unto Myself a son, and he belied Me by saying that he will not return to Me as he was when I first created him.

شَتَمَنِى اِبْنُ آدَمَ وَمَا يَنْبَغِى لَهُ ذلِكَ، وَكَذَّبَ بَنِى اِبْنِ آدَمَ وَمَا

يَنْبَغِى لَهُ ذلِكَ. فَأَمَّا شَتْمُهُ اِيَّاىَ فَقَوْلُهُ: إِنِّى اتَّخَذْتُ وَلَدًا

وَأَمَّا تَكْذِيبُهُ اِيَّاىَ فَقَوْلُهُ لَنْ يُعِيدُنِى كَمَا بَدَأَنِى.

While quoting this *Ḥadīth*, Ibn Taymiyyah acknowledges the differences between an insult and a lie, but he adds that there may be occasions when attributing a lie to another may amount to insult, and that this is a matter to be determined by reference to its context, linguistic nuances and to customary usage.[173]

In a similar vein, the attribution of a deliberate lie to the Prophet ﷺ (*takdhīb al-Rasūl*) is to be distinguished from an insult to the Prophet ﷺ (*sabb al-Rasūl*). This can be seen, for example, in the *Ḥadīth* which states: 'Let him who deliberately attributes a lie to me, take his seat in the Fire [of hell].'[174]

مَن كَذَبَ عَلَىَّ مُتَعَمِّداً فَلْيَتَبَوَّأْ مَقْعَدَهُ مِنَ النَّارِ.

This *Ḥadīth* is obviously silent on any punishment in this world for the conduct at issue. But, there is no doubt, as many commentators have stated, that deliberately accusing the Prophet ﷺ of lying is one of 'the gravest forms of all distortions of truth, and one that calls for the wrath of God Most High. For saying that the Prophet ﷺ has lied is essentially to attribute a lie to God Almighty Himself.'[175] However, unlike the offence of insulting God and the Prophet ﷺ, for which the majority of *'ulamā'* have assigned capital punishment, there is no specific punishment for attributing a lie to the Prophet ﷺ. The deliberate fabrication and forgery of *Ḥadīth*, wherein reports are invented and attributed to the Prophet ﷺ is a heinous sin, but one which is liable to *ta'zīr* punishment only. Thus, when a person relates a *Ḥadīth* which he knows to be a lie, he commits a major sin, but he does not become an infidel unless there is something in the report which indicates disbelief. If what is said amounts to *kufr* by itself, then it would be treated as such whether the statement is attributed to the Prophet ﷺ or otherwise. With regard to forgery, the scholars of *Ḥadīth* have isolated a vast number of fabricated statements which they have classified under the general heading of *al-mawḍūʿāt*.[176] Invented *Ḥadīth* are, however, to be distinguished from statements which deny the truth of the prophethood of Muḥammad ﷺ. As already indicated, a denial of this kind amounts to *kufr* if it is devoid of abuse and contempt, but when denial is accompanied by the latter two, it amounts to *sabb*. Infidelity or disbelief (*kufr*) is therefore to be distinguished, as Ibn Taymiyyah himself has stated, from blasphemy. A person who declares his disbelief is an apostate (*murtadd*), but one who conceals it is a heretic (*zindīq*). Ibn Taymiyyah adds that the distinction between blasphemy and apostasy is not always clear, as there may be instances when the matter is open to interpretation and *ijtihād*. This is also borne out by the fact that the jurists have held different views as to whether, and how, to distinguish apostasy from blasphemy.[177] The result that emerges from this analysis is that, despite a conceptual distinction that some jurists have acknowledged between blasphemy and apostasy, their attempts did not reflect the majority position which subsumed the one under the other, and applied the same punishment to both.

There is general agreement that slanderous accusation (*qadhf*) or the attribution of unchaste conduct to the Prophet ﷺ, the denial of the legitimacy of his descent, or the attribution of any of these insults to the mother of the Prophet ﷺ, amount to blasphemy (*sabb al-Nabī* ﷺ) and to automatic renunciation of the faith. *Sabb al-Nabī* ﷺ whether consisting of slander or other forms of insult can be committed by both Muslims and non-Muslims alike, and there is no difference between them in so far as the question of punishment is concerned.[178] Apostasy can, on the other hand, be committed only by Muslims.

Other expressions which the jurists have discussed under the explicit forms of insult to the Prophet ﷺ normally include statements which attack his personal integrity, such as saying that 'he was greedy, ignorant, an idiot, or that he abandoned the canonical prayer'.[179] Insults which are not explicit, and yet imply mockery and disrespect are liable to the discretionary punishment of *taʿzīr*, such as when one person tells another, 'even if you bring me the Prophet on your shoulders, I will not ... '. For this type of expression lacks clarity as both the element of contempt and its relation to the Prophet ﷺ are vague and indirect.[180] An explicit insult, whether to God or the Prophet ﷺ has been held to carry the capital punishment, whereas expressions in which there is doubt, and those which fall short of a direct insult are liable to *taʿzīr* punishment, the nature and quantity of which may be determined by the judge.[181]

The jurists are in agreement that insulting and attributing unchaste behaviour (*qadhf*) to the wife of the Prophet ﷺ, ʿĀ'ishah, amounts to blasphemy and disbelief, for her chastity is clearly affirmed by the Qur'ānic text XXIV:16. Charges of this kind not only compromise the honour of the Prophet ﷺ but also attribute a lie to the Qur'ān. Thus, Ibn Taymiyyah has stated that there is a consensus on this matter, and that all the leading imāms have concurred that insulting ʿĀ'ishah is tantamount to an affront to the Prophet ﷺ himself. Imām Mālik's ruling on this issue, which is widely quoted by others, is that this offence against ʿĀ'ishah invokes the same punishment as an insult to the Prophet ﷺ. While confirming Imām Mālik's ruling on the issue, Ibn Ḥazm stresses that insulting ʿĀ'ishah is apostasy in the full sense (*riddah tāmmah*) as it attributes falsehood to the words of God Most High. As for insult to and abuse of the other wives of the Prophet ﷺ, the *ʿulamā'* have recorded two different views; firstly, that it is like abusing the rest of the Companions, and as such is an offence which is liable to *taʿzīr* punishment only. The second view, which is considered to be preferable, holds that an affront to, or scandalous accusation against any of the Prophet's ﷺ wives is to be treated on the same footing as an insult to ʿĀ'ishah. The proponents of this view refer to a statement attributed to the prominent Companion, Ibn ʿAbbās, who equated affronting the wives of the Prophet ﷺ with insulting and dishonouring the Prophet ﷺ himself.[182] The jurists have also held that the abuse of other Prophets who are identified as such in the Qur'ān, Sunnah or *ijmāʿ*, by anyone who knows of this identification, or insulting all the Prophets without specifying any particular one by name, is tantamount to an affront to the Prophet Muḥammad ﷺ. For belief (*īmān*) in all of them is an article of the Muslim faith, and an insult to them is therefore 'apostasy and *kufr* on the part of any Muslim, and it is *muḥārabah* (open hostility and war) when committed by a *dhimmī*'.[183] This latter means that if the person charged with the insult is a *dhimmī*, that is a non-Muslim citizen of the Islamic state, then he loses his protected status and becomes liable to punishment for blasphemy. The jurists are equally in agreement that insulting and reviling the Angels in general, or any one of them in particular, falls under the same rules which are applicable to insulting the Prophets, provided that there is no disagreement on the identity and status of the Angel when such is specified.[184] This conclusion is drawn from the Qur'ānic reference to the Angels as all being messengers of God. Insult, mockery, and contempt in regard to them, therefore, fall under the same rules that are applied to insulting the Prophet Muḥammad ﷺ.[185]

6. THE RIGHT OF GOD AND THE RIGHT OF MAN

At the outset it should be noted that the *ʿulamā'* have surprisingly taken a more serious view of insult to the Prophet Muḥammad ﷺ as compared to reviling God Most High. This is not to say that the offence in either case is anything less than blasphemy; nevertheless, it has been said by way of explanation that the honour of God cannot, in any real sense, be touched by the nonsensical conduct of a misguided individual. In this case, the blasphemer merely brings disgrace upon himself, as he can in no way compromise the status of God in the eyes of the believers, but as a human being, the Prophet ﷺ is susceptible of abuse and therefore his rights must be protected. However, the vast majority of jurists have nevertheless held that insulting and mocking God is blasphemy, and that the perpetrator of the attack automatically becomes a *kāfir* on the grounds that 'no one would do so unless he is a disbeliever', as al-Buhūtī points out.[186]

The main purpose in drawing a distinction between reviling God (*sabb Allāh*) and insulting the Prophet (*sabb al-Rasūl*) ﷺ is to determine the admissibility or otherwise of repentance in each case. This distinction is also related in turn to the binary division of rights into the right of God and the right of man. Thus, according to the majority view, *sabb Allāh* consists of the violation of the right of God (*ḥaqq Allāh*), which is in principle pardonable when the offender repents and expresses regret over his conduct. Insult to the Prophet ﷺ, is, on the other hand, held to be a violation of the right of man, or *ḥaqq al-ʿabd* (also referred to as *al-ḥaqq al-ādamī*), that is, the personal right and honour of the Prophet ﷺ. There is disagreement among the *ʿulamā'* on the question of whether repentance by a person who insults the Prophet ﷺ is admissible at all, and whether repentance in this case absolves the offender from punishment.[187] According to the majority opinion, the punishment for reviling God Most High is cancelled upon repentance prior to arrest. But, there is reservation on this point when it comes to the question of insulting the Prophet Muḥammad ﷺ. This offence, it is said, is similar to slanderous accusation (*qadhf*), as both consist mainly of the violation of the right of man, and repentance in either case is of little consequence, for only a pardon which is granted by the injured party, not repentance as such, constitutes a valid ground for dropping the punishment in offences pertaining to the right of man. Thus, it is argued that blaspheming against the Prophet ﷺ consists of a violation of his personal right, and that only the Prophet ﷺ himself could pardon such conduct. As a result, punishment in this case is enforced regardless of whether the offender repents. This is the ruling of the Ḥanbalī and Mālikī schools, although in both different opinions have been recorded among their respective scholars. The Ḥanbalī/Mālikī ruling operates on the assumption that the right to pardon, in the case of insult to the Prophet ﷺ, only existed when the Prophet ﷺ was alive as he could grant it himself, but that it was discontinued thereafter. However, the Ḥanbalī/Mālikī position which overrules admissibility of repentance in the case of *sabb al-Rasūl* ﷺ is somewhat questionable. The correct view, in my opinion, is that after the demise of the Prophet ﷺ, the offence of *sabb al-Rasūl* ﷺ should be no different to *sabb Allāh* as both of these violate the right of God. This is, to all intents and purposes, the position maintained by the Ḥanafīs and Shāfiʿīs. But they arrived at this decision through a different route, for they consider blasphemy, whether in the form of *sabb Allāh* or *sabb al-Rasūl* ﷺ, as a sub-variety of apostasy, which is in turn considered as an offence which violates the right of God. My own view of this issue, which I have elaborated in an earlier section of this chapter, is that blasphemy need not be regarded as a sub-variety of apostasy; that the two are different concepts and each requires a different treatment. But, I still submit that blasphemy, in both of its varieties under discussion, consists of a violation of public rights. Therefore, it is not only reasonable, but also in the interests of consistency, that the head of state and competent judicial authorities, in their capacities as defenders and representatives of the right of God, should act in the same role, not only with regard to *sabb Allāh*, but also with regard to *sabb al-Rasūl* ﷺ.

Furthermore, the distinction between the right of God and the right of man is often determined by the preponderance of the respective interests of the individual and the community. Assigning a particular interest or right to one or the other of these categories is, to some extent, a matter of juristic opinion, for basically all rights in Islam, as the Mālikī jurist al-Qarāfī points out, consist primarily of the right of God, which is, in turn, exercised and represented by the community of believers and their lawful government.[188]

Moreover, it would appear eminently logical, and consistent with the central role of the Prophet Muḥammad ﷺ in the creed and dogma of Islam, that an insult to him is treated in the same way as a revilement of God; and that both of these are considered first and foremost violations of the religious beliefs of Islam and of the rights of the community of believers. Blasphemy in either of these two forms is, therefore, a blatant violation of the right of God.

7. THE QUESTION OF REPENTANCE

Differences of opinion have arisen among the schools of law with regard to whether the blasphemer should be asked to repent, and whether his repentance, if obtained, is admissible. In this context, the admissibility of repentance acquires special significance as it can lead to the absolute and unconditional acquittal of the accused. Sometimes there is disagreement over issues even among jurists of the same school, and this tends to introduce an element of doubt in ascertaining the representative view of the individual schools.

While the Ḥanafīs maintain that it is recommended to ask the blasphemer to repent (*istitābah*) and return to Islam, Imām Mālik has considered this to be unnecessary. The Shāfiᶜīs and Ḥanbalīs have each recorded two different views, one of which corresponds with that of the Ḥanafīs and the other with that of Imām Mālik. The majority opinion thus stipulates *istitābah* as a requirement prior to the enforcement of punishment: over a period of three days, the convict should be asked whether he or she wishes to repent. As just stated, the Mālikīs, however, have ruled out repentance on the basis that the *Ḥadīth* which states, 'Kill whoever changes his religion', is silent on repentance, and some Shāfiᶜīs and Ḥanbalīs accept this. The majority view of the latter rites, on the other hand, is based on the report from ᶜĀ'ishah that a woman renounced Islam on the day of the battle of Uḥud and the Prophet ﷺ ordered that she should be asked whether she wished to repent.[189]

In a chapter on apostasy, al-Shawkānī accommodates both views by maintaining that asking the apostate to repent is valid if the latter has acted from a position of ignorance, but not if he has a claim to knowledge and righteousness.[190]

On the slightly separate issue of whether repentance, solicited or otherwise, by one who reviles God and/or the Prophet Muḥammad ﷺ, is admissible, the majority have held that it is. The Ḥanbalīs and the Mālikīs have each recorded two different views. The dominant view in both of these schools is that repentance will not absolve the blasphemer from punishment in this world, although it may, if he is sincere, benefit him in the hereafter.[191] In this regard, the Ḥanbalīs and Mālikīs do not draw a distinction between reviling God and insulting the Prophet ﷺ, regarding them as two manifestations of the same offence and, therefore, liable to be treated on an equal basis. This view is, in turn, based on the precedent of Caliph ʿUmar b. al-Khaṭṭāb, who is known to have drawn a parallel between reviling God and insulting the Prophet ﷺ, and in neither case is he known to have asked the blasphemer to repent. Thus, it is said that the main difference between blasphemy and apostasy is that the latter is open to repentance but the former specifically is not.[192] However, the second view of the Ḥanbalī and Mālikī schools is that it is obligatory for the convicted blasphemer to be given an opportunity to repent and return to Islam.[193]

The Ḥanafīs and the majority of the Shāfiʿīs on the other hand, consider blasphemy to be in the same category as apostasy and have ruled that repentance is admissible in both cases. Thus, the blasphemer, like the apostate, is to be asked for repentance on three consecutive days, which will be counted from the time of conviction, and that during this time, the convict is entitled to food and other necessities. Repentance, in the case of the apostate, consists of his or her return to Islam by reciting the testimonial of the faith (*kalimat al-shahādah*). In the case of a *dhimmī*'s repentance, he should expressremorse over his conduct and affirm that he will not repeat it; the head of state may accept his repentance and the accused may consequently retain his own religion or embrace Islam.[194] According to another view, which appears preferable, the terms of repentance should be related to the nature and content of the offence, and the accused should specifically denounce what he has done or said in the first place.

Furthermore, repentance from an apostate and his return to Islam is acceptable, according to the Ḥanafīs and Shāfiʿīs, for a maximum of four occasions. Thus, if the apostate repents and returns to Islam for the fifth time, the latter act will be of no account, but on each of the preceding instances, the convict is to be granted the respite of three days. This ruling is based on the report that the Prophet ﷺ asked one Nabhān, 'for repentance four or five times'. Qāḍī ʿIyāḍ al-Yaḥsabī, who reports this, adds that Ibn Wahab reported from Imām Mālik that each time the apostate commits the offence, he should be asked for permanent repentance. This is also the ruling of Imāms al-Shāfiʿī and Ibn Ḥanbal.[195]

ʿAlī b. Abī Ṭālib is reported to have held that the apostate should be called to repentance over a period of two months. However, Ibrāhīm al-Nakhaʿī, the teacher of Imām Abū Ḥanīfah, and Sufyān al-Thawrī have held that the door of repentance always remains open to a defector from the faith for as long as he lives.[196]

8. THE BLASPHEMY OF A NON-MUSLIM

There are three possible situations where a non-Muslim may be involved in blasphemy against Islam:

(a) When a non-Muslim professes an article of his own faith which happens to contradict the Islamic creed, such as when a Christian states that Jesus is the son of God. However, this is, from the viewpoint of Islam, a simple variety of disbelief rather than actual blasphemy.

(b) When a non-Muslim says something which, although part of his belief, is said in an offensive manner. An example of this is the incident which occurred after the call to prayer, when a Jew addressed the muezzin with the words 'you lied'. The case here is similar to any involving a non-Muslim scorning an article of the Muslim faith or any of the injunctions of God that are contained in the Qur'ān. In this case, if the non-Muslim is a *dhimmī*, he loses his protected status and becomes liable to punishment.

(c) When the insult in question is not a part of the faith of its perpetrator, and consists of something which is equally forbidden in his own religion. No distinction is made, in regard to this type of blasphemy, between Muslims and non-Muslims, as anyone who reviles God commits a blasphemous offence, regardless of his or her religious denomination.

The jurists have differed, as stated earlier, on the admissibility or otherwise of repentance, but most regard it as admissible and hold that repentance may, in the case of a non-Muslim, consist of conversion to Islam. Some *ʿulamā'* of Medina have also held that repentance is acceptable from a *dhimmī* in the same way as it is from a Muslim, and that the non-Muslim does not lose his protected status either. Imāms al-Shāfiʿī and Aḥmad b. Ḥanbal, according to one of two reports, maintained that the *dhimmī* may not be asked to repent, but if he converts to Islam at his own initiative, he is not liable to any punishment. According to a variant report, Imām Mālik and Aḥmad b. Ḥanbal have held that the *dhimmī* is liable to the mandatory death penalty; however some Mālikīs maintained that if the insult perpetrated by a non-Muslim consists of attributing a lie to the Prophet (*takdhīb al-Rasūl*) ﷺ, then there is no liablility to capital punishment.[197] In yet another report, Imām al-Shāfiʿī is said to have held that the protected status of the *dhimmī* terminates when he commits blasphemy and that, consequently, he becomes an enemy of war (*ḥarbī*), in which case the head of state is within his rights to punish him as such. Imām al-Shāfiʿī adds that in this matter the head of state has discretionary powers similar to those he has with regard to prisoners of war, that is, over whether to kill the offender or ask for ransom, and over whether or not to expropriate his property.[198] On the other hand, Imām Abū Ḥanīfah and his disciples have maintained that the covenant with the *dhimmī* (*ʿahd al-dhimmah*) is not terminated as a result of blasphemy consisting of *sabb Allāh* and/or *sabb al-Rasūl* ﷺ, nor is the *dhimmī* liable to the death penalty, but he is liable to a deterrent punishment of *taʿzīr* in the same way as when he commits other evil acts (*munkarāt*) which are forbidden to him. In support of this view, the Ḥanafīs refer mainly to the *Ḥadīths* quoted earlier, in which some Jews addressed the Prophet ﷺ with the phrase, 'death be upon you' (*al-sām ʿalaykum*), but, in none of the reports did the Prophet ﷺ order any punishment.[199]

9. EVIDENCE IN THE QUR'ĀN AND SUNNAH

The most detailed treatment of blasphemy in the works of the *ʿulamā'* remains that of Taqī al-Dīn Ibn Taymiyyah (d. 728/1328) *al-Ṣārim al-Maslūl ʿalā Shātim al-Rasūl* where the distinguished author has addressed, *inter alia*, the punishment of apostasy and the Qur'ānic evidence relating to it. While giving a through presentation of the diverse opinions on the subject, Ibn Taymiyyah himself has consistently maintained that blasphemy is liable to the mandatory death penalty; that the sentencing judge has little choice but to enforce the punishment upon proof, and that the offender need not be asked to repent. In the following pages, a summary of Ibn Taymiyyah's interpretation of the Qur'ānic evidence on blasphemy is presented. The purpose here is not to enter into an exhaustive discourse but merely to draw attention to some of the conclusions that the learned author has drawn. Ibn Taymiyyah's erudition in the religious sciences is beyond question. He is one of the few towering figures in the tradition of Islamic scholarship of the post-classical era, who almost succeeded in establishing a legal school (*madhhab*) of his own. This should not, of course, deflect us from the need to renew contact with the primary legal sources and to re-examine the juristic opinions of even the most prominent *ʿulamāʾ* of the past in the light of the letter and spirit of the Qur'ān. In reaching their juristic conclusions, the *ʿulamāʾ* were naturally influenced by the prevailing conditions of their time, including such factors as the pressure to conform to the hallowed legacy of the past. We have seen the tendency, in almost all the great religions, to infuse political connotations into blasphemy and apostasy, and consequently many religious scholars of renowned piety and prominence were persuaded to adopt exceedingly punitive attitudes on sensitive religious issues. Ibn Taymiyyah is not alone in this. Indeed, the Mālikī jurist, Qāḍī ʿIyāḍ al-Yaḥṣabi (d. 544/1149) who preceded Ibn Taymiyyah, has written a treatise on the same subject and places an equal, if not greater, emphasis on the same conclusions that Ibn Taymiyyah has drawn. Qāḍī ʿIyāḍ's work, entitled *al-Shifāʾ bi Taʿrīf Ḥuqūq al-Muṣṭafā*, addresses the rights of the Prophet ﷺ in general and devotes large sections to the matter of blasphemy. In a chapter devoted to the textual authority of the Qur'ān in support of the death penalty for one who vilifies the Prophet ﷺ, Qāḍi ʿIyāḍ has discussed the same passages of the Qur'ān as Ibn Taymiyyah, and the two authors have drawn identical conclusions.[200]

The question I venture to raise here is whether Ibn Taymiyyah and his predecessor, Qāḍī ʿIyāḍ, were not carried a little too far in their interpretation of the Qur'ān on the subject of blasphemy. Both of these distinguished authors were primarily concerned, as the titles of their works suggest, with *sabb al-Rasūl* ﷺ, that is, words and behaviour that vilify the illustrious name and character of the Prophet Muḥammad ﷺ. The issue here is not over any particular author or individual. I am discussing Ibn Taymiyyah's interpretation, not because his interpretation is different from other well-known commentators, but to show that even Ibn Taymiyyah, having written so profusely on blasphemy, is at pains to establish that the death penalty for blasphemy is a Qur'ānic dispensation.

Ibn Taymiyyah begins his discussion of the Qur'ānic evidence with the premise that blasphemy, whether consisting of insult to God or to His Messenger ﷺ, carries the death penalty; and that this has a Qur'ānic mandate, and is a prescribed punishment (*ḥadd*) which leaves the sentencing judge with little choice but to enforce it. To this effect, the learned author has discussed seven Qur'ānic passages, which I have quoted in the following pages, and to which I add two more. It is perhaps text number five in the series below which is of central importance to Ibn Taymiyyah's conclusions. The author begins his analysis with a passage from the Qur'ān which has as its principal theme opposition and hostility to God and to the Prophet ﷺ, and it reads as follows:

> 1. Do they not know that for him who opposes *(yuḥādid)* God and His Messenger, there is the fire of hell, wherein he shall dwell permanently; that is the terrible disgrace.(IX:63)
>
> أَلَمْ يَعْلَمُوٓا أَنَّهُۥ مَن يُحَادِدِ ٱللَّهَ وَرَسُولَهُۥ فَأَنَّ لَهُۥ نَارَ جَهَنَّمَ خَٰلِدًا فِيهَا
> ذَٰلِكَ ٱلْخِزْىُ ٱلْعَظِيمُ

The main conclusion that Ibn Taymiyyah draws from this text is that opposing or annoying the Prophet ﷺ is tantamount to annoying God Most High. This conclusion is supported, the author maintains, by the immediately preceding passage which provides, 'And among them are those who annoy/insult (*yu'dhūna*) the Prophet and say that he is but ear[s] [he believes what he hears].'[201] (IX:61) It is precisely because of their hostile remarks in reference to the noble Prophet ﷺ, Ibn Taymiyyah goes on to say, that 'the opposers (*muḥāddīn*) shall dwell in hell-fire'.[202] He further concludes, from the juxtaposition of the two texts, that *adhā*, annoyance or insult, and *muḥādadah,* hostile opposition, have been used synonymously in the Qur'ān.[203] The discussion proceeds with a reference to two other Qur'ānic passages on the same theme:

> 2. Those who oppose *(yuḥaddūna)* God and His Messenger, will be among the most humiliated *(al-adhallīn)*. God has decreed: It is I and My Messengers who must prevail. God is Mighty and Powerful. (LVIII:20-21)
>
> إِنَّ ٱلَّذِينَ يُحَآدُّونَ ٱللَّهَ وَرَسُولَهُۥٓ أُو۟لَٰٓئِكَ فِى ٱلْأَذَلِّينَ • كَتَبَ ٱللَّهُ لَأَغْلِبَنَّ
> أَنَا۠ وَرُسُلِىٓ إِنَّ ٱللَّهَ قَوِىٌّ عَزِيزٌ

Here, the author comments on the word *adhall*, most humiliated, drawing attention to the fact that it is the superlative form of *dhalīl*; and that a person can only be described in such terms when his life and property is no longer inviolable (*maʿṣūm*); and that the Qur'ān refers to those who insult God and the Prophet ﷺ as 'most humiliated' because they enjoy no immunity and no protection.[204] To substantiate this conclusion further, Ibn Taymiyyah quotes another passage where the Qur'ān confirms, in equally emphatic terms, the degraded status of those who malign or oppose God and His Messenger ﷺ:

> 3. Those who oppose God and His Messenger will be humiliated *(kubitū)* as were those who came before them. (LVIII:5)

إِنَّ ٱلَّذِينَ يُحَآدُّونَ ٱللَّهَ وَرَسُولَهُۥ كُبِتُوا۟ كَمَا كُبِتَ ٱلَّذِينَ مِن قَبْلِهِمْ

Here, the author elaborates on the meaning of *kubitū* and its connotations of intense degradation and humiliation. The author maintains that, in this passage, the Qur'ān refers to sinners and hypocrites of bygone ages, and the fact that they met with destruction because they insulted and harmed their prophets. 'It is thus clear', Ibn Taymiyyah asserts, that 'the hypocrites (*munāfiqūn*) are enemies [of God] and have been humiliated by death and destruction. It is therefore obligatory that every enemy (*muḥādd*) should meet with the same predicament.'[205] The dominantly linguistic tone of this discussion, consisting mainly of comparing words, continues, and Ibn Taymiyyah next draws a parallel between *muḥādadah* - opposition, hostility, causing annoyance - and *mushāqaqah* - separation, contention, antagonism. The text in which the word *mushāqaqah* occurs is a more punitive text, but one which has little to do with blasphemy as such, being concerned with fighting the enemy in the battlefield, not with blasphemy:

> 4. And smite them above their necks and smite all their fingertips because they opposed *(shāqqū)* God and His Messenger, and those who oppose God and His Messenger [should know that for such] God is strict in punishment. (VIII:12-13)

فَٱضْرِبُوا۟ فَوْقَ ٱلْأَعْنَاقِ وَٱضْرِبُوا۟ مِنْهُمْ كُلَّ بَنَانٍ ۝ ذَٰلِكَ بِأَنَّهُمْ
شَآقُّوا۟ ٱللَّهَ وَرَسُولَهُۥ وَمَن يُشَاقِقِ ٱللَّهَ وَرَسُولَهُۥ فَإِنَّ ٱللَّهَ شَدِيدُ
ٱلْعِقَابِ

The occasion for the revelation of this text is well-known to have been the battle of Uḥud, and therefore what it says is primarily concerned with the enemy soldiers in that battle. It is thus evident, as Ibn Taymiyyah himself tends to suggest, that the text is quoted merely to compare the key words therein and to enable the following conclusion to be derived: 'Thus it is known that *muḥādadah*, derived from [the verbal root of] *ḥadd*, and *mushāqaqah*, derived from [the vebal root of] *shaqq*, both mean dissension, opposition and antagonism, and that the former (i.e. *muḥādadah*) comprises the meaning of the latter.'[206]

The next Qur'ānic passage that Ibn Taymiyyah has discussed is one from which he drew his main conclusion, namely that the death penalty for blasphemy is a Qur'ānic dispensation and that it is a prescribed punishment. He quoted the following text which occurs in *Sūrat al-Aḥzāb*:

> 5. Verily, those who insult/annoy *(yu'dhūna)* God and His Messenger, have been cursed by God in this world and in the Hereafter, and He has prepared for them a humiliating punishment. And those who insult/annoy believing men and women without due cause bear on themselves a calumny *(buhtānan)* and a glaring sin *(ithman mubīnan)*. (XXXIII: 57-8)

إِنَّ ٱلَّذِينَ يُؤْذُونَ ٱللَّهَ وَرَسُولَهُۥ لَعَنَهُمُ ٱللَّهُ فِى ٱلدُّنْيَا وَٱلْآخِرَةِ وَأَعَدَّ لَهُمْ
عَذَابًا مُّهِينًا ۝ وَٱلَّذِينَ يُؤْذُونَ ٱلْمُؤْمِنِينَ وَٱلْمُؤْمِنَٰتِ بِغَيْرِ مَا ٱكْتَسَبُوا۟
فَقَدِ ٱحْتَمَلُوا۟ بُهْتَٰنًا وَإِثْمًا مُّبِينًا

The author then comments: 'This verse makes obligatory the death penalty for one who insults God and His Messenger.'[207] Here, Ibn Taymiyyah also draws a parallel between insulting God and insulting His Messenger ﷺ, an equation on which the text is self-evident. Anyone, therefore, who annoys the Prophet ﷺ perpetrates exactly the same offence with respect to God Most High, and 'one who insults God is an infidel (*kāfir*) and legally liable to be executed (*ḥalāl al-dam*)'. Another point to be noted, as in Ibn Taymiyyah's interpretation of this text, is that a distinction is made therein between insulting God and His Messenger ﷺ, on the one hand, and insulting other believers, on the other: whereas the perpetrators of the former have been cursed and humiliated in the strongest language, those who hurt other believing men and women are committing, as the text tells us, only a glaring calumny and sin. The point that the author stresses here is that God Most High has cursed the perpetrator of blasphemy. 'Cursing (*laʿnah*) is the opposite of mercy (*raḥmah*): anyone whom God has cursed and precluded from His mercy both in this world and the next is certainly a non-believer (*kāfir*).' Further to substantiate this and accentuate the enormity that is attached to *laʿnah*, Ibn Taymiyyah quotes a *Ḥadīth* in which it is declared that 'cursing a believer is tantamount to killing him'.

لَعْنُ المُؤْمِنِ كَقَتْلِهِ

Neglecting the somewhat figurative nature of the language of this *Ḥadīth*, Ibn Taymiyyah goes on to conclude that one whom God has cursed is also liable to the death penalty: 'It is thus known that killing him is permissible (*fa ʿulima anna qatluhu mubāḥ*)'.[208] Two pages later, Ibn Taymiyyah reaffirms this analysis, observing that insulting a believer does not call for the curse of God in this world or the next, nor does it invoke a painful chastisement. This, Ibn Taymiyyah adds, is known from the distinction that the Qur'ān has drawn between insulting God and His Messenger ﷺ, on the one hand, and insulting one's fellow believers, on the other. For the latter amounts to a glaring sin (*ithman mubīnan*), that is, slanderous accusation, (*qadhf*), which is an offence, but not so grave as to be equated with insulting God and His Messenger ﷺ: only the latter invokes God's curse in this world and the next.[209]

The author then discusses two other passages, both of which occur in *Sūrat al-Nūr* and are concerned with slanderous accusation (*qadhf*). One is said to refer to the wives of the Prophet ﷺ, and the other is of general import. The point that Ibn Taymiyyah makes here is that God Most High once again curses those who insult the wives of the Prophet ﷺ, but that this is not the case in the text which expounds the ordinary offence of slanderous accusation (*qadhf*). The two passages read as follows:

> 6. Those who slander chaste women, careless but believing, cursed are they in this life and in the Hereafter. For them is a grievous punishment. (XXIV:23)

إِنَّ ٱلَّذِينَ يَرْمُونَ ٱلْمُحْصَنَٰتِ ٱلْغَٰفِلَٰتِ ٱلْمُؤْمِنَٰتِ لُعِنُوا۟ فِى
ٱلدُّنْيَا وَٱلْءَاخِرَةِ وَلَهُمْ عَذَابٌ عَظِيمٌ

7. And those who slander chaste women, then fail to bring forth four witnesses [to prove the charge they have laid] give them eighty lashes of the whip and nevermore accept their testimony; they, they are the transgressors. Except for such as subsequently repent and correct [themselves]; for verily, God is Forgiving, Merciful. (XXIV: 4-5)

وَٱلَّذِينَ يَرْمُونَ ٱلْمُحْصَنَٰتِ ثُمَّ لَمْ يَأْتُوا۟ بِأَرْبَعَةِ شُهَدَآءَ فَٱجْلِدُوهُمْ
ثَمَٰنِينَ جَلْدَةً وَلَا تَقْبَلُوا۟ لَهُمْ شَهَٰدَةً أَبَدًا وَأُو۟لَٰٓئِكَ هُمُ ٱلْفَٰسِقُونَ۝
إِلَّا ٱلَّذِينَ تَابُوا۟ مِنۢ بَعْدِ ذَٰلِكَ وَأَصْلَحُوا۟ فَإِنَّ ٱللَّهَ غَفُورٌ رَّحِيمٌ

In response to the question about the curse in the first of these texts, Ibn Taymiyyah points out that this particular text was revealed concerning the wives of the Prophet ﷺ, insulting whom is a heinous offence which invokes the curse of God, although the perpetrator does not thereby lose his status of 'believer' and his life is still protected. This interpretation is attributed to the renowned Companion, Ibn ʿAbbās, who stated that the text under discussion was revealed concerning ʿĀ'ishah and the other wives of the Prophet ﷺ, despite the absence in the text of a specific reference to that effect. To this Ibn Taymiyyah adds that, unlike the second passage, which makes a provision for repentance, the first passage, that is, the one concerning the wives of the Prophet ﷺ, is silent regarding the admissibility or otherwise of repentance. The conclusion is thus drawn that insulting and slandering women other than the wives of the Prophet ﷺ is an offence which does not invoke the curse of God and is open to repentance.[210] At this point, Ibn Taymiyyah refers to a variety of interpretations offered by other commentators on these passages. The issue which is debated here concerns the validity, in principle, of the attempt by Ibn ʿAbbās and others to confine the application of the first passage exclusively to the wives of the Prophet ﷺ. Had the text itself specified this, there would, of course, have remained no doubt. But in the absence of such a reference, the general principle of interpretation pertaining to the occasions of revelation (*asbāb al-nuzūl*) would seem to apply. Ibn Taymiyyah has himself pointed this out and said that the general rulings of the Qur'ān should be applied in their general capacity even if they are revealed in reference to particular occasions. Even if it is admitted that the text was revealed concerning the wives of the Prophet ﷺ, Ibn Taymiyyah holds that, since the wording of the text is general, its purport must apply to all believing women.[211] By stating this, it would appear that Ibn Taymiyyah himself dilutes the import of the argument he advanced earlier in which he attempted to reserve the curse of God exclusively for blasphemers who insult or malign God and His Messenger ﷺ. For it would seem that the first of the two texts (i.e. no. 5 ff. above) speaks in general terms and sends down the curse of God on 'those who slander chaste women, careless but believing'. Cursing is therefore no longer confined to those who vilify God and His Messenger ﷺ, that is, to the perpetrators of blasphemy proper, as Ibn Taymiyyah had initially asserted. Ibn Taymiyyah has thus departed from his initial premise (i.e. that the curse of God can only be sent down upon a blasphemer) when he admits that the general rulings of the Qur'ān should retain their generality notwithstanding the specificity of the occasion of their revelation. But this point need not be pressed any further. For it is one thing to say that God Most High curses only the most heinous of all conduct, and another that the conduct in question carries the capital punishment. In short, even if we admit Ibn Taymiyyah's argument on this point, it would still not prove his initial premise that the death penalty for blasphemy, in whatever capacity, is a Qur'ānic mandate.

I have thus summarised Ibn Taymiyyah's treatment of the Qur'ānic evidence concerning the death penalty for blasphemy, and I venture to say that it does not sustain the conclusions that he has drawn from it. To recapitulate, Ibn Taymiyyah's categorical statement that killing the perpetrator of blasphemy is a Qur'ānic obligation was founded primarily on some Qur'ānic passages wherein God Most High has cursed those who vilify Him and His Messenger ﷺ. From these Ibn Taymiyyah concludes that God curses only those who have renounced Islam and whose life is no longer sacrosanct, that the perpetrators of blasphemy are liable to death and that their repentance is of no account. The tone and tenor of this analysis are dominantly speculative and it does not, with due respect to Ibn Taymiyyah's unquestionable erudition and piety, stand the test of accuracy which is normally observed by the commentators (*mufassirūn*) on the Qur'ān. The Qur'ān has made no reference to the death penalty for blasphemy, and the text does not warrant the conclusion that it is a Qur'ānic obligation, or a prescribed punishment or a mandate. On the contrary, we would submit that the general language of the Qur'ān can only sustain the broad conclusion that the perpetrator of blasphemy disgraces himself and invokes the curse of God upon himself, and that it is a criminal offence which carries no prescribed or mandatory punishment, and, as such, automatically falls under the category of *taʿzīr* offences, whose punishment may be determined by the head of state or competent judicial authorities.

There is ample evidence in the Qur'ān that pagan Arabs, the disbelievers, and the hypocrites insulted and offended the Noble Prophet ﷺ on numerous occasions. Note, for example, the reference to Abū Lahab, who used to vilify the Prophet ﷺ (CXI:1), as did many others, by the use of such insulting expressions as 'possessed' (*majnūn*) in reference to him (XXXVI:35). The Qur'ān also provides evidence that the disbelievers often referred to the Prophet ﷺ as 'soothsayer' (*kāhin*), and 'magician' or 'sorcerer' (*sāḥir*). Another line of attack used by the opponents of Islam was to claim that the Qur'ān was the work of Muḥammad ﷺ himself. This opposition, too, took the form of verbal abuse by which the pagan leaders rejected and ridiculed the Qur'ānic teachings on the unity of God and belief in the resurrection.[212] The Qur'ān usually gives the lie directly to these charges, and, on numerous occasions, instructs the Prophet ﷺ, to exercise patience, sound reasoning, and persuasion.

To conclude my review of the Qur'ānic evidence, I refer to two more relevant passages. In one of these, the Prophet ﷺ and his Companions have been addressed as follows:

> 8. And you shall certainly hear much that will insult you *(adhan kathīra)* from those who received the Scripture before you and from the polytheists. But if you persevere patiently and guard against evil, this will be the best course with which to determine your affairs. (III:186)

وَلَتَسْمَعُنَّ مِنَ ٱلَّذِينَ أُوتُوا۟ ٱلْكِتَٰبَ مِن قَبْلِكُمْ وَمِنَ ٱلَّذِينَ أَشْرَكُوٓا۟ أَذًى
كَثِيرًا وَإِن تَصْبِرُوا۟ وَتَتَّقُوا۟ فَإِنَّ ذَٰلِكَ مِنْ عَزْمِ ٱلْأُمُورِ

This passage was revealed in Medina, and it leaves little doubt that the Prophet ﷺ and his Companions often encountered insulting and irritating incidents at that time. Given the nature of the Prophet's ﷺ mission and campaign, opposition verging on insult and abuse from the disbelievers was by no means unexpected. It would be neither feasible nor wise, under such circumstances, to have been too preoccupied with prosecution and punishment. This is precisely what the Qur'ān has recommended and also what the Prophet ﷺ actually did. But the juristic doctrine that was later developed followed a different course, one which moves more along punitive lines, rather than those of patience and perseverance. The substance of the text quoted above has also been confirmed elsewhere in the Qur'ān, wherein the hostile environment to which the Prophet ﷺ and his followers were exposed is characterised even more clearly:

> 9. Among the followers of the Book, many would wish that they could turn you back to infidelity after you have believed - because of their envy after the truth is manifest to them. But forgive and overlook until God accomplishes His purpose (*amr*, lit. 'command' or 'order'). (II:109)

> وَدَّ كَثِيرٌ مِّنْ أَهْلِ ٱلْكِتَٰبِ لَوْ يَرُدُّونَكُم مِّنۢ بَعْدِ إِيمَٰنِكُمْ كُفَّارًا حَسَدًا
> مِّنْ عِندِ أَنفُسِهِم مِّنۢ بَعْدِ مَا تَبَيَّنَ لَهُمُ ٱلْحَقُّ فَٱعْفُوا۟ وَٱصْفَحُوا۟ حَتَّىٰ
> يَأْتِىَ ٱللَّهُ بِأَمْرِهِۦٓ

This too is a Medinan verse, and the instruction it contains clearly advises the Prophet ﷺ and the early community to develop their inner resources through patience and resilience. It teaches that the success of Islam had naturally made the disbelievers insecure and envious, and that under such circumstances a punitive approach would not produce the desired result.

It is of interest to note that Ibn Taymiyyah discusses in detail some of the cases in which the Prophet ﷺ granted pardon to individuals who annoyed and insulted him. Included among these was the Jewish convert ʿAbd Allāh b. Abī Sarḥ, who used to be the scribe of the Prophet ﷺ and then renounced Islam, fled to Mecca and spread rumours that the Prophet ﷺ used to dictate the Qur'ān to him but that often he (Ibn Abī Sarḥ) would finish the sentence, and the Prophet ﷺ would not object. That Muḥammad ﷺ, in other words, was a self-styled prophet. Ibn Taymiyyah also recounts the story of the Jewish poet, Anas b. Zunaym al-Daylamī, who used to satirise the Prophet ﷺ and insult him and his Companions. They were both forgiven when they apologised. Ibn Taymiyyah then goes on to cite the two Qur'ānic passages quoted above, on the virtue of forgiveness, and informs us that after migrating to Medina, the Prophet ﷺ turned his attention to propagating the faith among its residents. It was not uncommon at that time for a man to embrace Islam while his father and relatives remained disbelievers, which situation led to resentment and discontent on the part of the non-Muslim relatives. Hence the Jews and polytheists (*al-mushrikūn*) of Medina used to insult and annoy the Prophet ﷺ and his Companions. But God Most High commanded the Prophet ﷺ and the believers to exercise patience and forgiveness. This was, in fact, the occasion of the revelation of both passages cited above.[213]

The recorded instances of *sabb al-Rasūl* ﷺ which were prosecuted all occurred in Medina when the Prophet ﷺ combined the office of head of state with his prophetic mission. Although he was frequently insulted and ridiculed during the Meccan period of his mission, he is on no occasion known to have taken up the issue against the offenders. This would suggest that blasphemy as a punishable offence materialised in a political context. The circumstances in Mecca at the early stages of the advent of Islam admittedly did not permit the enforcement of any punishment for blasphemy. All that is conveyed by the evidence in the Qur'ān and Sunnah is a resolute denunciation of such conduct, and an assurance that its perpetrators incur the wrath of God and will be punished in the Hereafter. It is also significant to note that the Prophetic Sunnah, during the Meccan period, does not provide the evidence by which to identify blasphemy as the serious offence it was later identified as under different circumstances in Medina.

I do not propose to discuss the evidence in the Sunnah in detail but shall only attempt to make some general observations. The reason I do so is that I have tried to ascertain the accuracy of the details concerning some of the recorded incidents of insult to the Prophet ﷺ during his lifetime and immediately after his demise, during the period of the Rightly-Guided Caliphs. However, the details tend to vary and it is difficult to be accurate, especially when one tries to look at the evidence from a different perspective. It seems likely that, of the countless incidents of blasphemy which occurred during the lifetime of the Prophet ﷺ, some were never recorded. Of the cases that were brought to the attention of the

Prophet ﷺ, it appears that the majority were pardoned, and only the most serious cases were prosecuted. It is almost certain that the Prophet ﷺ validated the death penalty in about a dozen cases, either directly or by tacit approval that was given after the event. However, the reports also indicate that these particular cases involved a combination of offences including treason, hostility to Islam and vilification of the Prophet ﷺ in the form of personal abuse contained in satirical poetry and prose which was also disparaging of Islam, as well as accusations of lying made against him. The reports I have consulted do not provide enough evidence to warrant a distinction *ex post facto* between the religious and the political contents of the cases that were prosecuted for blasphemy and insult. The jurists have not separated apostasy from blasphemy, and have shown little inclination to isolate the religious from the political. Note, for example, the following passage in which al-Samarā'ī has commented on some of the cases that were prosecuted at the time:

> As for the four persons who apostasised and whose blood was declared licit by the Messenger of God ﷺ, they had combined *(faqad jamaᶜū)* attacks upon the honour of the Messenger of God ﷺ, through insult and abuse, and a manifest contempt for Islam, with their apostasy. And yet the Prophet ﷺ did not order all of them to be killed. Indeed, he accepted repentance from some of them. [214]

It is therefore difficult to give a satisfactory answer to such questions as to whether these individuals were convicted to death for apostasy alone, or apostasy combined with high treason and subversive activity against the nascent state, or indeed for the personal insult and abuse against the Prophet ﷺ. It is pertinent to note that no Muslim was either accused of or punished for any offence such as high treason or conspiracy against the state, in Medina. Blasphemy and apostasy were the equivalent and, indeed the only, offences in that category. We also note that there is no separate terminology either in the Qur'ān or in the sayings of the Prophet ﷺ for 'high treason'. It is thus understood that the death penalty was designed not for blasphemy as a crime against religion alone but primarily as a crime against the community and state.

The Qur'ānic concept of blasphemy, that is opposition (*muḥādadah, mushāqaqah*) to and insult (*adhā*) against God and the Prophet ﷺ, as discussed above, comes close to the notion of high treason. The dominantly political character of these offences in the early days of Islam will be appreciated if one is reminded of the hostile response to the new faith, and the fact that the Prophet ﷺ had to fight or authorise some eighty-five battles after his migration to Medina at a time when he combined the office of head of state with his prophetic mission.

The attempt at drawing a distinction between the political and religious contents of blasphemy is warranted because of the predominantly political character of this offence in early Islam, and the fact that it is no longer a specifically political offence in our own time. Blasphemy presented a major threat to the existence and continuity of Islam at a time when neither the new faith nor the nascent Islamic state were secure against rampant hostility and challenge. This situation remained substantially unchanged during the period of the Rightly-Guided Caliphs.

While discussing apostasy in early Islam, Ibn Qayyim al-Jawziyyah has observed that it was a purely political issue and that assigning the death penalty for apostasy had nothing to do with freedom of conscience; and that this was so because apostasy threatened the very foundations of Islam and its political organisation.[215]

We also note that apostasy became a particularly serious issue when it was practised not only by the odd individual but by large groups of people who would openly renounce Islam and abandon it as an act of subversion. There is clear evidence on this in the Qur'ān, which refers to the people of the Book (*ahl al-Kitāb*) who would announce their conversion to Islam one day and would renounce it later the same day, so as to discredit Islam in the eyes of its followers (III:72). Many commentators, including Mutawallī, have noted that incidents of apostasy during the lifetime of the Prophet ﷺ and the reign of the first caliph, Abū Bakr, were largely committed by groups of individuals who acted in concert. The Jews and Christians during this period used to profess Islam in a group only to renounce it later in an attempt to weaken allegiance to the new faith.[216]

Commenting on Ibn Qayyim's observation that apostasy was a political offence, al-ᶜĪli has examined some of the cases and reached the conclusion that the Prophet ﷺ authorised the death penalty for apostasy in his capacity as political leader, and he exercised discretionary power in its application; and that as such the Prophet ﷺ himself has treated apostasy as a *taᶜzīr* offence. We know, for example, that the Prophet ﷺ exempted from the death penalty, several persons who renounced Islam and defamed and vilified him. Included among these were ᶜAbd Allāh b. Abī Sarḥ, ᶜIkrāmah b. Abī Jahl, Ṣafwān b. Umayyah, and Hind, the wife of Abū Sufyān. Al-ᶜĪli adds that the Prophet ﷺ allowed and accepted intercession in these cases, and this lends further support to the conclusion that apostasy is a *taʿzīr* offence.[217] Here, it should be noted that the word 'apostasy' is being used almost synonymously with blasphemy. Since most of the reported instances of apostasy also combined insult to the Prophet ﷺ and blasphemy against Islam, the two offences became indistinguishable.

Blasphemy and apostasy in this period were dominantly political offences which had religious overtones. The nearest parallel to these in our own time is high treason. There was, of course, no separation between religion and politics or religious and civil authority in the early days of Islam, and this, in principle, remains the case to this day, in that, in theory, Islam does not validate such a separation. But certain other changes have taken place in the course of history, one of which is the distinction between religious and political crimes that is now widely recognised and practised. The political crime of high treason is now treated differently from the religious offence of blasphemy. The gravity that is now attached to the former clearly outweighs that of the latter. This change has occurred partly as a result of the change in the foundation and character of the modern state. Whereas the state of Medina under the leadership of the Prophet ﷺ and the Rightly-Guided Caliphs, was clearly committed to, and rooted in, the ideology and religious law of Islam, and political loyalty was measured by these criteria, this is no longer the case with the nation-state of today. Consequently, a significant change has occurred in the nature and composition of the original concepts of apostasy and blasphemy, in that both of these have been largely divested of their political content. It would thus be reasonable to reflect that change in our perception of the gravity of this offence. Since blasphemy no longer has the political crime of high treason as a concomitant, it would seem unwarranted for us to treat it in the same way as it used sometimes to be treated in the Islamic state of Medina. Blasphemy today continues to be a dangerous offence, which can incite violence and loss of life, and pose a threat to law and order in society, as was seen in the aftermath of Salman Rushdie's misguided venture. But even so, blasphemy today can in no sense threaten the existence or continuity of Islam as a great religion, a legal system and a major civilisation.

I thus conclude that the Sunnah authorised capital punishment for apostasy primarily because apostasy in the early years of Islam was equivalent to high treason and posed a serious threat to both the religious and political foundations of the new community in Medina. Apostasy and blasphemy shared the same attributes, and were hardly distinguishable from one another, since instances of apostasy, among other things, involved hostility towards, and abuse of, the Prophet ﷺ.

This situation continued substantially unchanged during the period of the Rightly-Guided Caliphs, and also in the early years of the Umayyads. As Islam triumphed and the Umayyad state grew in strength, apostasy no longer presented a threat to the security of either. However, no parallel change in the law was attempted. Although the circumstances that had once provided a persuasive argument in support of capital punishment for apostasy no longer existed, the legal provisions that initially addressed the issue nevertheless remained unchanged; however, the character of apostasy had in fact changed from being a predominantly political offence to one which was predominantly religious. Whether for reasons of piety or caution, the *ʿulamāʾ* did not address the question of whether apostasy could continue to be viewed in the same light as in the early years of Islam.

The scholastic doctrines of the *madhāhib* treated blasphemy and apostasy on the same footing and viewed blasphemy as an extension of apostasy, a position which is no longer justified. Furthermore, due to a change in the character of the nation-state, they can no longer be seen as political crimes in the first place, nor do they present a serious challenge to the security of the state. It would therefore be eminently justified for these changes to be reflected in the law that is applied to blasphemy and apostasy respectively.

My enquiry has also led me to the conclusion that blasphemy carries a *taʿzīr* punishment, which is open to a measure of discretion and the influence of circumstantial factors. Based on this appraisal, the precise definition of blasphemy, the acts and words that incur this offence, and then the quantum of the punishment, may be determined and specified, or amended and refined as the case may be, by the legitimate political authority and legislative organ of the state in modern times.[218]

NOTES

1. Cf. Abū Ḥabīb, *Dirāsah*, p. 745.
2. 'Essential benefits' are those on which the life of the community depends, and

neglect of which causes the collapse of normal life. The five essential interests (*maṣāliḥ*) identified in the *Sharīʿah* are faith, life, property, intellect and lineage.

3. Cf. Zaydān, *Majmūʿah*, p. 129.
4. Shaltūt, *Min Tawjīhāt al-Qur'ān al-Karīm*, p. 330.
5. Ibid., p. 331.
6. Munayminah, *Mushkilat al-Ḥurriyyah*, p. 8.
7. Muslim, *Mukhtaṣar Ṣaḥīḥ Muslim*, Kitāb al-Īmān, Bāb al-muslim man salima, p. 23, *Ḥadīth* no. 69.
8. Ali, *A Manual of Ḥadīth*, p. 27.
9. Cf. ʿAwdah, *al-Tashrīʿ al-Jinā'ī*, II, 459.
10. Cf. *The Holy Qur'ān*, XXIV: 1-5.
11. Note for exmple the Egyptian penal code (*Qānūn al-ʿUqūbāt al-Miṣrī*), sec. 302 ff, which defines as '*qādhif*' anyone who attributes to another person a matter, which, if true, would render the person to whom the attribution is made liable to a penalty 'under this law and would invoke humiliation from his compatriots'.
12. Ibn Rushd al-Qurtubī, *Bidāyat al-Mujtahid wa-Nihāyat al-Muqtaṣid*, II, 440 ff.
13. Bahnasī, *al-Jarā'im fi'l-Fiqh al-Islāmī: Dirāsah Fiqhiyyah Muqāranah*, pp. 149 ff.
14. ʿAwdah, *al-Tashrīʿ al-Jinā'ī*, II, 455.
15. Ḥammād, *Ḥurriyyah*, p. 279.
16. Ibn Rushd al-Qurtubī, *Bidāyat*, II, 441.
17. Ibid., II, 442; al-Jazīrī, *Kitāb al-Fiqh ʿalā al-Madhāhib al-Arbaʿah*, V, 222-23 and 236.
18. Ibid., II, 443; al-Jazīrī, *Kitāb al-Fiqh*, V, 230.
19. Cf. ʿAwdah, *al-Tashrīʿ al-Jinā'ī*, II, 478.
20. Al-Tabrīzī, *Mishkāt* II, 1061, *Ḥadīth* no. 3570; al-Jazīrī, *Kitāb al-Fiqh*, V. 215.
21. Ibid., V, 238.
22. Note, e.g., *Sūrat Yūnus*, X:38 & 69; also *Sūrat al-Mumtaḥinah*, LX:12, where *iftirā'* and its derivatives are synonymously used with 'lying' (*kidhb*).
23. *Al-Mawsūʿah al-Fiqhiyyah*, V, 276.
24. Ibn Taymiyyah, *al-Siyāsah*, p. 164.
25. Abū Sinnah, 'Naẓariyyat al-Ḥaqq', in Muḥammad Tawfiq ʿUwaydah (ed.), *al-Fiqh al-Islāmī*, p. 209.
26. *Al-Mawsūʿah al-Fiqhiyyah*, V, 276.
27. Cf. al-ʿĪlī, *al-Ḥurriyyah*, p. 423.
28. Ibn Taymiyyah, *al-Siyāsah*, p. 164.
29. Shaltūt, *al-Islām*, p. 427. This is primarily a ruling of Shāfiʿī law which allows *taʿzīr bi'l-māl* or financial compensation, payable to the plaintiff. The Ḥanafis and others have expressed reservations on the validity of *taʿzīr bi'l-māl*.
30. Shaltūt, *Tawjīhāt*, p. 333.
31. For details see Ibn Qayyim al-Jawziyyah, *al-Ṭuruq al-Ḥukmiyyah fi'l-Siyāsah al-Sharʿiyyah*, p. 118.

32. Ibid., p. 111.
33. Ibn Taymiyyah, *al-Ṣārim al-Maslūl ʿalā Shātim al-Rasūl*, p. 541.
34. Al-Sharabāṣī, *Min al-Ādāb al-Nabawiyyah*, p. 237.
35. ʿAwdah, *al-Tashrīʿ al-Jināʾī*, p. 506.
36. Al-Tabrīzī, *Mishkāt*, vol. 3, *Ḥadīth* no. 4916.
37. Al-Maqdisī, *al-Ādāb al-Sharʿiyyah*, I, 10.
38. Al-Bahī, *al-Dīn wa'l-Dawlah*, p. 244-45.
39. Al-Tabrīzī, *Mishkāt*, vol. 3, *Ḥadīth* no. 4814.
40. Ibid., vol. I, *Ḥadīth* no 1678. In another *Ḥadīth*, it is stated 'When a person dies, remember him for his virtues.'
41. Al-Tabrīzī, *Mishkāt*, vol. I, *Ḥadīth* no. 1664.
42. Al-Tabrīzī, *Mishkāt*, vol. I, *Ḥadīth* no. 4847.
43. Muslim, *Ṣaḥīḥ Muslim*, Kitāb Faḍā'il al-Ṣaḥābah, Bāb taḥrīm sabb al-Ṣaḥābah, IV, 197.
44. Ismāʿīl, *Manhaj al-Sunnah*, p. 135.
45. Ibn ʿĀbidīn, *Ḥāshiyat al-Radd al-Mukhtār ʿalā al-Durr al-Mukhtār* (known as *Ḥāshiyat Ibn ʿĀbidīn*), IV, 74.
46. Ibid., IV, 230.
47. Cf. Lester K. Little, 'Cursing' *The Encyclopedia of Religion*, III, 184.
48. Ibid., p. 182.
49. Al-Maqdisī, *al-Ādāb*, I, 314.
50. Muslim, *Mukhtaṣar Ṣaḥīḥ Muslim*, Kitāb al-Birr wa'l-Ṣilah, Bāb karāhiyyat al-laʿnah, p. 481, *Ḥadīth* no. 1822; Al-Maqdisī, *al-Ādāb*, I, 304.
51. Ibid., I, 306.
52. Abū Jahl, who became the Makhzumite leader in Mecca was a contemporary of the Prophet ﷺ, and a most vehement enemy to him. He was behind the social/economic boycott against the Hashmites, and the attempted assasination of the Prophet ﷺ. Cf. XVII:62; XLIV:43; XCVI:6.
53. Al-Sharabāṣī, *Min al-Ādāb al-Nabawiyyah*, p. 237.
54. Al-Maqdisī, *al-Ādāb*, I, 303.
55. Ibid., I, 312; al-Sharabāṣī, *Min Ādāb*, p. 238; al-Bahnasāwī, *al-Ḥukm wa-Qaḍiyyat Takfīr al-Muslim*. p. 65.
56. Al-Sharabāṣī, *Min Ādāb*, p. 238.
57. Al-Bahnasāwī, *al-Ḥukm*, p. 151.
58. Al-Tirmidhī, *Sunan*, *Ḥadīth* no. 1978; al-Maqdisī, *al-Ādāb*, I, 11; This *Ḥadīth* is said to be 'isolated' (*gharīb*) but its chain of transmitters is considered to be reliable.
59. Al-Maqdisī, *al-Ādāb*, I, 311-12.
60. Abū Zahrah, *al-Jarīmah*, p. 182.
61. Ibn Ḥazm, *al-Fiṣal fi'l-Milal wa'l-Ahwā' wa'l-Niḥal*, III, 138.
62. Ibn ʿĀbidīn, *Ḥāshiyah*, III, 289.
63. Al-Bahnasāwī, *al-Ḥukm*, p. 128.

64. Al-Tabrīzī, *Mishkāt*, vol. 1, *Ḥadīth* no. 13.

65. Muslim, *Ṣaḥīḥ Muslim*, Kitāb al-Īmān I, 79.

66. Al-Tabrīzī, *Mishkāt*, vol. 3, *Ḥadīth* no. 4817. For detail on utterances which amount to clear instances of *kufr*, see the section of this book on blasphemy.

67. Al-Tabrīzī, *Mishkāt*, vol 3, *Ḥadīth* no. 4816; Abū Zahrah, *al-Jarīmah*, p. 182; al-Bahnasāwī, *al-Ḥukm*, p. 50.

68. Abū Zahrah, *al-Jarīmah*, p. 182.

69. Ibn ʿĀbidīn, *Ḥāshiyah*, I, 582; al-Buhūtī, *Kashshāf al-Qinnāʿ ʿan Matn al-Iqnāʿ*, II, 117; *al-Mawsūʿah al-Fiqhiyyah*, XIII, 234-35.

70. Al-Bahnasāwī, *al-Ḥukm*, p. 376.

71. Abū Zahrah, *al-Jarīmah*, p. 176.

72. Al-Bahnasāwī, *al-Ḥukm*, p. 148.

73. Majmaʿ al-Lughah, *al-Muʿjam al-Wasīṭ*, II, 698; al-Zāwī, *Tartīb al-Qāmūs al-Muḥīṭ*, III, 446; Wajdī, *Da'irat al-Maʿārif Qarn al-ʿIshrīn*, VII, 124; Cowan ed., *The Hans Wehr Dictionary of Arabic*, P. 696; Hughes, *A Dictionary of Islam*, p. 129; Muhsin Khan, *The Translation of the Meanings of Sahih al-Bukhari*, IX, 13.

74. Hughes, *Dictionary*, p. 129.

75. Cf. Ibn Qayyim, *Ighāthat al-Lahfān min Makāyid al-Shayṭān*, II, 125.

76. Cf. Riḍā, *Tafsīr al-Manār*, IX, 644.

77. Ibid., IX, 666.

78. Ibn Qayyim, *Ighāthah*, p. 123.

79. Riḍā, *Tafsīr al-Manār*, II 209. The polytheists used to persecute Muslims for having embraced Islam. For instance, they persecuted ʿAmmār b. Yāsir and his family, Bilāl and Ṣuhayb. For details see *Tafsīr al-Manār* II, 316.

80. Muhsin Khan, *The Translation of al-Bukhari*, IX, 267, *Hādīth* no. 215.

81. Riḍā, *Tafsīr al-Manār*, X. 112.

82. Cf. Hughes, *Dictionary*, p. 129; *The Translation of al-Bukhari*, Kitāb al-Fitan, IX, 143 ff.

83. Cf. Ghazawī, *al-Hurriyyāh*, p. 43.

84. This could also be said of Najibullah's predecessors, Karmal and Amin who, in the early 1980s, led an unrepresentative communist regime in Kabul thanks to the Soviet military occupation. Cf. Kamali, *Law in Afghanistan*, p. 58 ff.

85. Cf. Ismāʿīl, *Manhaj*, p. 141.

86. Note, for example, the *Ḥadīth* quoted by Ibn Qayyim, *Ighāthah*, II. 123 and al-Tabrīzī, *Mishkāt*, vol. 2, *Ḥadīth* no. 3678, 'If you are all united under one leader and then someone attempts to split you asunder and destroy your unity, kill him.'

87. Abū Zahrah, *al-Jarīmah*, p. 162.

88. See note 139 at page 114 above.

89. Abū Zahrah, *al-Jarīmah*, pp. 162-63.

90. Ibid., pp. 155-56, Ghazawī, *al-Hurriyyāh*, p. 58.

91. Ibid., pp. 156, El-Awa, *On the Political System of the Islamic State*, p. 43.

92. Al-Sibāʿī, *Ishtirākiyyah*, p. 49.

93. Major sins (*kabā'ir*) are, according to one definition, those which are severely punished. Another view specifies that the punishment for the *kabā'ir* approximates that of the prescribed punishments (*ḥudūd*).

94. Abū Zahrah, *al-Jarīmah*, p. 155, Ghazawī, *al-Hurriyyāh*, p. 58.

95. Cf. Hughes, *Dictionary*, p. 484; al-Kindī, *The Governors and Judges of Egypt*, 445-46. Reports have it that when Imam Abū Ḥanīfah was confronted with the question whether the Qur'ān was created or uncreated, he refused to expatiate and advised silence. Cf. Abū Zahrah, *Abū Ḥanīfah: Ḥayātuh wa-ʿAsruh, Ārā'uh wa-Fiqhhuh*, p. 181.

96. Al-Makdisi, 'Magesterium and Academic Freedom in Classical Islam and Medieval Christianity', in. Nicholas Heer, ed., *Islamic Law and Jurisprudence, p.* 131.

97. The 'arbitration' in question involved ʿAlī's decision to accept Muʿāwiyah's proposal to consult the Qur'ān with regard to their dispute. The dispute was the result of Muʿāwiyah's dissatisfaction with ʿAlī's efforts to find and prosecute the caliph ʿUthmān's assassins. In effect, Muʿāwiyah was attempting to gain the caliphate for the Umayyads. See also note 139 of Part Two.

98. Al-Shahristānī, *Al-Milal wa'l-Niḥal*, I, 168; al-Jundī, *Maʿālim al-Niẓām al-Siyāsī fi'l-Islām*, p. 203; Chejne, *Succession to the Rule in Islam*, p. 38.

99. Khadduri, M, *The Islamic Law of Nations: al-Shaybani's Siyar*, p. 231.

100. Al-Shawkānī, *Nayl al-Awṭār: Sharḥ Muntaqā'l-Akhbār*, VII, 187; see also al-ʿĪlī, *al-Ḥurriyyāh al-ʿĀmmah*, p. 384; Mutawallī, *Mabādi'*, p. 284; Ḥammād, *Ḥurriyyāh*, p. 124.

101. Abū Zahrah, *al-Jarīmah*, p. 172.

102. Khadduri, M, *The Islamic Law of Nations: al-Shaybani's Siyar*, p. 231.

103. Ibid., p. 230, al-Sarakhsī, *al-Mabsūṭ*, X 124.

104. Al-Shawkāni, *Nayl al-Awṭār*, VII, 190; El-Awa, *Political System*, p. 56; Ismāʿīl, *Manhaj*, p. 319.

105. Ismāʿīl, *Manhaj*, p. 319; Abū Zahrah, *al-Jarīmah*, p. 165; Ghazawī, *al-Ḥurriyyah*, p. 59.

106. Khadduri, M, *The Islamic Law of Nations: al-Shaybani's Siyar*, p. 230.

107. See ʿAwdah, *al-Tashrīʿ al-Jinā'ī al-Islāmī Muqāranan bi'l-Qānūn al-Waḍʿī*, I, 101.

108. Al-Mawardī, *Kitāb al-Aḥkām al-Sulṭāniyyah*, p. 67.

109. ʿAwdah, *Al-Tashrīʿ al-Jinā'ī*, I, 104-5.

110. Ibid., p. 105.

111. Ibn Qayyim, *Ighāthah*, II. 129.

112. Ibid., II, 144.

113. Ibid., II, 129.

114. Ibid., II, 114.

115. Kamali, 'Varieties of Raʿy', *American Journal of Islamic Social Sciences* 7, 39-64.

116. See Qur'ān XXVI:160-173; XXVII:54-58; XXIX:28-35; LIV:33-39.

117. Ibn Qayyim, *Ighāthah*, II 130.

118. Ibid.
119. Ibid.
120. Ibn Taymiyyah, *Public Duties in Islam: The Institution of Ḥisbah*, trans. Mukhtar Holland, p. 88.
121. Ibn Taymiyyah, *al-Siyāsah*, p. 123; see also Abū Zahrah, *al-Jarīmah*, p. 157, who quotes Ibn Taymiyyah at length on the subject.
122. Al-Sarakhsī, *al-Mabsūṭ*, I. 125.
123. Abu Zahrah, *al-Jarīmah*, p. 159.
124. Al-Ghazālī, *Iḥyā'*, VIII, 18.
125. Both *Ḥadīths* quoted in ibid. VIII, 185, and al-Sarakhsī, *al-Mabsūṭ*, X, 152-3.
126. Al-Sarakhsī, *al-Mabsūṭ*, X, 153.
127. Al-Ghazālī, *Iḥyā'*, VIII, 185 and further detail at VI, 159.
128. Cf. al-Sarakhsī, *al-Mabsūṭ*, X, 154.
129. Al-Ghazālī, *Iḥyā'*, VIII, 188.
130. Both *Ḥadīths* are quoted by al-Ghazālī in, *Iḥyā'*, VIII, 190.
131. Ibid., IX, 12-14.
132. Ibid., VI, 160.
133. Ibid., VI, 150-60, where al-Ghazālī discusses the issues in detail.
134. Cf. ibid., VI, 143.
135. For details on *siyāsah sharʿiyyah* see my article 'Siyāsah Sharʿiyyah or the Policies of Islamic Government', *American Journal of Islamic Social Sciences*, vol. 6 (1989).
136. Ibn Qayyim, *al-Ṭuruq*, pp. 258-9 (Beirut edn. by Dār al-Maʿrifah).
137. Ibid., p. 258 (Beirut edn. by Dar al-Maʿrifah).
138. Ibn ʿĀbidīn, *Ḥāshiyah*, IV, 65.
139. Ibn Qayyim, *al-Ṭuruq*, p. 256.
140. Cf. Ibn ʿĀbidīn, *Ḥāshiyah*, IV, 65.
141. Cf. ʿAwdah, *al-Tashrīʿ al-Jinā'ī*, pp. 138 ff.
142. Kamali, 'The Limits of Power in an Islamic State', *Islamic Studies* 28 (1989), 323-53.
143. Al-Shāṭibi, *al-Iʿtiṣām*, II, 293.
144. Ibn ʿĀbidīn, *Ḥāshiyah*, IV, 66-7.
145. Cf. al-Samarā'ī, *Aḥkām al-Murtadd*, p. 116 ff.
146. Ibid., pp. 43-46.
147. The full texts of these and other Qur'ānic passages have been discussed under a separate section below entitled 'Evidence in the Qur'ān and Sunnah'.
148. Ibn Taymiyyah, *al-Ṣārim*, p. 561.
149. Al-Samarā'ī, *Aḥkām al-Murtadd*, p. 99.
150. Ibn Taymiyyah, *al-Ṣārim*, p. 514. While recording this view, Ibn Taymiyyah adds, on the same page, that the Qāḍī Abū Yaʿlā al-Farrā, and Ibn Ḥazm al-Andalūsī, also recorded the same opinion. Some of the jurists of Iraq advised the caliph Hārūn al-Rashīd with regard to someone who had insulted the Prophet ﷺ, that the offender

should be flogged, as insult in his case was not accompanied by any claim to validity. Having stated this however, Ibn Taymiyyah goes on to say that when Imām Mālik was informed of this *fatwā*, he rejected it. Ibn Taymiyyah himself agrees with Imām Mālik and says that the view attributed to the *fuqahā'* of Iraq is somewhat obscure and that Abū Ya'lā has probably taken it from the works of some '*mutakallimūn*' (i.e. the Mu'tazilah).

151. Cf. al-Bahnasāwī, *al-Ḥukm*, p. 62.

152. Ibn Ḥazm, *al-Fiṣal*, II, 137-38.

153. Abū Zahrah, *al-Jarīmah*, p. 82; see also al-Bahnasāwī, *al-Ḥukm*, p. 50.

154. Al-Ghazālī, *al-Munqidh* (MacCarthy's trans.) p. 150.

155. Ibid., p. 162.

156. Ibn 'Ābidīn, *Ḥāshiyah*, IV, 237.

157. Cf. Abū Zahrah, *al-Jarīmah*, p. 196; al-Zuhaylī, *al-Fiqh al-Islāmī wa Adillatuhu*, VI, 184; al-Jazīrī, *Kitāb al-Fiqh*, V, 428.

158. Aḥmad Amīn, *Fajr al-Islām*, pp. 154-57.

159. Al-Bahnasāwī, *al-Ḥukm*, p. 373.

160. Carl Ernst, 'Blasphemy: The Islamic Concept,' *The Encyclopedia of Religion*, II, 242-43.

161. Aḥmad Amīn, *Ḍuḥā*, p. 158; al-Bahnasāwī, *al-Ḥukm*, p. 373; al-Jazīrī, *Kitāb al-Fiqh*, V, 428; al-Samarā'ī, *Aḥkām al-Murtadd*, p. 206.

162. Ibn Ḥazm, *al-Muḥallā*, XI, 411-12.

163. *Al-Mawsū'ah al-Fiqhiyyah*, XIII, 230-31; al-Jazīrī, *Kitāb al-Fiqh*, V, 436.

164. Ibn Taymiyyah, *al-Ṣārim*, p. 539.

165. Ibid.; Ibn Ḥazm, *al-Muḥallā*, XI, 416.

166. Ibn Taymiyyah, *al-Ṣārim*, p. 539.

167. Ibn Ḥazm, *al-Muḥallā*, XI, 416.

168. Ibn Taymiyyah, *al-Ṣārim*, p. 539.

169. Ibid., pp. 541, 543.

170. Bahnasī, *al-Jarā'im fi'l-Fiqh al-Islāmī: Dirāsah Fiqhiyyah Muqāranah*, p. 147.

171. Ibn Taymiyyah, *al-Ṣārim*, p. 541.

172. A *Ḥadīth Qudsī*, literally 'Divine Utterance', is to be distinguished from *Ḥadīth Nabawī*, 'Prophetic *Ḥadīth*', in as much as the former are the very words of God Himself, uttered upon the tongue of the Prophet ﷺ, while the latter are the words of the Prophet ﷺ. The word *Ḥadīth* usually refers to *Ḥadīth Nabawī*, Prophetic *Ḥadīth*, as throughout this book, unless stated otherwise. Although *Ḥadīth Qudsī* are the words of God, they do not constitute a part of the Qur'ān.

173. Ibid., p. 543.

174. Abū Dāwūd, *Sunan* (Hasan's trans.), III, 1036, *Ḥadīth* no. 3643.

175. Al-Sharabāṣī, *Min al-Ādāb al-Nabawiyyah*, p. 197.

176. Ibid., p. 202; Ibn Taymiyyah, *al-Ṣārim*, pp. 172, 174.

177. Ibn Taymiyyah, *al-Ṣārim*, p. 531.

178. Ibn Qudāmah, *al-Mughnī*, VIII, 232; al-Dusūqī, *Ḥāshiyat al-Dusūqī ʿalā'l-Sharʿ al-Kabīr li-Abī'l-Barakāt Sīdī Aḥmad al-Dardīr*, IV, 309; al-Jazīrī, *Kitāb al-Fiqh*, V, 4290.

179. Al-Dusūqī, *Ḥāshiyat* IV, 309; al-Sharbīnī, *Mughnī al-Muḥtāj ilā Maʿrifat Maʿānī Alfāẓ al-Minhāj*, IV, 135.

180. Ibid., IV, 311.

181. Ibid., IV, 312.

182. Ibn Taymiyyah, *al-Ṣārim*, pp. 566-67; Ibn Ḥazm, *al-Muḥallā*, XI, 415; *al-Mawsūʿah al-Fiqhiyah*, XIII, 231.

183. Ibn Taymiyyah, *al-Ṣārim*, p. 565; see also al-Buhūtī, *Kashshāf*, VI, 177; *al-Mawsūʿah al-Fiqhiyyah*, XIII, 231; al-Jazīrī, *Kitāb al-Fiqh*, V, 423.

184. Thus, it is somewhat uncertain whether al-Khiḍr and Luqmān were Prophets, and whether Hārūt and Mārūt are Angels. Cf. *al-Mawsūʿah al-Fiqhiyyah*, XIII, 231; al-Dusūqī, *Ḥāshiyat*, IV, 312.

185. Ibn Ḥazm, *al-Muḥallā*, XI, 412; Ibn ʿĀbidīn, *Ḥāshiyah*, IV, 235.

186. Al-Buhūtī, *Kashshāf*, VI, 168; al-Yaḥsabī, Qāḍī ʿIyāḍ, *al-Shifā' bi-Taʿrīf Ḥuqūq al-Muṣṭafā*, II, 270.

187. Cf. Ibn Taymiyyah, *al-Ṣārim*, p. 547-48; al-Yaḥsabī, *al-Shifā'*, II, 271; al-Samarā'ī, *Aḥkām*, p. 94.

188. Al-Qarāfī, *al-Furūq*, p. 141.

189. Cf. al-Yaḥsabī, *al-Shifā'*, II, 254; Ibn Qudāmah, *al-Mughnī*, X, 74 ff; al-Shawkānī, *Nayl al-Awṭār*, VII, 221; Rahman, *Apostasy*, p. 116.

190. Al-Shawkānī, *Nayl al-Awṭār*, VII, 221.

191. *Al-Mawsūʿah al-Fiqhiyyah*, XIII, 231; al-Buhūtī, *Kashshāf*, VI, 168; Ibn Ḥazm, *al-Muḥallā*, XI, 411.

192. Ibn Taymiyyah, *al-Ṣārim*, p. 300.

193. Al-Jazīrī, *Kitāb al-Fiqh*, V, 425; al-Samarā'ī, *Aḥkām*, p. 104.

194. Ibn Taymiyyah, *al-Ṣārim*, p. 302.

195. Ibid., V, 437-38; al-Yaḥsabī, *al-Shifā'*, II, 260.

196. Al-Yaḥsabī, *al-Shifā'*, II, 260; Ibn Qudāmah, *al-Mughnī*, VIII, 125; al-Shawkānī, *Nayl al-Awṭār*, VII, 221.

197. Ibn Taymiyyah, *al-Ṣārim*, pp. 559-61; Ibn Ḥazm, *al-Muḥallā*, XI, 415; *al-Mawsūʿah al-Fiqhiyyah*, XIII, 231.

198. Ibn Taymiyyah, *al-Ṣārim*, p. 8.

199. Ibid., pp. 10-24, and 254-55; Ibn Ḥazm, *al-Muḥallā*, XI, 416.

200. Al-Yaḥsabī, *al-Shifā'*, vol.2, p 219 ff.

201. This being a reference to the fact that the Prophet ﷺ believed in the revelations he received.

202. Ibn Taymiyyah, *al-Ṣārim*, p. 20.

203. Ibid. p. 22.

204. Ibid.

205. Ibid. p. 23.
206. Ibid. p. 24.
207. Ibid. p. 40.
208. Ibid. p. 42.
209. Ibid. p. 44.
210. Ibid. pp. 43-45.
211. Ibid. pp. 50-51.
212. Cf. Ernst, 'Blasphemy, the Islamic Concept', *The Encyclopedia of Religion*, II, 243.
213. Ibn Taymiyyah, *al-Ṣārim*, p. 79 ff.
214. Al-Samarā'ī, *Aḥkām al-Murtadd*, p. 199.
215. Ibn Qayyim al-Jawziyyah, *Zād al-Maʿād fī Hudā Khayr al-ʿIbād*, II, 419.
216. Mutawallī, *Mabādi'*, p. 302.
217. Al-Samarā'ī, *Aḥkām al-Murtadd*, p. 199.
218. The reader's attention is drawn to Appendix III below, in which a resumé of the law of Malaysia and Pakistan pertaining to blasphemy has been presented. Also included in this Appendix are some recent case-histories of blasphemy and apostasy in Indonesia, Egypt, and the Sudan.

CONCLUSION

The weight of the *Sharīʿah* evidence I have reviewed and presented on the various aspects of freedom of expression supports the dignity of the individual and his freedom of conscience. At the root of this evidence lies the basic moral issue of freedom versus responsibility, which could hardly be resolved on an ethically sound foundation unless the individual is granted the freedom to speak and act in harmony with his conviction and what he or she believes to be of benefit to society. When an upright individual of sound judgement encounters abusive conduct which upsets his sense of commitment to justice and truth, he ought to be able to take a stand to denounce it, and express an opinion to that effect. This is the basic message of a great many of the moral and legal teachings of Islam that I have reviewed. While providing the necessary authority for freedom of expression, the *Sharīʿah* also maintains a tolerant outlook toward other religions and legal traditions, and grants non-Muslim residents in Muslim communities the right to speak for justice, decency and truth, and to denounce the opposite of these.

Ethical values are upheld in Islam through affirmative moral teachings which inculcate uprightness of speech and conduct in the individual. Compassion, self-restraint, respect for the rights of others and avoiding harm to them, be it in the form of backbiting, acrimonious speech, or exposing the weaknesses of others, are among the major themes of the moral edifice of Islam and the foundation of its moral integrity and piety (*taqwā*). The basic rights and dignity of the citizen are in turn protected through a series of legal prohibitions concerning slanderous accusation, defamation and insult. The *Sharīʿah* adopts a similar stance regarding sedition and blasphemy so as to prevent sacrilege and serious threats to peace and order in society. In all of this we find that the evidence in the source materials of the *Sharīʿah* aims at a high standard of withstraint in the application of the law so that charges of slander, insult, and sedition are only made when deviation from the correct norms exceeds the limits of propriety and justified tolerance. Punitive measures are seen as the last resort which must be taken only when compellingly warranted. Thus, we note a remarkable degree of emphasis in the Qur'ān and the Sunnah on moral persuasion, good advice, appeal to the good conscience of individuals, repentance and forgiveness. These are some of the most important aspects of social fraternity which Islam strongly advocates. The emphasis on persuasive methods is clearly overwhelming; moral advice must naturally come before punitive measures and all efforts must be made to reform the individual who might have breached acceptable norms of conduct. Reformation through moral advice (*naṣīḥah*), expiation (*kaffārah*), and repentance (*tawbah*), is the essence and objective of the legal directives and moral teachings of the Qur'ān and the Sunnah, which should be given proper institutional expression in any judicial system which aspires to Islamic norms.

Many constitutions of contemporary Muslim countries have adopted provisions which declare freedom of speech and freedom of religion among the basic rights of the citizens. Notwithstanding the fact that most of these constitutional declarations were inspired by western models, they tend nevertheless to be in harmony with the normative guidance of the Qur'ān and the Sunnah, which proscribes compulsion in religion on the one hand, and on the other, demands the individual to be an active participant in the quest for moral integrity and the vindication of truth. Those who are subject to these Islamic norms enjoy full freedom of expression but are also required to observe all the necessary restraints that ensure a responsible use of this freedom and prevent abuses of it. Modern constitutional proclamations on basic rights are conceptually sound, but seem to lack a satisfactory practical implementation. Constitutional proclamations on civil liberties in many Muslim countries have yet to be transformed into reality and become part of the applied law of the land. There is, also, a need for taking new measures that would enhance the scope and substance of freedom of expression. This can be done, perhaps, through articulating in detail the state laws on aspects of this freedom which have not received proper attention. Statutory legislation in Muslim countries would do well to enrich the Islamic content of its provisions on basic liberties by assigning, perhaps, a more visible role to some of the Qur'ānic concepts and principles such as *ḥisbah, naṣīḥah, shūrā*, and co-operation in good work (*taʿāwun*). How these are to be articulated in the form of pragmatic formulae incorporating the rights and duties of the citizen and state, merits the attention of scholars and legislators in Muslim countries, especially those among them that are more resourceful and influential. The *Sharīʿah* provisions on these and other themes pertaining to the rights of the individual are decidedly in favour of enhancing the status of the individual vis-à-vis the state. From the viewpoint of the *Sharīʿah*, the state is under a basic duty to implement these provisions and protect the rights and liberties of the individual through all legitimate means at its disposal.

We do not envisage a seriously wide gap between the state law and the *Sharīʿah* on the subject of our concern. It is perhaps more a question of policy orientation and style rather than substantive alteration and reform. For the pro-liberty and consultative substance of modern constitutional law in Muslim countries tends to conform with the basic principles of the *Sharīʿah*. But since the *Sharīʿah* has its own concepts and postulates, a *Sharīʿah*-orientated policy can enrich the substance of freedom of expression most effectively only when it is allowed to express its own identity and character. This is to be recommended, especially when one bears in mind the generally pro-western orientation of the nation-state and constitutional law of the post-colonial period in Muslim countries. Many Muslim countries have, on the other hand, made efforts and adjustments so as to move closer to their own history and heritage. This is a process that merits greater attention and support and which should hopefully be facilitated through consultation and consensus.

Freedom of expression is the principal theme in the democratic substance of any constitution, and advancement in this area is in many ways seen as a yardstick by which to assess the representative capacity of a government. To articulate an Islamic legislative approach with regard to human dignity and people's rights and immunities, as well as their duties and responsibilities, will undoubtedly require sustained and dedicated effort. But the reward would be that the Muslim personality and culture would have expressed itself in the legislative, judicial and policy-making spheres of the modern nation-state.

APPENDIX I:

Ḥaqq, Ḥukm Sharʿī and ʿAdl

1. MEANING AND DEFINITION OF *ḤAQQ*

Among the primary meanings of the word *ḥaqq* in Arabic are 'established fact', 'reality' or 'truth'. In law it is taken to mean the last, namely, 'truth', or that which corresponds to facts, which is in fact the word's predominant meaning.[1] 'Right', 'power', and 'claim' constitute some of the other equally prominent meanings of *ḥaqq*, and some writers have even added 'beneficence and public good' (*al-khayr wa'l-maṣlaḥah*) to the list.[2]

The word '*ḥaqq*' occurs frequently in the Qur'ān, and is often used to imply the certainty of values, rewards, promises and punishments. Al-Ṣābūnī has listed at least six different meanings of *ḥaqq* in the Qur'ān, but he concludes that the concepts of certainty and proof generally underlie the Qur'ānic usage of this word.[3] In the language of the Qur'ān, *ḥaqq* is interchangeable with duty (*wājib*). Although instances can be found where '*ḥaqq*' means 'a right' as opposed to 'an obligation' - such as the passage which entitles 'the beggar and the indigent' to a certain right (*ḥaqq*) with regard to the wealth of an affluent society (LI:19) - there is no attempt in the Qur'ān to distinguish either of these as the predominant meaning of *ḥaqq*. Occasionally, *ḥaqq* is used to denote the ultimate victory and salvation of the believers as a certain outcome of some action. (cf. X:103; XXX:47). Killing is forbidden save 'in [the cause of] justice' (*bi'l-ḥaqq*); and '... do not conceal the truth (*al-ḥaqq*) while you know it' (II:42), are two examples, along with other similar usages of *ḥaqq*, which lead al-Bahī to the conclusion that *ḥaqq* in the Qur'ān is inextricably linked with justice and benevolence (*ʿadl wa iḥsān*) and that these are the ultimate values which are intended wherever there is a mention of *ḥaqq* in the Qur'ān.[4] Finally, *ḥaqq* is sometimes used without conveying an emphatic obligation, but as a way of encouraging a specific type of behaviour. For example, in a *Ḥadīth* recorded by Muslim, Abū Hurayrah has narrated that 'A Muslim has a right (*ḥaqq*) over other Muslims in six matters ...', namely, to have his greeting (*salām*) returned, to have his invitation accepted, to receive sincere advice (*naṣīḥah*), and so forth. These are obviously moral rights, but, to emphasise observance, they are all referred to as constituting a '*ḥaqq*'. This, incidentally, serves as an example of the concept of moral, as opposed to legal, rights in Islam. Classical Muslim jurists have not articulated a juridical definition for *ḥaqq*, but have instead relied on the linguistic meaning of the word.[5] As ʿAlī al-Khafīf has observed, the jurists perhaps have not felt the need to do so, as the word is clear and versatile and its juridical usage is often closely related to its literal meaning.[6]

A somewhat vague definition of *ḥaqq* appears in the *Baḥr al-Rā'iq* of Ibn Nujaym, where *ḥaqq* is defined as 'the entitlement of a person to a thing' (*al-ḥaqq ma yastaḥiqquhu'l-rajul*). This definition is circumlocutory, as it defines *ḥaqq* by its own derivative. The same author has, however, given an accurate definition of the right of ownership which he terms 'an exclusive assignment' (*ikhtiṣāṣ ḥājiz*).[7] An exclusive claim or assignment in favour of the right-bearer is a basic ingredient of the general concept of *ḥaqq*, and it is in this respect that *ḥaqq* is distinguished from 'permissibility' (*ibāḥah*). The right of ownership is a typical example of *ḥaqq* as an exclusive assignment. On the other hand, freedom of movement and freedom of speech are examples of *ḥaqq* in the sense of *ibāḥah*. For these are advantages to which people are generally entitled, and thereby no exclusive claim is established in favour of anyone in particular.[8]

Modern scholars have advanced several definitions for *ḥaqq*, varying in respect of the emphasis that they place on its different elements. Some of these definitions view *ḥaqq* from the perspective of *ḥukm sharʿī*, while others tend to emphasise the concept of public interest (*maṣlaḥah*). To avoid engaging in technicalities, I shall quote only one definition; in it *ḥaqq* is described as 'an exclusive appropriation of or power over something, or a demand addressed to another party which the *Sharīʿah* has validated in order to realise a certain benefit'.[9]

In this definition, exclusive appropriation (*ikhtiṣāṣ*) precludes things which are merely permissible, that is, the *mubāḥāt*, from the scope of *ḥaqq*. A right must also be validated by the *Sharīᶜah*, and this requirement prevents factual appropriation which is not valid, such as stolen items in possession of the thief. A right may likewise be exclusive to God, a human being, to real persons or to corporate persons. And, lastly in this definition, a right is the means to a benefit, but it is not identical with that benefit. For example, the right-bearer who is entitled to conclude a contract of sale may not use it in order to procure usury (*ribā'*), nor may this right be used in order to harm another person or the community by means, for example, of hoarding (*iḥtikār*). For these actions are all forbidden by the expressed will of the Lawgiver. Thus the benefit that is pursued by *ḥaqq* is distinguishable from the *ḥaqq* itself, and can be separately identified. A *ḥaqq* is a benefit (*maṣlaḥah*) only when it consists of an exclusive assignment, but in its objective sense, a *maṣlaḥah* which is unrelated to anyone in particular is not a *ḥaqq*. Nevertheless, it appears that *ḥaqq* in Islamic law is intertwined with *maṣlaḥah*. Although the two are not identical, *ḥaqq* is essentially goal-oriented (*ghā'iyyah*), and its valid exercise is determined on that basis. When a right is used in a manner that violates the *maṣlaḥah* on which it is predicated, the exercise amounts to abuse of that right. According to al-Shāṭibī, 'The acts that the *Sharīᶜah* validates are not goals in themselves but the means to certain other objectives, and these are the benefits (*al-maṣāliḥ*) in pursuit of which the acts have been validated in the first place.'[10] Thus we understand that in Islam, notwithstanding the fact that *ḥaqq* is essentially an individualistic concept, the rights and interests of individuals are subservient to higher values, such as justice and *maṣlaḥah*.

The power (*sulṭah*) that is established by *ḥaqq* may be over a person, such as the right of custody (*ḥaḍānah*) over a child, or it may be over a thing, such as the right of a legal heir to a share in the estate of his deceased relative. However, due to the overriding influence of *maṣlaḥah* on *ḥaqq*, the right-bearer does not have unqualified latitude in exercising his right. For example, the 'right' to life is sacrosanct not only against aggression by others, but also against aggression by oneself. Similarly, the owner of property is not entitled to destroy it without any useful purpose. To do so would violate the basic objective of the Lawgiver and of the *maṣlaḥah* on which it is founded.

2. *ḤAQQ* AND *ḤUKM*

The scholars of the roots or sources of Islamic law (*uṣūl al-fiqh*) discuss *ḥaqq* and its varieties under the general subject of *ḥukm sharʿī*, which concerns *Sharīʿah* laws and values.[11] *Ḥukm* is a broad subject which comprises a variety of concepts, including commands, prohibitions, permissibility, and others. All *aḥkām* (pl. of *ḥukm*) in the *Sharīʿah* originate in principle in the Qur'ān and the Sunnah, which constitute the sum total of God's communication to mankind. The Qur'ān has however, in turn authorised those who are in charge of affairs, the *ulū'l-amr*, to issue *aḥkām*.

Ḥukm is the cause (*sabab*) of *ḥaqq*, in that the latter originates in the former, but *ḥaqq* and *ḥukm* are not identical. In other words, *ḥaqq* is the result or effect of *ḥukm*. In *uṣūl al-fiqh*, *ḥukm* is defined as 'communication from the Lawgiver pertaining to the conduct of a legally competent person' (*mukallaf*), which may consist of a demand, an option or an enactment (*al-waḍʿ*).[12] This definition is broad enough to subsume *ḥaqq* in almost all of its varieties. A demand is usually communicated either in the form of a command or a prohibition. Whenever a demand is conveyed in decisive terms it constitutes either something obligatory (*wājib*), or something totally forbidden (*ḥarām*). But, if the demand does not have an absolute emphasis, then it constitutes either what is recommendable (*mandūb*), or what is reprehensible (*makrūh*). An option (*takhyīr*), on the other hand, leaves the individual at liberty to do or not to do something, and the *ḥukm* that is so produced is known as *mubāḥ*. An enactment (*al-waḍʿ*) is neither a demand nor an option but an objective exposition of the requirements of a *ḥukm* which designates something as a cause, a condition, or a hindrance to something else. This aspect ensures that a *ḥukm* of the *Sharīʿah* is properly applied only when its cause (*ʿillah*) is present, all the necessary conditions (*shurūṭ*) fulfilled, and there is nothing to hinder its proper enforcement.[13] The fact that 'rights' are, for the most part, subsumed under the general subject of *ḥukm sharʿī* is significant insofar as it suggests that rights in Islamic law originate, directly or indirectly, in the clear injunction of the *Sharīʿah*.[14]

As noted earlier, *ḥukm* has a wider definition than *ḥaqq*, as it is not confined to regulating relations among individuals in society, which is the main theme of *ḥaqq*, but also regulates relations between man and his Creator. This last meaning is often subsumed by the juristic concept of *ḥaqq Allāh*, but in reality *ḥaqq Allāh* is a *ḥukm* more than it is a right. Thus, it appears that every right in Islamic law is a *ḥukm*, but that every *ḥukm* does not necessarily consist of a right. This can be seen more clearly, perhaps, in the case of *ḥukm waḍʿī* which may expound a certain aspect of a *ḥukm taklīfī*,[15] but may not create a right or an obligation at all.[16] Every *ḥukm sharʿī*, as al-Shāṭibī points out, has a devotional (*taʿabuddī*) aspect, which means that in the *Sharīʿah* no *ḥukm* is totally separable from the right of God. Al-Qarāfī also expresses basically the same idea when he states that in Islam there is no right of man in total isolation from the right of God.[17]

Some *ʿulamā'* concerned with *uṣūl*, such as Ṣadr al-Sharīʿah, have spoken of public rights and permissibilities such as 'freedom, honour, and ownership' (*al-ḥurriyyah wa'l-ʿiṣmah wa'l-mālikiyyah*) as the basic right of every human being,[18] while others have spoken of the right of ownership as a basic right and an 'exclusive appropriation' (*ikhtiṣāṣ ḥājiz*) of the owner. It is also noted that many rights in Islamic law fall under the category of so-called duty-oriented rights. Although Muslim jurists do not apply such a classification, the tendency in Islamic law to unify right and duty under the single concept of *ḥukm*, and then to seek a balanced orientation of both under the general concept of justice (*ʿadl*), indicates an emphasis toward integration. Many rights in Islam are in fact duty-oriented rights, for example, the father's right to discipline his child is in reality a duty. Likewise is the right of a guardian in respect of requiring equality in marriage (*kafā'ah*) for his ward, which in fact ensures that the prospective spouse is a suitable match.[19]

3. RIGHT AND JUSTICE *(ḤAQQ AND ʿĀDL)*

I have noted the tendency in the *Sharīʿah* toward integrating rights and obligations into the broad concepts of *ḥaqq* and *ḥukm*, and also the view that a balanced implementation of rights and duties is governed by the Qur'ānic standards of justice. The usage of *ḥaqq* in the Qur'ān is inextricably linked with justice which is, in fact, one of the Qur'ānic meanings of *ḥaqq*. We know, of course, that justice in any legal system is concerned with the correct implementation of rights and duties, but the question here is of an organic integration of these under the rubric of justice. This is something which is arguably unique to the Qur'ān and distinguishes the Islamic approach as typically unitarian in comparison to other legal systems.

As stated earlier, the *Sharīʿah* does not seek to eliminate the distinction between rights and obligations, nor does it, on the other hand, emphasise this distinction in the familiar pattern of a modern constitution. In fact, right and duty in the Qur'ān merge into the concept of *ʿadl,* so much so that they become, in principle, an extension of one another. While I noted that *ḥukm* subsumes both rights and obligations, the relationship between *hukm* and *ʿadl* is also one of a means to an end. *Ḥukm* is the means toward *ʿadl,* as is *ḥaqq* the fulfilment and realisation whereof, in both of its dual capacities of right and obligation, is predicated upon *ʿadl.* Thus, Islam seeks to establish justice through the enforcement of *ḥukm sharʿī*, which is at the same time expected to mean the proper fulfilment of rights and duties. The Qur'ān's ubiquitous emphasis on *ʿadl* makes this clearly one of the cardinal objectives of Islam and an overriding theme of the Holy Book itself. To underscore this, I refer to a passage where justice is declared to be not only the ultimate goal of religion, but that of prophethood and divine revelation: in other words, it is the core and essence of Islam itself. 'We sent Our Messengers with clear signs, and sent down with them the Book and the measure so that people should practise justice.' (LVII:25)

لَقَدْ اَرْسَلْنَا رُسُلَنَا بِالْبَيِّنٰتِ وَاَنْزَلْنَا مَعَهُمُ الْكِتٰبَ وَالْمِيزَانَ
لِيَقُومَ النَّاسُ بِالْقِسْطِ.

The phrase 'Our Messengers' suggests that justice has been the goal of all revealed religious guidance throughout human history. This emphasis on justice implies its innateness and universality.

> O believers! Stand out firmly for justice as witnesses for God, even if it be against yourselves, (your) parents or relatives; and whether it concern the rich or the poor... (IV:135)

يٰاَيُّهَا الَّذِينَ اٰمَنُوا كُونُوا قَوَّامِينَ بِالْقِسْطِ شُهَدَاءَ لِلّٰهِ وَلَوْ على
اَنْفُسِكُمْ اَوِالْوَالِدَيْنِ وَالْاَقْرَبِينَ. اِن يَكُنْ غَنِيًّا اَوْ فَقِيرًا.

... and let not the hatred of a people wrong you into being unjust. (V:8)

وَلَا يَجْرِ مَنَّكُمْ شَنَانُ قَوْمٍ علـى اَلَّا تَعْدِلُوا.

... and when you judge among people, judge with justice. (IV:58)

وَاِذَا حَكَمْتُمْ بَيْنَ النَّاسِ اَن تَحْكُمُوا بِالْعَدْلِ.

The Qur'ān also enjoins Muslims to be just towards non-Muslims, specifically those who are not oppressive and have not committed acts of aggression against the believers.

> God does not forbid you from being kind towards, and dealing justly with those who fought you not about the faith and did not drive you from your homes. (LX:8)

لَا يَنْهٰكُمُ اللهُ عَنِ الَّذِينَ لَمْ يُقَاتِلُوكُمْ فِى الدِّينِ وَلَمْ
يُخْرِجُوكُمْ مِّن دِيَارِكُمْ اَنْ تَبَرُّوْهُمْ وَتُقْسِطُوا اِلَيْهِمْ.

In a recent address given at the International Islamic University, Malaysia, the Chief Justice of Pakistan, Muhammad Afzal Zullah, attempted to ascertain a certain order of priority in the value and belief structure of Islam. He proposed that if there were three such values which commanded absolute priority, these were *tawḥīd*, *risālah* and *ʿadl*, that is, belief in the Oneness of God, in the truth of Muḥammad's ﷺ prophethood and in justice. The speaker then added that the order of priority in this scale had become the subject of deliberation between himself and one of the other judges of the Supreme Court of Pakistan, and both had agreed that, owing to the high profile that *ʿadl* is given in the Qur'ān, it should precede *risālah*, and as such it was to come next to *tawḥīd*.[20] This would warrant the conclusion that *ʿadl* is a fundamental right of everyone without any discrimination whatsoever. When we recognise the basic unity of purpose in *ʿadl, ḥukm, ḥaqq*, and *wājib*, there remains no objection to a functional distinction between the various rights and their division into categories according to the nature of each particular right, and the weight and character of affirmative evidence that is found to support it.

As standards of justice in the Qur'ān transcend all levels of discrimination among people, this high concern for objectivity in the Qur'ānic vision of justice could hardly be sustained in a situation of bipolarity between rights and obligations. For, placing any undue emphasis on one at the expense of the other is likely to compromise the objectivity of justice. In other words, a comprehensive approach to *ᶜadl* necessitates that rights and obligations be integrated. At present, in many modern constitutions there is a general acceptance of the binary division between rights and obligations, and then a commitment of varying degrees to the pursuit of one or the other. On the other hand, the Qur'ānic approach to justice is typically unitarian. In Islam, rights and obligations are naturally integral to *ᶜadl*, and yet are subsidiary to the essence of justice itself. Thus justice is not identical with rights, for if it were then it could simply be waived by anyone who had a claim to it. As a concept, justice is more objective than that, and is free of the bias which 'rights' might entail in favour of their bearer.[21]

Insofar as it relates to the binary division of rights into 'the right of God' and 'the right of man', Islam seeks to establish an objective balance between the two, protecting the interests of both the individual and the community under the umbrella concept of *ᶜadl*. Contrary to the philosophical orientations of individualism, liberalism, and socialism, the *Sharīᶜah* does not seek to emphasise the one at the expense of the other. *ᶜAdl* itself is the philosophy of Islam and this necessitates an integrated and unitarian approach toward rights and obligations.[22]

Within the general framework of *ᶜadl*, the precise adjustment of rights and obligations in favour of one or the other may be open to other interests such as considerations of public policy and *maṣlaḥah*, insofar as they remain in harmony with the Qur'ānic scheme of values. Therefore, placing emphasis on a particular right or obligation would be acceptable if this proved to be beneficial, and ultimately reflected an integrated approach to justice, a greater refinement of *ijtihād*, and a better accommodation of the legitimate aspirations of society.

CONCLUSION

It would appear that many aspects of *ḥaqq* in Islamic law were developed in the absence of a clearly articulated definition. However, we find on the other hand that Muslim jurists had from an early stage articulated a definition for *ḥukm sharʿī* and each of its various components.[23] The availability of a clear definition for *ḥukm* may in fact have retarded progress on the definition of *ḥaqq* and encouraged the tendency for the one to be subsumed under the other. Moreover, *ḥukm* exhibits a closer affinity with obligation (*wājib*) rather than *ḥaqq*. Rights and duties are, of course, mutually related even if they are not mirror-image reflections of each other, and although they are not always correlative in that one can exist without the other, non-correlative rights and duties are nevertheless specific exceptions of a marginal rather than a central significance.[24]

The analysis I have presented here and in Part One supports the primacy of *ḥukm* and *wājib* over *ḥaqq* in Islamic law, but neither of these has ever meant relegating *ḥaqq* into insignificance. Nor has it deterred the *ʿulamāʾ* from paying exclusive attention to developing the various aspects of *ḥaqq*, such as its causes (*asbāb*); varieties and classifications; its uses (*istiʿmāl al-ḥaqq*) and abuses (*taʿassuf fī istiʿmāl al-ḥaqq*); the fulfilment of a right (*istifāʾ al-ḥaqq*); and the termination of a right (*inqiḍāʾ al-ḥaqq*).[25] I have also developed a certain perspective on the relationship of *ḥaqq* with *ʿadl* under the unitarian influence of *tawḥīd*, and I have, in the same light, discussed the recognition of fundamental rights as a separate category in Islamic law.

Western jurists are divided on the relative significance of 'right' versus 'duty'. Wesley Hohfeld was not the first, for example, to recognise 'right' as a very ambiguous term. In his work, *Fundamental Legal Conceptions*, he elaborated this theme to a greater extent than have his predecessors. In his view, a right is an advantage, and as such is a general concept as compared to a duty which is specific. A person under duty must be told specifically, not in general terms, what he may or may not do. But a right to life and property, statable as it is, is very general and may be correlated with not one, but a long catalogue of duties. To correlate a right with a specific duty is, therefore, not always self-evident, as this relationship, certain as it is, can be either clear and immediate, or dilute and remote. With this in the background, Western thinkers have advanced two different theories, one of which advocates the relative primacy of rights as the origin of duties. The opposite theory is often referred to as that of redundancy of rights: 'Whether we speak of rights or duties is at the end of the day merely a matter of perspective or style since nothing extra is conveyed by using instead of duty the language of right.'[26] 'Being a right against' can be alternatively stated as 'having a duty towards' without, in any material sense, detracting from, or denying the substance or the two-party relationship of either. It is, perhaps, due to the correlativity of right and duty that recognition of one must of necessity mean a corresponding recognition of the other.

NOTES

1. Cf. 'Ḥaqq', *al-Mawsūʿah al-Fiqhiyyah*, n. 10 at 7; 'Ḥakk', *The Encyclopedia of Islam*, New Edition; Wehr, Dictionary of Modern Arabic, p. 192.

2. Ḥammād, *Ḥurriyyat al-Ra'y*, p. 433.

3. Al-Ṣābūnī, *Muḥāḍarāt fi'l-Sharīʿah al-Islāmiyyah*, pp. 341-42.

4. Al-Bahī, *al-Islām fī Ḥall Mashākil*, p. 68.

5. Cf. Zarqā, *al-Madkhal al-Fiqhī al-ʿĀm*, III, 10. The tendency to rely on the literal meaning has also prevailed in *al-Mawsūʿah al-Fiqhiyyah* ('The Encyclopaedia of Fiqh') of Kuwait where the article on 'Ḥaqq' (vol. 18) does not give a definition of *ḥaqq*.

6. Al-Khafīf, *al-Ḥaqq wa'l-Dhimmah*, p. 36.

7. Ibn Nujaym, *al-Baḥr al-Rā'iq Sharḥ Kanz al-Daqā'iq*, 148 ff. This definition is also quoted by *al-Mawsūʿah al-Fiqhiyyah*, vol. 18. p. 10.

8. Cf. al-Darīnī, *al-Ḥaqq wa-Madā Sulṭān al-Dawlah fī Taqyīdih*, p. 182.

9. Al-Darīnī, ibid., n. 11 at p. 193.

10. Al-Shāṭibī, *al-Muwāfaqāt fī Uṣūl al-Aḥkām*, II, 385.

11. Cf. al-Darīnī, *al-Ḥaqq*, n. 11 at p. 211.

12. Cf. *al-Mawsūʿah*, n. 10 at p. 8. The *fuqahā'* on the other hand define *ḥukm* as the ruling that a *mujtahid* arrives at, based on the evidence in the sources and general principles of the *Sharīʿah*, concerning the conduct of the *mukallaf*. Cf. Ahmad Zaki Hammad, 'Ghazali's Juristic Treatment of the Sharīʿah Rules in al-Mustaṣfā,' *The American Journal of Islamic Social Sciences*, 4 (1987), 158.

13. For a detailed discussion of this definition see M.H. Kamali, *Jurisprudence*, pp. 321 ff.

14. *Al-Mawsūʿah*, n. 10 at p. 11.

15. *Ḥukm taklīfī*, or a 'defining law', consists of rules that define and evaluate the conduct of persons into such categories as obligatory (*wājib*), recommendable (*mandūb*), and forbidden (*ḥarām*), whereas *ḥukm waḍʿī*, or a 'declaratory law', lays down the necessary conditions, causes and impediments as to how the *ḥukm taklīfī* should be properly implemented.

16. Al-Khafīf, *al-Ḥaqq wa'l-Dhimmah*, n. 9 at p. 41; al-Darīnī, *al-Ḥaqq*, n. 11 at p. 210.

17. Al-Shāṭibī, *al-Muwāfaqāt,* n. 13 at II, 317; al-Qarāfī, *Kitāb al-Furūq*, I, 140–41.

18. ʿUbayd Allāh b. Masʿūd al-Bukhārī known as Ṣadr al-Sharīʿah, *al-Tawḍīḥ fī Ḥall Ghawāmiḍ al-Tanqīḥ*, II, 161.

19. Cf. Al-Darīnī, *al-Ḥaqq,* n. 11 at p. 176.

20. 'The Application of Islamic Law in Pakistan,' an address by Muhammad Afzal Zullah, Chief Justice of Pakistan, on 6th September 1991. Although the learned speaker did not mention this, his position here has a precedent in the theological doctrines of the Muʿtazilah. In their formulation of the five principles of the faith (*al-uṣūl al-khamsah*) *ʿadl* comes second only to *tawḥīd*. The five principles are: (1) *tawḥīd*; (2) *ʿadl* (3) belief in the promise of reward and threat of punishment (*al-waʿd wa'l-waʿīd*); (4) belief in the intermediate status (*al-manzilah bayna'l-manzilatayn*), that is between Islam and disbelief (and accordingly between Paradise and Hell); (5) commanding good and forbidding evil. Cf. Abū Zahrah, *Tārīkh al-Madhāhib*, p. 119.

21. Cf. ʿImārah, *al-Islām wa Ḥuqūq al-Insān*, p. 57.

22. Cf. Al-Darīnī, *al-Ḥaqq* n. 11 at pp. 148–49.

23. These are the Lawgiver (*ḥakīm*), the subject matter of *ḥukm* (*maḥkūm fīhi*), the party of incidence (*maḥkūm ʿalayhi*) and, of course, the *ḥukm* itself.

24. The correlativity of rights and duties is a much debated subject of jurisprudence. But it seems that a duty can exist independently of 'right'. In Islamic law, this is true of many of the obligatory duties in the area of *ʿibādāt*, which are not necessarily predicated on a particular right. Similarly, duties in criminal law, whether Islamic or Western, are imposed on members of society, none of whom have concomitant rights (cf. Dias, *Jurisprudence*, p. 37). A right, on the other hand, seems to be more dependent on 'duty', and it is the duty in this pair which appears to be the stronger or more independent component.

25. See for details al-Sanhūrī, *Maṣādir al-Ḥaqq fi'l-Fiqh al-Islāmī*, I, 35 ff; Abū Sinnah, 'Naẓariyyat al-Ḥaqq', at p. 175 of *al-Fiqh al-Islāmī,* ed. M T ʿUwaydah; Yūsuf Mūsā, *al-Fiqh al-Islāmī*, pp. 211 ff; and al-Zarqā, *al-Madkhal al-Fiqhī al-ʿĀm*, II, 15 ff.

26. See for details Stoljar, *An Analysis of Rights*, p. 47 ff.

APPENDIX II: ON *BID^cAH*

Matters pertaining to the religion of Islam in Malaysia are regulated under State Enactments rather than federal law. Usually bearing the title 'Adminstration of Muslim Law Enactment', these legal decrees normally contain a chapter on offences against the religion of Islam, including such matters as the propagation of false doctrines and teachings. Notwithstanding some variation in the law from one state to another, the enactments which are discussed here do not differ a great deal, and may, therefore, be regarded as representative of the general approach of Malaysian law to the issues of our concern. These provisions also serve as an example of how a basically moral tenet of the *Sharī^cah* has been made the subject of legislation. Broadly speaking, teaching a false doctrine may perhaps fall under the category of a reprehensible act (*makrūh*), but the head of state has powers under the *Sharī^cah* to legislate on such matters, and to impose a total ban on what is *makrūh* should this prove to be beneficial and in the interests of good government. For example, the Selangor Administration of Muslim Law Act, 1952 (as amended by the Administration of Muslim Law (Amendment) Enactment No. 9 of 1983), which is also applicable in the Federal Territory of Kuala Lumpur, provides the following under the heading of 'false doctrine'.

> Whoever shall teach or publicly expound any doctrine or perform any ceremony or act relating to the Muslim religion in any manner contrary to the Muslim Law shall be guilty of an offence punishable with imprisonment for a term not exceeding six months, or with a fine not exceeding one thousand dollars (§. 18).

This provision also appears *in toto* in the 1965 Administration of Muslim Law of Perak (§. 169.1). But the Perak Enactment goes on to add in subsection 2 of the same section that in the case of a person who is convicted of a false *fatwā*, or teaching, and has printed or published any material to which the conviction relates, the materials shall be forfeited and destroyed.

The 1986 Administration of Muslim Law Enactment of Terengganu, in Section (204), reproduces *in toto* the foregoing provisions of the Perak Enactment with the only difference that the penalty for the offence in question ' ... shall be a fine not exceeding five thousand ringgit or imprisonment not exceeding three years, or both'. The next clause in the same section is concurrent with that of the Perak provision on the forfeiture or destruction of the material to which the conviction relates.

These provisions are broad enough to comprise the propagation of false doctrines and teachings that partake of heresy (*bidʿah*) or transgression of the principles of Islam. There may be cases of *bidʿah* which may not be obviously 'contrary to the Muslim law', as some instances of *bidʿah* may also claim to be a true interpretation of Muslim Law on matters which may not have any precedent in the established *Sharīʿah*. However, it seems correct in principle that the law should operate on the basis of certainty, and that penal sentences can only be justified in cases of proven violation of the principles and doctrines of Islam. This is also the test in the Administration of Muslim Law Enactment of Perak which provides a maximum imprisonment of six months and a fine of five hundred dollars for any person who may be involved in the publication, printing and distribution of books and documents which are found to contain 'any matter contrary or repugnant to the true tenets of Islam or to any lawfully issued *fatwā*' (§. 168). The phrase 'true tenets of Islam' in this section would appear to go beyond obvious levels of 'repugnancy' and would seem to authorise probing into the veracity, or otherwise, of a dubious claim to truth. Be that as it may, the law here does not seem to concern itself with genuine scholarship or even with the speculative, but otherwise sincere, exposition of doctrines. I also note here that instances of violation are not always expected to be complex or difficult to identify.

The provision of Section 169(1) of the Perak Enactment was recently invoked in a case which was given publicity in the Malaysian press. According to one report, Haji Mohamed, a graduate of al-Azhar University who taught at an Anglo-Chinese School in Perak, and was the leader of a religious group, was jailed for deviant teachings. He was found guilty of having 'taught his followers that there was no Friday in the Qur'ān and the lunar calendar ...

[and] that it was against Islamic teachings to designate that particular day for congregational prayers'. He was also charged with giving sermons and for holding the normal Friday congregational prayers on Saturday evenings between sunset (*maghrib*) and late evening (*ʿishā'*).[1] There was not sufficient evidence to prove this latter charge, but the defendant was still sentenced to three months imprisonment for denying an established principle of Islam which has been consistently practised by the Muslim masses through unanimous consensus. Moreover, there is a chapter in the Qur'ān bearing the title '*Al-Jumʿah*', or 'The Congregation', which contains a passage addressing the believers as follows: 'When the call to the prayers on Friday (*min yawm al-jumʿah*) is given, then rush to the remembrance of God and abandon trading ...'. (LXII:9) In the face of a clear text such as this, which has been continuously put into practice by Muslims, there would seem to be little room for any divergent interpretation of the kind Haji Mohamed attempted to propagate.

At around the same time, in August 1991, the Malaysian National Council for Islamic Affairs, which is attached to the Prime Minister's Department, issued a circular to all Government Departments which communicated the decision to ban the publication and propagation of a book written by the Darul Arqam leader, Ustaz Ashaari Muhammad. Bearing the title *Aurad Muhammadiah Pegangan Darul Arqam*, this publication, although basically a prayer book, also contained controversial teachings on certain aspects of the faith. The reasons given for the ban on its circulation included the following:

(a) The book claims that Shaykh Suhaymi, the founder of Aurad Muhammadiah (who only died within the last few decades) has met with the Prophet Muḥammad and received the Aurad from him in the Holy Kaʿbah.

(b) It also claims that Shaykh Suhaymi is not dead but has disappeared, only to reappear as Imām al-Mahdī (i.e. the Messiah).

(c) The book modifies the 'confession of faith' *(shahādah)* in such a way as to reflect Shaykh Suhaymi as *Khalīfah* (successor) to the Prophet Muḥammad, thereby placing him on a par with [the] *Khulafā' al-Rāshidūn*.

Furthermore, the circular pointed out that the followers of al-Arqam firmly adhere to the teachings of their leaders and claim that the success of the Darul Arqam Movement has been due to the blessings of *Aurad Muhammadiah*. Consequently, the Government of

Malaysia imposed a ban not only on the book, but on all Darul Arqam propaganda activities within government departments.[2]

Once again we note that claims of direct contact with the Prophet Muḥammad ﷺ, or claims of the supernatural nature of Shaykh Suhaymi are not entirely new. Some of these claims, especially the one concerning the occultation (*ghaybah*) and reappearance of Shaykh Suhaymi, obviously resemble the theological doctrines of the Shīʿah Imāmiyyah about the disappearance of their twelfth imām, al-Mahdī, who is believed to be still alive and due to reappear. Belief in the occultation of the twelfth imām and his being the Mahdī, is one of the points over which the Sunnī and the Shīʿī followers of Islam are divided, and the Government of Malaysia has not hesitated to uphold the Sunnī/Shāfiʿī doctrines on this matter. This may be a slightly more complex case compared to that of Haji Mohamed of Perak, yet there is little doubt that these claims are contrary to established Muslim law. As far as the Sunnīs of Malaysia are concerned, these allegations are against the true tenets of Islam, and would, as such, represent unacceptable innovation (*bidʿah*).

NOTES

1. *The Star*, Tuesday Oct. 1, 1991, p. 13.

2. Circular dated 7th August 1991 by the Islamic Affairs Division, Prime Minister's Department, Kuala Lumpur.

APPENDIX III:
ON *FITNAH*

A Glance at Modern Law

A. SEDITION

Statutory enactments on the subject of sedition in present-day Muslim countries are, on the whole, wide-ranging and open to interpretation, often so much so as to impinge on freedom of speech. The Federal Constitution of Malaysia, 1957, for example, grants freedom of speech and expression to all Malaysian citizens, but also authorises parliament to pass laws that may impose restrictions on this freedom. This is, in principle, a correct approach in that only parliament has been granted such powers, but the list of restrictions that parliament can impose is wide-ranging. Parliament may thus, by law, impose on the freedom of speech whatever restrictions it deems necessary or expedient in the interest of the security of the Federation. This includes: friendly relations with other countries; public order or morality; restrictions to protect the privileges of parliament, or to provide against contempt of court; defamation; or incitement to any offence (Art. 10). Further restrictions are envisaged, under clause (4) of the same Article, which provides that parliament may pass laws prohibiting the questioning of sensitive matters such as racial issues or the prerogatives of Malay Rulers.

In the Conference on Freedom of Expression, December 1989, held in Kuala Lumpur, several of those who presented papers discussed aspects of Malaysian law pertaining to the restrictions that are imposed on this freedom. The speakers tended to approve of the guidelines contained in the Constitution, but were critical of some of the provisions of the Sedition Act, 1948. One of the participants, Shad Fārūqī, reviewed the Sedition Act in his paper entitled 'Laws Relating to Press Freedom in Malaysia'. He observed that the concept of sedition in Malaysia was much broader than in the United Kingdom, Ireland, India and Australia. A Malaysian lawyer was, therefore, unable to give a clear definition of what constitutes free speech and what constitutes sedition, with the consequent effect that 'this legal uncertainty is very much in favour of the prosecutor'.[1] Under the Sedition Act of Malaysia, sedition could be committed in any one of the following ways: inciting disaffection against any Malay Ruler or government; inciting unlawful changes to any lawful matter; inciting contempt for the administration of justice; raising discontent among the people; promoting ill-will between races or classes, or questioning 'sensitive issues' such as citizenship, the national language, special privileges of Malays and natives of Sabah and Sarawak and the status of the Malay Rulers. Section (3) of this law also penalises any act, speech, words or publication that have a 'seditious tendency', a phrase which to a large extent renders the question of intention irrelevant. But, the test here is once again whether the speech in question 'seeks to bring the government into hatred or contempt, excite disaffection against it, or promote ill-will and hostility among races or classes of population in the country'.[2] 'Disaffection' in the context of the Sedition Act means more than political criticism; it means the absence of affection, and the presence of disloyalty, enmity, and hostility. To 'excite disaffection' in relation to the government refers to implanting, arousing or stimulating in the minds of people a feeling of antagonism, enmity and disloyalty which tends to make the government insecure.[3] The law does not proscribe honest and reasonable criticism of the government, which is generally regarded to be beneficial: 'It is of course true that the greatest latitude must be given to freedom of expression. It would also seem to be true, as a general statement, that free and frank political discussion and criticism of government policies cannot be developed in an atmosphere of surveillance and constraint.'[4] The fact remains, however, that restrictive legislation on freedom of speech is quite elaborate. Some of the provisions of the Sedition Act are also reiterated in the Malaysian Penal Code (§. 298A) which penalises unlawful utterances and publications that cause disharmony, disunity, enmity and hatred. In another paper presented at the Kuala Lumpur Conference on Freedom of Expression, the author Lee Min Choon commented that some of the restrictions imposed under the Sedition Act 'may be unreasonable'. The writer further pointed out that judicial construction and elaboration by the judges has not helped matters. One particular judicial remark on the meaning of 'disaffection' (quoted above) was thus analysed, and the assessment it invoked from the writer was that 'this restriction tends to stifle the legitimate activities and aims of political opposition'.[5]

In its chapter entitled 'Offences Relating to Religion', the Penal Code of Malaysia provides that acts of oppression and violence against religion are punishable with imprisonment and fines: anyone who 'destroys, damages or defiles any place of worship, or any object held sacred by any class of persons, with the intention of thereby insulting the religion of any class of persons' is thus liable to maximum imprisonment of two years or with fine, or both (§. 295). A subsequent section of the Penal Code provides the following:

> Whoever by words, either spoken or written, or by signs, or by visible representations ... causes or attempts to cause disharmony ... or feeling of enmity, hatred or ill-will ... on grounds of religion between persons or groups of persons professing the same or different religions shall be punished with imprisonment for a term which may extend to three years, or with fine or with both (§. 298 A).

Under the Printing Presses Publications Act, 1984, malicious publication of false news is an offence which renders 'the printer, publisher, editor and the writer thereof', upon conviction liable to a maximum imprisonment of three years or a fine 'not exceeding twenty thousand ringgit or both' (§. 8A). The next clause in the same section clarifies the position with regard to malice, which is to 'be presumed in default of evidence showing that, prior to publication, the accused took reasonable measures to verify the truth of the news'.

The Constitution of the Islamic Republic of Pakistan, 1973, grants freedom of speech and expression 'to every citizen' and it protects freedom of the press. But then it goes on to provide that these freedoms are subject to 'any reasonable restriction imposed by law in the interests of the glory of Islam or the integrity, security or defence of Pakistan ... public order, decency or morality ... [and guarding against] defamation or incitement to an offence' (Art. 19).

In a commentary on this, Muhammad Munir points out that by virtue of this constitutional provision, all laws relating to the defence and security of the country, for instance, laws relating to the suppression of mutiny and internal rebellion, and laws relating to sedition and treason will be held valid even if they impose restrictions on freedom of speech, provided the court is satisfied that the restrictions so imposed have a reasonable relationship with the preservation of security. 'Reasonable relationship' in this context means 'not a remote or fanciful relation, but an intimate and proximate relation between the law and the security of the State'.[6] While commenting on the reference in the same Article to public order, Munir adds that words which promote enmity between classes may thus properly be punished. The Pakistan Penal Code thus penalises such utterances (§. 153-A), and so does the Public Safety Act, and the Security of Pakistan Act, 1952. Similarly, an order under Section 144 or Section 107, Criminal Procedure Code, prohibiting speeches likely to disturb public order, is protected. These restrictions also apply, the same author adds, to speeches prejudicially affecting the supply of essential commodities and services.[7] And lastly, constitutional references to morality and decency normally contemplate restrictions on obscene and prurient publications.

Another modern law offence which relates to the *Sharīʿah* concept of *fitnah* is contempt of court and contempt of parliament, both of which are recognised as statutory offences in the legislation of many Muslim and non-Muslim countries. Under Common Law, any speech or conduct, whether within the courtroom or outside, that tends to bring the authority and administration of the law into disrepute or interferes with court proceedings is a contempt of court. If, for example, the lawyer or the witness addresses the court in a manner that compromises the dignity of the court, the presiding judge may punish the offender for contempt of court.

In England, the overriding aim of the law of criminal contempt is to ensure that the jury is not exposed to prejudicial information prior to issuing its verdict. Hence, when the mass media publishes material in the course of a jury trial which could prejudice the jury, the publication may be held to be in contempt of court. Contempt of court under most jurisdictions remains an offence which is almost entirely governed by the discretionary powers of the judges who tend to exercise unrestricted power in the matter of deciding when newspapers and others are guilty of contempt.[8]

The Federal Constitution of Malaysia provides that the Supreme Court or High Court shall have the power to punish any contempt of itself (Art. 126). The procedure for contempt proceedings in the Supreme Court is governed by the Rules of the High Court, 1980, and similar rules regulating proceedings of the Supreme Court. In addition, the court can adopt summary contempt procedure on its own motion in cases where it is urgent to act immediately against contumelious conduct committed during its proceedings. It is equally important that the dignity of the court be protected even against contempt that is committed outside the court. In such cases the Attorney-General or any private party may initiate the contempt proceedings.

The discretion of the court in punishing contempt of court (and contempt of law) has, however, been regulated in Malaysia insofar as it relates to the *Sharīʿah* courts. Thus, we find in the 1988 Sharīʿah Criminal Code Enactment of Kedah, 1988 (and its equivalent 1985 Enactment of Kelantan), provisions which specify a maximum term of imprisonment or equivalent fine for contempt of court. Section 31 in each of the two Enactments thus provides:

> Any person who fails to comply with, contravenes, objects to, derides or refuses to obey any order of court shall be liable, on conviction, to a fine not exceeding one thousand ringgit or to imprisonment for a term not exceeding one year or both.

The Kedah and Kelantan Enactments also make liable to imprisonment of up to six months anyone who 'derides or despises any law' which is in force in their respective states (§. 18 and §. 28 respectively).

Furthermore, legislative enactments on the administration of Muslim law in the various states of Malaysia contain provisions on contempt of religious authorities. Consequently, anyone who is found guilty of contempt of the lawful authority of the Sultan as the Head of Religion of the State or other officials of the Council of Islamic Religion are liable to imprisonment for up to one year and a maximum fine of three thousand ringgit (the exact quantities vary in different states. Cf §§. 171, 207 and 32 of Administration of Muslim Law Enactments of Selangor, 1983, Terengganu, 1986, and Kedah, 1988, respectively).

While summarising the Malaysian law, Professor Ahmad Ibrahim writes that in Malaysia both the executive and the judiciary have ample powers to deal with criticism which exceeds the permissible limits. The courts can punish for contempt any criticism which they consider to be lacking in reasonable courtesy and good faith. The executive can act under the Sedition Act and can also have recourse to the powers of detention under the Internal Security Act. The right to free speech is therefore limited. It ceases at the point when it comes within the category of mischief as defined by the Sedition

Act or the Internal Security Act, or when it is considered to be in contempt of court.[9]

B. OBSCENITY

The test of obscenity in an old but basic English legal decision was held to be whether the tendency of the matter charged as obscenity or obscene publication is to pervert and corrupt those whose minds are open to such immoral influences, and into whose hands the publication is likely to fall.[10] In later cases, the probable effect, and not the mere tendency of the publication has been emphasised. A publication can be said to pervert and corrupt if it suggests to the minds of the young of either sex, or even to persons of more advanced years, thoughts of a libidinous character.[11] But, do books on sex in marriage fall within the purview of this description? Do we know when and how and to what extent the reading of a particular book will arouse sexual passions, and how these are to be balanced against the literary, scientific or educational value of a publication? Harry Street sums up the position of English law by saying that 'so far the charge against the law of obscenity is that it failed to face up frankly to the difficulties of defining obscenity.'[12]

Malaysia has, on the whole, followed the British Common Law on the basic concepts and definition of obscenity and obscene publication. Malaysian legislation on this subject is, however, scattered, and provisions relating to it are found in several statutes including the Penal Code, the Printing Presses and Publications Act, and the Cinematography Act. The Penal Code makes it a punishable offence for anyone publicly to exhibit, sell, distribute or in any manner put into circulation, import or export 'any obscene book, pamphlet, paper, drawing, painting, representation, or figure, or any obscene object whatsoever', and the offence is liable to imprisonment of up to three years, or fines, or both (§. 292). However, obscene acts which are committed in public places 'to the annoyance of others', obscene songs, ballads and words 'in or near any public place' are punishable with a maximum imprisonment of three months, or with a fine, or both. (§. 294)

The Printing Presses Publications Act, 1984, grants the Interior Minister of Malaysia unlimited discretionary powers to 'control undesirable publications' by an order which is to be published in the Gazette. The Minister may thus 'prohibit absolutely or subject to such conditions as may be prescribed, the printing, importation, sale, distribution or possession of obscene materials in any form including notes, photographs, music and sound recordings' (§. 7). The next section renders the possession of any prohibited publication an offence liable 'on conviction to a fine not exceeding five hundred ringgit' (§. 8).

Obscenity under the State legislation of Kelantan and Kedah in peninsular Malaysia is a punishable offence which carries up to six months imprisonment. The Sharīʿah Criminal Code of Kelantan, 1985, and of Kedah, 1988, under both their respective Sections 6, bearing the title 'Utterance of Indecent Words', provides the following:

> Any person who in any place wilfully utters or disseminates any word which is contrary to *ḥukm syarak* (a variant rendering of *ḥukm sharʿī*) and likely to cause a breach of peace shall be guilty of an offence and shall be liable on conviction to a fine not exceeding one thousand *ringgit* (about US$375) or to imprisonment for a term not exceeding six months or to both.

The Kedah and Kelantan Enactments also penalise indecent acts by anyone who 'commits in a public place any act or behaves in an indecent manner which is contrary to *ḥukm syarak*'. The acts so committed carry upon conviction up to six months of imprisonment, a maximum of one thousand ringgit or both (§. 5.1).

The Pakistan Penal Code prohibits possession, production, sale and distribution of 'any obscene book, pamphlet, paper ... or ... any obscene act in any public place ...'. The offence so committed is punishable with imprisonment 'which may extend to three months or with fine or with both'.[13] The question of providing a precise legal definition for 'obscene' has remained unresolved. In 're D. Pandurangan and Another v. State Prosecutor' (1953) (*Criminal Law Journal*, p. 763-64), the High Court of Madras considered the prosecutors' argument that certain pornographic books were obscene and fell within the mischief of 5.292, Indian (also Pakistan) Penal Code. The court identified the main problem as follows:

> The word 'Obscene' is not defined in the code. The natural and ordinary meaning of the term as given by the dictionaries is this:
> Webster's New International Dictionary: Obscene: Offensive to chastity or modesty; expressing or presenting to the mind or view something that delicacy, purity and decency forbid to be expressed; impure as obscene language, obscene picture[s] ... lustful ideas, indecent, lewd ...

Having expounded the dictionary meaning of 'obscene', the court went on to add that in the absence of a legal definiton, it remains 'a question of fact in each case whether a particular book falls within the meaning of this word. In this case a perusal of the book will convince anyone that it falls within the meaning given above.'

Muhammad Munir's description of obscenity is based on, and substantially concurrent with the foregoing. He seems to depart from the conclusion only where he says that the words 'decency' and 'morality' have a much wider signification under the penal law of Pakistan than 'obscenity'.[14] However, in the absence of a clear definition of 'obscenity', or, indeed, of its allied words such as 'indecency' and 'immorality', the difference between these concepts is not as self-evident as Munir has tended to suggest. Unless the concepts in question are given a definition, it would seem difficult to consider the scope of one as being 'much wider' than the other.

NOTES

1. Shad Fārūqī, 'Law Relating to Press Freedom in Malaysia', unpublished paper presented to the Conference on Freedom of Expression held in commemoration of World Human Rights Day, Kuala Lumpur, December 1989, p. 3.
2. Lee Hun Hoe, Chief Justice of Borneo, in Public Prosecutor v. Ooi Kee Saik, (1971), *Malayan Law Journal*, 2, p. 108.
3. Ibid., statement by Raja Azlan Shah, Jr (as he then was).
4. Ibid.
5. Choon, 'Should there be any Restrictions to the Freedom of Expression?', unpublished paper presented to the Conference on Freedom of Expression held in commemoration of World Human Rights Day, Kuala Lumpur, December 10, 1989, p. 5.
6. Munir, *Constitution of the Islamic Republic of Pakistan: Being a Commentary of the Constitution of Pakistan 1973*, p. 159.
7. Ibid., p. 161.
8. For details see Street, *Freedom of the Individual and the Law*, p. 152. ff.
9. Ahmad Ibrahim, 'Freedom of Speech and Expression Under the Federal Constitution: Sedition and Contempt of Court', *Law Info*, 1987, p. 19.
10. Street, *Freedom*, p. 122.
11. Cf. Munir, *The Constitution of Pakistan*, p. 162.
12. Street, *Freedom*, p. 127.
13. Section 292 & 294 Pakistan Penal Code.
14. Munir, *The Constitution of Pakistan*, p. 162.

APPENDIX IV:
ON BLASPHEMY

A Glance at Modern Law with Special Reference to Malaysia

Although Malaysia does not claim to be an Islamic state, Islam has a visible presence both in the Constitution and the social reality of Malaysia. Islam, side by side with Malay custom (*adat*), could be said to be among the strongest forces in society. It is partly due to the presence of sizeable minorities of Chinese (about 30%), Indians (about 10%) and others (about 10%) that Malaysian leaders describe their country as a multi-religious and multi-cultural society. This has, in turn, provided the government with a case for its secular orientation. Muslims constitute about fifty per cent of the population and the Malay rulers or sultans must necessarily be Malay, professing the religion of Islam. There is, however, nothing in the Constitution which provides that the Prime Minister or any Minister or Federal high officials must be Muslim.[1] The Federal Constitution declares Islam as 'the religion of the Federation', and also provides that 'other religions may be practised in peace and harmony in any part of the Federation' (Art. 3(1)). Article 11 of the Federal Constitution provides that every person has the right to profess and practise his or her religion and, subject to clause (4), to propagate it. Clause (4) provides that 'state law and in respect of the Federal Territories of Kuala Lumpur and Labuan, Federal Law may control or restrict the propagation of religious doctrine or belief among persons professing the religion of Islam.' The state legislature may consequently take the necessary measures to protect Islam against distortion and the propagation of false doctrine.

Commenting on Islam in the Malaysian Constitution, Professor Ahmad Ibrahim observed that 'the special position of Islam in the constitution' is also seen in the form of the oath taken by the Yang di-Pertuan Agong (i.e. the King) upon assuming office.[2] The oath is in the solemn Islamic form and reads in part that 'We shall at all times protect the religion of Islam and uphold the rules of law and order in this country.' In response to the suggestion that Islamic law is not recognised in Malaysia, as it is not included in the definition of law in Article 16 of the Constitution, the same author is of the view that, given a more positive attitude to matters of interpretation, it can be argued that the definition of the law in question uses the term 'includes', and so can be extended to embrace the Islamic law.[3] In Professor Ahmad Ibrahim's assessment, there is room for argument, within the terms of the Constitution, by the Muslims of Malaysia 'that they are entitled under Article 3 (1) to lead their way of life according to the teachings of Islam. If they wish to follow the Islamic Law and not the English Common Law, they should be allowed to do so.'[4]

As noted above, under the Federal Constitution, matters pertaining to the religion of Islam are to be regulated by state enactments (except for the Federal Territory). This is also the case with regard to the affairs of the *Sharīᶜah* courts which are governed by the state enactments rather than Federal Law. With reference to blasphemy, the Administration of Muslim Law Enactment of Selangor, 1952 (amended in 1983), which is also applicable in the Federal Territory of Kuala Lumpur, only contains a provision on 'contempt of religion'. The provision appears in part IX of the enactment which exclusively deals with offences concerning the religion of Islam, and reads as follows:

> Whoever by words spoken or written or by visible representations insults or brings into contempt or attempts to insult or bring into contempt the Muslim religion or the tenets of any sect thereof or the teaching of any lawfully authorised religious teacher or any *fatwā* (religious edict) lawfully issued by the President (of the State Religious Council) or under the provisions of this Enactment shall be punishable with imprisonment for a term not exceeding six months or with a fine not exceeding one thousand dollars. (§. 172.)

The terms of this provision are broad enough to comprise all words and acts of contempt against Islam, and as such, they are not confined to blasphemy in particular. But blasphemy would still remain the principal concern of this provision. The broad terms of the law here also extend to 'attempts to insult or bring into contempt' the laws and principles of Islam.

The Terengganu Administration of Muslim Law Enactment 1986 contains a similar provision on contempt of religion. But the offence so created here carries a heavier penalty. Section (209) thus reads:

> Whoever, whether orally or in writing or by any act or in any manner whatsoever, treats with contempt the Religion of Islam or the ways of any of the four Mazhabs, or any religious officer or religious teacher or authorised Imam or any *fatwā* lawfully issued under this Enactment commits an offence and shall be punishable with a fine not exceeding three thousand ringgit or with imprisonment not exceeding one year or with both.

Like that of the Selangor Enactment, the scope of this provision is also wider in that it is not confined to blasphemy but comprises a range of contemptuous acts, including contempt of the religious edict (*fatwā*) of an authorised religious officer. Since blasphemy is the most objectionable of all forms of contempt to religion, it would be expected to carry the maximum punishment that is stipulated in this enactment.

The Sharīᶜah Criminal Code of Kedah Enactment (No. 8 of 1988) has a general provision on the 'utterance of indecent words' which reads as follows:

> Any person who, in any place, wilfully utters or disseminates any word which is contrary to *Hukum Syarak* and likely to cause a breach of peace shall be guilty of an offence and shall be liable on conviction to a fine not exceeding one thousand ringgit or to imprisonment for a term not exceeding six months or both (§. 6).

Once again, the wording of this Section is broad enough to comprise not only blasphemy but also *bidᶜah* or any distortion of the principles of the established *Sharīᶜah*. Be that as it may, and minor variations apart, these provisions are fairly representative of the laws of other Malaysian states. Section (6) of the Sharīᶜah Criminal Code of Kelantan, 1985, for example, is identical with the foregoing provision under Kedah law. One year of imprisonment under the law of Terengganu and six months in most other states, an equivalent fine in each case or both, would thus seem to be the standard punishment for contempt of religion including blasphemy. The 1986 Administration of Islamic Religious Affairs Enactment of Terengganu contains a provision which carries the more specific title of 'contempt of Qur'ānic verses' and the offence in this case carries a heavier penalty. Section (206) thus reads:

> Whoever, whether orally or in writing or by any act or in any manner whatsoever, treats with contempt, or causes to be treated with contempt, any verse from the Qur'ān or any Ḥadīth or any word or sentence regarded as holy by Muslims commits an offence and shall be punished with a fine not exceeding three thousand ringgit or with imprisoment not exceeding one year or with both.

The equivalent provision to this in the 1952 Selangor Enactment is entitled 'misuse of the Koran' and although slightly less emphatic in tone, it contemplates the same offence, which is punishable in the Federal Territory and Selangor with 'imprisonment for a term not exceeding six months or with a fine not exceeding one hundred dollars' (§. 170 and §. 21 of the amending Enactment No. 9, 1983 of Selangor). Notwithstanding the specific reference to 'contempt of Qur'ānic verses' in the Kedah Enactment, the provision is, nevertheless, capable of general application to contemptuous expressions concerning 'any word or sentence regarded as holy by Muslims'.

As to whether the perpetrator of the said offence would still be regarded as a Muslim or is an apostate, the Terengganu Enactment provides that 'No person, except the Majlis (i.e. the Islamic Religious Council of Terengganu) or the Mufti shall ... make or issue any *fatwā*, relating to the Religion of Islam or *hukum syarak*, or accuse any person professing the religion of Islam [of] being a *murtad* (apostate), *syirik* (polytheist) or an infidel.' (§. 205.) The next clause in the same Section also provides that, 'No person, except *Hakim Sharʿi* shall decide' whether a person professing the religion of Islam has become an apostate or infidel. The term '*Hakim Sharʿi*' here means a competent *qāḍī* who is knowledgeable about the *Sharīʿah*.

Given the conditions of Malaysian society where large minorities of non-Muslims, Chinese, Christians and Hindus live side by side with their Muslim compatriots, and where everyone is exposed to each other's divergent religious and cultural influences, it is no surprise to find that the law takes a serious stand on the question of unfounded charges of blasphemy and infidelity. The Terengganu Enactment thus provides further that anyone who contravenes the provisions of Section (205) and declares another an infidel, apostate, or blasphemer commits an offence punishable with 'a fine not exceeding five thousand ringgit or with imprisonment not exceeding three years or with both' (§. 205.3).

A similar provision exists in the 1952 Selangor Enactment which renders the issuance of religious edicts by unauthorised persons, including religious scholars and leaders, into a punishable offence. This enactment is explicit on the point that issuing a *fatwā* in matters pertaining to offences against the religion of Islam is the sole prerogative of the state religious authorities. Persons who may issue such a *fatwā* are the State Mufti or anyone who acts under powers conferred by the religious authorities of the state, namely, the Sultan and the Religious Council. An unauthorised person who issues a *fatwā* is consequently liable to a punishment of up to six months of imprisonment or a fine not exceeding 'one thousand dollars or with both' (§.168 - amended in 1983). These provisions may fall under the broad doctrine of *siyāsah sharᶜiyyah*, or *Sharīᶜah*-oriented policy, which authorises the ruling authorities to introduce such rules and regulations as they deem necessary and beneficial. Given the sensitive nature of the issues involved and the pluralist character of Malaysian society, the Malay Sultans and rulers in almost all Malaysian states have apparently been persuaded to adopt the policy of disallowing unauthorised religious edicts on matters pertaining to offences against the religion of Islam.

The Pakistan Penal Code and the Code of Criminal Procedure were amended under the late president, General Zia ul-Haq, and they now contain provisions which make any utterance that implies disrespect to the Prophet of Islam ﷺ, or to any member of his family (i.e. the *ahl al-bayt*) or his Companions, as well as words of contempt concerning the ceremonies and rituals of Islam (*shaᶜā'ir-i Islām*) into a punishable offence. The amended version of the Penal Code thus renders the offence in question liable to death or life imprisonment:

> Whoever by words, either spoken or written, or by visible representation, or by any imputation, innuendo, or insinuation, directly or indirectly, defiles the sacred name of the Holy Prophet Muhammad (peace be upon him) shall be punished with death, or imprisonment for life, and shall also be liable to fine.[5]

The offence here is obviously treated as a *taᶜzīr* offence which may be punished, in its most aggravated instances, by death. In other instances, the offence carries life imprisonment and a fine. The Penal Code also provides that anyone who 'wilfully defiles, damages, or desecrates ... the Holy Qur'ān .... or an extract therefrom ... shall be punishable with imprisonment for life' (§. 295-B). Furthermore, the penal code makes liable to a term of imprisonment 'which may extend to three years, or with fine, or with both', anyone who 'directly or indirectly defiles the sacred name of any wife (*ummul mumineen*), or members of the family (*ahle bait*) of the Holy Prophet' (S. 298-A). And finally, anyone who wilfully 'insults or attempts to insult' the religious feelings of any class of the citizens of Pakistan' is liable to imprisonment 'which may extend to two years or with fine, or both' (§ 295-A).

Blasphemy prosecutions are somewhat rare. I have known of only two cases which were reported in 1991: one in Indonesia and the other in Egypt, and both were widely publicised in the media. In the first case, the editor of a weekly periodical, *Monitor*, which used to be the best-selling tabloid in Indonesia, was sentenced to five years imprisonment for blasphemy against Islam. Arswendo Atmowiloto, a Roman Catholic aged 42, was charged in the district court of Jakarta after publishing an opinion poll in October 1990 which rated 'pop singers, politicians, and even himself as more popular than the Prophet Muhammad . . . The poll ranked Prophet Muhammad eleventh in popularity behind the likes of President Suharto and Iraqi President Saddam Hussein.' Under Indonesia's criminal code, blasphemy carries a maximum of five years imprisonment. The defendant was found guilty of 'intentionally and publicly disgracing one of the religions of Indonesia'. While announcing this, the presiding judge Sarwono sentenced the defendant to the maximum term of five years. The judge added that because Arswendo had apologised he was ordered to pay only 2,500 rupiah in costs compared with ten million rupiah of the fine which the prosecutor had demanded. The newspaper was also closed in October 1990 'after the Muslims demostrated violently across the country following the poll'. The presiding judge added that the defendant's conduct had upset Muslims 'and could disrupt, directly or indirectly, the nation's unity, stability and resilience'.[6]

In December 1991 a blasphemy prosecution also took place in Egypt, where the judicial authorities convicted a novelist, ʿAlā' Ḥāmid together with his publisher-distributor to eight years of imprisonment each for blasphemy, which consisted of a fictionalised satire about the Prophet of Islam ﷺ. The case was tried in a special security court in Cairo, and the sentences were passed under the anti-subversion law which included the publisher and printer as accomplices. The reports do not give much detail but it seems that this case was in many ways similar to that of the British author, Salman Rushdie, who blasphemed against Islam in his novel *The Satanic Verses*. ʿAlā' Ḥāmid's publication, entitled *Masāfah fī ʿAql*

Rajul ('Distance in a Man's Mind') also consisted of stories based on dream sequences of a disparaging nature to the Prophet Muḥammad ﷺ, resembling the theme and context of Salman Rushdie's novel. The newspaper comments highlighted the point that it was unusual for this case to be tried by the security courts. For in the past, security courts in Egypt have almost exclusively dealt with political offences deemed threatening to the state. Sentences passed by the security courts are appealable only to the Prime Minister of Egypt. Anti-religious publications in Egypt are normally treated under the provisions of the Penal Law no. 29 of 1982 which penalise offenders to a term of 'imprisonment ranging from six months to five years and fine of 500 to 1000 Egyptian pounds' (Art. 928).

In a BBC World Service broadcast of 27 December, 1991, it was announced that no appeal was expected to be allowed in this case.[7] Notwithstanding this, two weeks later, a newspaper report stated that the Egyptian Organisation for Human Rights, which is a private lobbying group, had appealed to the Prime Minister of Egypt on Mr Ḥāmid's behalf.[8] Naguib Mahfouz, the 1988 Nobel laureate, wrote in a news column, just before the Ḥāmid verdict was announced, that he and a number of other Egyptian writers were surprised at the severity of the sentence and the manner in which Ḥāmid was tried and prosecuted. Mahfouz wrote concerning this episode: 'Would it not have been better to rationally analyse and criticise the book and then shelve it, if you will, among all those other books that have, since the Middle Ages, attacked Islam?' Be that as it may, it is quite obvious that blasphemy can and does disrupt public order, and incite large-scale hysteria and violence. It would appear that the Egyptian authorities were particularly apprehensive not to let this episode incite the kind of upheval that the world had just experienced following the publication of *The Satanic Verses*. Despite the fact that among the Third World nations Egypt has taken pride over its lively press and respect for freedom of speech, it seems certain that ʿAlā Ḥāmid and his associates had underestimated the sensitivity of their fellow citizens in Egypt over blasphemous attacks on the Prophet of Islam ﷺ.

I conclude this section with reference to a case of apostasy in the Sudan under Numeiri, in which the accused was tried and executed. It seems that the whole issue became enmeshed in the politics of crisis which made it exceedingly difficult for the courts to remain objective and impartial. This was the case of Maḥmūd Muḥammad Ṭāhā, the 76-year-old leader of the Muslim Republican Brothers, who was executed in 1985 for his heretical views on aspects of Islam which he preached for nearly two decades. In 1976 al-Azhar University offically declared him to be an apostate from Islam, and many other Muslim organisations recorded their disapproval of Ṭāhā's views. The case was so controversial that it became the catalyst for the downfall of Numeiri, whose regime was overthrown within weeks of Ṭāhā's execution. As of the early 1980s, Numeiri had begun an Islamisation programme which was less than convincing, and lacked public support. In an attempt to save his fledgling regime from imminent collapse, Numeiri turned to Islam and started on a course of activities which were seen to be politically motivated and contrived. Because of their criticisms of Numeiri's policy, many Republicans were thrown in jail. Ṭāhā - well-spoken and articulate - persisted in his controversial views on Islam. Included among these was his view that the obligatory prayers (*ṣalāh*), could become a mere mechanical act: that a Muslim can reach a stage in devotion and piety whereby the ritual prayer becomes no more than an unnecessary act of formalistic conformity. Another equally controversial view that Ṭāhā advocated was the denial of the article of the Muslim faith concerning the finality of the prophethood of Muḥammad ﷺ. Ṭāhā maintained that Muḥammad ﷺ was a true prophet but that he was not the last of the prophets. With regard to the pilgrimage to the Kaʿbah (*Ḥajj*), Ṭāhā held the view that a believer need not go to Mecca to pay homage to his Creator. He can perform a similar act of devotion anywhere at any time. Numeiri arrested him and many of his followers who were tried in January 1985, apparently for offences other than apostasy. Ṭāhā boycotted his trial for offences against the Sudan Penal Code of 1983 and the State Security Act of 1973, as being illegal. On review, the trial court's judgement, which did not deal with apostasy, was replaced by the higher court ruling which convicted Ṭāhā of apostasy, and sentenced him to death. In ruling Ṭāhā an apostate, the appellate court also relied on an *ex parte* civil proceeding that was brought in 1968 by private plaintiffs offended by Ṭāhā's opinions on Islam. That case had resulted in a ruling that he was an apostate. The appeal court also relied on declarations by al-Azhar and the Muslim World League. Numeiri approved the sentence and Ṭāhā was publicly hanged on January 18, 1985. One of the unresolved issues of this case was a reference to Articles 47 and 48 of the Constitution on freedom of expression and belief. The court did not address this issue and simply ignored the constitution.[9]

NOTES

1. Ahmad Ibrahim, 'The Position of Islam in the Constitution of Malaysia' in Ahmad Ibrahim et al, *Readings on Islam in Southeast Asia*, p. 215.

2. Idem, 'The Principles of an Islamic Constitution and the Constitution of Malaysia', (1989), *International Islamic University Law Journal* 1 (No. 2) p. 7.

3. Ibid., p. 8.

4. Ibid., p. 7.

5. The Pakistan Penal Code, 1960 (amended up to 15th November 1991), §. 195-B.

6. *New Straits Times*, Kuala Lumpur, April 9, 1991, p. 21.

7. BBC Radio Broadcast heard by the present writer.

8. *New Straits Times*, January 6, 1992, p. 8. See also the report and interviews on this case in *al-Bilād* (Beirut) No. 78, 25 April 1992, p. 50.

9. I am grateful to my Sudanese colleague at the International Islamic University, Malaysia, Professor Muhammad 'Ata al-Sid, for his information and comments on Maḥmud Ṭāhā's case during a conversation with me on 6th Feb. 1992. For further information on Numeiri's Islamisation episode, see S. Safwat, 'Islamic Laws in the Sudan', in al-Azmeh, ed., *Islamic Law*, p. 242 ff. Also for details on Ṭāhā's case see Mayer, *Islam and Human Rights*, p. 182 ff.

APPENDIX V: THE SALMAN RUSHDIE AFFAIR

Ever since Salman Rushdie's novel *The Satanic Verses* was published on 26 September, 1988, in the United Kingdom by Viking Penguin, it has not ceased to arouse controversy, and has evoked denunciation and protest among Muslims throughout the world. Muslim communities in Britain and elsewhere demanded a ban on the sale and publication of this book which was seen as deliberate and aggressive blasphemy against Islam. Protests against *The Satanic Verses* escalated with remarkable speed and resulted in the death of five people in Pakistan, and one in Kashmir in February 1989. The following month, two men, the imām of Belgium's Islamic community and his assistant, were shot dead, and in June 1991 the Japanese translator of Rushdie's novel was also killed in Tokyo. The aftermath of Rushdie's inflammatory publication has been widely debated and publicised, which is why I propose to be brief on the factual coverage of events concerning this case.[1]

Some of the responses that I will review here are the opinions (*fatāwā*) of the late Ayatollah Khomeini of Iran, those of the *ʿulamā'* of al-Azhar University of Egypt, and the Islamic Law Academy of the Muslim World League. I will also discuss the views of three individual writers, namely, Shabbir Akhtar, Rafʿat Aḥmad, and ʿAlā'uddīn Kharūfah who have each published a book on the subject and formulated responses which merit attention.

The Satanic Verses reviles and defames the Prophet of Islam ﷺ, the wives of the Prophet ﷺ and his leading Companions. The book also contains contemptuous passages concerning the Holy Qur'ān and some of the cardinal values and principles of the Islamic faith.

Initially, I had directly quoted some of the blasphemous contents of Rushdie's novel concerning the Prophet ﷺ himself, his wives and Companions, but decided, upon revision, to report only indirectly those outrageous expressions. His contemptuous remarks about God and the Qur'ān on pp. 363-64 are not only blasphemous but also flippant. To describe the Qur'ān, for example, as 'a hotch-potch of trivial rules' (p. 363), smacks of ignorance about the Qur'ān and the profound contribution it has made to civilisation. Rushdie's inflammatory aspersions on the Prophet ﷺ on page 366, and the gratuitously indecent language he uses in reference to the wives of the Prophet ﷺ, the 'mothers of the believers' (*ummahāt al-mu'minīn*) on pages 381-82 are simply too outrageous, and far below the standards of civilised discourse. The Prophet Abraham عليه السلام and the Companions of the Prophet ﷺ are reviled in the most ugly and despicable terms (pp. 101, 117, 374). 'It therefore mattered little', as the Muslim community in Britain said in a statement of protest to Penguin Books Ltd, 'what praises or prizes are lavished on such a work.'[2] The mere incidence of phrases such as these leaves little doubt as to the extent of the author's insensitivity - an insensitivity which has caused offence and outrage beyond measure to countless millions of Muslims within and outside Britain.

Rushdie has often claimed that *The Satanic Verses* was a fictional account, and that the question of truth or falsity cannot therefore properly arise. This assertion seems to have made little impact on critics like M.H. Faruqi, editor of *Impact International*, who stated: 'It doesn't matter if it's a fiction, a serious book, or a dream—the point is that the language should be decent.'[3] Shabbir Akhtar's remark, that *The Satanic Verses* 'remains too close to actual Islamic history for Rushdie's claim to be convincing', finds support in Rushdie's own statement, given in an interview in January 1989, where he said: 'Almost everything in those sections - the dream sequences - starts from an historical or quasi-historical basis ...'.[4]

Another commentator, Galeyn Remington, has stated that Rushdie 'manipulated his material in just the way that hurts; he played on Moslem sensibilities in a very knowing way'. John Esposito is also categorical in his assessment that he knew of no Western scholar of Islam 'who would not have predicted that [Rushdie's] kind of statements would be explosive'.[5] Even before the out-break of riots and protest rallies that led to actual loss of life, *Impact International* wrote the following report, soon after the publication of *The Satanic Verses*:

> The Muslim community in Britain - and so would be others as information reaches them in course of time - is shocked and outraged beyond any describable measure by the unprecedented enormity of this sacrilege and by the fact that a so far respectable publisher, Penguin, has been

insensitive enough to lend its name to this extreme profanity.[6]

It is also interesting to note that the official Vatican newspaper denounced *The Satanic Verses* as blasphemous. Furthermore, the Chief Rabbi of England expressed disapproval of Rushdie's novel, and Israel's prominent Rabbi, Avraham Shapira, attempted to prevent publication of the book in Israel, as he judged it to be offensive to the religious sensibilities of Muslims.[7]

On 14 February 1989, Iran's Ayatollah Khomeini issued a *fatwā* in which 'the author of the book entitled *The Satanic Verses*, which abuses Islam, the Prophet, and the Koran, and all those involved in its publication who were aware of its content, are sentenced to death'. To this the Ayatollah further added: 'I ask the Muslims of the world at large to swiftly execute the writer and the publishers, wherever they find them, so that no one in the future will dare to abuse Islam. Whoever is killed on this path will be regarded as a martyr, God willing.'[8]

Following the broadcast of Ayatollah Khomeini's appeal over Tehran Radio, the relatively moderate president of Iran, ʿAli Khamene'i said, however, that 'the wretched man might still be pardoned if he repented and said, "I made a blunder", and apologised to Muslims and the Imam'.[9] On 18 February, Rushdie issued the following carefully worded statement in which he expressed regret but no repentance over the course the events had taken:

> As the author of *The Satanic Verses* I recognise that Moslems in many parts of the world are genuinely distressed by the publication of my novel. I profoundly regret the distress that publication has occasioned to the sincere followers of Islam. Living as we do in a world of many faiths this experience has served to remind us that we must all be conscious of the sensibilities of others.[10]

Ayatollah Khomeini issued another statement on 19 February which declared in no uncertain terms:

> Even if Salman Rushdie repents and becomes the most pious man of all time, it is incumbent on every Muslim to employ everything he has got, his life and his wealth, to send him to hell.[11]

The Ayatollah's *fatwā* evoked mixed responses from the *ʿulamā'* and Muslim leaders who expressed reservations over the wisdom of his verdict addressing the Muslims at large to kill Rushdie without any reference to due judicial process. This was, perhaps, the only procedural flaw in the Ayatollah's verdict which became the focus of media attention. But those who were exposed to media coverage of the whole episode would know that no serious Muslim commentator has challenged the basic validity of the Ayatollah's *fatwā*. Adjudication was generally viewed to be necessary if only to find out whether Rushdie was willing to repent. This was the view of the Chairman of the *Fatwā* Committee of the Azhar University, Shaykh Dr. ʿAbd. Allāh al-Mashhad who said, in a statement concerning the death sentence issued by Ayatollah Khomeini, that 'Islam requires the claimant to present evidence, and the defendant to defend himself either by counter evidence or by taking a solemn oath. Issuing a judgement in the manner it was [issued in], denied such an opportunity ...'.[12]

The Rector of the Azhar University of Egypt, Shaykh Jād al-Ḥaqq, also advised quiet deliberation and adjudication, as opposed to mass demonstrations and sensational responses, which have, as he observed, only stimulated demand for the book and its distribution. The verdict, Jād al-Ḥaqq added, shot up the sales of this book beyond even the author's own wildest dreams.[13]

The Mufti of Egypt, Dr. Ṭanṭāwī, the country's senior Muslim authority, also officially confirmed the need for a full and fair trial: The court must ask the writer to explain his intentions so that its judgement is not influenced by misreading and misunderstanding. The accused, even if proven guilty, can seek clemency and forgiveness.[14]

At its eleventh session held in Mecca, from 10 to 26 February 1989, the Islamic Law Academy of the Muslim World League (*Rābiṭat al-ʿĀlam al-Islāmī*) issued a statement on Salman Rushdie. The session, chaired by one of Saudi Arabia's most prominent *ʿulamā'*, Shaykh ʿAbd al-ʿAzīz Ibn Bāz, issued a six-point statement which declared Rushdie an apostate, and recommended that he and his publishers should be prosecuted under criminal charges in a British court, and that the Organisation of Islamic Conference should take up the case against them. The Academy similarly recommended that Rushdie should be tried in absentia in an Islamic country under the rules of the *Sharīʿah*, and that the decision, even if not enforceable, should serve the purpose of expressing the anger and denunciation of the Muslims over this affront. Furthermore, the Academy dismissed the expression of regret by Rushdie (made earlier on 18 February 1989) for the hurt he had caused to the

Muslims as 'idle and meaningless' for it failed to renounce the contents of the offensive publication. And lastly, the Academy called upon Muslim countries and governments to ban the importation and sale of *The Satanic Verses* in their respective territories.[15]

The Organisation of Islamic Conference, in its twelfth session of Foreign Ministers held in Riyad, from 13 to 16 March 1989, issued a statement which actually denounced Rushdie's book as a flagrant violation of the right to freedom of expression. Referring to the Universal Declaration of Human Rights and its limitations on the freedom of speech, the statement stressed that 'this right is not to be exercised at the expense of the rights of others, nor should Islam be made the target of sacrilege in the name of freedom of expression'. The member states recorded their 'strong denunciation of *The Satanic Verses* whose author is considered an apostate'. The statement adds that the book ignores the principles of morality, civilised conduct and respect for the sensibilities of over one billion Muslims. The statement then calls upon all member states to take immediate steps to ban the book and cause it to be withdrawn from circulation in their countries.[16]

As for the literary and artistic value of Rushdie's novel, Shabbir Akhtar has reached the conclusion that 'there is nothing in *The Satanic Verses* which helps to bring Islam into fruitful confrontation with modernity, and nothing to bring it into thoughtful contact with contemporary secularity and ideological pluralism'. Akhtar goes on to characterise the book as 'a calculated attempt to vilify and slander Muhammad' ﷺ.[17]

This is substantially confirmed by another commentator who says that there is a difference between the kind of writing that provokes healthy anger in people such that it ultimately opens their eyes to new thoughts, and hurtful prose that serves only to offend and blind them. Rushdie's book falls into the second category: 'The ignorance, ridicule, humiliation and resentment that parts of this book have nourished will neither illumine the human condition nor open the minds and hearts of people on different sides of the great divide between tradition and modernity.'[18]

Is it right for a man of letters to overturn basic social values in the name of art? This is the question Khalid Sayeed has raised: 'If I were to tell you that I had a dream in which Hitler appeared and said he had been maligned, that he didn't kill the Jews, and then I wrote about this in lyrical prose, are you going to say to me that this is a work of art and should be judged by different standards!'[19]

In his book, *Ḥukm al-Islām fī Jarā'im Salman Rushdie* (*Islam's verdict on the crimes of Salman Rushdie*), ʿAlā'uddīn Kharūfah, one of the *ʿulamā'* at Muḥammad Ibn Saud University of Medina (currently of the International Islamic University, Malaysia), has summarised the views and doctrines of the leading schools of Islamic law and has attempted to ascertain Rushdie's position as follows:

> The offences that Rushdie has committed amount to apostasy *(riddah)* under the rulings of all of the *madhāhib* that we have quoted. Rushdie is undoubtedly an apostate; I endorse this and consider him an offender who has renounced Islam and became an apostate. The jurists have, however, differed in regard to whether or not it is obligatory to ask the apostate to repent, and then they have differed as to the admissibility, or otherwise, of his repentance.[20]

Kharūfah explains that the preferred view of the Ḥanafī school is that repentance should be solicited over three consecutive days following conviction by a competent court, and that the death penalty is not enforceable prior to soliciting repentance. It is further stated that 'repentance by an apostate like this (i.e. Rushdie) would be admissible to Imām Abū Ḥanīfah.'

The Shāfiʿīs have held that repentance is admissible even in cases of repeated apostasy. They would require 'someone like Salman Rushdie to recite the two testimonials of the faith (*al-shahādatayn*) and declare his penitence and remorse for vilifying Islam'.[21]

The preferred ruling of the Ḥanbalī school concerning Salman Rushdie would be, Kharūfah adds, to admit his repentance on condition that he declares this clearly, recites the two testimonials, and clearly expresses his aversion to what he has done. In the meantime, it is required to discipline the apostate with a stern deterrent punishment. However, according to the Ḥanbalī scholar Ibn Taymiyyah, the likes of Salman Rushdie would be considered infidels whose repentance is neither necessary nor acceptable, with no respite being given prior to their execution.

Having stated this, Kharūfah adds that any of these rulings may be implemented, however, 'on condition that it be for the benefit of Islam (*li-maṣlaḥat al-Islām*) ... and in the meantime presents a good image of Islam (*diʿāyah ṭayyibah li'l-Islām*)'. Bearing in mind that Islam is a religion of tolerance, magnanimity and breadth, contemporary Muslims need to prove the reality of these, especially in the context of relations between Muslims and non-Muslims at the present time.

Consequently, according to the majority opinion of the Ḥanafis, Shāfiʿīs and Ḥanbalīs, Rushdie's repentance is acceptable only on condition: that it is unequivocal and expresses regret over his conduct; that he will not attempt to publish his book again; and finally, that he withdraws the existing copies from the market. When he does all of these things, it then becomes obligatory to accept his statement on face value as Islam does not permit contrived soul searching.

But, Kharūfah adds, if Rushdie refuses to apologise with these conditions, then he will remain in fear for the rest of his life, and it shall remain obligatory on Muslims 'to reach him so long as he is still alive (*an yulāḥiquh madā ḥayātih*) and never to neglect this duty'.[22]

On 28 December 1990, *The Times* of London published an article by Salman Rushdie entitled, 'Why I Have Embraced Islam'. In this article, Rushdie stated 'Although I come from a Muslim family background, I was never brought up as a believer, and was raised in an atmosphere ... broadly known as secular.' He then added that he had a meeting with six Muslim scholars on Christmas Eve and that the meeting was a victory for compassion, understanding, and tolerance. Rushdie went on to say, 'This is not a disavowal of my works, but the simple truth, and to my pleasure it was accepted as such.'

Then he added 'in spite of everything, *The Satanic Verses* is a novel that many of its readers have found to be of value. I cannot betray them. I believe the book must continue to be available so that it can gradually be seen for what it is.'

On 7 January 1991, the American magazine, *Newsweek*, wrote that in February 1989 Salman Rushdie had declared 'I am not a Muslim.' Then 'last week at a Christmas Eve meeting with Islamic leaders in England, Rushdie publicly asserted "There is no god but Allāh, and Muḥammad is His last prophet"' ﷺ.

As can be seen, Rushdie's statements fall short of a categorical renunciation of the blasphemous content of his novel. The persistent ambivalence in Rushdie's statements and the contrast between his words and his conduct, is bound to be reflected in any attempt at evaluating the case. Professing the testimonial of the faith is an interesting development but it could only produce the anticipated consequence when Rushdie explicitly repents, stops defending and justifying his blasphemous publication and indicates his intentions to that effect. What weight a merely verbal proclamation can carry in absolving Rushdie of the charge of blasphemy against the backdrop of his persistent defence of the book, whether for financial gain or a moral claim to righteousness, needs to be determined (if only on grounds of procedural propriety) by a competent judicial tribunal. The court that adjudicates this case must exercise full judicial authority and be able to issue a binding decision. It is one thing for Rushdie to make statements in the knowledge that he does not have to comply with a binding order, and quite another when he knows that he would have to face the consequences of his conduct.

NOTES

1. Further details of events, press reviews, scholarly opinions and conference resolutions concerning Rushdie can be found in Lisa Appignanesi and Sara Maitland, *The Rushdie File*; Rafʿat S. Aḥmad's *Āyāt Shayṭāniyyah: Naqd Kitāb Salman Rushdie*, pp. 82 ff; Kharūfah's *Ḥukm al-Islām fī Jarā'im Salman Rushdie*, pp. 13ff, and Shabbir Akhtar, *Be Careful with Muhammad: The Salman Rushdie Affair*. The last three were all published in 1989. For full details of publication see the bibliography below.
2. Quoted in Appignanesi, *The Rushdie File*, p. 65.
3. Quoted in Ibid., p. 27.
4. Akhtar, *Be Careful with Muhammad*, p. 129; Appignanesi, *The Rushdie File*, p. 22.
5. Both quoted in Appignanesi, *The Rushdie File*, p. 250.
6. M. H. Faruqi 'Sacrilege, Literary but Filthy: The Satanic Verses', *Impact International*, 28 October–10 November 1988.
7. Appignanesi, *The Rushdie File*, pp. 235-6.
8. Front page article 'Battle of the Book', *Newsweek*, February 27, 1989; Aḥmad, *Āyāt Shayṭāniyyah*, p. 84.
9. Ibid.
10. Quoted in Appignanesi, *The Rushdie File*, pp. 97-8.
11. Ibid., p. 99.
12. Quoted in Aḥmad, *Āyāt Shayṭāniyyah*, p. 91.
13. Ibid., pp. 112, and 119.
14. Quoted in Appignanesi, *The Rushdie File*, p. 139.
15. The text of the statement appears in Kharūfah, *Ḥukm al-Islām*, pp. 111-13. For a shorter version see Aḥmad, *Āyāt Shayṭāniyyah*, p. 112.
16. Quoted in Kharūfah, *Ḥukm al-Islām*, pp. 114-15.
17. Akhtar, *Be Careful with Muhammad*, p. 6.
18. Quoted in Appignanesi and Maitland, *The Rushdie File*, p. 140.
19. *Globe and Mail*, Toronto, 18 February 1989.
20. Kharūfah, *Ḥukm al-Islām*, p. 105.
21. Ibid, p. 107.
22. Ibid., pp 106-109.

Bibliography

ʿAbd Allāh, ʿAbd al-Ghanī Basyūnī, *Naẓariyyat al-Dawlah fi'l-Islām*, Beirut: al-Dār al-Jāmiʿiyyah, 1986.

ʿAbd al-Bāqī, Muḥammad Fu'ād, *al-Muʿjam al-Mufahras li-Alfāẓ al-Qur'ān al-Karīm*, 2dn edn., Cairo: Dār al-Fikr li'l-Ṭibāʿah wa'l-Nashr, 1401/1981.

ʿAbd al-Ḥalīm, Rajab Muḥammad, *al-Riddah fī Ḍaw' Mafhūm Jadīd*, Cairo: Dār al-Nahḍah al-ʿArabiyyah, 1985.

ʿAbd al-Raḥmān, ʿĀ'ishah, *al-Qur'ān wa-Qaḍāyā'l-Insān*, Beirut: Dār al-ʿIlm li'l-Malāyīn, 1982.

ʿAbduh, Muḥammad, *Risālat al-Tawḥīd*, 6th edn., Cairo: Dār al-Manār, 1973.

Abū Dāwūd, *Sunan Abū Dāwūd*, Eng. trans. Ahmad Hasan, 3 vols., Lahore: Ashraf Press, 1984.

Abū Ḥabīb, Saʿdī, *Dirāsah fī Minhāj al-Islām al-Siyāsī*, Beirut: Mu'assasat al-Risālah, 1406/1985.

Abū Sinnah, Aḥmad Fahmī, 'Naẓariyyat al-Ḥaqq', in Muḥammad Tawfīq ʿUwaydah (ed.), *al-Fiqh al-Islāmī*, Cairo: Maṭābiʿ al-Ahrām al-Tijāriyyah, 1391/1971, pp. 175-235.

Abū Sulaymān, ʿAbd al-Wahhāb, 'al-Naẓariyyāt wa'l-Qawāʿid fi'l-Fiqh al-Islāmī', *Majallat Jāmiʿat al-Malik ʿAbd al-ʿAzīz*, no. 2, Jamāda al-Thānī 1398/May 1978.

Abu Sulayman, Abdul-Hamid: *The Islamic Theory of International Relations: New Directions for Islamic Methodology and Thought*, Herndon, Va: International Institute of Islamic Thought, 1987.

Abū Yūsuf, Yaʿqūb Ibrāhīm, *Kitāb al-Kharāj*, 2nd edn., Cairo: al-Maṭbaʿah al-Salafiyyah, 1352/1933.

Abū Zahrah, Muḥammad, *al-Jarīmah wa'l-ʿUqūbah fi'l-Fiqh al-Islāmī*, Cairo: Dār al-Fikr al-ʿArabī, n.d.

__*Tanẓīm al-Islām li'l-Mujtamaʿ*, Cairo: Maṭbaʿat Mukhaymar, n.d.

__*Uṣūl al-Fiqh*, Cairo: Dār al-Fikr al-ʿArabī, 1377/1958.

__*Abū Ḥanīfah: Ḥayātuhu wa-ʿAṣruhu, Ārā'uhu wa-Fiqhuhu*, Cairo: Dār al-Fikr al-ʿArabī, 1385/1947.

__*Tārīkh al-Madhāhib al-Islāmiyyah*, Cairo: Dār al-Fikr al-ʿArabī, 1977.

Administration of Islamic Law Enactment of Selangor, 1989.

Administration of Islamic Religious Affairs Enactment of Terengganu, 1986.

Administration of Muslim Law Enactment of Perak, 1965.

Administration of Muslim Law Enactment of Selangor, Malaysia, 1952 (and its amendments of 1983 and 1991 respectively).

ʿAfīfī, Muḥammad al-Ṣādiq, *al-Mujtamaʿ al-Islāmī wa-Uṣūl al-Ḥukm*, Cairo: Dār al-Iʿtiṣām, 1400/1980.

Aḥmad, Rafʿat Sayyid, *Āyāt Shayṭāniyyah: Naqd Kitāb Salman Rushdie*, Cairo: al-Dār al-Sharqiyyah, 1409/1989.

Akhtar, Shabbir, *Be Careful with Muhammad: The Salman Rushdie Affair*, London: Bellew Publishing, 1989.

Ali, Abdullah Yusuf, *The Holy Qur'ān: Text, Translation and Commentary*, Jeddah: Islamic Education Centre, n.d.

Ali, Maulana Muhammad, *A Manual of Hadith*, London: Curzon Press, 1977.

Al-Alusī, Maḥmūd b. ʿAbd Allāh, *Rūḥ al-Maʿānī fī Tafsīr al-Qur'ān al-ʿAẓīm*, Deoband (India): Idārat al-Ṭibāʿah al-Muṣṭafā'iyyah, 1970.

Al-Āmidī, Sayf al-Dīn, *al-Iḥkām fī Uṣūl al-Aḥkām*, ed. ʿAbd al-Razzāq ʿAfīfī, Beirut: al-Maktab al-Islāmī, 1402/1982.

Amīn, Aḥmad, *Fajr al-Islām*, 14th edn., Cairo: Maktabat al-Nahḍah al-Miṣriyya, 1986.

Al-Anṣārī, ʿAbd al-Ḥamīd Ismāʿīl, *al-Shūrā wa-Āthāruhā fi'l-Dimuqrāṭiyyah*, 2nd edn., Beirut: al-Maktabah al-ʿAṣriyyah, 1400/1980.

Appignanesi and Maitland, *The Rushdie File*, New York: Seracuse University Press, 1990.

Al-ʿArabī, ʿAbd Allāh, *Niẓām al-Ḥukm fi'l-Islām*, Cairo: Dār al-Fikr, n.d.

Arnold, Thomas Walker, *The Preaching of Islam*, Lahore: Shah Muhammad Ashraf Press, 1961.

Asad, Muhammad, *Principles of State and Government in Islam*, Berkeley: University of California Press, 1966.

Al-ʿAsqalānī, Aḥmad ibn ʿAlī ibn Ḥajar, *Fatḥ al-Bārī Sharḥ Ṣaḥīḥ al-Bukhārī*, ed. Fu'ād ʿAbd al-Bāqi and Muḥayyuddīn al-Khaṭīb. Beirut: Dar al-Maʿrifah, n.d.

El-Awa, Mohamed Selim, *On the Political System of the Islamic State*, Indianapolis, Indiana: American Trust Publication, 1980.

__*Fi'l-Niẓām al-Siyāsī li'l-Dawlah al-Islāmiyyah*, Cairo: al-Maktab al-Miṣrī al-Ḥadīth, reprint 1983.

__'Pluralism in Islam', *The American Journal of Islamic Social Sciences*, 8, (1991).

__*Punishment in Islamic Law*, Indianapolis: American Trust Publications, 1982.

ʿAwdah, ʿAbd al-Qādir, *al-Tashrīʿ al-Jinā'ī al-Islāmī Muqāranan bi'l-Qānūn al-Waḍʿī*, Cairo: Maktabat Wahbah, 1401/1981.

Azzam, Salem, ed., *Universal Islamic Declaration of Human Rights*, London: Islamic Council of Europe, 1981.

Al-Badawī, Ismāʿīl, *Daʿā'im al Ḥukm fi'l-Sharīʿah al-Islāmiyyah wa'l-Nuzūm al-Dusturiyyah al-Muʿaṣarah*, Cairo: Dār al-Fikr al-ʿArabī, 1400/1980.

Al-Bahī, Muḥammad, *al-Dīn wa'l-Dawlah min Tawjīhāt al-Qur'ān al-Karīm*, Beirut: Dār al-Fikr, 1391/1971.

__*al-Islām fī Mashākil al-Mujtamaʿāt al-Islāmiyyah*, Cairo: Maktabat Wahbah, 1401/1981.

Al-Bahnasāwī, Sālim, *al-Ḥukm wa Qaḍiyyat Takfīr al-Muslim*, 3rd edn., Kuwait: Dār al-Buḥūth al-ʿIlmiyyah, 1405/1985.

Bahnasī, Aḥmad Fatḥī, *al-Jarā'im fi'l-Fiqh al-Islāmī*: Dirāsah Fiqhiyyah Muqāranah, 5th edn., Beirut: Dār al-Shurūq, 1403/1983.

Bailey, David H., *Public Liberties in the New States*, Chicago: Rand McNally & Co., 1964.

Al-Banʿalī, Aḥmad b. Ḥajar al-Buṭāmī, *Taḥdhīr al-Muslimīn ʿan al-Ibtidāʿ wa'l-Bidaʿ fi'l-Dīn*, Doha, Qatar: Maṭābiʿ ʿAlī b. ʿAlī, 1402/1983.

Barendt, Eric, *Freedom of Speech*, Oxford: Oxford University Press, 1985.

Al-Bayhaqī, Abū Bakr Aḥmad b. al-Ḥusayn, *al-Sunan al-Kubrā*, Beirut: Dār al-Fikr, n.d.

Bridge, J.W., et al., *Fundamental Rights*, London: Sweet & Maxwell, 1973.

Al-Buhūtī, Manṣūr b. Yūnus b. Idrīs, *Kashshāf al-Qinnāʿ ʿan Matn al-Iqnāʿ*, Riyadh: Maktabat al-Naṣr al-Ḥadīthah, 1968.

Al-Bukhārī, ʿUbayd Allāh b. Masʿūd (Ṣadr al-Sharīʿah), *al-Tawḍīḥ fī Ḥall Ghawāmiḍ al-Tanqīḥ*, Cairo: Maṭbaʿat Dār al-Kutub, 1327.

Al-Bukhārī, Muḥammad b. Ismāʿīl, *Jawāhir Ṣaḥīḥ al-Bukhārī*, ed. ʿIzz al-Dīn Sirwān, Beirut: Dār al-Iḥyā', 1407/1987.

Chejne, Anwar G., *Succession to the Rule in Islam*, Lahore: Sh. Muhammad Ashraf, 1960.
Choon, Lee Min, 'Should there be any Restrictions to the Freedom of Expression?', unpublished paper presented to the conference on Freedom of Expression held in commemoration of World Human Rights Day, Kuala Lumpur, December 10, 1989.
Constitution of the Islamic Republic of Pakistan, 1973.
Cranston, Maurice, *What Are Human Rights?*, London & Sydney: The Bodley Head, 1973.
Al-Darīnī, Fatḥī, *al-Ḥaqq wa-Madā Sulṭān al-Dawlah fī Taqyīdihi*, 3rd edn., Beirut: Mu'assasat al-Risālah, 1404/1984.
Dias, R.W., *Jurisprudence*, 4th edn., London: Butterworths, 1976.
Dicey, A.V., *Introduction to the Study of the Law of the Constitution*, 10th edn., London: Macmillan, 1964.
Al-Dusūqī, Shams al-Dīn Muḥammed ʿArafah, *Ḥāshiyat al-Dusūqī ʿalā'l-Sharʿ al-Kabīr li-Abī'l-Barakāt Sīdī Aḥmad al-Dardīr*, Cairo: ʿIsā al-Bābī al-Ḥalabī, n.d.
Enayat, Hamid, *Modern Islamic Political Thought*, London: Macmillan Press, 1982.
Encyclopedia Americana, International Edition, Danbury, Connecticut: Grolier Incorporation, 1991.
The Encyclopedia of Islam, new edn., Leiden: E.J. Brill, 1965.
The Encyclopedia of Religion, New York: Macmillan Publishing Co., 1987.
The Encyclopedia of Religion and Ethics, ed. James Hastings. New York: T&T Clark, 1908.
Fārūqī, Shad S., 'Law Relating to Press Freedom in Malaysia', unpublished paper presented to the Conference on Freedom of Expression held in commemoration of World Human Rights Day, Kuala Lumpur, December 1989.
Federal Constitution of Malaysia, 1957 (as at 25th June 1990), Kuala Lumpur: International Law Book Services, 1990.
Fikrī, ʿAlī, *al-Muʿāmalāt al-Māddiyyah wa'l-Adabiyyah*, Cairo: Muṣṭafā al-Bābī al-Ḥalabī, 1366/1947.
Gardet, Louis, 'God in Islam', *The Encyclopedia of Religion*, New York: Macmillan Publishing Co., 1987.
Al-Ghazālī, Abū Ḥāmid Muḥammad, *al-Munqidh min al-Ḍalāl*, Eng. trans. R.J. MacCarthy, Boston: Twayne Publishers, 1980.
__*Iḥyā' ʿUlūm al-Dīn*, 2nd edn., Cairo: Dār al-Fikr, 1400/1980.
__*Kitāb Ādāb al-Ṣuḥbah wa'l-Muʿāsharah maʿah Aṣnāf al-Khalq*, ed. Muḥammad Saʿūd al-Muʿīnī, Baghdad: Maṭbaʿat al-ʿAnī, 1984.

___*al-Mustaṣfā min ʿIlm al-Uṣūl*, 2 vols., Cairo: al-Maktabah al-Tijāriyyah, 1356/1937.

Ghazawī, Muḥammad Salīm, *al-Ḥurriyyah al-ʿĀmmah fi'l-Islām*, Alexandria: Mu'assasat Shabāb al-Jāmiʿah, n.d.

Gibb, H.A.R., 'Constitutional Organization', in M. Khadduri, ed., *Law in the Middle East*, Washington D.C.: The Middle East Institute, 1955.

Goldziher, Ignaz, *Introduction to Islamic Theology and Law*, Princeton: Princeton University Press, 1981.

Ḥammād, Aḥmad Jalāl, *Ḥurriyyat al-Ra'y fi'l-Maydān al-Siyāsī*, Cairo: Dār al-Wafā' li'l-Tibāʿah wa'l-Nashr, 1408/1987.

Ḥammād, Aḥmad Zakī, 'al-Ghazālī's Juristic Treatment of the Sharīʿah Rules in Mustaṣfā', *The American Journal of Islamic Social Sciences*, 4 (1987).

Hasan, Ahmad, *The Doctrine of Ijmāʿ in Islam*, Islamabad: Islamic Research Institute, 1984.

Hohfeld, Wesley, *Fundamental Legal Conceptions*, New Haven, 1964.

Hughes, Thomas P., *Dictionary of Islam*, reprint Lahore: The Book House, n.d.

Ḥusayn, Muḥammad Khiḍr, *al-Ḥurriyyah fi'l-Islām*, Cairo: Dār al-Iʿtiṣām, 1324/1906.

___*Rasā'il al-Iṣlāḥ*, 2 vols., Cairo: Dār al-Iṣlāḥ li'l-Nashr wa'l-Tawzīʿ, n.d.

— *Naqd Kitāb al-Islām wa Uṣūl al-Ḥukm*, Tunis: Maktabah al-Zaytūniyyah, 1925.

Ibn ʿĀbidīn, Muḥammad Amīn, *Ḥāshiyat al-Radd al-Mukhtār ʿalā'l-Durr al-Mukhtār* (known as *Ḥāshiyat Ibn ʿĀbidīn*), Cairo: Dār al-Fikr, 1399/1979; and 2nd edn, Cairo: Maṭbaʿat al-Bābī al-Ḥalabī, 1386/1966.

Ibn Ḥanbal, Aḥmad, *Fihris Aḥādīth Musnad al-Imām Aḥmad b. Ḥanbal*, compiled by Abū Hājir Zaghlūl, Beirut: Dār al-Kutub, 1405/1985.

Ibn Ḥazm, Muḥammad ʿAlī b. Aḥmad b. Saʿīd al-Ẓāhirī, *al-Fiṣal fi'l-Milal wa'l-Ahwā' wa'l-Niḥal*, Cairo: Maktabat al-Salām al-ʿĀlamiyyah, n.d.

___*al-Muḥallā*, Cairo: Idārat al-Ṭibāʿah al-Munīriyyah, 1351/1932.

Ibn Hishām, ʿAbd al-Mālik, *al-Sīrah al-Nabawiyyah*, Cairo: Muṣṭafā al-Bābī al-Ḥalabī, 1936; also Cairo: Dār al-Taḥrīr, 1348/1929.

Ibn Nujaym, Zayn al-ʿĀbidīn, *al-Baḥr al-Rā'iq Sharḥ Kanz al-Daqā'iq*, Cairo: al-Maktabah al-ʿIlmiyyah, 1311 A.H.

Ibn Qayyim, see al-Jawziyyah below.

Ibn Qudāmah, Muwaffaq al-Dīn Ibn Qudāmah al-Maqdisī, *al-Mughnī*, 3rd edn., Cairo, Dār al-Manār, 1367 A.H.

Ibn Taymiyyah, Taqī al-Dīn, *al-Ṣārim al-Maslūl ʿalā Shātim al-Rasūl*, ed. Muḥammad Muḥyi'l-Dīn ʿAbd al-Ḥamīd, Beirut: Dār al-Kitāb, 1398/1978.

__*Iqtiḍā' al-Ṣirāṭ al-Mustaqīm li-Mukhālafat Aṣḥāb al-Jaḥīm*, annotated by Nāṣir b. ʿAbd al-Karīm al-ʿAql, n.p., 1404/1984.

__*Majmūʿat Fatāwā Shaykh al-Islām Ibn Taymiyyah*, compiled by ʿAbd al-Raḥmān b. Qāsim, Beirut: Mu'assasat al-Risālah, 1398 A.H.

__*Majmūʿat al-Rasā'il wa'l-Masā'il*, 2 vols., Riyadh, n.p., n.d.

__*al-Siyāsah al-Sharʿiyyah fī Iṣlāḥ al-Rāʿī wa'l-Raʿiyyah*, 2nd edn., Cairo: Dār al-Kitāb al-ʿArabī, 1951.

__*Public Duties in Islam: The Institution of Ḥisbah*, trans. Mukhtar Holland, Leicester: Islamic Foundation, 1982.

Ibrahim, Ahmad, 'Freedom of Speech and Expression Under the Federal Constitution: Sedition and Contempt of Court', *Law Info* Published by the Student Society, International Islamic University Malaysia, 1987.

__'Principles of an Islamic Constitution and the Constitution of Malaysia', *International Islamic University Law Journal*, vol. 1, no.2 (1989).

__'The Position of Islam in the Constitution of Malaysia', in Ahmad Ibrahim et al., *Readings on Islam in Southeast Asia*, Singapore: Institute of Southeast Asian Studies, 1986.

Al-ʿĪlī, ʿAbd al-Ḥakīm Ḥasan, *al-Ḥurriyyah al-ʿĀmmah*, Cairo: Dār al-Fikr, 1403/1983.

ʿImārah, Muḥammad, *al-Islām wa-Ḥuqūq al-Insān: Ḍarūrāt lā Ḥuqūq*, Cairo: Dār al-Shurūq, 1409/1989.

Impact International, London.

International Institute of Islamic Thought (Cairo), Conference Report on Pluralism in Islam, *American Journal of Islamic Social Sciences*, 8 (1991), p. 353.

Islāmiyyat al-Maʿrifah, al-Maʿhad al-ʿĀlamī li'l-Fikr al-Islāmī, Herndon, VA., 1981.

Ismāʿīl, Yaḥyā, *Manhaj al-Sunnah fi'l-ʿIlāqah Bayn al-Ḥākim wa'l-Maḥkūm*, Cairo: Dār al-Wafā', 1406/1986.

Al-Jawziyyah, Ibn Qayyim, *Iʿlām al-Muwaqqiʿīn ʿan Rabb al-ʿĀlamīn*, ed. Muḥammad Munīr al-Dimashqī, Cairo: Idārat al-Ṭibāʿah al-Munīriyyah, n.d.

__*al-Ṭuruq al-Ḥukmiyyah fi'l-Siyāsah al-Sharʿiyyah*, ed. Muḥammad

Jamīl Ghāzī, Jeddah: Maṭbaʿat al-Madanī, n.d. Also used: the Cairo edition published by al-Mu'assasah al-ʿArabiyyah li'l-Ṭibāʿah wa'l-Nashr, 1380/1961, and the Beirut edition by Dār al-Maʿrifah.

__*Zād al-Maʿād fī Hudā Khayr al-ʿIbād*, Mecca: al-Maṭbaʿah al-Makkiyyah, n.d.

__*Ighāthat al-Lahfān min Makāyid al-Shayṭān*, ed. Muḥammad Anwar al-Baltājī, Cairo: Dār al-Turāth al-ʿArabī, 1403/1983.

Al-Jazīrī, ʿAbd al-Raḥmān, *Kitāb al-Fiqh ʿalā'l-Madhāhib al-Arbaʿah*, Beirut: Dār al-Fikr li'l-Ṭibāʿah wa'l-Nashr, 1392 A.H.

Jennings, Ivor, *The Law and the Constitution*, 5th edn., London: University of London Press, 1959.

Joynboll. Th.W., 'Blasphemy', *Encyclopedia of Religion and Ethics*, II, p. 672.

Al-Jundī, Muḥammad, *Maʿālim al-Niẓām al-Siyāsī fi'l-Islām*, Cairo: Dār al-Fikr, 1406/1986.

Kamali, Mohammad Hashim, *Principles of Islamic Jurisprudence*, revised edition, Cambridge: The Islamic Texts Society, 1991.

__ 'Have We Neglected the Sharīʿah Law Doctrine of Maṣlaḥah?', *Islamic Studies*, 27 (1988), pp. 287-304.

__ '*Siyāsah Sharʿiyyah* or the Policies of Islamic Government', *American Journal of Islamic Social Sciences*, vol. 6 (1989), pp.39-81.

__ *Law in Afghanistan: A Study of the Constitutions, Matrimonial Law and the Judiciary*, Leiden: E.J. Brill, 1989.

__ 'The Limits of Power in an Islamic State', *Islamic Studies*, 28 (1989), pp. 323-353.

__ 'The Approved and Disapproved Varieties of Ra'y (Personal Opinion) in Islam', *American Journal of Islamic Social Sciences*, vol. 7 (1990), pp. 39-64.

__ 'Freedom of Expression in Islam: An Analysis of *Fitnah*', *American Journal of Islamic Social Sciences*, vol. 10 (1993), pp. 178-201.

__ 'An Analysis of Rights in Islamic Law', *American Journal of Islamic Social Sciences*, vol. 10 (1993), pp. 340-367.

Al-Kāsānī, *Badāʾiʿ al-Ṣanāʾiʿ*, Cairo: Maṭbaʿat al-Istiqāmah, 1956.

Khadduri, Majid, *The Islamic Law of Nations: al-Shaybani's Siyar*, Baltimore: The John Hopkins Press, 1966.

Al-Khafīf, Shaykh ʿAlī, *al-Ḥaqq wa'l-Dhimmah*, Cairo: Maktabat Wahbah, 1945.

Al-Khālidī, Maḥmūd ʿAbd al-Majīd, *Qawāʿid Niẓām al-Ḥukm fi'l-Islām*, Kuwait: Dār al-Buhūth al-ʿIlmiyyah, 1980.

__*Al-Shūrā*, Beirut: Dār al-Jil, 1404/1984.

Khalīl, ʿImād al-Dīn, *Fi'l-Naqd al-Islāmī al-Muʿāṣir*, 3rd edn., Beirut: Mu'assasat al-Risālah, 1404/1984.
Khallāf, ʿAbd al-Wahhāb, *al-Siyāsah al-Sharʿiyyah*, Cairo: al-Maṭbaʿah al-Salafiyyah, 1350/1971.
Khan, Muhammad Muhsin, *The Translation of the Meanings of Sahih al-Bukhari*, Lahore: Kazi Publications, 1979.
Khan, Muhammad Zafrulla, *Human Rights in Islam*, London: Higginson, 1967.
Kharūfah, ʿAlā'uddīn, *Ḥukm al-Islām fī Jarā'im Salman Rushdie*, Jeddah: Dār al-Iṣfahānī li'l-Ṭibāʿah, 1410/1989.
Al-Khudarī, Muḥammad, *Muḥāḍarāt fī Tārīkh al-Umam al-Islāmiyyah*, Cairo: al-Maktabah al-Tijāriyyah, 1370/1969.
Al-Kindī, N., *The Governors and Judges of Egypt*, ed. R. Guest, Leiden: E.J. Brill, 1912.
Lambton, A.K.S., *State and Government in Medieval Islam*, Oxford: Oxford University Press, 1981.
Laylah, Muḥammad Kāmil, *al-Nuẓūm al-Siyāsah*, Cairo, Dār al-Fikr al-ʿArabī, 1963.
Little, Lester K., 'Cursing', *The Encyclopedia of Religion*, New York: Macmillan Publishing Co., 1987.
Luca, C., 'Discrimination in the Arab Middle East', in Willem A. Veenhoven, ed., *Case Studies on Human Rights and Fundamental Freedoms*, vol. 1, The Hague, 1975, pp. 211-40.
MacDonald, D.B., 'Ḥakk', *The Encyclopedia of Islam*, new edition, Leiden: E.J. Brill.
Madkūr, Muḥammad, *al-Qaḍā' fi'l-Islām*, Cairo: Dār al-Nahḍah al-ʿArabiyyah, 1964.
Mahmassānī, Ṣubḥī, *Arkān Ḥuqūq al-Insān fi'l-Islām*, Beirut: Dār al-ʿIlm li'l-Malāyīn, 1979.
Ibn Mājah, Muḥammad b. Yazīd al-Qazwīnī, *Sunan Ibn Mājah*, Istanbul: Cagri Yayinlari, 1401/1981.
Majmaʿ al-Lughah al-ʿArabiyyah, *al-Muʿjam al-Wasīṭ*, 3rd edn. Cairo: Sharikat al-Iʿlānāt al-Sharqiyyah, 1405/1984.
Makdisi, George, 'Magesterium and Academic Freedom in Classical Islam and Medieval Christianity', in. Nicholas Heer, ed., *Islamic Law and Jurisprudence*, Seattle: Washington University Press, 1990.
Malayan Law Journal, Kuala Lumpur, Malaysia.
Al-Maqdisī, Muwaffaq al-Dīn Ibn Qudāmah, *al-Mughnī*, Riyadh: Maktabat al-Riyāḍ al-Ḥadīthah, 1401/1981.
Al-Maqdisī, Shams al-Dīn ʿAbd Allāh b. Maflah al-Ḥanbalī, *al-Ādāb al-Sharʿiyyah wa'l-Minaḥ al-Marʿiyyah*, Cairo: Maṭbaʿat al-Manār, 1348 A.H.

Mawdūdī, S. Abu'l-A'la, *Islamic Law and Constitution*, Lahore: Islamic Publications Ltd., reprint 1979.

__*al-Ḥukūmah al-Islāmiyyah*, trans. Ahmad Idris, n.p., al-Mukhtar al-Islami, 1977.

Al-Māwardī, Abū'l-Ḥasan, *Kitāb al-Aḥkām al-Sulṭāniyyah*, Cairo: Maṭba'at al-Sa'ādah, 1327/1909.

Al-Mawsū'ah al-Fiqhiyyah, Kuwait: Wizārat al-Awqāf wa'l-Shu'ūn al-Islāmiyyah, 1405/1984.

Mayer, Ann Elizabeth, 'Law and Religion in the Muslim Middle East', *The American Journal of Comparative Law*, 35 (1987), pp. 135-84.

—*Islam and Human Rights*, Boulder, Colorado: Westernview Press, 1991.

Al-Miṣrī, 'Adnān Darwīsh, *al-Kulliyyāt: Mu'jam fi'l-Muṣṭalaḥāt wa'l-Furūq al-Lughawiyyah*, Damascus: Wizārat al-Irshād, 1974.

Montgomery-Watt, W, *Islamic Political Thought: the Basic Concepts*, Edinburgh: Edinburgh University Press, 1968.

Al-Mubārakfūrī, Ṣaī al-Raḥmān, *al-Aḥzāb al-Siyāsiyyah fi'l-Islām*, al-Jāmi'ah al-Salafiyyah, India, 1407/1987.

Munayminah, Jamīl, *Mushkilat al-Ḥurriyyah fi'l-Islām*, Beirut: Dār al-Kitāb al-Lubnānī, 1974.

Munir, Muhammad, *Constitution of the Islamic Republic of Pakistan: Being a Commentary of the Constitution of Pakistan 1973*, Lahore: Law Publishing Co., 1975.

Murphy, Jeffrie G., *An Introduction to Jurisprudence*, Totowa, New Jersey: Rownan & Allenheld, 1984.

Mūsā, Muḥammad Yūsuf, *al-Fiqh al-Islāmī*, Cairo: Dār al-Kutub al-Ḥadīthah, 1374/1954.

Muslim, Ibn al-Ḥajjāj al-Nīshāpūrī, *Mukhtaṣar Ṣaḥīḥ Muslim*, ed. Muḥammad Nāṣir al-Dīn al-Albānī, 2nd edn., Beirut: Dār al-Maktab al-Islāmī, 1404/1984.

Muṭahharī, Murtaḍā, 'Islam and the Freedom of Thought and Belief.' Trans. 'Alī Ḥusayn. *Al-Tawḥīd*. Vol. XI, No. 2, pp. 143-63, 1412 A.H.

Mutawallī, 'Abd al-Ḥamīd, *Mabādi' Niẓām al-Ḥukm fi'l-Islām*, Alexandria: Mansha'āt al-Ma'ārif, 1974.

Al-Nabhān, Muḥammad Fārūq, *Niẓām al-Ḥukm fi'l-Islām*, Kuwait: Jāmi'at al-Kuwait, 1974 Also consulted: the Beirut edition of this book published by Mu'assasat al-Risālah, 1408/1988.

Al-Nabhānī, Shaykh Taqī al-Dīn, *Muqaddimat al-Dustūr*, Kuwait, no publisher given, 1964.

Nadwat al-Riyāḍ: Nadwah ʿIlmiyyah Ḥawl al-Sharīʿah al-Islāmiyyah wa Ḥuqūq al-Insān fi'l-Islām, Beirut: Dār al-Kitāb al-Lubnānī, 1973.
Naḥwī, ʿAdnān ʿAlīriḍā, *Malāmiḥ al-Shūrā fi'l-Daʿwah al-Islāmiyyah*, 2nd edn., Riyadh: 1984.
Al-Nawawī, Muḥyī'l-Dīn, *Riyāḍ al-Ṣāliḥīn*, 2nd edn. by Muḥammad Nāṣir al-Dīn al-Albānī, Beirut: Dār al-Maktab al-Islāmī, 1404/1984.
New Straits Times, Kuala Lumpur.
Newsweek, USA.
Nieuenhuijze, C.A.O., *The Lifestyles of Islam*, Leiden: E.J. Brill, 1985.
The Pakistan Penal Code 1860 (amended up to 15th November 1991), Lahore: PLD Publishers, 1991.
Penal Code of Malaysia (Straits Settlement Ordinance No. IV of 1871).
Printing Presses and Publications Act of Malaysia (Act 301), 1984.
Qanūn al-ʿUqbāt al-Miṣrī (The Egyptian Penal Code).
Al-Qarāfī, Shihāb al-Dīn, *Kitāb al-Furūq*, Cairo: Maṭbaʿat Dār Iḥyā' al-Kutub al-ʿArabiyyah, 1346 A.H.
__*al-Iḥkām fī Tamyīz al-Fatāwā ʿan al-Aḥkām wa-Taṣarrufāt al-Qāḍī wa'l-Imām*, ed. ʿAbd al-Fattāḥ Abū Ghaddah, Aleppo: Maktab al-Maṭbūʿāt al-Islāmiyyah, 1387/1967.
Al-Qāsimī, Ẓāfir, *Niẓām al-Ḥukm fi'l-Sharīʿah wa'l-Tārīkh*, 2nd edn., Beirut: Dār al-Nafā'is, 1977.
Al-Qurṭubī, Abū ʿAbd Allāh Muḥammad, *al-Jāmiʿ li-Aḥkām al-Qur'ān* (known as *Tafsīr al-Qurṭubī*), Cairo: Maṭbaʿat Dār al-Kutub, 1387/1967.
Al-Qurṭubī, Abū'l-Walīd Muḥammad b. Rushd, *Bidāyat al-Mujtahid wa-Nihāyat al-Muqtaṣid*, 5th edn., Cairo: Muṣṭafā al-Bābī al-Ḥalabī, 1401/1981.
Rahman, Fazlur, *Islam*, 2nd edn., Chicago and London: University of Chicago Press, 1979.
Rahman, S.A., *The Punishment of Apostasy in Islam*, 2nd edn., Lahore: Institute of Islamic Culture, 1978.
Rahman, Tanzilur, *Essays on Islam*, Lahore: Islamic Publications, 1988.
__*Islāmi Qānūn-e Irtidād*, Lahore: Qānūnī Kutubkhāna, n.d.
Ramadan, Said, *Islamic Law: its Scope and Equity*, 2nd edn., n.p., 1971.
Riḍā, Muḥammad Rashīd, *Tafsīr al-Qur'ān al-Ḥakīm* (also known as *Tafsīr al-Manār*), Beirut: Dār al-Maʿrifah, 1328.

__*Ta'rīkh al-Ustādh al-Imām Muḥammad ʿAbduh*, Cairo: Maṭbaʿat al-Manār, 1324/1904.

Al-Sābiq, Sayyid, *ʿAnāṣur al-Quwwah fi'l-Islām*, Cairo: Maktabat Wahbah, 1382/1983.

Al-Ṣābūnī, ʿAbd al-Raḥmān, *Muḥāḍarāt fi'l-Sharīʿah al-Islāmiyyah*, n.p. 1392/1972.

Safwat, Safiya, 'Islamic Laws in the Sudan', in Aziz al-Azmeh, ed., *Islamic Law: Social and Historical Contexts*, London & New York: Routledge, 1988, pp. 231-49.

Al-Samarā'ī, ʿAbd al-Razzāq Nuʿmān, *Aḥkām al-Murtadd fi'l-Sharīʿah al-Islāmiyyah*, Beirut: Dār al-ʿArabiyyah li'l-Ṭibāʿah wa'l-Nashr, n.d.

Said, Abdul Aziz, 'Precepts and Practice of Human Rights in Islam', *Universal Human Rights*, vol. 1, no. 1 (Jan. 1979),

Al-Sanhūrī, ʿAbd al-Razzāq, *Maṣādir al-Ḥaqq fi'l-Fiqh al-Islāmī*, Cairo: Maʿhad al-Dirāsāt al-ʿArabiyyah al-ʿĀliyah, 1956.

Al-Sarakhsī, Shams al-Dīn Muḥammad, *al-Mabsūṭ*, Cairo: Maṭbaʿat al-Saʿādah, 1324 A.H., also Beirut: Dār al-Maʿrifah, 1406/1986.

Sardar, Ziauddin, *The Future of Muslim Civilisation*, London: Croom Helm, 1979.

Schacht, Joseph, 'Law and Justice', in P.M. Holt (ed.), The *Cambridge History of Islam*, Cambridge: Cambridge University Press, 1971.

Al-Shahristānī, Abu'l-Fatḥ Muḥammad, *al-Milal wa'l-Niḥal*, ed. ʿAbd al-ʿAzīz Muḥammad al-Wakīl, Cairo: Mu'assasat al-Ḥalabī, 1378/1968.

__*Kitāb al-Muṣāraʿat al-Falāsifah*, ed. S M Mukhtar, Cairo: 1976.

Shākir, al-Shaykh Aḥmad, (ed.), *Fahāris Sunan al-Tirmidhī*, Beirut: Dār al-Kutub al-ʿIlmiyyah, 1407/1987.

Shaltūt, Maḥmūd, *Min Tawjīhāt al-Qur'ān al-Karīm*, Kuwait: Maṭābiʿ Dār al-Qalam, n.d.

__*al-Islām ʿAqīdah wa-Sharīʿah*, Kuwait: Maṭābiʿ Dār al-Qalam, n.d.

Al-Sharabāṣī, Aḥmad, *Min al-Ādāb al-Nabawiyyah*, Cairo: Maṭābiʿ al-Ahrām, 1971.

Al-Shaʿrānī, ʿAbd al-Wahhāb, *Kitāb al-Mīzān*, Cairo: al-Maṭbaʿah al-Ḥusayniyyah, 1329 A.H., also Beirut: Dār al-Fikr, 1401/1981.

Al-Sharbīnī, Muḥammad al-Khaṭīb, *Mughnī al-Muḥtāj ilā Maʿrifat Maʿānī Alfāẓ al-Minhāj*, Cairo: Dār al-Fikr, n.d.

Sharīʿah Criminal Code Enactment of Kelantan, Malaysia 1985.

Sharīʿah Criminal Code Enactment of Kedah, Malaysia 1988.

Al-Shāṭibī, Abū Isḥāq Ibrāhīm, *al-Muwāfaqāt fī Uṣūl al-Aḥkām*,

annotated by Muḥammad Khiḍr al-Ḥusayn, Cairo: al-Maṭbaᶜah al-Salafiyyah, 1341.
__*al-Iᶜtiṣām*, Cairo: Maṭbaᶜat al-Manār, 1332/1914, also Beirut: Dār al-Maᶜrifah, 1402/1982.
Al-Shawkānī, Yaḥyā b. ᶜAlī, *Irshād al-Fuhūl min Taḥqīq al-Ḥaqq ilā ᶜIlm al-Uṣūl*, Cairo: Dār al-Fikr, n.d., also Cairo: Dār al-Ḥadīth, 1413/1993.
__*Nayl al-Awṭār: Sharḥ Muntaqā'l-Akhbār*, Cairo: Muṣṭafā al-Bābī al-Ḥalabī, n.d.
Al-Sibāᶜī, Muṣṭafā, *Ishtirākiyyat al-Islām*, 2nd edn., Damascus: Dār al-Qawmiyyah li'l-Ṭibāᶜah wa'l-Nashr, 1379/1960.
Siegman, Henry, 'The State and the Individual in Sunni Islam', *The Muslim World*, 54 (1964), p. 230.
Al-Sirwān, ᶜIzz al-Dīn ᶜAbd al-ᶜAzīz, ed., *Jawāhir Ṣaḥīḥ al-Bukhārī*, Beirut: Dār Iḥyā' al-ᶜUlūm, 1407/1987.
The Star, Malaysia.
Stoljar, Samuel J., *An Analysis of Rights*, Wiltshire: The Macmillan Press, 1984.
Street, Harry, *Freedom of the Individual and the Law*, Bristol: Migibbon & Kee, 1967.
Al-Subkī, Tāj al-Dīn ᶜAbd al-Wahhāb, *al-Ashbāh wa'l-Naẓā'ir*, ed. ᶜĀdil ᶜAbd al-Mawjūd, Beirut: Dār al-Kutub al-ᶜIlmiyyah, 1411/1991.
Al-Suyūṭī, Jalāl al-Dīn, *al-Jāmiᶜ al-Ṣaghīr*, 4th edn., Cairo: Muṣṭafā al-Bābī al-Ḥalabī, 1954.
Al-Ṭabarī, Muḥammad b. Jarīr, *Tafsīr al-Ṭabarī*, 3rd edn., Cairo: Muṣṭafā al-Bābī al-Ḥalabī, 1968.
Al-Tabrīzī, ᶜAbd Allāh al-Khaṭīb, *Mishkāt al-Maṣābīḥ*, ed. Muḥammad Nāṣir al-Dīn al-Albānī, 2nd edn., Beirut: al-Maktab al-Islāmī, 1399/1979.
The Times, London.
Al-Tirmidhī, Abū ᶜĪsā Muḥammad, *Sunan al-Tirmidhī*, Istanbul: Cagri Yayinlari, 1981, also Beirut: Dār al-Fikr, 1400/1980.
Tuffāḥah, Aḥmad Zakī, *Maṣādir al-Tashrīᶜ al-Islāmī wa Qawāᶜid al-Sulūk al-ᶜĀmmah*, Beirut: Dār al-Kitāb al-Lubnānī, 1405/1985.
Tyser, C R, *The Mejelle: Being an English Translation of Majallah el-Ahkam el-Adliya*, Lahore: Law Publishing Co. 1967.
Universal Islamic Declaraion of Human Rights, New York: U.N.G.A, n.d.; and the Islamic Council of Europe.
ᶜUthmān, Fatḥī, *al-Farḍ fi'l-Mujtamaᶜ al-Islāmī*, Cairo: Shirkat Maṭābiᶜ al-Iᶜlānāt al-Sharqiyyah, 1382/1962.

__*Ḥuqūq al-Insān Bayn al-Sharīʿah al-Islāmiyyah wa'l-Fikr al-Qānūnī al-Gharbī*, Beirut: Dār al-Shurūq, 1401/1982.

Wafī, ʿAbd al-Wāḥid, *Ḥuqūq al-Insān fi'l-Islām*, Cairo: Maṭbaʿat al-Risālah, n.d.

Wajdī, Muḥammad Farīd, *Da'irat al-Maʿārif Qarn al-ʿIshrīn*, 3rd edn., Beirut: Dār al-Maʿrifah, 1971.

Waṣfī, Muṣṭafā Kamāl, *al-Niẓām al-Dustūrī fi'l-Islām Muqārinan bi'l-Nuẓum al-ʿAṣriyyah*, Cairo: Maktabat Wahbah, 1974.

Wehr, Hans, *Arabic-English Dictionary*, ed. J.M. Cowan, New York: Spoken Language Services Inc., 1976.

Al-Yaḥsabī, al-Qāḍī Abū'l-Faḍl ʿIyāḍ, *al-Shifā' bi-Taʿrīf Ḥuqūq al-Muṣṭafā*, annotated by Aḥmad al-Shamanī, Cairo: Dār al-Fikr li'l-Ṭibāʿah wa'l-Nashr, n.d.

Al-Zamakhsharī, Jār Allāh Maḥmūd, *al-Kashshāf ʿan Ḥaqā'iq al-Tanzīl*, Beirut: Dār al-Maʿrifah, n.d.

al-Zarqā, Muṣṭafā Aḥmad, *al-Madkhal al-Fiqhī al-ʿĀm*, 3 vols., Damascus: Dār al-Fikr, 1967-68.

Al-Zāwī, al-Ṭāhir Aḥmad, (ed.), *Tartīb al-Qāmūs al-Muḥīṭ*, 3rd edn., Beirut: Dār al-Fikr, n.d.

Zaydān, ʿAbd al-Karīm, *Majmūʿat Buḥūth Fiqhiyyah*, Baghdad: Maktabat al-Quds, 1395/1975.

__*al-Farḍ wa'l-Dawlah fi'l-Sharīʿah al-Islāmiyyah*, al-Ittiḥād al-ʿĀlamī li'l-Munaẓẓamāt al-Ṭullābiyyah, Gary, Indiana, 1390/1970.

__*al-Madkhal li-Dirāsat al-Sharīʿah al-Islāmiyyah*, Baghdad: Mu'assasat al-Risālah, 1405/1985.

Al-Zuhaylī, Wahbah, *al-Fiqh al-Islāmī wa Adillatuhu,* 8 vols., 3rd edn., Damascus: Dār al-Fikr, 1409/1989.

Glossary

ʿAdalah: Uprightness of character.
*Adat (*Malay*):* Custom.
ʿAdhāb: Punishment.
Adhall: Most abased; most humiliated - superlative of *dhalīl* (below).
Adhā or *Adhan*: Annoyance; insult; damage; harm.
Adhān: The call to prayer.
ʿĀdil: An upright, just person.
ʿAdl: Justice.
Āfāt al-lisān: The calamaties of speech.
Āḥād: Solitary *ḥadīth* transmitted through a single chain of individuals.
ʿAhd al-dhimmah: Covenant of protection; covenant with the *dhimmī*.
Aḥkām (sing. *ḥukm):* Principles; regulations; textual ordinances; the pillars of Islam. See also *ḥukm* below.
Ahl al-ʿadl: The just community, i.e. the Sunnis; just people.
Ahl al-baghy: Rebels.
Ahl al-bayt: A member of the Prophet's ﷺ household; in the Qur'ān, specifically his wives.
Ahl al-bidʿah wa'l-shubuhāt: Innovators; sceptics; sophists.
Ahl al-fasād: The morally corrupt.
Ahl al-Ḥadīth: The partisans of Tradition.
Ahl al-hawā: Mischievous or capricious people.
Ahl-al-Kitāb: Lit. 'the people of the Book, i.e. the Jews and Christians.
Ahl al-ra'y: The partisans of personal opinion.
Ahl al-shūrā: People worthy of being consulted, whose opinion should be sought.
Aḥmaq: Foolish person.
ʿAjam: Non-Arab.

Akh (pl. *ikhwān*): Brother.
ʿĀlim: Scholar; learned person.
Amārāt (sing. *amārah*): Indications; signs; characteristics.
ʿAmal: Act; deed.
ʿĀmm: General, as opposed to specific.
Amr: Order; command; ordinance.
Anṣār: The Helpers, the early Muslims of Medīna who took in the Prophet ﷺ and the Meccan Emigrants *(muhājirūn).*
ʿAql: Intelligence; reason.
Asbāb al-nuzūl: The historical context of, or causes for, the revelation of a verse/verses of the Qur'ān.
Asbāb jalliyyah: Self-evident causes.
ʿĀshūrā': The tenth day of Muḥarram, observed as a voluntary fast in commemoration of the martyrdom of Ḥusayn, the grandson of the Prophet ﷺ.
Aṣl al-ṣiḥḥah: Principle of presumption of validity.
Aṣl al-tashrīʿ: a norm of the *Sharīʿah.*
Al-Asmā' al-Ḥusnā: The Most Beautiful Names of God.
Āyah (pl. *āyāt*): A verse of the Qur'ān.
ʿAyb: Defect; shortcoming; shame.
Bahata: To slander.
Baghy: Transgression; rebellion.
Bayʿah: Pledge of allegiance.
Bidʿah: Innovation, usually pernicious innovation as opposed to valid precedent. *Bidʿah* is often used in contradistinction to the Sunnah.
Bidʿah ḍalālah: Misguided innovation.
Bidʿah ḥaqīqiyyah: Actual, total, intrinsic innovation.
Bidʿah ḥasanah: A good innovation.
Bidʿah iḍāfiyyah: Partial, additional, relative innovation.
Bidʿah mustaḥsanah: Beneficial innovation.
Bidʿah qabīḥah: A bad (lit. ugly) innovation.
Bidʿah Sharʿiyyah: An innovation in matters pertaining to the *Sharīʿah.*
Bidʿah tarkiyya: An innovation involving the forsaking or abandonment of something lawful in the *Sharīʿah.*
Bidʿah ghayr tarkiyya: An innovation which does not consist of abandoning any part of the *Sharīʿah* but may involve an alteration to part of the *Sharīʿah*, or may advance a perspective different to that of the established norm.
Birr: Piety; righteousness; pious work.

Bughghāt: Rebels.
Bughghāt muḥāribūn: Treasonous rebels.
Buhtān: False accusation.
Burnus: Burnoose; hooded cloak.
Ḍalāl: Error; misguidance; deviation from the truth.
Ḍarar: Harm; injury; damage.
Ḍarūrah: Necessity.
Ḍarūriyyāt: 'Essential values', often referring to the five values of life, faith, property, intellect and lineage. The term is also used in contradistinction to *ḥājiyyāt* and *taḥsīniyyāt.*
Dawām al-dahr: The permanence of this world.
Dhalīl: An abased or humiliated person.
Dhanb (pl. dhunūb): Sin.
Dhikr: Remembrance; mention; invocation (of a Name of God); Reminder: a reference to the Qur'ān and the guidance therein.
Dhimmī: Free non-Muslim subjects living in Muslim lands, who, in return for capital tax payment, enjoy protection and safety.
Dīn: Religion.
Duʿā': Supplication; prayer; summons; call.
Duʿā' al-khayr: A call to good.
Fahm fāsid: Misconception.
Falāḥ: Success.
Faqīh (pl. fuqahā'): Jurist.
Farḍ ʿayn: Emphatic personal obligation, often referring to religious duties, which are established by the decisive injunctions of the Qur'ān and Sunnah.
Farḍ kafā'ī: Collective obligation of the community as a whole, which is discharged even if some, and not all, members of the community perform it.
Fasād: Invalidity.
Fasād al-qaṣd: Ill intent; corrupt intention.
Fāsiq: Transgressor; a corrupt person; one who violates the moral and religious values of Islam. The term is often used in contradistinction to *ʿādil*, an upright person.
Fatwā: Considered opinion given by a qualified scholar, a muftī (jurisconsult), or a *mujtahid* (one who is competent enough to conduct *ijtihād*) concerning a legal/religious issue; a religious edict.
Fatwā al-Ṣaḥābī: The considered personal opinion of a Companion of the Prophet ﷺ.
Fay': Spoils of war.

Fiqh: Islamic law as developed by Muslim jurists. The term is often used synonymously with *Sharīʿah*; the main difference being that *Sharīʿah* bears a closer link with divine revelation, whereas *fiqh* mainly consists of the works of religious scholars and jurists.
Firyah: Slander; calumny; falsehood; lie. Synonymous with *iftirā'*.
Fisq: Transgression; often used in contradistinction to *kufr*, disbelief.
Fisq al-aʿmāl: Sinful deeds.
Fitnah (pl. *fitan*): Sedition, affliction and tumult. In the Qur'ān it is often used to imply oppression and persecution which denies its victim the freedom of religion.
Fitnat al-shahawāt: Fitnah pertaining to sensuality.
Fitnat al-shubuhāt: Fitnah pertaining to doubts.
Fuqahā': See *faqīh*.
Furūʿ: The detailed branches of jurisprudence.
Fusūq: Iniquity; outrage.
Ghaḍab: Anger.
Ghā'iyyah: Goal-oriented.
Ghaybah: Occultation.
Ghībah: Backbiting; calumny.
Ghusl: A full bath - a ritual requirement after sexual intercourse, at the end of a period of menstruation or after having been in contact with what is considered ritually impure.
Ḥaḍānah: The right of custody.
Ḥadd: Prescribed penalty; see *ḥudūd*.
Ḥadīth (pl. *aḥādīth*): Lit. speech; the reported sayings and teachings of the Prophet Muḥammad ﷺ. It is used interchangeably with Sunnah.
Ḥajj: Pilgrimage to the holy Kaʿbah in Mecca; an obligatory duty which all capable Muslims must perform at least once in their life-time.
Ḥājiyyāt: Complementary benefits which come next in order of priority to *ḍarūriyyāt*.
Hajr: To deny access to someone; a form of social boycott, signified by the refusal to answer the greeting of the person concerned, refusing to speak to them, and refusing to approve of their views.
Al-Ḥakīm: The Lawgiver (God).
Ḥākim: Ruler, governor; deciding (factor etc).
Ḥākim sharʿī: A competent *qāḍī*, knowledgeable about the *Sharīʿah*.
Ḥalāl: Legitimate; allowed by the *Sharīʿah*.
Ḥalāl al-dam: Legally liable to be executed; lit. a person or animal whose blood is lawful.

Ḥaqq: Truth; (pl.) *ḥuqūq:* rights.
Ḥaqq Allāh: The right of God - generally used in reference to public or community rights, as opposed to private rights.
Ḥaqq al-ᶜabd: The right of man.
Al-ḥaqq al-ādamī: Personal or private rights.
Ḥaqq al-muᶜāraḍah: The right of criticism.
Ḥarām: Totally forbidden.
Ḥarbī: An enemy of war.
Ḥaṣr asbāb al-taᶜzīr: Confining the application of *taᶜzīr* to its proper grounds.
Hawā (pl. *ahwā'*)*:* Caprice; whimsical desire; or mischievous whim that takes one away from correct guidance and from the approved principles of Islam.
Hidāyah: Correct guidance.
Ḥilm: Gentleness; forbearance.
Ḥirābah: High treason.
Ḥisbah: Commanding or promoting good and forbidding or preventing evil *(al-amr bi'l-maᶜrūf wa'l-nahy ᶜan al-munkar)*. It is a collective obligation *(farḍ kafā'ī)* of the Muslim community to take an affirmative stand towards *ḥisbah* and put it into effect whenever the occasion arises.
Ḥizb (pl. aḥzāb): Group; band; party.
Hudā: Guidance, specifically Divine guidance.
Ḥudūd (sing. *ḥadd*)*:* Prescribed punishments which the Qur'ān or Sunnah have determined for a handful of offences, including adultery and indefensible theft.
Ḥukm (pl. *aḥkām*)*:* Law, injunction, or value of the *Sharīᶜah* which seeks to regulate the conduct of competent individuals who are capable of bearing legal obligations.
Ḥukm sharᶜī: Legal ruling: a *Sharīᶜah* command.
Ḥukm taklīfī: A defining law.
Ḥukm waḍᶜī: Declaratory law.
Hukum syarak/Ḥukm syarak (Malay): *Ḥukm sharᶜī.*
Ḥurriyyah: Freedom.
Ḥurriyyah Dīniyyah: Freedom of religion; religious freedom.
Ḥurriyyah Ijtimāᶜiyyah: Social liberty.
Ḥurriyyat al-muᶜāraḍah: Freedom to criticise.
Ḥurriyyat naqd al-ḥākim: Freedom to criticise the governor or government activity.
Ḥurriyyat al-qawl: Freedom of speech.
Ḥurriyyat al-ra'y: Freedom of opinion.

Ḥurriyyat al-ra'y al-siyāsī: Freedom of expression in political affairs.
Ḥusn al-khulq: Good character.
ʿIbādah: Worship; a rite of worship.
ʿIbādāt: Devotional matters and rituals of worship; often referring to obligatory duties such as the daily prayers, giving charity and fasting. The term is often used in contradistinction to *muʿāmalāt.*
Ibāḥah: Permissibility, being the verbal noun of *mubāḥ* (permissible), which represents a value point in the Islamic scale of five values, coming next after *wājib* and *mandūb.*
Iftirā': Attributing lies to a person; libel; calumny.
Iftitān al-nisā': A temptation to women.
Iḥsān: Goodness; excellence; benevolence.
Iḥtikār: Hoarding.
Iʿjāb: Self-gratification; self-complacency; conceit.
Ijmāʿ: General consensus of jurists and scholars concerning a juridical matter. It is often used in contradistinction to *ikhtilāf.*
Ijtihād: Lit. Self-exertion; independent reasoning usually by a qualified person (i.e. *mujtahid*) in order to deduce the juridical ruling of an issue from the source materials of the *Sharīʿah.*
Ijtihād bi'l-ra'y: Ijtihād which is founded on considered personal opinion.
Ikhlāṣ: Sincerity.
Ikhtilāf: Disagreement and difference of opinion, often used in contradistinction to *ijmāʿ;* dissension.
Ikhtilāf al-taḍādd: A substantial difference of opinion amounting to contradiction.
Ikhtilāf al-tanawwuʿ: An insubstantial difference of opinion.
Ikhtilāf fi'l-ra'y: Difference of opinion.
Ikhtiṣāṣ: Exclusive appropriation.
Ikhtiṣāṣ ḥājiz: Exclusive assignment.
ʿIllah: Cause.
ʿIlm: Knowledge; science.
ʿIlm al-ikhtilāf: The science of disagreement.
Imām: Lit. a leader; often referring to the eponym and leading authority of a legal school (*madhhab*); any leading scholar; the prayer leader who leads congregational prayers in the mosque; the head of state.
Īmān: Faith, consisting of professing Islam in one's words, which is also indicative of an affirmative state of mind towards Islam.
Immaʿah: A person of weak character; someone easily led by others.
Inqiḍā' al-ḥaqq: The termination of a right.

Iqāmah: Standing to begin the canonical prayer; the call to indicate this.
ʿIrāḍ: Shunning. See also *hajr.*
ʿIrḍ: Dignity.
ʿIshā': Late evening; night.
ʿIṣmah: Honour; immunity; protection.
Isnād: The chain of transmitters for a *ḥadīth.*
Istibdād bi'l-ra'y: The arbitrary imposition of a personal opinion on others.
Istifā' al-ḥaqq: The fulfilment of a right.
Istiḥsān: To deem something good; juristic preference, that is, when one of the two or more possible solutions to an issue is given preference over the other(s) on grounds of it being more conducive to the general objectives of the *Sharīʿah.*
Istihtār: Disdain; scorn.
Istiʿmāl al-ḥaqq: Use of a right.
Istiṣḥāb: Presumption of continuity.
Istiṣlāḥ: Consideration of public interest. See *maṣlaḥah* for which it is a synonym.
Istitābah: To call on a person to repent.
Al-iʿtibār al-munāsib: Consideration of what is proper and appropriate under the circumstances.
Iʿtidā': Transgression against another. Synonym for *al-taʿaddī.*
Izālat al-munkar: Removal of evil.
Al-jabr wa'l-ikhtiyār: Predestination and free-will.
Jadal: Disputation; argument; discussion.
Jahl: Ignorance.
Jāhil: Ignorant person.
Jamāʿah: Multitude; group; community.
Jannah: The Garden, Paradise.
Jarḥ al-shuhūd: The impugning of witnesses; declaring the testimony of a witness invalid.
Jahr bi'l-sū': Pulic utterance of wicked, hurtful,or malicious speech.
Jidāl: See *Jadal.*
Jihād: Lit. struggle, in both the moral sense of struggling against evil or striving for excellence, and also in the physical sense of armed struggle for a holy cause.
Jizyah: The Islamic poll-tax.
Juḥd: Denial of the truth and veracity of the opinion and conduct of another party over minor differences.
Al-kabā'ir: The major sins.

Kafā'ah: Adequacy; equality, for instance, between the spouses in a marriage.
Kaffārah: Expiation.
Kāfir: Disbeliever; infidel.
Kāhin: Soothsayer.
Kalām: Lit. speech; the scholastic theology of Islam developed by such schools as the Ashʿarites and Muʿtazilites.
Kalimah khabīthah: An evil word; evil speech.
Kalimah ṭayyibah: A good word; good speech.
Kalimat al-shahādah: The Islamic testimonial of faith, namely to testify that 'there is no god save God, and Muḥammad ﷺ is His messenger'.
Kathrat al-su'āl: Excessive questioning.
Kātib: Scribe.
Khalīfah: Caliph; vicegerent; successor.
Khalwah: Illicit proximity, intimacy or privacy between members of the opposite sex.
Khayr: That which is good or for the best; good work; beneficence.
Al-Khulafā' al-Rāshidūn: The Rightly-Guided Caliphs, a reference to the first four caliphs in office after the the demise of the Prophet ﷺ, namely Abū Bakr al-Ṣiddīq (died 12 A.H./634 A.D.), ʿUmar ibn al-Khaṭṭāb (died 23/643), ʿUthmān ibn ʿAffān (died 35/656) and ʿAlī ibn Abī Ṭālib (died 40/661). They ruled for a total of forty years.
Khuṣūmah: Argumentation; dispute; controversy.
Kidhb: Lies; lying.
Kufr: Lit. concealing or covering; denial of Islam by one's words and conduct; disbelief; infidelity. The term is often used in contradistinction to *īmān* and *islām*.
Al-kufr al-akbar: The greater *kufr*, which is the explicit and unequivocal renunciation of the faith.
Al-kufr dūn al-kufr: Lit. 'disbelief other than disbelief'; the lesser *kufr* which is a degree below the greater *kufr*. *Kufr* in this sense does not mean total or outright disbelief: it is used metaphorically in order to accentuate the gravity of conduct which actually amounts to transgression (*fisq*).
Laghw: Foolish talk; nonsense.
Laʿn or *Laʿnah*: A curse.
Maʿānī khafiyyah: Hidden meanings.
Madh: Flattery; sycophancy; praise.
Madhhab (pl. *madhāhib*): Theological or legal school. The four main

Sunni schools of law are: 1. the Ḥannafiyyah, founded by Imām Abū Ḥanifah al-Nuʿmān ibn Thābit (d. 150/767); 2. the Mālikiyyah, founded by Imām Mālik ibn Anas (d. 179/795); 3. the Shāfiʿīyyah, founded by Imām Muḥammad ibn Idrīs al-Shāfiʿī (d. 204/820); and 4. the Ḥanbaliyyah, founded by Imām Aḥmad ibn Ḥanbal (d. 241/855).

Madhmūm: Reprehensible; objectionable; blameworthy.

Mafhūm al-mukhālafah: Divergent implication.

Maghrib: Sunset; dusk.

Mahr: Dowry.

Maḥẓūr: Forbidden; out of bounds.

Majlis al-shūrā: The consultative assembly.

Majnūn: Possessed.

Makrūh: Reprehensible; something which is blameworthy yet legally not punishable. It is one of the five value points on the well-known Islamic scale of values, coming after *mubāḥ*.

Māl yaṣīr: A small amount; a paltry gain or profit.

Mālikiyyah: Ownership; the right thereto.

Mandūb: Recommended, praiseworthy; a course of conduct which earns moral reward if followed; however a person who does not follow such a course of conduct is not open to punishment. It is also synonymous with *mustaḥabb*.

Mansūkh: Abrogated.

Al-manzilah bayna'l-manzilatayn: The intermediate state between Islam and disbelief (a Muʿtazilite doctrine).

Maqāṣid al-Sharīʿah: The objectives of the *Sharīʿah*.

Maqbūl: Acceptable.

Maqdhūf: A victim of slanderous accusation.

Maqṣid (pl. *maqāṣid*): Aim; objective; intention.

Maʿrūf: Good, in accordance with the *Sharīʿah*, and the approved custom of society. The term is often used in contradistinction to *munkar*.

Maṣāliḥ mursalah: Unrestricted interests.

Maṣāliḥ muʿtabarah: Accreditd interests, namely those that have been clearly recognised by the *Sharīʿah*.

Maʿṣiyah: Disobedience; sedition; rebellion; sin.

Maṣlaḥah (pl. *maṣāliḥ*): Public good, benefit or interest; often used in contradistinction to *mafsadah*, mischief, evil. The rules of the *Sharīʿah* are all deemed to be for the realisation of the general benefit of the people.

Maṣlaḥah ʿāliyah: A higher cause or interest.

Maṣlaḥah murṣalah: Consideration of public interest.
Maᶜṣūm: Inviolable; innocent.
Mawḍūᶜāt: Forged or fabricated *Ḥadīths*.
Miḥnah: Inquisition.
Mirā': Acrimony; acrimonious contention; negative disputation.
Mu'adhdhin: Muezzin; the man who, with the *adhān,* summons Muslims to the prayers in a mosque.
*Muᶜāmalāt (*sing. *muᶜāmalah):* Civil or commercial transactions, often used in contradistinction to *ᶜibādāt,* devotional matters.
Mu'awwal: Allegory.
*Mubāḥ (*pl. *mubāḥāt):* Permissible; neutral; actions for which neither any reward nor any punishment is accorded.
Mubtadiᶜ (pl. *mubtadiᶜūn*): Innovator.
Al-mubtadiᶜ al-ᶜāmī: A non-influential commoner who indulges in *bidᶜah.*
Mufāriq li'l-jamāᶜah: One who splits off, or separates himself from the community.
*Mufassir (*pl. *mufassirūn):* Commentator; usually referring to the author of a work of *tafsīr*, or commentary on the Qur'ān.
Mufsid: Instigator of corruption.
Muftī: Jurisconsult; mufti.
Muḥādadah: Hostile opposition.
Muhājirūn: Emigrants; specifically, the early Muslims who emigrated from Mecca to Medīna.
Muḥārabah: Open hostility; war.
*Muḥkamāt (*sing. *muḥkam):* The perspicuous verses of the Qur'ān.
Muḥṣan: A married Muslim of upright character who is not guilty of *zinā'* or *riddah*; a chaste person; of unblemished reputation.
Muḥsinīn (sing. *muḥsin*): People noted for their piety and good works; virtuous people.
Mujāhir bi'l-maᶜāṣī: A person who publicises their misbehaviour or sinful conduct.
Mujtahid (pl. *mujtahidūn*): a legist competent enough to formulate an independent opinion based on the traditional sources, in matters legal or theological.
Mukallaf: Legally responsible individual.
Mukhāṣamah: Hostile debate or exchange of words.
Mumārāt: Acrimonious talk or behaviour.
*Munāfiqūn (*sing. *munāfiq):* Hypocrites.
Munkar: Not good, that which is disapproved and contrary to the established values of Islam.

Munkarāt: Highly reprehensible acts; wicked deeds.
Murtadd (pl. *murtaddūn*): Apostate; a person who, after embracing Islam, renounces it by their explicit words and conduct.
Mushāqaqah: Separation; dissension; contention; antagonism; adverse behaviour.
Mushrikūn (sing. *mushrik*): Polytheists; idolators; those who associate other gods with God.
Mustaḥabb: see *mandūb.*
Musta'man: Person of protected status.
Mutaṣawwifah: Sufis/mystics.
Mutashābihāt (sing. *mutashābih*): Ambiguous, obscure, difficult to understand - the abbreviated letters which occur at the beginning of some chapters of the Qur'ān are typical examples; the ambiguous passages in the Qur'ān.
Muṭlaq: Absolute; unlimited; unrestricted.
Mutrak al-ẓāhir: Abandonment of the literal.
Al-Nabī: See *al-Rasūl* ﷺ.
Nafs: Soul.
Nāʿiyah: Hired mourner.
Naql kādhib: False narration.
Nāṣiḥ: Sincere advisor.
Naṣīḥah: Sincere advice, often offered at the initiative of its donor.
Nāsikh: Abrogating.
Naskh: Abrogation.
Nuṣūṣ (sing. *naṣṣ*): Clear textual injunctions of the Qur'ān or Sunnah which convey meanings that are self-evident and do not require interpretation.
Qaḍā': The Divine decree.
Qadar: Predestination; fate; destiny; power.
Qadhf: Slanderous accusation, being one of the offences which carries a prescribed punishment (*ḥadd*) of eighty lashes of the whip.
Qādhif: The perpetrator of *qadhf*; slanderer.
Qāḍī: Judge.
Qarā'in: Circumstantial evidence.
Qaṭʿī: Decisive; definitive; not speculative. It is used in opposition to *ẓannī*.
Qawlan maʿrūfan: Courteous and correct speech.
Qawwā'id kulliyah: Legal maxims.
Qiblah: The direction faced during prayer; for Muslims, the *Kaʿbah* in Mecca.
Qīmat al-mithl: The fair market price.

Qiṣāṣ: Retaliation.

Qiyās: Analogical reasoning aimed at extending a given ruling of the Qur'ān and Sunnah to a new case, on grounds of an effective cause common to both the new and the original case.

Qiyās al-awlā: Analogy of the superior.

Rafʿ al-ḥaraj: Removal of hardship.

Raḥmah: Mercy.

Rāʿī: Shepherd.

Rajm: Punishment by stoning.

Al-Rasūl: The Messenger, the Prophet Muḥammad ﷺ.

Ra'y: Considered personal opinion, often used in contradistinction to *naṣṣ* (see *nuṣūṣ).*

Ra'y bāṭil: Invalid opinion.

Ra'y fī mawdiʿ al-ishtibāh: A dubious opinion.

Ra'y madhmūm: Blameworthy or objectionable opinion.

Ra'y ṣaḥiḥ: Valid or praiseworthy opinion.

Ra'y tafsīrī: An opinion which interprets and clarifies textual injunctions *(nuṣūṣ).*

Ra'y ijtihādī: A considered personal opinion consisting of the independent reasoning of a qualified individual.

Ribā': Usury.

Riddah: Apostasy.

Rifq: Gentleness.

Riyā': Hypocrisy.

Rukūʿ: Bowing with hands on knees during the canonical prayer.

Sabb: Insult; vilification.

Sabb Allāh: Blasphemy.

Sabb al-Nabī ﷺ: See *Sabb al-Rasūl* ﷺ.

Sabb al-Rasūl ﷺ: To vilify, or blaspheme against the Prophet ﷺ.

Sabb al-ṣaḥābī: To insult one of the Companions of the Prophet ﷺ.

Sabbāb: Blasphemer.

Ṣabr: Patience; perseverance.

Sadd al-dharā'iʿ: Blocking recourse to expedients; blocking the means to some end.

Al-ṣaghā'ir: The minor sins.

Sāhir: Magician; sorcerer.

Ṣā'igh: Permissible.

Ṣalāh (pl. *ṣalawāt):* Canonical prayers that a Muslim is obliged to perform five times daily.

Salām: Peace; the Islamic greeting 'Peace be upon you', exchanged among Muslims whenever they meet.

Ṣalāt al-tarāwīḥ: Prayers recited after midnight and before dawn, performed during the month of Ramaḍān.

Ṣalāt al-khawf: 'The prayer in fear', i.e. the shortened version of the daily canonical prayers, permitted when one is in fear for one's safety.

Ṣāliḥīn/ṣāliḥūn: Upright and pious people who act righteously.

Ṣawm: Fast, obligatory during the month of Ramaḍān.

Satr al-fawāḥish: Concealment of misdeeds.

Shaᶜā'ir -i-Islam (Urdu): The ceremonies and rituals of Islam.

Shahādah: The Islamic declaration of faith, 'There is no god save God and Muḥammad ﷺ is His messenger', also referred to as *al-shahādatayn,* 'the two testimonials of faith', the first testifying to the unity of God and the second to the prophethood of Muḥammad ﷺ; testimony.

Shahawāt (sing. *shahwah*): Lusts; the carnal appetites; desires.

Shāᶜir: Poet.

Shan-i-nuzūl (Urdu): The historical context for the revelation of a verse/verses of the Qur'ān.

Al-sharᶜ: the law; the *Sharīᶜah.*

Sharᶜī: Juridical, legal.

Sharīᶜah: Islamic law as contained in the divine guidance of the Qur'ān and Sunnah. 'Islamic law' is the nearest English translation of *Sharīᶜah*, yet the latter is not confined specifically to legal subject matter and extends to the much wider areas of moral and religious guidance.

Shatm: See *sabb.*

Shayṭān: Satan.

Shubhah (pl. *shubhāt*): Doubt.

Shufᶜ: Pre-emption.

Shūrā: Consultation.

Shurūṭ (sing. *sharṭ*): Conditions; pre-requisites.

*Ṣifāt (*sing. *ṣifah)*: Attributes; qualities. Often used in reference to the Names of God.

Ṣiḥḥa: Validity.

Siyāsah sharᶜiyyah: Sharīᶜah-oriented policy; often refers to discretionary decisions taken by the Head of State or *qāḍī* in pursuit of public good, in response to emergency situations, or in cases where a strict application of the established law would lead to undesirable results.

Sū' al-ta'wīl: Ill-conceived interpretation.

Sū' istiᶜmāl al-ḥaqq: The misuse or abuse of a right.

Sulṭah: Authority; power.
Sunnah: The teaching and exemplary conduct of the Prophet Muḥammad ﷺ which constitutes the most authoritative source of Islam next to the Qur'ān. The Sunnah of the Prophet is known through authentic reports of his sayings, *Ḥadīth.*
Sūrah (pl. *suwar):* Chapter of the Qur'ān.
Syirik (Malay): Polytheist.
Taʿabbudī: Devotional.
Taʿaddī: See *Iʿtidāʾ.*
Taʿassuf fī istiʿmāl al-ḥaqq: Abuse of a right.
Taʿāwun: Mutual assistance; co-operation in good work.
Tadākhul: Overlap; intersection; amalgamation.
Taghrīb: Banishment; exile.
Tahattuk: Impudence; insolence.
Taḥsīniyyāt: Embellishments, or things which are merely desirable, as opposed to *ḍarūriyyāt* which are deemed to be essential.
Takdhīb ṣarīḥ: Explicit denial.
Takfīr: Accusing someone of being a disbeliever.
Takhṣīṣ: Specification.
Takhyīr: Option.
Ṭalāq: Divorce.
Taʿlīm: Teaching, instruction, direction, schooling, training.
Taqdīr: Measurement.
Taqiyyah: Dissimulation; expedient concealment - a principle of Shīʿite theology which permits the believer to conceal the truth when in danger.
Taqlīd: Lit. imitation; often implying an indiscriminate following of the rulings and opinions of the *ʿulamāʾ* of the past. It is often used in contradistinction to *ijtihād.*
Taqyīd: Qualification; condition; limitation.
Taqwā: Piety; God-fearingness; God-consciousness.
Tarāwīḥ: See *Ṣalāt al-tarāwīḥ.*
Taʿrīḍ biʾl-adhā: Attempted harm, annoyance or hurt.
Taʿrīḍ biʾl-qadhf: Attempted slander.
Taʿrīf: Informing; apprising; making known.
Tarjīḥ: Preference (of one legal opinion over others).
Tasalsul: A chain of events.
Taṣdīq biʾl-qalb: An inner affirmation with the heart, as opposed to an affirmation with the tongue (*lisān*).
Tashbīb: Extolling the beauty of women.
Tawbīkh: Reprimand.

Tawḥīd: Monotheism; belief in the oneness of God; the Divine Unity.

Ta'wīl: Allegorical explanation.

Tayammum: The ritual ablution before the canonical prayers, performed with clean earth in the absence of water.

Taᶜzīr: Lit. deterrence or a deterrent punishment which a *qāḍī* may impose at his discretion by reference to attending circumstances. It is often used in contradistinction to *ḥadd.*

Taᶜzīr bi'l-māl: Damages for the plaintiff; financial compensation payable to the plaintiff.

Thubūt: Established; certain; certainty.

Tuhmah: Accusation; charge; insinuation; suspicion.

Ṭuhr: Ritual purity.

Ukhūwah: Fraternity; brotherhood.

ᶜUlamā' (sing. *ᶜālim):* Religious scholars; theologians.

Ulū'l-amr: Lit. 'those with authority'; government and community leaders, as well as the *ᶜulamā'*, who exercise authority and influence in community affairs. The Qur'ān requires that they must be respected and obeyed.

Ummah: The Muslim community at large, irrespective of colour, race, place of residence, language, and nationality. The only bond of unity within the *ummah* is unity of faith.

Ummahāt al-mu'minīn: Lit. the 'mothers of the believers', referring to the wives of the Prophet ﷺ.

Uṣūl al-fiqh: Sources or roots of Islamic law and jurisprudence; refers mainly to the Qur'ān and Sunnah as the principal sources of the *Sharīᶜah*, but also to a number of other sources and methods which are used in order to facilitate the proper exercise of *ijtihād.*

Al-uṣūl al-khamsah: The five principles of the faith.

Al-waᶜd wa'l-waᶜīd: The Divine promise of reward and threat of punishment.

Waḍᶜ: Enactment.

Al-Wāḥid: The One (God).

Wāḥid: One.

Wājib: Obligatory; an obligation or duty arising from the decisive injunctions of the Qur'ān and Sunnah.

Walī al-ḥisbah: The market controller.

Waᶜẓ: Kindly admonition.

Wuḍūᶜ: The ritual ablution before the canonical prayers, performed with water.

Wujūb: Necessary; indispensability.

Yaqīn: Certitude.
Zakāh: Lit. purity; legal alms incumbent upon a Muslim, to help the poor and the needy, at the rate of approximately two and a half percent, payable annually on certain types of assets held for over a year.
Ẓālim: Tyrant; oppressor; unjust person.
Zanādiqah (sing. *zindīq):* Atheists; heretics.
Zandaqah: Heresy.
Ẓann: Conjecture; suspicion; speculation.
Ẓann ghālib: Overwhelming probability.
Ẓann al-mubāḥ: Speculation based on probability, as opposed to speculation based on doubt (*shakk*), where the chances of a thing being right or wrong are equal. *Ẓann* is often admitted as a valid basis of adjudication.
Ẓannī: Speculative.
Ẓihār: A form of pre-Islamic divorce with the following formula of repudiation: 'you are to me as my mother's back'.
Zinā': Adultery and fornication, sexual intercourse outside marriage.

Index

Terms that appear in both English and as transliteration are cross-referenced. An initial capital indicates another entry, whilst small initial letters either refer to a sub-entry or are translations. If no translation is given please refer to the glossary or the text itself.

D

G

H

Q

R

S